GIBBS·SMITH
P
PUBLISHER

SALT LAKE CITY

An Architectural
Guidebook to

BROOKLYN

FRANCIS MORRONE ✴ PHOTOGRAPHY BY JAMES ISKA

For Francis Morrone's Brooklyn bibliography and an "index for specialists" based on this book, as well as for updates to information from the book, go to www.francismorrone.com.

First Edition
05 04 03 02 01   5 4 3 2 1

Book published by
Gibbs Smith, Publisher
P.O. Box 667
Layton, Utah 84041

Orders: (1-800) 748-5439
www.gibbs-smith.com

Edited by Suzanne Taylor
Designed and produced by J. Scott Knudsen
Printed and bound in the United States of America

Library of Congress Cataloging-in-Publication Data

Morrone, Francis, 1958–
    An architectural guidebook to Brooklyn / by Francis Morrone;
    photographs by James Iska.— 1st ed.
        p. cm.
Includes index.
    ISBN 1-58685-047-4
    1. Architecture—New York (State)—New York—Guidebooks.
2. Brooklyn (New York, N.Y.)—Guidebooks. 3. New York (N.Y.)—
Buildings, structures, etc.—Guidebooks. 4. Brooklyn (New York,
N.Y.)—Buildings, structures, etc.—Guidebooks. I. Iska, James. II.
Title.
    NA735.N5 M639 2001
    720'.9747'1—dc21
                      00-012250

An Architectural
Guidebook to
Brooklyn

Contents

To Patricia, again

Introduction

This is a book about the built environment of Brooklyn, New York. I have lived in Brooklyn for twenty-one years. When I moved to New York from Chicago, I had no particular intention to settle in Brooklyn. I did so out of financial expediency. My neighborhood, Park Slope, was attracting many refugees from what, even in the immediate wake of New York City's fiscal crisis, were the soaring rents of Manhattan. I knew few such people at the time who actually preferred living in Brooklyn over Manhattan. That, in a very short time, I realized how much I preferred Brooklyn to any other place shows how fate is a funny thing.

For many of the people in my position at the time, Brooklyn was what one saw from the F train when it climbed above ground for two stops between Seventh Avenue and Carroll Street. One saw the fetid Gowanus Canal, with its factories and warehouses and its tall, raucous signs proclaiming Eagle Clothes and Goya Foods and Domino Sugar. On a clear day one saw the Statue of Liberty. One saw countless church spires. And one saw the grail, the skyline of Manhattan, the island one would reach in just a few stops. There was Park Slope, there were a couple of Viewmaster slides of a gritty old Brooklyn, and then there was Manhattan. Seldom did we turn in the other direction, into the interior of Brooklyn. The experience was roughly the same, though the odds and ends of a briefly glimpsed Brooklyn differed somewhat, for friends who had similarly settled for—not in—Brooklyn neighborhoods such as Carroll Gardens, Cobble Hill, Boerum Hill, and Fort Greene. (Brooklyn Heights was too expensive.)

For me it all began to change when I started to work as well as to live in Brooklyn. My place of work for a number of years was near Grant Square, in either the northern part of Crown Heights or the southern part of Bedford-Stuyvesant (no one seems quite sure which). Though this was several miles from my Park Slope abode, I, a dedicated walker, chose to walk to work. This afforded me views of a Brooklyn I'd hardly imagined existed. I passed through some scenes of urban devastation, which did not surprise me, since I'd grown up in a big city and had witnessed firsthand some of the processes by which once-fine inner-city neighborhoods were physically ruined. What I was unprepared for was the beauty. I'd always fancied myself a connoisseur of cities, one who could see that a dense and aged urban environment could be as beautiful as any natural scenery. Yet the Brooklyn I was slowly getting to know was so diversely beautiful, so clearly the product of successive ideals of the good city (however failed many of these visions ultimately proved to be), that I became a Brooklyn addict. I set out to experience as much of Brooklyn as I could.

Back in Park Slope, I became aware that if I were to sit down and draw up my own urban utopia, it would probably come out looking an awful lot like my neighborhood, with no need of the "Gogmagogsville" (as Saul Bellow calls Manhattan) across the river. Here was an astonishingly diverse collection, block after block after block, of high-quality row houses and apartment houses, most of them exceptionally well maintained. Here were tree-lined streets where old and young, families and singles, blacks and whites, straights and gays all mingled freely while feeling that this was home. Park Slope edges and derives its name from Prospect Park. Though today the park is in much better condition than it was twenty or so years ago, even at its nadir one could sense immediately that this was a masterpiece of landscape design. Grand Army Plaza, even for those weaned on the aesthetics of modernism, excited visitors with its fully realized turn-of-the-century vision of urban grandeur. And the nearby institutions—the Brooklyn Museum, the Brooklyn Botanic Garden, and the Brooklyn Public Library—were, in the aggregate, something that is given to very few people in this world to have right in their own backyard. Before long I could confidently say that there was no Manhattan neighborhood I would prefer to Park Slope. (I might, however, be just as content to live in Cobble Hill or Fort Greene, and there is a little corner of my soul that strangely hankers for Greenpoint.)

In any event, this book is not an autobiography. It is a guidebook. The chapters and their entries are arranged geographically. I focus on architecture and include a variety of things that, if not quite architectural, nonetheless are inspired by looking at buildings. I regret deeply not being able to cover more of Brooklyn. That is partly the fault of the nature of commercial book publishing and partly the fault of Brooklyn. When one writes a book, one is limited to a certain number of pages, a certain number of words. The publisher decides beforehand how big the book can be so that a price can be set. A publisher who wishes to produce a guidebook to Brooklyn architecture first decides what kind of book will sell, including at what price. He may conclude that, say, $19.95 is the highest price most people will pay for such a book. Once these calculations are made, the author has his "program," much in the way an architect does when he is hired to design a building. The architect must work within certain limits and do the best he can within those limits. So too the author of a book. For to go beyond a certain number of words may require an additional "signature" being added to the book, which will of necessity drive up the price, perhaps to the point where no one will buy the book. This is all my way of saying that early on in the process of composing this book I had to make some very hard choices. Brooklyn was simply too big for me to be able to cover all its neighborhoods in the fairly leisurely manner of this book as I envisioned it. I decided therefore to concentrate on the contiguous areas of northern and central Brooklyn. This includes the oldest urbanized areas of Brooklyn as well as the vast "brownstone belt" and some of the principal industrial areas. It takes in Prospect Park and the Flatbush district to its south. It leaves out Sunset Park, Bay Ridge, Bensonhurst, and Coney Island, places filled with interesting things, places that in their own ways are parts of the quintessential Brooklyn, and places I love. I was particularly distressed to have to do without Sunset Park (home of the amazing Green-wood Cemetery, of St. Michael's Church, and of so much more) and Bay Ridge. The loss of Coney Island I can live with. It is fascinating, and I've led tours of it, but of all topics in Brooklyn history, Coney Island has hardly been neglected. I also, at the last moment, decided to drop Bushwick, which I'd pretty much written up already.

In this book I do not write about things I do not like. Those familiar with my other writings may be taken aback by the sanguinity of my tone in this book. I do not think it is a boosterish tone. It is, I hope, a loving tone. I employ many superlatives in this book. An awful lot of things are "great," "wonderful," "marvelous," "superb," and "magnificent." Blame it on Brooklyn. I also try to steer clear of sentimentality. Unique though Brooklyn may be, there are times I've been reduced to tears by how similar some things here seem to what I knew growing up in Chicago. I could have adopted a more sentimental tone or a more elegiac tone. I did not for a couple of reasons. First, this is not an elegy for Brooklyn. Brooklyn is very much alive. Many of the neighborhoods with which I deal are alive in much the way they ever were, though the skin color of the inhabitants may have changed. It's also true that neighborhoods thought down and out a few years ago are now on the upswing. I don't mean the obvious examples such as Park Slope and Fort Greene, which have been or are being "gentrified." I mean parts of Bedford-Stuyvesant, for example, that seem today to be nearly as bourgeois as they were in 1900. (The reader will sense throughout the book that I use "bourgeois" not as academics use the term, as one of opprobrium, but as an encomium, harkening to its true meaning of "city dweller" or "citizen" with all that that implies about the peculiarly urban values of privacy, decorum, and public-spiritedness. Think Jane Jacobs.) Second, the sentimental thing has been done already and, in some cases, superbly, by writers more gifted than I, such as Elliot Willensky in *When Brooklyn Was the World*. (Another outstanding general overview of Brooklyn in recent years is Paul Gardner and Grace Glueck's *Brooklyn: People and Places, Past and Present*.)

As for what I do cover, one may note a few seemingly inexplicable omissions. Let me say at the outset that I have chosen to focus on those things that are of most interest to me. Sometimes I am expansive—the book was conceived to allow me the opportunity of such expansiveness. Sometimes I am not. Some entries run to a thousand or more words, others may be twenty words. Brooklyn Heights is filled with fine pre–Civil War houses. They deserve to be looked at and loved. I love them. I just found I did not have a lot to say about them, at least not without being betrayed into a lengthy, general disquisition on, for example, the Greek Revival. I have tried in this book to avoid this, principally for reasons of space. Sometimes one feels reduced to saying, "Look at that—isn't it beautiful?" and then moving on. Institutional buildings and churches tend to merit more verbiage than houses. This is as it should be. The houses are wonderful and they define our experience of the city's streets. In the end, though, houses were built by and for individuals or families. Other types of buildings were built for the larger public. Brooklyn, though known as the borough of homes and churches, is also a place where throughout its history numerous attempts by both private and public concerns have been made to enrich and to embellish the public environment, and some among these attempts—Prospect Park and Grand Army Plaza and the Brooklyn Museum—are among the most notable of modern times anywhere in the world. This leads me to what has become an overriding interest of mine in recent years, and that is the legacy of the City Beautiful movement of the late nineteenth and early twentieth centuries, that efflorescence of civic art that for me marks the highest stage of American urbanism. Seldom is the City Beautiful written about without some studied academic distance, which is in itself no bad thing, except that today academics tend to view the American past through the lenses of irony, sarcasm, disdain, or a kind of (generally perfectly irrelevant) quasi-Marxism. I am tired of irony, sarcasm, disdain, and quasi-Marxism. I am tired, above all, of the prevailing sense, particularly among academics, that we view the past from a privileged perspective. We do not know *more* than the men and women of 1900 knew. We know things differently, and not necessarily better. Indeed, in the final accounting, we may turn out to know a good deal *less* than they knew. I long to know what they knew, however impossible that dream may be. Some of that longing, I hope, comes across in what follows. It will be the major portion of my forthcoming book tentatively titled *Brooklyn 1900*, an examination of the architectural and social realities of Brooklyn at the time of its consolidation with New York City, with particular emphasis upon the City Beautiful and its impact on Brooklyn.

The guidebook comes first. It is above all my attempt to sift through the stores of Brooklyniana lodged in my head and to come to terms with my own feelings about the place and to try to express them in a more or less cogent manner that allows others to learn what I know and to form their own opinions, all of which is preparatory to the greater works on Brooklyn's built environment—my own forthcoming book as well as forthcoming works by scholars far more gifted than I—that shall inevitably flood the bookstores in the years to come.

On the outside of the apartment building on Cumberland Street in Fort Greene, where Marianne Moore lived for many years, is a plaque bearing a quotation from her. With a poet's grace, she said: "Brooklyn has given me pleasure, has helped educate me; has afforded me, in fact, the kind of tame excitement on which I thrive."

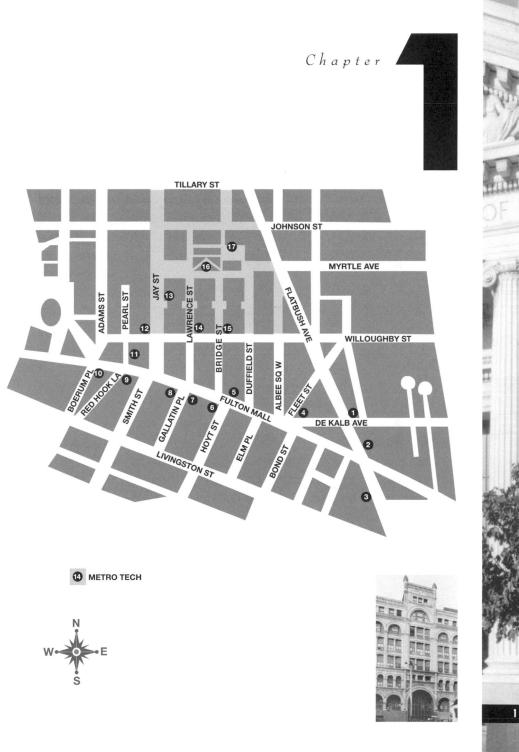

Chapter 1

TILLARY ST

JOHNSON ST

MYRTLE AVE

FLATBUSH AVE

WILLOUGHBY ST

ADAMS ST

PEARL ST

JAY ST

LAWRENCE ST

BRIDGE ST

DUFFIELD ST

ALBEE SQ W

FLEET ST

DE KALB AVE

BOERUM PL

RED HOOK LA

SMITH ST

GALLATIN PL

HOYT ST

ELM PL

BOND ST

FULTON MALL

LIVINGSTON ST

14 METRO TECH

N W E S

OF BR

4 Dime Savings Bank

1 BROOKLYN PARAMOUNT THEATRE

Northeast corner of Flatbush Avenue Extension and DeKalb Avenue
1928, Rapp & Rapp

The Paramount was Brooklyn's most famous movie palace. Its architects, the firm of Rapp & Rapp, were specialists in razzle-dazzle theaters. They designed the mountainous Paramount Building in Times Square, with the Paramount Theater in its base, a few years before they worked for the same company across the river. (Actually, neither of the brothers C. W. and G. W. Rapp had anything to do with the Brooklyn Paramount, since the former died in 1926 and the latter in 1916. The firm, however, carried on.) In the 1920s, movie houses in outlying neighborhoods and the outer boroughs were often more lavish than the movie houses of Times Square. Movie-production companies tended to own the theaters, so a particular theater would be a Warner Brothers theater, or a Fox theater, or a Paramount theater. The competition among these theaters was intense and got to the point where the movies took a backseat to the architecture. In the 1920s and 1930s, the theater architecture, as well as the movies themselves, provided a fantastic respite from often-dreary neighborhood life. (Apropos of the owners of the Brooklyn Paramount, the great director Ernst Lubitsch once said, "I've been to Paris, France, and I've been to Paris, Paramount. I prefer

Paris, Paramount.") The Brooklyn Paramount, with 4,400 seats, was Brooklyn's largest and, at the time of its opening, the second largest in New York City, after the Roxy on Seventh Avenue and 50th Street. (The Loew's Kings, in Flatbush, also designed by Rapp & Rapp, had 3,690 seats.) The Paramount was an example of what is called the "atmospheric theater." In this type of theater, according to a 1928 article in a professional architectural magazine, "the scenic effects are not confined to the stage, but are made to envelop the audience by carrying a scenic architectural treatment completely around the auditorium." Typically, atmospheric theaters featured domed ceilings in their auditoriums, painted and illuminated to look like the sky on a beautiful day. Often, as at the Brooklyn Paramount, there were fountains, and "color organs" sprayed the walls with light through different colored filters. The theater opened on November 23, 1928, with a movie called, of all things, *Manhattan Cocktail,* starring Nancy Carroll. The theater closed on August 21, 1962, with a screening of Howard Hawks's *Hatari,* that cult favorite of New Wave French directors Godard and Truffaut. The Paramount was not only a movie theater. The leading performers in American popular music graced its stage across three decades that saw plenty of change in popular tastes. The great Bing Crosby practically lived at the Brooklyn Paramount in February and March of 1932. In a slightly different vein, Buddy Holly appeared there several times in 1957 and 1958. (Holly's last performance there came eleven months and six days before he was killed in an airplane crash.) In 1955, the Brooklyn Paramount was where disc jockey Alan Freed presented his very first rock-and-roll stage show. (That show broke the all-time one-day attendance record at the Paramount that crooner Russ Columbo had set twenty-four years earlier.) Freed and Murray the K presented many shows at the Paramount, making it the early headquarters of rock and roll in New York City. (They also presented shows down Flatbush Avenue at the Fox.)

The Brooklyn Paramount was appended to a tall, bulky, rather nondescript, eleven-story office building. (Paramount, which had been founded in 1916, liked its theaters to be in the bases of income-producing office buildings, as here and in Manhattan's Paramount Building.) The office building is at the corner, and the external wall of the theater is visible to the east along DeKalb Avenue. Look hard and you can see a faded painted sign with the theater's name on the DeKalb Avenue wall. The office building was converted in 1950 into administrative offices and classrooms for Long Island University. Unprepossessing though this exterior architecture may be, once it was seriously enlivened by signage. The theater marquee wrapped around the corner at the base of the office building. Its signs pointed north, south, east, west, and diagonally across Flatbush Avenue in a southwest direction. The south and west faces of the office building featured narrow, projecting, electrically illuminated signs saying "Paramount," rising from the top of the marquee all the way to the top of the office building. The pièce de résistance, though, was the enormous neon sign, the equivalent of perhaps four stories in height, that stood atop the office building. In simple bold lettering it spelled out, on its top line, "PARAMOUNT," and, on its bottom line, "THEATRE." The sign was oriented diagonally across Flatbush Avenue, in a southwest direction, into the heart of Brooklyn, turning its back on the Borough of Manhattan so close by, just on the other side of the Manhattan Bridge.

Try to imagine downtown in its heyday. There is still much here to see and do, of course. Once, though, there were movie palaces, the Paramount and the Fox and the RKO Albee, and department stores, Abraham & Straus and Martin's. They are all gone. A&S became Macy's. The movie palaces have shut down and the Fox and Albee buildings have been knocked down, the former for a modern office building, the latter for a glass-enclosed shopping center. The Paramount remains, however, albeit in a different function. Thirty-four years after the theater was built, it became the Arnold and Marie Schwartz Athletic Center of Long Island University. The auditorium is now the stadium of the Long Island University Blackbirds. In the late 1990s it was chic to attend Blackbirds games here. The team was doing very well. Charles Jones led the nation in scoring. Spike Lee, who lived nearby in Fort Greene at the time, went to the games. The most interesting thing, though, is that the games of this Division I NCAA basketball team were being played not in some state-of-the-art sports facility but amid the ornate Rococo decorations of the old movie palace, under the original "sky ceiling," the team and the crowd whipped up by the theater's original Wurlitzer organ. Some organ enthusiasts say that the 1928 Wurlitzer sounds better now than it did in the theater days when heavy draperies and plush seats absorbed its sound. (I am indebted to the web site of the New York Theater Organ Society, www.nytos.org, for information about the Paramount's organ.)

2 *Bell Atlantic Building*

2 BELL ATLANTIC BUILDING
(Originally the New York Telephone Company Building)
395 Flatbush Avenue Extension between DeKalb Avenue
and Fulton Street, east side
1975, Skidmore, Owings & Merrill

This was Skidmore, Owings & Merrill's second building for the Brooklyn Center Project initiated in 1969 by Mayor Lindsay and the Office of Downtown Brooklyn Development. Though by the standards of modernist architecture the earlier Skidmore, Owings & Merrill building is considered superior to this one, I and most people prefer this one, because with its pedestrian arcade the building did not, as other modern buildings in this area did, destroy street life in downtown Brooklyn. One emerges into this pedestrian arcade from the vast subway interchange below, where seemingly every line in the city converges, to be greeted by a particularly commodious McDonald's that provides sustenance to the student body of Long Island University.

3 CONSOLIDATED EDISON COMPANY, BROOKLYN DIVISION
30 Flatbush Avenue, between Fulton and Livingston Streets, west side
1972, Skidmore, Owings & Merrill

In 1967, a man named Dennis Durden, vice president for Urban Affairs of Federated Department Stores (owners of Abraham & Straus), spearheaded the formation of the Downtown Brooklyn Development Committee to study and make recommendations about the future of the downtown area. Two years later, Mayor John V. Lindsay announced a major urban-renewal project to be implemented over a fifteen-year period in a vast area bounded by Myrtle Avenue on the north, Boerum Place/Adams Street on the west, Ashland Place on the east, and Atlantic Avenue on the south—in other words, the entirety of what we call downtown Brooklyn. This plan had "scorched earth" written all over it, promising to do with downtown what the Cadman Plaza project had done with the adjoining Civic Center area several decades earlier. Nothing of the sort transpired, of course, though there was considerable piecemeal rebuilding under the plan, including the creation of Fulton Mall. In 1970, the subarea bounded by Ashland Place on the east, Lafayette Avenue on the south, Nevins Street and Flatbush Avenue on the west, and DeKalb Avenue on the north was designated for redevelopment by Stephen and George Klein, the owners of the nearby Barton's candy factory, as the Brooklyn Center Project. Two years later, the new office building by Skidmore, Owings & Merrill for the Consolidated Edison Company was the project's first building. The building conforms to its triangular site and is horizontally accentuated with continuous ribbon windows that are a sleeker version of the Corbusier-inspired thing that we see at Shreve, Lamb & Harmon's Supreme Court Building at Cadman Plaza from fifteen years earlier. Probably more noteworthy than the architecture of the Consolidated Edison building is that it replaced the Brooklyn Fox Theatre, one of the several great movie palaces of downtown Brooklyn. The Fox, designed by C. Howard Crane, was built in 1928 and demolished in 1971.

4 DIME SAVINGS BANK

9 DeKalb Avenue, northeast corner of Fleet Street
1906–8, Mowbray & Uffinger
Expanded 1931–32, Halsey, McCormack & Helmer

Mowbray & Uffinger designed the original building. They were the architects a few years earlier of the People's Trust Company on Montague Street. Halsey, McCormack & Helmer substantially enlarged the Dime during the Great Depression. That was a couple of years after the construction of their masterpiece, the Williamsburgh Savings Bank Tower. Both firms, in other words, were exceptionally adept at designing banks. It shows. This is one of the four or five most magnificent banking buildings in New York City. The site is a triangle bounded by DeKalb and Flatbush Avenues and Fleet Street. The entrance is at the southern point of the triangle, facing across Albee Square to Fulton Street. It is hard to think of a space with more potential to be a beautiful, European-style plaza. The entrance to the bank is splendid, holding the space with all the authority and skill that architecture can muster. It is a projecting tetrastyle Ionic portico from which the east and west sides of the building flare to the north. The portico is crowned by one of the best triangular pediments in Brooklyn, filled, as such pediments should be, with sculpture— semi-reclining figures flank a beautiful clock. Colonnades of fully modeled Ionic columns are recessed within the east and west walls of the building. The top floor, with anthemion cresting, forms a platform for a fine, broad saucer dome. Sometimes such domes are not visible from close up, but here the composition rises up in such carefully modulated stages that the dome is fully visible from the square below. Here is that sort of skillfully crafted classical building that is designed to be enjoyed both close-up and at a distance. At the front door is a great deal of bronze decoration. Look for the relief showing the Dime Savings Bank with the Brooklyn Bridge behind it, just below the prominent figure of Mercury. The exterior is fully revetted in marble. As great as the exterior is, the interior takes the breath away. It is one of New York's most magnificent rooms, really quite unlike any other banking room I know. In the center, under the dome, is a rotunda ringed by twelve soaring Corinthian columns of red marble. Similar columns flank each of the three exits. The capitals are embellished with gilded Mercury dimes, the bank's symbol. Everything here is of the highest quality: the Cosmatesque floor, the pilasters all along the walls, the gilded anthemia, the colorful coffered ceiling, the beautiful hanging bronze

4 *Dime Savings Bank*

light fixtures with bare bulbs, and so on. For me, it feels more like a great department store than a bank. This is an interior in which one would like to hang around and relax with a drink. The design, inside and out, borrows from several classical traditions, particularly that of the Italian Renaissance, and it is not quite right to call this, as some people have, a Roman temple.

An amusing footnote here is that the brief comment on this building in the third edition of the *AIA Guide* calls it "domical, columned." This appears in the fourth edition as "comical, columned." I rather hope that it's the fourth edition that contains the misprint.

The Dime Savings Bank was founded in Brooklyn in 1859. Savings banks emerged in the first half of the nineteenth century as largely philanthropic enterprises to aid working people in saving money. New York's first savings bank was sponsored by the Society for the Prevention of Pauperism, and another early one, the Emigrant Industrial Savings Bank, was formed with the imprimatur of the Roman Catholic Archbishop John Hughes as a way of instilling the habit of thrift among working-class Irish residents of the city. Savings banks' investment portfolios were therefore very conservative. This soon changed, however, as savings banks became ever more profitable. Nonetheless, savings banks always were an institution of the hoi polloi, the small depositors, and they tended to be more conservative than commercial banks, which is why they tended better to withstand the Great Depression, and can explain in part how the Dime Savings Bank was able to undertake a significant expansion of its flagship building during a period we tend to think of as not particularly propitious for banks.

Just outside the Dime Savings Bank is Albee Square, the small triangular open space formed by the confluence of five streets—Fulton, Bond, Gold, and Fleet Streets and DeKalb Avenue. It is named after the RKO Albee movie theater that once stood on the site of the glass-enclosed shopping mall that is now called the Galleria at Metrotech, at the northwest corner of DeKalb Avenue and Fleet Street. Originally called Albee Square Mall, it was designed by Gruen Associates (the nation's most famous firm of shopping-mall architects) and opened in 1980. The movie theater, demolished in 1977, was opened in the 1920s and contained two thousand seats. Edward F. Albee, who built the RKO Albee, was a major vaudeville promoter who also built the legendary Palace Theater on Seventh Avenue and 47th Street in Times Square. He was the father of the playwright of the same name.

Fulton Street has been Brooklyn's most important commercial thoroughfare since the seventeenth century. Known at various times as the Old Ferry Road and as King's Highway, it was named for Robert Fulton in 1814. A huge part of Fulton Street was basically scorched from the earth after World War II as part of the Cadman Plaza urban-renewal project. Perhaps the only other piece of deliberate devastation of an urban commercial core to be carried out on a comparable scale, or at least resulting in so much loss of historically and architecturally noteworthy buildings, was Philadelphia's Independence Park project from around the same time. Today's Cadman Plaza West follows the route of Fulton Street between Joralemon and Front Streets, where an old short stretch of the original Fulton Street continues to the East River as "Old Fulton Street." The elevated railway ran clangorously above Fulton Street for many years, darkening the sidewalks and, at least in steam days, blanketing with soot all in its trail. Here between the Brooklyn Bridge, which the el traversed, and City Hall was that visual chaos decried by sensitive critics such as Montgomery Schuyler, and that, many years later, still stuck in the craw of planners who dreamed of raising order from the urban clutter. Fulton ran basically north to south from the East River until Joralemon Street, where it turned east. It's that whole north-south stretch that no longer exists. Fulton today begins at Adams Street, where Joralemon turns into Willoughby Street, right near City Hall. Downtown Fulton Street runs to Flatbush Avenue. On the other side of Flatbush Avenue, Fulton Street runs through Fort Greene, a long way through Bedford-Stuyvesant, into Cypress Hills to the county line. In the late-nineteenth century, as the interior of Brooklyn developed, the commercial core of Brooklyn moved into the present-day downtown stretch of Fulton Street from the part that was obliterated after World War II. In 1939, the Federal Writers' Project's *New York City Guide* said that Fulton Street had "a bustling Main Street air, not unlike State Street, Chicago, or Euclid Avenue, Cleveland. Today the neon signs blink all day long in the false twilight of an overhead el structure, surface cars bang and clatter incessantly, the subway entrances expel and admit passengers, while the streets are clogged with pedestrian and automobile traffic." In those days before suburban malls, residents of Nassau and Suffolk Counties rode the Long Island Railroad to Flatbush Avenue to shop and dine on Fulton Street. It was not just Brooklyn's, but all Long Island's, downtown. Soon the el came down. Still the street bustled. As recently as the 1960s, Fulton Street, even as Brooklynites were moving to the suburbs in droves, was reckoned to be the sixth busiest shopping street in the United States. Then came hard times. The great department stores, Martin's and Abraham & Straus, closed. The glorious movie palaces nearby, the Paramount and the Fox and the RKO Albee, closed. You know what? Fulton Street may still be one of the busiest shopping streets in the country. A stroll between Adams Street and Flatbush Avenue in the year 2000 reveals that there is scarcely an empty storefront. Some rather rich national chains are moving in. Building façades are likelier to be restored nowadays than "modernized" as they were in those last-ditch efforts to appear up-to-date in the 1950s and 1960s. The crowds cannot conceivably be less than they were in the 1920s or 1930s. Fulton Street is now, of course, Fulton Mall: in the 1980s, private automobiles were banned between Adams Street and Flatbush Avenue. Buses still use the street, but there is a commodious feeling and on the whole this "malling" of the street has been notably more successful than many similar efforts around the country. It may not have so many pockets of elegance as in the days of Martin's or Oppenheim & Collins. Here may be the premier working-class shopping street of New York City, a place to buy CDs and children's toys and jeans and sneakers. What's happened—as has happened on Chicago's State Street—is that while the neighborhood shopping streets throughout Brooklyn declined, or never recovered from 1960s riots, or otherwise became disreputable, Fulton Street in downtown Brooklyn took up the slack and became the biggest neighborhood shopping strip in the city. Fulton Street, too, is an architectural wonderland, at which in my allotted space I can only hint.

5 *Wechsler Brothers Block*

5 WECHSLER BROTHERS BLOCK (aka Offerman Building)
Fulton Street between Bridge and Duffield Streets, north side,
and Duffield Street between Fulton and Willoughby Streets, west side
1890–91, Lauritzen & Voss

Both the Fulton and the Duffield Street façades are Romanesque Revival extravaganzas. The Fulton façade is eight stories of dark brick and sandstone with superb terra-cotta ornamentation in the spandrels and on the piers. There is a big arched entrance in a center section that rises a story above the flanking sections. Note the "18" and the "90" worked into the terra-cotta. The ground floor, as with just about every old building along Fulton Street, has been mutilated. The building is sited midblock on Fulton but extends deep to the north, wrapping around the buildings at the northwest corner of Fulton and Duffield so that there is a long façade on Duffield Street. This façade partakes of much the same Romanesque formal vocabulary as the Fulton façade, though the effect is much different. Here the elements are employed in a much more austere manner. Eight bold arches range along the ground floor, and eight high-arched bays rise from the third through the fifth stories. At the top floor is a series of twenty-three smaller arches below a band of corbeling. Above the second floor appears "1890 Offerman Building 1891." This façade is very much in the Richardsonian mode of such buildings as H. H. Richardson's R. and F. Cheney Building of 1875–76 in Hartford, Connecticut. Lauritzen & Voss designed this building just after P. J. Lauritzen designed the Union League Club at Grant Square in Crown Heights. The club and the Wechsler Brothers Block have more than a few stylistic affinities.

6 LIEBMANN BROTHERS BUILDING
446 Fulton Street, southwest corner of Hoyt Street
1888, William H. Beers

It is pure Brooklyn, with its dark red brick, ogee-domed corner tower, rough stone trim, terra-cotta ornamentation, and its oriels. Atop the Hoyt Street façade once were seven terra-cotta urns: six remain. The top, or fourth, floor is a superb arcade with Romanesque arches but with classical keystones. Two more urns crown the Fulton Street façade. The ground floor has been mutilated. W. H. Beers also designed the wonderful house at 87 Remsen Street in Brooklyn Heights one year after the Liebmann building.

6 Liebmann Brothers Building

7 ABRAHAM & STRAUS DEPARTMENT STORE

Fulton Street between Hoyt Street and Gallatin Place, south side
Main building: 1929, Starrett & Van Vleck

Abraham & Straus, now Macy's, evolved into an enormous complex of eight interconnected buildings in the block bounded by Fulton, Hoyt, and Livingston Streets and Gallatin Place. Along Fulton Street, it is not until one steps back and looks up that one realizes how architecturally diverse the assemblage is. (It is comparable to the full-block evolution of the St. George Hotel in Brooklyn Heights.) At street level, continuous show windows unify all the disparate elements. If one part of the complex etches itself in the mind as the essential A&S, then surely it is the high Art Deco building by Starrett & Van Vleck, with its vertically banded reeds of brick rising the full height of the building. The main building is L-shaped around the old Liebmann Brothers Building at the southwest corner of Fulton and Hoyt Streets. On Fulton Street it's deliriously sandwiched between, on the west, two cast-iron façades, both rusted and crumbling-looking, one wide and in the French Second Empire style, the other narrow and in a sort of Flemish Renaissance style, and, on the east, the Liebmann Brothers Building. What a stew of styles and materials! The best building in the A&S stew is the one at the northeast corner of Livingston Street and Gallatin Place. It is a seven-story Romanesque Revival structure built in 1885 and faced in Roman brick and brownstone. It has an elegantly rounded corner and, in the first-floor arches, exquisite terra-cotta decoration worthy of Louis Sullivan. The store began in 1865 as Wechsler & Abraham, a partnership of Joseph Wechsler and Abraham Abraham. Wechsler & Abraham moved to the present location twenty years later. It is said that by 1889, Wechsler & Abraham was the largest dry-goods store in New York State. At the time, this stretch of Fulton, which we all think of as the heart of downtown, was the new downtown, as the center of gravity of retailing moved south of Willoughby Street from the part of Fulton Street felled for Cadman Plaza after World War II. By the late nineteenth century, Brooklyn was orienting herself ever inward toward the newly populous regions between City Hall and Prospect Park, rather than between City Hall and the East River ferries. Retailing thus nudged southward and eastward. So too culture: the Brooklyn Academy of Music would soon move from Montague Street (where its building burned down) to a new site all the way east at Lafayette Avenue. In 1893, Wechsler & Abraham became Abraham & Straus, as Bedford-Stuyvesant resident Abraham Abraham teamed with Macy's brothers Straus, Isidor (who died with his wife on the *Titanic*) and Nathan, of Manhattan. (The Montague Street lawyer William Jay Gaynor represented Abraham and steered him through the deal's thickets. Gaynor, a Park Slope resident, would later become mayor of New York City.) Corporately, A&S and Macy's were siblings until 1920, so it is not too unjust that the store should today be Macy's, even though "Abraham & Straus," like "Daily Eagle" and "Brooklyn Dodgers," was so long a part of the borough's nomenclatorial identity. A&S opened its first branch in 1934, in Jamaica, Queens, and soon spread throughout suburbia. It was one of the original Federated Department Stores in 1949. When I came to Brooklyn around 1980, A&S was in the process of upgrading itself, and was as fine a department store as New York City could boast. It was a delight to shop in. In the 1980s, the first Manhattan A&S opened as the anchor of the A&S Plaza, carved out of the old Gimbel's building at Herald Square. It, too, was a good store. Alas, a few years later A&S went under, having outlasted many other American department stores of its vintage. I think we should all be thankful that the Fulton Street store continues to operate as a respectable department store.

*7 Abraham & Straus
Department Store*

The architects of Abraham & Straus's main building were Starrett & Van Vleck, a firm that designed all kinds of buildings in New York City but is probably most famous for its numerous department stores. They designed Lord & Taylor (1914), Saks Fifth Avenue (1924), and Bloomingdale's (1930), all in Manhattan. One of their major non-department store designs was the Leverich Towers Hotel (1928) in Brooklyn Heights.

At the northeast corner of Fulton and Lawrence Streets is a building with a rounded corner and a balustrade near its top wrapping around the whole building. At the top of the rounded corner can be made out a crest bearing the insignia of the store that erected this building in 1922, Oppenheim & Collins. This elegant women's store was among those that lent class to Fulton Street in the 1920s and 1930s. Eventually, Oppenheim & Collins opened branches in Manhattan, Garden City, Buffalo, and Philadelphia. They yielded this building in 1957 to E. J. Korvette. Several retailers now occupy the handsome structure, the ground floor of which was long ago mutilated.

8 Former BOND STORE
400 Fulton Street, southwest corner of Gallatin Place
1949, Louis Allen Abramson

Abramson designed the dignified Brooklyn Jewish Center on Eastern Parkway in 1922. Twenty-seven years later, the restrained Beaux-Arts classicism of that building yielded to the International Style modernism we see here. The four-story building is almost square at ninety-five by one hundred feet. The strip windows on the otherwise blank limestone façcade recall the 1934 Spear & Company store by DeYoung & Moscowitz on West 34th Street in Manhattan, as well as the 1957 State Supreme Court Building by Shreve, Lamb & Harmon at Cadman Plaza. That is to say, this style of strip window, a trademark tic of a certain wave of modernist architecture, persisted through three decades (at least) of New York architecture. As was for many years the case with the Spear & Company store, a gigantic billboard, at the time I am writing this, heavily obscures the clean modernist lines of the old Bond's. The billboard features Brooklyn's own hip-hop star Li'l Kim, tugging suggestively at the waistband of her denim short-shorts. One wonders what Adolf Loos would have thought.

9 GAGE & TOLLNER RESTAURANT

372 Fulton Street between Smith Street and Red Hook Lane, south side
Building: 1875
Restaurant: 1892

Charles Gage opened a restaurant in 1879 at 302 Fulton Street, slightly to the west of the present location. Eugene Tollner joined Gage the following year. In 1892, the restaurant relocated to its present site. The dating of things here is a tad complicated. The building itself was originally an Italianate house built in 1875, seventeen years before the restaurant moved in. I believe that the restaurant added the marvelous wooden storefront. Not only is it special today as a rare survivor, but this storefront was probably among the loveliest in its time in Brooklyn. It is the interior of Gage & Tollner, however, that captivates people. It is remarkably intact from the way it probably appeared at the turn of the century. It is a long, narrow, gaslit room defined on its sides by walls with magnificent full-height mirrors in cherry-wood arch frames forming a

9 Gage & Tollner Restaurant

rhythmical arcade. The gaslights are original and are suspended from the ceiling in marvelous wrought-iron fixtures. The beautiful wooden bar and the mahogany tables were, I believe, transported here from the original restaurant. The flickering light, the mirrors, the Lincrusta wall coverings, and the dark wood combine to create an atmosphere, not of luxury so much, but of rich bourgeois comfort. Somehow, amid ownership changes and changes in restaurant fashion, the place has hung on, and through each incarnation manages proudly to retain much of what's been drawing people to this splendid room for more than a century now. The restaurant critic Seymour Britchky, who wrote about the atmosphere of restaurants better than any critic I know, said of Gage & Tollner that it was redolent with the graces of old Brooklyn Heights families, members perhaps of the Renaissance Club and of Mrs. Field's, wearing their sensible clothing from Abraham & Straus and utterly comfortable in their Brooklyn skin, tucking into that quintessential Brooklyn dish, still served here, of clam bellies on toast. Those clam bellies, incidentally, are delicious. They are the tender center part of the clam, breaded and broiled, and traditionally served with toast. The clam bellies are but one of the traditional dishes still served here and perhaps nowhere else in New York. It's said that this is the last place to sample the sort of fare one might have been served at Delmonico's in its heyday. The peripatetic gourmands Jane and Michael Stern have written that the only other places left where one can eat the things Gage & Tollner serves are private eating clubs in Philadelphia and private homes in Baltimore. It is true that amid the frenetic swirl of foodie fads, G & T can get lost in the shuffle. This may be especially so nowadays, when a new wonderful restaurant opens in Brooklyn every week. Folks in Fort Greene and Boerum Hill and Park Slope no longer need to trek to G & T for their special-occasion dinners, as I, a Park Sloper, did fifteen or twenty years ago. But maybe we all still should. And maybe the Landmarks Preservation Commission should hold a hearing about those clam bellies.

10 FULTON SAVINGS BANK
Fulton Street, southeast corner of Boerum Place
1955, DeYoung, Moscowitz & Rosenberg

This granite, white brick, and glass International Style structure is now a branch of HSBC and also houses parts of the Brooklyn Law School. (HSBC, which seems to be taking over many old banks in New York, is the Hong Kong and Shanghai Banking Corporation, headquartered in London.) The architects were among the first to bring a full-blown European modernism to New York in their De Stijl–influenced Spear & Company store on West 34th Street in Manhattan in 1934. Later, in the 1970s, the same long-lived firm designed the campus of Fashion Institute of Technology in Chelsea. Their bank on Fulton Street is really the gateway from the Civic Center to downtown. The building is crisper and better maintained than many of its ilk. It reads as a cube on Fulton Street, but around the corner on Boerum Place it has a four-part staggered façade extending all the way to Red Hook Lane and nicely articulating the building's tricky triangular site. It replaced a burlesque theater on the site, when planners in this period of Cadman Plaza wished to render order out of the chaos of Fulton Street.

11 BROOKLYN LAW SCHOOL (now Brooklyn Friends School)
375 Pearl Street between Fulton and Willoughby Streets, east side
1929, Mayers, Murray & Philip

Pearl Street is a sort of alley that runs for only about a block from Fulton Street north until it dead-ends at the south side of the Brooklyn Marriott Hotel. There's not heavy traffic on Pearl Street, either automotive or pedestrian. This gem of a building is therefore seldom noted. Originally the home of the Brooklyn Law School (founded in 1901), which later moved to Joralemon Street, it is now the home of the distinguished Brooklyn Friends School. Mayers, Murray & Philip, the building's architects, were the successor firm to Bertram Grosvenor Goodhue, one of New York's greatest architects. If the successors never quite achieved the master's poetry, nonetheless they often produced very interesting and handsome buildings. Perhaps their best-known works are the dome (1930) and community house (1926–28) of St. Bartholomew's Church on Park Avenue, begun by Goodhue, who died in 1924 before the complex was completed. Another well-known work by Mayers, Murray & Philip is the Church of the Heavenly Rest (1926–29) on Fifth Avenue and 90th Street. Here on Pearl Street we have a limestone base with brick above, then limestone again at the top of the building. Five-story wings flank an eight-story center section. The style is Romanesque Revival with a little of the flavor of Art Deco. (The web site of the Brooklyn Friends School refers to their "art deco building in downtown Brooklyn.") The building is ornamented with light-colored polychromatic tile work, and with elaborate reliefs in the limestone of the recessed entrance bay. At the top, Romanesque columns carry nine arched windows below a shallow stone balcony lifted on heavy, crude brackets. Look up and see the fenced-in rooftop space that must be very nice for the students. The building is next door to and provides a striking contrast to the Board of Transportation Building of only about twenty years later. The Brooklyn Friends School was founded in 1867 (ten years after the meeting-house was built on Schermerhorn Street) and stresses academic excellence along with the traditional Quaker virtues of "tolerance, compassion, equality, and pacifism." It is interesting to note that at least three truly distinguished private preparatory schools are located within a few blocks of one another in this area of Brooklyn: Brooklyn Friends, St. Ann's, and Packer Collegiate.

12 BOARD OF TRANSPORTATION BUILDING
370 Jay Street, northwest corner of Willoughby Street
1950, William E. Haugaard and Andrew J. Thomas

*12 Board of
Transportation Building*

When this building was built, Lewis Mumford was America's foremost architectural critic. A lifelong hater of the classical, Mumford extolled what he believed to be a morally virtuous modernism. Mind you, he could be as harshly critical of International Style– and Bauhaus-inspired buildings as could any classicist. To read Mumford's architectural criticism is to encounter a mind capable of making the subtlest distinctions rendered in crystal-clear prose. Even those who disagree with everything he ever said love to read him. Here is something he said about this building in the *New Yorker:* "a new structure in this area, finished last year, has already set the right precedent for a modern office building, and I am hopeful that its sobriety and efficiency will leave a mark on the whole neighborhood." He dreamed of a whole business district composed of buildings like this one. Such sobriety, such healthfulness, such virtue as this building possesses, said Mumford, "we" would trade in a heartbeat for all the columns floating in the air, all the cartouches, all the swags and rosettes in the world. (Every time I read a Mumford "we," I cannot help fantasizing myself in Charlton Heston's place in *The Omega Man.*) On Jay Street, the building's principal façade, it seems rather like an ice cube. It is a thirteen-story limestone box with 420 equal-sized windows punched out of it like the cells of a spreadsheet. These windows are flush with the wall, not set within frames to give a sense of depth and solidity to the building. It is raised on piers—Corbusian "pilotis." These create a not unattractive street-level "arcade" in which can be found stairs and escalators descending to the Jay Street/Borough Hall station of the IND subway. The subway signage is in illuminated, blocky green letters, and is rather elegant in an Art Moderne sort of way. All the other sides of the building are similarly arcaded and fenestrated. The building rises to the flattest roof in the universe. For office workers, it was and is a boon that all the hundreds (one is tempted, like Carl Sagan, to say "billions and billions") of windows are of the openable casement type. We can see why Mumford found this a healthful design. The sheer quantity of openable windows, together with the slab-like form of the building (356 feet long by 82 feet wide), must truly make for outstanding cross-ventilation, an undeniable virtue in any kind of construction. This building seems to be striving to take such virtues and to make them the basis for the building's expression. It says, look—*cross ventilation!* I cannot imagine that Lewis Mumford could have dreamed how purely quaint this building would one day seem, but that, indeed, is the chief virtue of this building today. Being the headquarters of what was then called the New York City Board of Transportation, this building housed the vaults where all the money collected by the city's token-booth clerks was brought by trains that pulled into special sidings below the building. The design actually dates from before World War II, placing this in the first generation of New York modernism, kin to such buildings as Hunter College (1940) on Park Avenue and 68th Street. The original architect of the Board of Transportation Building, and presumably its chief form-giver, was William E. Haugaard, who had earlier codesigned the handsome New York State Office Building (1928–30) in a restrained classical style on Centre and Worth Streets in Manhattan. By the time the Board of Transportation Building was to be realized, after the war, Haugaard had died, and Andrew J. Thomas took over as architect. Thomas had earlier been not only the architect but also the developer of many of the renowned garden-apartment complexes in Jackson Heights, Queens, in the 1920s. He also codesigned Queens Borough Hall (1941) on Queens Boulevard.

13 BROOKLYN FIRE HEADQUARTERS
365–367 Jay Street between Willoughby Street
and Myrtle Avenue, east side
1892, Frank Freeman

The somber-hued Romanesque Revival that is the ostensible style of this building was a Brooklyn and New York staple of the 1880s and early 1890s, when this was built, and merely to enumerate the elements of the style hardly tells the story of the surety and compacted power of a design by Frank Freeman that is uniquely fine. Freeman was an architect of fecund imagination, as exemplified not only in his Romanesque works such as this, his house for Herman Behr on Pierrepont Street, and his Eagle Warehouse and Storage Company Building in DUMBO, but also in classical designs such as his Brooklyn Savings Bank that once stood on Pierrepont Street. This building is three bays wide but reads as two distinct parts. The two bays on the right are unified at the ground floor, by one of the boldest and most mellifluously carved arches of its arch-happy day in Brooklyn, and at the top, in a pyramidal tile roof with an eyelid dormer. The part to the left is a tower, rising a full story over the rest of the building and culminating in a tiled pyramid. The tower sports its own magnificent arch, this time a thrillingly receding one, at the top. But the elements that perhaps make the building, unifying the composition across its variegated parts and lending to the façade its exciting plasticity, are the three turrets. Though

13 *Brooklyn Fire Headquarters*

not all of the same height or thickness, they still bring a strong resolution to the design. The tower is sandwiched by them, with the one on the tower's right side working with one at the far right of the building to sandwich the double-bay section as well. The building's palette derives from its materials: rock-faced sandstone, a tawny Roman brick, and terra-cotta. The whole thing seems strongly influenced by Henry Hobson Richardson's Allegheny County Courthouse and Jail (1883–88) in Pittsburgh.

This much-admired building served Brooklyn as its fire headquarters for a mere six years. Note the date of construction: six years hence the City of Brooklyn would be no more. The fire headquarters of the consolidated city was in Manhattan, and this became, simply, the most splendid neighborhood firehouse in Greater New York. In the 1980s it was converted to housing.

FRANK FREEMAN (1861–1949)

Canadian-born Frank Freeman came to Brooklyn in 1885, at the age of only twenty-four, and hit the ground running. He lived in Brooklyn Heights (he was a parishioner of Holy Trinity Episcopal Church) and established offices in both New York City and Brooklyn; though he did work in Manhattan, it is his Brooklyn work for which he shall forever be renowned. In his time he was prolific, and if it does not seem that way to us, it is because so many of his buildings have been demolished. Still, as entries in this book attest, enough of Freeman still exists in Brooklyn that we can all see why Norval White has called him "Brooklyn's greatest architect." Whether or not that's true, it is not an outrageous claim. One highly notable thing about Freeman was his versatility. His most touted buildings are in a basically Richardsonian Romanesque vein. Of these, none has been more praised than the Brooklyn Fire Headquarters (1892), though the Herman Behr house (1888–90) on Pierrepont Street in Brooklyn Heights and the Eagle Warehouse and Storage Company Building (1893) on Old Fulton Street are also much praised. Two still-standing buildings by Freeman that are classical rather than Romanesque are the Crescent Athletic Club (1906) on Pierrepont and Clinton Streets, and the Brooklyn Union Gas Company Building (1914) on Remsen Street between Court and Clinton Streets.

Among Freeman's Brooklyn buildings no longer standing, we may count the following: the Hotel Margaret (1889) on Columbia Heights and Orange Street, the Guido Pleissner house (1889) on Plaza Street and Lincoln Place in Park Slope, the Thomas Jefferson Association Building (1889–90) on Boerum Place and Fulton Street, the Germania Club (1889–90) on Schermerhorn Street between Smith Street and Boerum Place, the Bushwick Democratic Club (1892) on Bushwick Avenue and Hart Street, and the Brooklyn Savings Bank (1894) on Pierrepont and Clinton Streets.

Freeman also worked in Manhattan in critically acclaimed houses (now gone) on Riverside Drive. The Samuel Gamble Bayne house (1888–91) stood on the southeast corner of Riverside Drive and 108th Street, and the Henry F. S. Davis house stood on the northeast corner of the same intersection.

Notice that all the Romanesque designs mentioned above date from a five-year period, 1888 to 1893. The classical designs range from 1894 to 1914. In 1893, something happened called the World's Columbian Exposition. Many Brooklyn architects shifted from Romanesque and Queen Anne to classical around that time, including Montrose W. Morris and R. L. Daus. Before the Great Divide, Daus designed buildings such as the houses for William M. Thallon and Edward Bunker (1887–88) on St. John's Place in Park Slope, and the Lincoln Club (1889) in Bedford-Stuyvesant. After 1893, Daus began to produce such buildings as the New York and New Jersey Telephone Company Building (1898) on Willoughby and Lawrence Streets and the John W. Weber house (1909) on Eighth Avenue in Park Slope. As for Morris, before 1893, he did such work as his own house from 1885 on Hancock Street in Bedford-Stuyvesant, the Arlington Apartments (1887) on Montague Street, the Henry Carlton Hulbert house (1889) on Prospect Park West, the Alhambra Apartments (1889–90) on Nostrand Avenue, and the Imperial Apartments (1892) on Pacific Street and Bedford Avenue. After 1893, Morris gave us the houses at Nos. 18 and 19 Prospect Park West (1898) and at Nos. 16 and 17 Prospect Park West (1899) and the apartment houses at 143 Eighth Avenue and 10 Montgomery Place (1910–11) in Park Slope. On one block in Fort Greene we see both halves of Montrose Morris. On South Oxford Street between Lafayette and DeKalb Avenues can be seen the San Carlos Hotel (now called the Roanoke Apartments) from 1890, and the remodeled façade of the house at 26 South Oxford Street from 1893. What's amazing is that these architects were skilled enough to do outstanding work in very contrasting veins. Some architects belong to the pre-1893 world, such as the Parfitt Brothers and William B. Tubby who, though they worked until well after 1893 and occasionally employed classical elements in their designs, never embraced the new Beaux-Arts Classicism. Other architects, such as Helmle & Huberty and Mowbray & Uffinger, belong wholly to the post-1893 world.

Though many will disagree with me—and judging solely from photographs since I never saw it in real life—I would say that the Brooklyn Savings Bank on Pierrepont and Clinton Streets may have been Freeman's finest work—and it was classical.

---

14 NEW YORK AND NEW JERSEY TELEPHONE COMPANY BUILDING

81 Willoughby Street, northeast corner of Lawrence Street
1898, R. L. Daus

This is one of the glories of downtown Brooklyn and perhaps its remarkable architect's masterpiece. The base is limestone with light-colored brick above. The entrance is on the east end of the Willoughby Street front. A triangular pediment crowns the doorway, deeply recessed within an enormous arch. Note the shield with a superimposed "T" and "C," for Telephone Company. Old-fashioned telephones, earpieces, and bells are worked into the decoration. Magnificent eagles top the piers framing the entrance arch. The building rises eight stories to a superb modillioned cornice in verdigris copper. On Willoughby are three arched bays across the façade rising from the fifth through the seventh floors, with Corinthian columns rising from the fifth through the sixth floors. The rounded corner at Lawrence Street is breathtaking. At its top is a wreathed oculus featuring a Mercury head. On the Lawrence Street façade are three more arches rising from the fifth through the seventh floors. The style might be thought of as a subset of the Beaux-Arts: the Cartouche style. This was the heyday of the Cartouche style. Think of this building as one of the great Upper East Side town houses of the period, such as Ernest Flagg's Oliver Gould Jennings house or Carrère & Hastings's Henry T. Sloane house, both on East 72nd Street, blown up to office-building scale. Count them, and one will see that there are no fewer than seventeen cartouches (not one of them a shrinking violet) worked into the design of this building.

This is an absolutely gorgeous building, handled with great skill by its École des Beaux-Arts–trained architect who added so much to the streets of Brooklyn throughout his distinguished career. Daus created buildings as diverse as the Queen Anne–style Lincoln Club (1889) in Bedford-Stuyvesant, the 1890 French Renaissance–style house at 47 Montgomery Place in Park Slope, and the Arts & Crafts–like Saratoga Branch (1908) of the Brooklyn Public Library in

Bedford-Stuyvesant. The Telephone Company Building may exhibit what he learned at the École des Beaux-Arts better than anything else he designed in Brooklyn. It is only a block away from the Board of Transportation Building, built half a century though seemingly light-years later. This was as profound a repudiation as can be imagined of every principle on which the Telephone Company Building was based. About the later building, Lewis Mumford, to whom it was a masterpiece, wrote: "We could cheerfully trade the imitative classic monumentality of the old civic centers, with their reliance on columns and cornices . . . for some of this honesty, this straightforwardness, this matter-of-fact decency." One gets the impression that, though he does not mention it, Mumford had to have seen the Telephone Company Building so near the Board of Transportation Building, and found the older building wanting in every respect. What a curious interlude it was in architectural criticism when skillful embellishment was decried in the most heavily moralizing terms as "dishonest" and "indecent." Mumford praised the "sobriety" of the Board of Transportation Building. I suppose that makes the Telephone Company Building drunken. Give me the drunken building any time.

14 *New York and New Jersey*
Telephone Company

15 *New York Telephone Company,*
Long Island Headquarters

15 NEW YORK TELEPHONE COMPANY, LONG ISLAND HEADQUARTERS

101 Willoughby Street, northeast corner of Bridge Street
1931, Voorhees, Gmelin & Walker

This and the earlier telephone building at the northeast corner of Lawrence Street make Willoughby one of the most exciting streets in downtown Brooklyn. This complexly massed setback skyscraper, 348 feet high, was designed by Ralph Walker, one of the best and most innovative of the skyscraper architects of the 1920s and 1930s. We call the style Art Deco, and Walker, in his New York Telephone Building of 1923–26 on West Street in Manhattan, basically invented the Art Deco skyscraper. New York Telephone often employed Walker. He was born in Waterbury, Connecticut, in 1889. He worked for a small architectural firm in Providence, Rhode Island, and then attended the Massachusetts Institute of Technology. He chose not to attend the École des Beaux-Arts, and it is said of Walker that at no point in his career was he a classical architect. He served in the Army Corps of Engineers in World War I, after which he moved to New York and entered the office of another architect,

Bertram Grosvenor Goodhue, who rejected the Beaux-Arts approach. Goodhue's office had an atelier-like atmosphere, and several of the architects to rise to prominence in the 1920s and 1930s, including Raymond Hood and Wallace K. Harrison as well as Walker, put in time there. Walker's next move was to join the workmanlike firm of McKenzie, Voorhees & Gmelin in 1919. (This was the successor firm to Eidlitz & McKenzie, architects of the Times Tower in Times Square. Eidlitz was Cyrus L. W. Eidlitz, son of Leopold Eidlitz, who designed the original Brooklyn Academy of Music on Montague Street.) The firm was still called McKenzie, Voorhees & Gmelin when Walker designed the Telephone Building on West Street as well as when, around the same time, the firm designed the Brooklyn Municipal Building on Joralemon Street. By the time the Willoughby Street New York Telephone Building was built, the firm had become Voorhees, Gmelin & Walker. Walker designed the Irving Trust Company Building (1929–31) at No. 1 Wall Street, the Western Union Building (1928–30) at 60 Hudson Street in what we now call TriBeCa, and numerous other noteworthy buildings, most of them immediately identifiable as Ralph Walker designs. What makes them so identifiable are, first, the massing, conforming to the setback requirements of the 1916 zoning law not simply by stacking cubes one atop the other, but through careful manipulation of projecting and receding planes, chamfered corners, and a generally sculptural quality often lacking in the works of other skyscraper architects. Second, Walker paid fastidious attention to the "skins" of his buildings, using subtle gradations of color and subtle ripplings of the surface to achieve expressive effects. The Willoughby Street building is an outstanding example of his mature style. In his only slightly earlier Irving Trust Company Building, Walker rendered the building's limestone curtain wall as a vertically rippled drapery. On Willoughby Street, he translated that innovation into brick. The subtle vertical ripples were even more faceted than at the Wall Street building. By doing this and by using countless gradations in the color of the brick, Walker's intent was to create "ribbons of light and shadow running up and down the façade" (Stern, Gilmartin, and Mellins, *New York 1930*). The quality of the bricklaying is extraordinary, and the façades here repay close scrutiny. Also note the patterned brickwork and the lush bronze grilles at the building's base. The recessed, faceted entryway on Bridge Street is highly reminiscent of the entrance to the Irving Trust Company Building, with its seeming bow to German Expressionist stage design.

    Next door to the east of the Ralph Walker building is Skidmore, Owings & Merrill's Chase Manhattan Bank Building (4 Metrotech Center), a very careful attempt to harmonize with the earlier building. Note also that the firm responsible for the master plan of Metrotech—Smith, Smith, Haines, Lundberg & Waehler—is the successor firm to Voorhees, Gmelin & Walker.

16 METROTECH
Bounded roughly by Flatbush Avenue and Jay, Willoughby, and Tillary Streets
1989–

In the last ten or so years, Metrotech has redefined downtown Brooklyn. Downtown weathered some pretty serious storms in the 1960s, 1970s, and 1980s but emerged as still one of the busiest shopping areas in Greater New York. Many people nonetheless felt that downtown could and should be so much more. With Manhattan's burgeoning financial services economy, downtown Brooklyn was a logical choice for companies to locate their "back office" space. To keep such space, Manhattan, near company headquarters, proved prohibitively expensive in the booming 1980s. A great deal of this "back office" space was being relocated to less-expensive real estate, sometimes in the New York suburbs, sometimes in other parts of the country and even the world. A bank, for example, might be headquartered in Manhattan, but when one pays one's credit card bill to that bank, the check is sent to Wilmington, Delaware, or to Boise, Idaho. Why not Brooklyn? This was one impetus for the rethinking of downtown Brooklyn that resulted in Metrotech. Another was that in the 1980s, some of the most booming areas in the country were high-tech "corridors" located near major scientific and engineering universities. New York City lagged behind as a high-tech "incubator." Yet smack in downtown Brooklyn was Polytechnic University, a major engineering institution. Why couldn't it develop the same symbiotic relationship with start-up businesses that other such schools had done elsewhere in the country? A master plan was drawn up by the large architectural firm of Haines Lundberg Waehler, the successor firm to Voorhees, Gmelin & Walker, designers of the nearby Long Island headquarters of the New York Telephone Company on Willoughby Street, and to McKenzie, Voorhees & Gmelin, designers of the Municipal Building on Joralemon Street. Several major companies signed on. Chase Manhattan Bank, Brooklyn Union Gas (now Keyspan), and Securities Industry Automation Company (which runs the computers at the New York Stock Exchange) all became tenants. The master plan called for the wholesale redevelopment of the downtown stretch of Myrtle

Avenue. Myrtle was closed to traffic between Jay Street and Flatbush Avenue, a stretch of four blocks. A landscaped pedestrian promenade and a large landscaped plaza were created. A group of large office towers was constructed along the south side of Myrtle (now called Myrtle Promenade). To the north were new and preexisting buildings of Polytechnic University. Polytechnic, old and distinguished as it was, had never had a proper campus. That changed with Metrotech, which can be thought of as a combination corporate campus—the kind now found throughout suburbia—and university campus. Metrotech is still very much a work in progress.

The office buildings along the south side of Myrtle Promenade partake of a largely 1980s design vocabulary, either a softened modernism or a hardened postmodernism—take your pick. They are mostly faced in brick, sometimes ornamentally patterned, and they form a continuous pedestrian arcade along Myrtle. The arcades also feature storefronts—an urbanistic bow that one does not find in suburban office parks. Restaurants and cafés have opened in

16 *Metrotech*

these storefronts, and in nice weather spill tables onto the sidewalks. Skidmore, Owings & Merrill designed the Chase Manhattan Bank buildings at Nos. 3 and 4 Metrotech Center (as the addresses are officially rendered), which form an "L" around Ralph Walker's fine New York Telephone Company Building of 1931 at the northeast corner of Willoughby and Bridge Streets. The designers of these Metrotech buildings clearly admired the Walker building and tried very hard to be deferential neighbors. Critically the most acclaimed of Metrotech's buildings are the new New York City Fire Department Headquarters (9 Metrotech Center) on the southeast corner of Johnson and Bridge Streets, and Polytechnic University's new Bern Dibner Library (5 Metrotech Center) on Johnson Street between Lawrence and Bridge Streets. Swanke Hayden Connell designed the Fire Department Headquarters, built in 1997. This is the fire headquarters of all New York City and is located only a couple of blocks from the Frank Freeman building on Jay Street, which was once the City of Brooklyn Fire Headquarters before consolidation changed all that. The new fire headquarters is to the immediate north of the old First Free Congregational Church (now Polytechnic's student center) and, with its red brick, its pediments, and its "antae," bows to the design of the church. Davis Brody Bond designed the library, which was built in 1992 and features a pre-cast concrete grid with bits of traditional detailing.

Metrotech is not without its critics. Some see this as a reprise of 1950s- and 1960s-style urban renewal, the same sort of scorched-earth approach that created Cadman Plaza. Others believe that it embodies a number of lessons learned from the failure of past urban-renewal efforts. What is more, support-ers say, Polytechnic got the proper campus it deserved while at the same time a decrepit part of downtown received a much-needed economic jolt. Only time will tell, of course. For my part, though I have not decided what I think of it, I will say this. There is a pleasant workaday hum about the place on weekdays. The mixture of office workers and students is pleasing. On nice afternoons the promenade and the plaza are quite urbane places. On the downside, the place is dead on weekends. This may change to some degree when Polytechnic's new dormitories are completed, a date projected as the fall of 2002, when there will be a continuous student presence in the area. Another thing to look out for is the continuing development of Metrotech as a hub for high-tech start-ups. Thus far, the Metrotech scene has been dominated by big corporate logos. I recall, though, that when Metrotech was first broached in the 1980s, high-tech start-ups were very much a part of the raison d'être. Left-wing and free-market critics alike are made very uneasy by the presence of so many big corporate logos. The left-wingers worry about the eroding manufacturing base and what they view as pie-in-the-sky dreams of a Rockefellerized city of shiny, sterile office towers and apartments for the affluent. The free marketeers claim that New York City is shooting itself in the foot by catering to large corporations that can afford the armies of lawyers needed to navigate the bureaucratic maze and to take advantage of complicated tax incentives. The free marketeers say that the dynamism of Silicon Valley or Route 128 will be impossible to repli-cate in New York City unless there is radical change. Left-wingers and free marketeers have very different visions of the future. What they agree on is that development centered around big corporations is ultimately self-defeating, and a vestige of the shopworn corporatist mentality of the post–World War II period that gave us urban renewal and modernist architecture. At this writing, the DUMBO area has begun to attract significant numbers of "dot-com" start-up companies. With that in mind, Forest City Ratner, the large real-estate developer, is planning a new Metrotech building to be dedicated exclusively to dot-com companies. This thirteen-story, 520,000-square-foot building, sched-uled for completion in the fall of 2001, is rising to the immediate south of the old First Free Congregational Church. Designed by Swanke Hayden Connell, it will be called 9 Metrotech South, at which time the Fire Department Headquarters, which the same firm designed to the immediate north of the church, will be called 9 Metrotech North.

BROOKLYN POLYTECHNIC UNIVERSITY

Polytechnic University began as the Brooklyn Collegiate and Polytechnic Institute in 1853. It was another in the remarkable flurry of cultural and educational institutions created at the time by lead-ing figures in Brooklyn society. In this case, the names included Isaac H. Frothingham, who was also a founder of the Brooklyn Academy of Music; J. Carson Brevoort, an historian and a founder of the Long Island Historical Society; Josiah Low, brother of Abiel Abbot Low and uncle of Seth Low; and James S. T. Stranahan, who gave Brooklyn its Prospect Park. The Institute was to be an elementary and secondary school for boys from families of means. It opened in 1855 in a building on the then still largely unbuilt Livingston Street in what would later be downtown Brooklyn. John H. Raymond,

Polytechnic's first president, later became the first president of Vassar College, founded in 1861, in Poughkeepsie, New York.

In its early years, the secondary education at the Institute was at a very high level, and graduates, at age seventeen, often entered Harvard or Columbia as sophomores and even juniors. It was not at first a technical and engineering school. Indeed, most of its early students opted for its classical course preparing them for admission to Ivy League colleges. Toward the end of the nineteenth century, however, the scientific and engineering course had grown more popular and would eventually come to define the Institute. The name was changed in 1889 to the Polytechnic Institute of Brooklyn, and the preparatory and collegiate divisions became separate. The preparatory division became known as Poly Prep, and in 1917 moved to Bay Ridge, where it is still going strong as a bastion of the Brooklyn elite. A watershed event was the first meeting of the American Society of Engineering Education, held at the Institute in 1894. From this point on, engineering dominated the school, and the liberal arts degree option was dropped in 1908. The school first awarded the Ph.D. degree in the 1930s. Women were first admitted in the 1940s, a decade that also saw the school hit its stride as an important research institution where, among other things, much of the work was done toward the invention of radar.

In 1954, the expanding school moved into the old American Safety Razor Company Building on Jay Street. The 1960s were a rough time at Polytechnic, which saw declining enrollment that exacerbated an already tight financial situation. This was partly rectified in 1973 when Polytechnic merged with the engineering school of New York University, which had been located at NYU's Bronx campus. Polytechnic crawled back from its 1960s low point, first by becoming involved in the Metrotech development, then by being beneficiaries of the totally unexpected largess of Donald and Mildred Othmer. Donald Othmer was a professor of chemical engineering at Polytechnic, and he and his wife Mildred lived in Brooklyn Heights. The Othmers seemed the quintessence of middle-class thriftiness, and no one had any idea that they were so rich. It turned out that they had made some wise investments, partly with the help of an old family friend named Warren Buffett. The Othmers left $175 million of their $750 million estate to Polytechnic, the largest private cash gift ever left to a university in the United States. (The Othmers also left a substantial sum of money to the Brooklyn Historical Society. At this writing, the Historical Society has closed down its landmark building on Pierrepont Street for an Othmer-funded overhaul, and is temporarily ensconced in office space in Two Metrotech Center, appropriately Polytechnic's neighbor.) At this writing, the school is building an eight-story structure on Jay Street just north of Myrtle Avenue to house a gymnasium and laboratories, and a sixteen-story dormitory building, to be named for the Othmers, at Johnson Street just east of Jay Street. Davis Brody Bond designed both buildings, which are expected to open by fall 2002.

Seth Low and Alfred Tredway White, who grew up next door to each other on Pierrepont Place, both attended Polytechnic. Brooklyn architects William B. Tubby, Raymond F. Almirall, Woodruff Leeming, and J. Monroe Hewlett were all Polytechnic alumni. Almirall, Leeming, and Hewlett all went on from Polytechnic to the École des Beaux-Arts in Paris.

Though Polytechnic's emphasis since the 1880s and 1890s has been on engineering, it is interesting to note that in recent decades the school has boasted some stellar non-engineering faculty, including the great historian of slavery Eugene D. Genovese, and the renowned free-market economist Murray Rothbard, both native Brooklynites who would eventually end up far from home: Genovese in South Carolina, Rothbard (until his death a few years ago) in Las Vegas. The poet Louis Zukofsky taught for nearly twenty years at Polytechnic.

---

17 FIRST FREE CONGREGATIONAL CHURCH
(now Wunsch Student Center of Polytechnic University)
311 Bridge Street between Myrtle Avenue and Johnson Street
1846–47

The 1830s and 1840s were the heyday of the Greek Revival, a style that was used for just about every conceivable type of building. Churches of all denominations adopted it. In Brooklyn, perhaps the most noteworthy Greek

Revival church was the First Reformed Dutch Church, designed by Minard Lafever (whose pattern books popularized the style) and built in 1834–35 on Joralemon and Court Streets, where the Municipal Building now stands. This and any number of other churches in the style have been knocked down, but not this Congregational church, now owned and used by Polytechnic University. On the line of what used to be Bridge Street, the church is now an ornament of the Metrotech development that incorporates office buildings and the campus of Polytechnic. This church may well have been drawn from one of Lafever's pattern books, as so many similar, simple Greek Revival churches were. Unlike Lafever's own Reformed Dutch Church, which had a full temple front of freestanding columns, this one is "distyle in antis," in which two full Doric columns are set within a slightly recessed portico, up a broad flight of stairs. On either side of the portico are pedimented windows framed by pilasters. A broad, unadorned pediment tops the whole building. As with other churches in the style, it is quite austere. I know of no other extant churches in the style in Brooklyn, but in Manhattan comparable works include St. James Church on St. James Place, from the 1830s, and Oliver Street Baptist Church (Mariners' Temple), from the 1840s, both of which were at one time erroneously attributed to Lafever, though both were probably inspired by his pattern books.

Of historical interest is that this church—built for the New England Congregationalists who flooded into Brooklyn in the first half of the nineteenth century—became, in 1854, the home of the oldest African American congregation in Brooklyn, the African Wesleyan Methodist Episcopal Church (founded in 1818), and served as a stop on the Underground Railroad for escaped slaves. In 1863, it was also a sanctuary for African Americans fleeing the mob violence of the horrendous draft riots. Known as Bridge Street Church, the congregation remained here until 1938, when it moved to Bedford-Stuyvesant. After thirty years in which the old Bridge Street Church was used as, among other things, a postcard factory, it was purchased by Polytechnic, and, though it is a church no longer, is in a fine state of preservation as the Wunsch Student Center. The restoration and renovation of the building was completed in 1996; James Wong was the architect.

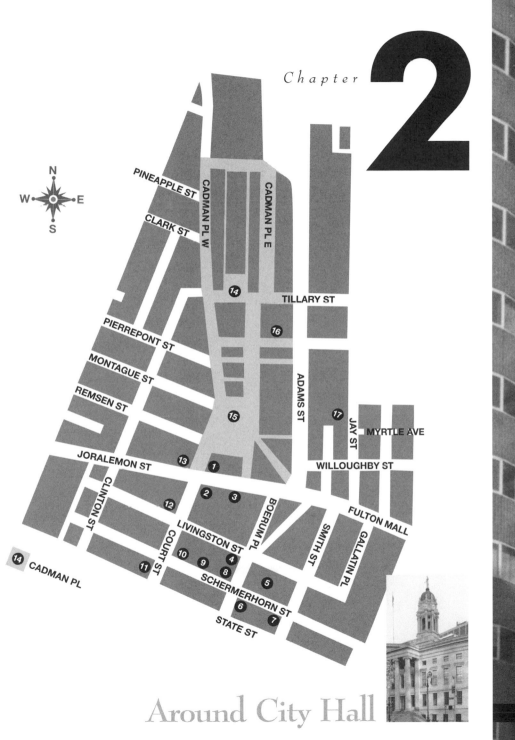

2

W · N · E · S

PINEAPPLE ST

CLARK ST

CADMAN PL W

CADMAN PL E

TILLARY ST

PIERREPONT ST

MONTAGUE ST

REMSEN ST

ADAMS ST

JAY ST

MYRTLE AVE

JORALEMON ST

WILLOUGHBY ST

CLINTON ST

FULTON MALL

LIVINGSTON ST

BOERUM PL

SMITH ST

GALLATIN PL

COURT ST

SCHERMERHORN ST

STATE ST

CADMAN PL

Around City Hall

15 *Statue of Henry Ward Beecher*

HENRY WARD BEECHER
1813 ✠ 1887

Chapter 2

Around City Hall

1 CITY HALL
209 Joralemon Street, northeast corner of Court Street
1845–48, Gamaliel King
1898, Vincent Griffith and Stoughton & Stoughton

It is now, of course, *Borough* Hall. When it opened, the City of Brooklyn was but ten years old with another fifty to go. The New York State Legislature granted Brooklyn its city charter on April 8, 1834. At the time, Brooklyn's population was less than 25,000. City Hall was sited on a plot of land that was donated by the owners of parts of it, the Pierrepont and the Remsen families, remembered in the names of nearby streets. A prominent New York architect named Calvin Pollard was entrusted in the following year with the commission to design the new city hall. Its cornerstone was laid a year after that. Pollard is scarcely remembered today. He is unmentioned in *The Encyclopedia of New York City,* nor does his name appear in the *AIA Guide*. Yet he was one of several New York architects once quite prominent whose misfortune is that not a single one of his buildings has survived. Indeed, there are survivors among buildings by architects once much less prominent than Pollard, and we've all heard of those other architects. It is an illustration of how sheer chance plays a role in establishing architectural reputations! Be that as it may, the reader will have inferred that if Brooklyn City Hall as built were Pollard's design, we'd

1 *City Hall*

then know Pollard's name. In fact, though the cornerstone was laid and foundations dug, the nation was plunged almost immediately thereafter into a depression, and work on the building was halted. Building resumed in 1845. By that time Pollard was out of the picture, and the design and supervision of construction passed to a man named Gamaliel King, a carpenter and a grocer who in 1835 had been runner-up to Pollard in the City Hall design competition. King was then hired to supervise the construction. By 1845, with King in charge, much of Pollard's design was retained, though somewhat reduced in scale. We can infer from the fact that with City Hall originally planned to be much larger than it turned out, the city fathers of the nascent burg must have had something like the visions (delusions?) of grandeur that would, some half a century later, affect the planners of the Brooklyn Museum, another landmark that never quite achieved its intended dimensions. City Hall curiously parallels another Brooklyn landmark, as well. King had to make use of the existing foundation dug for Pollard's unbuilt City Hall. Just so, almost a century later, Githens & Keally had to make use of an already existing foundation when they were hired to design the Brooklyn Public Library thirty or so years after work had to be suspended on the building designed by Raymond Almirall. And let us not forget that the Roman Catholic Diocese of Brooklyn dug a foundation for a magnificent cathedral in Fort Greene that remained nothing but a hole in the ground for several decades before the Diocese decided to abandon the project. This is almost a leitmotif in Brooklyn's architectural history.

City Hall is one of New York's most impressive works in the Greek Revival style. I have to admit to feeling sometimes that buildings of the American Greek Revival have perhaps too great a tendency to the chaste and austere. However handsome their proportions, crisp their detailing, or stately their presence, many buildings in the style, for me, cry out for ornament. The big, blank pediment, for example, can be an imposing thing, as intended, but can also be dull. Later in the nineteenth century, architects, many of them trained at the École des Beaux-Arts, embellished New York with sculptural pediments that are today among the city's greatest treasures. The Greeks themselves, of course, made extensive use of ornament and color, including embellished pediments. Yet in the nineteenth-century Greek Revival, chastity was the rule. It may explain why, of all the historical "revivals" of the nineteenth century, the Greek Revival was the one most favored by modern architects. (For a sense of how the Greeks themselves went at things, look at the model of the Parthenon displayed at Manhattan's Metropolitan Museum of Art.) That said, though she wears a blank pediment, Brooklyn City Hall is a lively building with strongly modeled façades and a sculpturally elaborate cupola that lends a great deal to the success of the building. For one thing, the sheer number of pediments almost makes up for their absence of embellishment. There are five roof pediments. One surmounts the fine, imposing hexastyle Ionic portico facing north onto Cadman Plaza. Roof pediments can be seen topping off the slightly projecting center sections of the east and west sides as well as the projecting east and west wings of the south side of the building. Triangular pediments cap fifty of the building's 166 windows. (I was amazed by this number when I counted!) All the pediments, great and small, are very shallow and outlined by heavy moldings, so that there is much plasticity and play of shadow over the façades. Adding to this dimensionality are twenty-four Doric pilasters rising from the base of the building through the attic story.

41

In 1895, the original wooden cupola was destroyed by fire. In 1898, the new cupola, designed by Stoughton & Stoughton (the architects of the splendid Soldiers' and Sailors' Monument in Riverside Park) and Vincent Griffith, was installed. That was the same year this ceased to be City Hall: in 1898, Brooklyn was fatefully absorbed into New York City, and City Hall became Borough Hall. In 1902, the old Common Council room, by then obsolete, was renovated into a courtroom. This resplendent Beaux-Arts design, a marvelous addition to the building showing the continuity of the classical language of architecture, was designed by the Brooklyn architect Axel Hedman, whose row houses and apartment houses dot the streets of Park Slope and Bedford-Stuyvesant. As the decades went by, however, and as thoughts turned (beginning in the 1930s and reaching a crescendo in the postwar years) to remaking the civic core of Brooklyn—thoughts ultimately issuing in Cadman Plaza and many of its surrounding buildings—some planners seriously proposed leveling old City Hall. They charged that its functions were obsolete, that its architecture was never any great shakes to begin with, and that the history it represented—that of a city that lasted a mere sixty-five years—was thin gruel. Yet, perhaps miraculously, like its Manhattan counterpart, which was also repeatedly threatened, it never was knocked down. In 1966, amid the upheavals of the urban renewal that had vastly altered the Brooklyn civic center, the then recently formed New York City Landmarks Preservation Commission designated City Hall as a landmark, ensuring its survival. In what condition it would survive was an open question until 1980 when, at the behest of long-serving borough president Howard Golden, the Manhattan architectural firm of Conklin & Rossant was hired to carry out a long-desired restoration of the building. The restoration and renovation were completed by 1989, and the results are stunning. Perhaps the most exciting part of the project was the restoration of the exquisite copper shingling of the 1898 cupola, work carried out by Les Metalliers Champenois, the same outstanding French firm involved in the copper restoration of the Statue of Liberty and of A. A. Weinman's great *Civic Fame* statue atop the Manhattan Municipal Building. Inside, the courtroom, with its coffered and gilded dome and excellent woodwork and plasterwork, was beautifully restored to Axel Hedman's specifications. New fittings were installed in the rotunda that, though not duplicating Gamaliel King's original work, were inspired by it. Altogether, old City Hall ended up looking better than anyone dreamed it could. Every Tuesday at 1:00 P.M., there is a free tour of the building, including the courtroom. I highly recommend it.

LOST BROOKLYN

Near City Hall was the exuberantly colonnaded, domed, pedimented, balustraded, and rusticated Kings County Courthouse at the southwest corner of Joralemon and Fulton Streets, built in 1861–65 to the designs of Gamaliel King (architect of City Hall) and Herman Teckritz, and clad, like City Hall, in Tuckahoe marble. It extended through to Livingston Street. King and Teckritz beat out Peter B. Wight's Ruskinian design in a competition. While the old Montague Street corridor was Victorian Gothic, the new civic center would be classical. Next door to the west, on the south side of Joralemon Street between Fulton and Court Streets, was the old Municipal Building by Ditmars & Mumford, from 1876–78. Also clad in marble, this was a mansarded French Second Empire pile with a rusticated ground story and a small dome. Rounding out the classical core of the City of Brooklyn was the Hall of Records, 1885–87, by William A. Mundell (architect of the Long Island Safe Deposit Company of more than fifteen years earlier). On the southwest corner of Fulton Street and Boerum Place, this was a white limestone classical structure with a crisply defined pedimented entranceway and a balustraded attic. Indeed, City Hall, the County Courthouse, and the Hall of Records, all along Fulton Street, each had a similarly scaled, prominent triangular entrance pediment, none filled with sculpture, such that the austere classical pediment might have served as a symbol of the City of Brooklyn itself. One saw these pediments one after the other, practically at eye level, as one rode the Fulton Street el into Brooklyn. All might have taken their cue from the First Reformed Dutch Church built in 1834–35, which stood until 1886 on part of the site of the Municipal Building on the south side of Joralemon Street near Court Street. One of the greatest of the Greek Revival churches to be built in New York, it was the only one in that style by Minard Lafever that has been positively attributed. In addition to its magnificent octastyle Ionic portico, the church sported a broad, blank pediment. One of Brooklyn's most prominent buildings in its day, it was completed in the year of, and undoubtedly affected the competition for, the design of City Hall. (The Lafever church was its congregation's fourth home and was succeeded by the present Old First Reformed Church, designed by George L. Morse and built in 1888–91 on Seventh Avenue in Park Slope.) It is perhaps significant that the Lafever church, a symbol of old Brooklyn, came down the year before the completion of the Fulton Street elevated railway, a symbol of the new Brooklyn. Of pediment row, only City Hall remains.

Further architectural distinctiveness, though not of a classical kind, was added to the civic center area by Frank Freeman's Thomas Jefferson Association Building of 1889–90, built for the Kings County Democrats, on Boerum Place and Fulton Street opposite the Hall of Records. It was in the same highly creative Richardsonian Romanesque vein as Freeman's Fire Headquarters, which still stands on Jay Street. An even more impressive work by Freeman and closer in spirit to the Fire Headquarters was his Germania Club, nearby at 120 Schermerhorn Street between Smith Street and Boerum Place. It was built in the same years, 1889–90, as the Thomas Jefferson building.

In spite of the many architecturally distinctive and even distinguished buildings hereabouts, critics such as Montgomery Schuyler saw an overbearing visual clutter about the Fulton Street spine, a clutter exacerbated by the presence (from 1887) of the el, which ran above Fulton Street from the Brooklyn Bridge, and which contributed as well to what must have been tremendous auditory clutter. It seems no one was quite prepared for how visually disruptive the el—for which local businessmen had clamored—would prove.

Montgomery Schuyler decried the disfigurement wrought by the el, as well as the general architectural chaos of the civic center: "It looks, indeed, like a mining camp and a 'boom' in active operation. It does not look like a Western city. It is much too 'Western' and too crude. . . . Yet it is suffused without remonstrance by the inhabitants of the fourth city of the Union with a history going back two hundred years."

2 Municipal Building

2 MUNICIPAL BUILDING
210 Joralemon Street, southeast corner of Court Street
1927, McKenzie, Voorhees & Gmelin

The fifteen-story Municipal Building was completed in the same year as McKenzie, Voorhees & Gmelin's masterpiece, the New York Telephone Company Building on West Street in Manhattan. Considered in the abstract, the Municipal Building is perhaps rather dull. The abstract, however, is not how it was designed to be considered. It had three main urbanistic responsibilities, and fulfilled them all with considerable aplomb. First, it had to be a harmonious neighbor to Borough Hall. The Municipal Building provides an excellent backdrop. The larger building's horizontally tripartite design, with a high central section and flanking end pavilions, lightly echoes, without copying, the composition of the main façade of Borough Hall. The Municipal Building's plain shaft does nothing to call attention to itself, while its two-story-high Joralemon Street colonnade echoes the colonnaded portico of Borough Hall. The little cupola atop the Municipal Building, which, considered in the abstract, might have seemed a false touch, echoes the cupola atop the older building. The second urbanistic responsibility was to provide a new

entrance to the IRT subway station. In this instance, the stately Tuscan colonnade on Joralemon Street lends a touch of the ceremonious to the mundane
task of entering and exiting the subway. The building's designers could scarcely
have foreseen the third responsibility. They had no idea that thirty or so years
later Fulton Street would be leveled and the vast open space of Cadman Plaza
created. Borough Hall by itself could hardly have managed to contain the
space at its southern end. The Municipal Building, however, manages the feat.
Up close along Joralemon Street, the Municipal Building is a fine piece of
design, with the aforementioned colonnade and a rusticated granite base yielding above the second story to a limestone shaft. The building is topped by a
series of hipped roofs.

3 BROOKLYN LAW SCHOOL
250 Joralemon Street between Boerum Place and Court Street,
   south side
1994, Robert A. M. Stern & Associates

This is, in my opinion, hands down the best building erected in Brooklyn
since World War II. Stern, at this writing the dean of the school of architecture
at Yale University, was a leader of the postmodernist movement of the 1980s
and has long been a peripatetic figure in the architectural culture of New York
City, doing as much as anyone to ignite interest in all the varied forms and
facets of the city's physical heritage. Most of his major buildings, alas, are outside New York. Here is an exception. He had a daunting problem of design on
Joralemon Street. This building was inserted, sliver-like, between the
Municipal Building to the west and Brooklyn Law School's existing building on
the southwest corner of Joralemon Street and Boerum Place. The law school
(founded in 1901) had moved into that building in 1968, after almost four
decades in the building on Pearl Street that now houses Brooklyn Friends
School. The firm of Praeger-Kavanagh-Waterbury designed the 1968 building,
a glass and white marble modernist box set behind a large plaza. The space
Stern had to negotiate, therefore, was between two wildly dissimilar buildings
with a large plaza thrown into the equation. The 1968 building replaced one
of the great landmarks of Brooklyn, the old Kings County Courthouse, built in
the 1860s, that Gamaliel King, architect of City Hall across the street,
designed. Everything about the law school building did damage to its setting.
The stretch of Joralemon fronted by the Municipal Building on the south and

3 *Brooklyn Law School*

the rear of Borough Hall on the north is marvelously atmospheric, with building heights, materials, classical details, façade indentations, and so on all coming together in just the right way. I can only imagine that the old courthouse
added to the scene. The 1968 law-school building added a plaza that was not
only not needed, considered from the standpoint of urban planning, but that
paid no heed to the carefully modulated volumes along the street. Add to
Stern's program the necessity of restoring some of the lost urban charm to
Joralemon Street. Stern dealt with the problem of the plaza by setting his building a little back from the line of the façade of the Municipal Building and well
in front of the façade of the 1968 building, thus creating a staggered effect
along the south side of Joralemon. This also allows a little of the east side of
the Municipal Building to be visible from the east, the first of Stern's several
bows to the architecture of the Municipal Building. This also made it so that
two façades, the north and the east, of Stern's building were highly visible and
had to be given the full design treatment. Stern used a light-colored stone that
makes a smooth transition between the gray limestone of the Municipal
Building and the blinding white marble of the 1968 building. He made the cornice atop his three-story base even with the cornice of the colonnaded base of

the Municipal Building. The shaft of Stern's building is set back slightly from the base. The fourth-floor setback provides the space for a loggia-like balcony screened by an abstracted colonnade, the center two of the four columns of which are on the line of the two columns rising from the first through the second stories flanking the main doorway on Joralemon Street. (This fourth-floor colonnade may also have been intended to echo the upper-level colonnades of the nearby Central Court Building and 110 Livingston Street.) That doorway, by the way, sports a blank triangular pediment—a bow to the tradition of blank pediments that once defined the Brooklyn Civic Center's architecture. The line of these columns continues up through the next four stories, separating the windows in a manner that echoes, albeit in a classier dress, the window treatment of the 1968 building. Above the ninth floor rises another balcony, similar to though more elaborately designed than the one above the third floor. This not only functions as part of the composition of the building's crown but also expresses the tenth-floor conference room that is the most elaborate interior space in the building. Viewed from the north, the building appears to terminate above its eleventh story in a flat roof. Viewed from the east, the building terminates in a nicely molded round pediment. This east façade is otherwise basically the same as the north façade. Because of the floor-height requirements, Stern could not keep his window levels even with those of the Municipal Building. He did, however, keep everything even that he could. The AIA Guide called this building "bland." That is to consider it in the abstract, however, and that's not how it was designed. The 1968 building is an example of a building conceived purely as an abstract problem of design. Stern, however, showed a remarkable sensitivity to the urban context, and created a building that belongs to the category of works that add to the urban fabric rather than merely to their own aggrandizement.

4 110 LIVINGSTON STREET
Southwest corner of Boerum Place
1926, McKim, Mead & White

Originally the Benevolent and Protective Order of Elks clubhouse, it is now the headquarters of the New York City Board of Education, though, at this writing, for how much longer is uncertain. The local papers have speculated that it is to be converted to apartments. This twelve-story limestone building is by McKim, Mead & White, the same firm that designed the Brooklyn

Museum and countless other treasures of New York and other cities. By 1926, however, it was not the same McKim, Mead & White it had once been. Stanford White had been dead for twenty years and Charles Follen McKim for seventeen. By the 1920s, McKim, Mead & White existed in name only. Leland M. Roth, the leading scholar of McKim, Mead & White, has written: "After 1920 the firm came to specialize in educational and medical complexes, perhaps even earning in part the label 'plan factory' suggested of them. Still, the quality of design and construction remained high, so that the successors were able to accomplish much through the momentum created by the founders." The firm, as Roth has suggested, did continue to produce fine buildings, and this is one of them. It is quite bulky, comprising 361,000 square feet, and little is done, as might have been by White or McKim, to make it less bulky. The architects just accepted the dimensions as requested and set about making it as handsome a bulky building as they could. Gone was the old flair of the firm. Still, not many firms in 1926 could more creditably design classical details than McKim, Mead & White, and it is in certain fine details that this building shines. Particularly fine is the imposing arched entrance set within the rusticated lower section of the building. Three-coffer-deep vaults lead to the front doors, while overhead is a fine filigreed iron screen. Cartouches are placed at the keystones, just below a balustrade. How many handsomer entryways were done at the time? Not many, I should think. It is reminiscent of the entrance to a much earlier McKim, Mead & White building, the Century Association clubhouse on West 43rd Street in Manhattan.

5 METROPOLITAN TRANSPORTATION AUTHORITY HEADQUARTERS

Bounded by Schermerhorn, Smith, and Livingston Streets
and Boerum Place
1989, Murphy/Jahn

This is an enormous structure by Helmut Jahn, the Chicago architect who made a big splash in the 1980s—first in his hometown, then in other cities, including New York—with his jazzy skyscrapers that were usually lumped into the "postmodernist" category. In Chicago, Jahn was known as an enfant terrible. For decades in Chicago, it seemed everything looked like Mies van der Rohe designed it. Jahn was a leading figure in a sort of "brat pack" of Windy City architects (along with Stanley Tigerman, Laurence Booth,

5 *Metropolitan Transportation*
Authority Headquarters

Thomas Hall Beeby, and others) who very self-consciously broke with the Miesian tradition. Indeed, Chicago's most prolific Miesian firm for years was C. F. Murphy Associates, which metamorphosed into Murphy/Jahn. (The architectural historian Reyner Banham once puckishly said that C. F. Murphy Associates' Richard J. Daley Center in Chicago was the best building Mies van der Rohe ever designed, even though Mies didn't design it.) A crescendo of sorts was achieved with Jahn's State of Illinois Center (1979–85). Soon Jahn was in great demand all over the country. The Philadelphia skyline was irrevocably altered by Jahn's One Liberty Place, completed in 1987. Manhattan got plenty of Jahn, too. He designed CitySpire (1987) on West 56th Street, Park Avenue Tower (1987) on East 55th Street, 425 Lexington Avenue (1988) at 43rd Street, and 750 Lexington Avenue (1988) at 59th Street. Helmut Jahn, it seems, likes Brooklyn architecture. CitySpire was dramatically crowned with a Byzantine-style dome, which Jahn said was inspired by that of the Williamsburgh Savings Bank Tower, which was one of the skyscrapers that architects of Jahn's generation had rediscovered as a counterpoint to Miesian austerity. Here, at the MTA Headquarters, Jahn seems to refer to two traditions in Brooklyn architecture. One is the rich tradition of polychromatic masonry, evident in the present building in its "zebra stripes" of alternating horizontal bands of dark and light brick. More than that, Jahn seems inspired by the Brooklyn tradition of strong, rounded corner towers, such as one finds in James W. Naughton's Boys' High School or Montrose W. Morris's apartment buildings. Jahn's are designed with horizontal banded windows that seem a little more like Sir Owen Williams's Daily Express Building in London than like anything Montrose Morris designed. Nonetheless, I am sure that Brooklyn was Jahn's immediate inspiration. The round towers hinge the building as it fills its large trapezoidal site, with a little bite taken out for a small plaza at the southeast corner of Livingston Street and Boerum Place.

Note how many headquarters of New York City agencies are located in Brooklyn's downtown/civic center area. The MTA, the Board of Education, and the New York City Fire Department are all headquartered in this vicinity. This has partly to do with the city's desire to keep its offices in easily accessible areas where the real estate is not as expensive as it is in Manhattan. It has also to do with the way central governments will sometimes spin off certain functions to areas thought in need of an economic boost.

6 FRIENDS MEETING HOUSE
110 Schermerhorn Street, southeast corner of Boerum Place
1857, attributed to Charles T. Bunting

The design of the Meeting House is very similar to that of the Friends' Meeting House at Stuyvesant Square in Manhattan, which was built a couple of years later, and that is why many believe that the same architect designed both. Like most Quaker Meeting Houses, Brooklyn's is very simple. It's a brick box with a low-angled gabled roof, multipaned and shuttered windows, a single semi-elliptical window set within the gable, and a projecting, white-painted, wood-frame entrance with a low-angled pediment. The gable and the pediment are outlined in thick moldings, but beyond that there's virtually nothing to report. It has that beguiling simplicity expressive of the still, small inner voice that we know from the Quaker tradition. By the way, the other famous Manhattan Quaker Meeting House, the one at Gramercy Park that was long used by the Orthodox Quakers and then became the Brotherhood Synagogue, was codesigned by Gamaliel King, the architect of Brooklyn City Hall.

It is fitting that the Friends Meeting House should be located directly behind the Men's House of Detention, built almost a century later (1956) on

Atlantic Avenue between Smith Street and Boerum Place (LaPierre, Litchfield & Partners, architects). Not only did Quakers pioneer the American penal system, they have for three centuries and more been the most vociferous advocates for prison reform. When Tocqueville and Beaumont visited America in 1831–32, their purpose was to study Cherry Hill Penitentiary (now called Eastern State Penitentiary) in Philadelphia. That prison was considered the model of Quaker ideas of penal reform. The Atlantic Avenue House of Detention is nothing like Eastern State Penitentiary in its architecture, in its penal philosophy, or even in its specific function. It is not a penitentiary, of course, but a house of detention where inmates are held awaiting trial. It is like the Eastern State Penitentiary, however, in that in its day it was considered a model of humane penal reform. The building looks like any number of middle-class modern apartment buildings in neighborhoods from Forest Hills to Yorkville. That's just the point, it seems. This has been nicknamed the "Brooklyn Hilton." (At one point, the hotel at Renaissance Plaza that became the Marriott was slated to be a Hilton. It would have caused confusion to have two Brooklyn Hiltons.) Faced in granite, brick, and glass, the eleven-story slab contained rooftop recreation space, medical and dental clinics, and a chapel. It had to have seemed like sweetness and light compared to the facility it replaced, the old Raymond Street Jail, a castellated Gothic hulk built in 1880 on Willoughby Street between St. Edward's Street and Ashland Place in Fort Greene. In 1939, the *New York City Guide* of the Federal Writers' Project said of Raymond Street Jail: "Obsolete, inadequate, and unsanitary, it has been repeatedly condemned by investigating Grand Juries." There must have been a certain number of inmates familiar with both facilities. One would love to hear their commentaries on the differences between the two buildings.

7 CENTRAL COURT BUILDING
120 Schermerhorn Street, southwest corner of Smith Street
1932, Collins & Collins

This building is an often overlooked gem, probably one of the last of the essays in full-bore Beaux-Arts classicism in New York City. This isn't "Depression Doric" like the Appellate Division Courthouse on Monroe Place. The Schermerhorn Street façade is limestone and divided in halves horizontally. The lower half has a hammered surface and is fully rusticated, and the upper half is smooth. Three gargantuan Tuscan arches dominate the façade.

These lead into recessed entryways behind fine black iron gates. In the spandrels of the Tuscan arches are two large, lovely cartouches topped by superb eagles. The upper part of the façade features nine stately Corinthian columns above a balustrade that extends the full width of the building, continuing around to the Smith Street façade. On Smith Street, the lower half of the façade features nine Tuscan-arched windows with rusticated voussoirs. This massive building shares its block of Schermerhorn Street with the diminutive Friends Meeting House, and somehow the juxtaposition works. By the way, I think the best approach by far to the Central Court Building is from the direction of the Friends Meeting House. It was no doubt designed for the approach from the north on Smith Street, from which perspective the full Schermerhorn Street façade becomes visible. The Schermerhorn Street approach, however, with the building on one's right, maximizes the impact of the big arches, which are so unexpected, particularly after the Friends Meeting House. One can then turn the corner to the north on Smith Street to take in the building as a whole.

Note that by looking east from in front of this building, one has one of the best of all possible views of the Williamsburgh Savings Bank Tower.

8 NEW YORK TRANSIT MUSEUM
Northwest corner of Schermerhorn Street and Boerum Place, in the former Court Street IND station

The New York Transit Museum is a wonderful place located in the bowels of the earth, a decommissioned 1930s IND subway station. Here vintage subway and elevated cars are exhibited along the old platforms. One can board and inspect these cars. There are also antique turnstiles and a working signal tower. Every year in September, Schermerhorn Street between Boerum Place and Court Street is host to the "Bus Festival." Examples of city buses from throughout the twentieth century line the street. The museum's expert guides provide commentary, and horse-drawn omnibus rides are offered through Brooklyn Heights. At this writing, the Transit Museum is scheduled to close in fall 2000 for six months or so as it is renovated. The Transit Museum was founded in 1974 with the more modest name of New York Transit Exhibit, and was intended to be a temporary exhibit of subway memorabilia. It proved popular, though, and as it evolved into a true museum, the name was changed. While it is closed for renovation, one might visit the museum's satellite gallery and shop in Grand Central Terminal.

9 Former GERMAN EVANGELICAL LUTHERAN CHURCH
63 Schermerhorn Street between Boerum Place and Court Street,
north side
1888, Josiah Cleveland Cady

10 Former BROOKLYN PUBLIC LIBRARY
67 Schermerhorn Street between Boerum Place and Court Street,
north side
1887, William B. Tubby

Two architects who contributed greatly to the Brooklyn scene designed these two buildings built one year apart and tucked away right next to each other on Schermerhorn Street. The architect of the former German Evangelical Lutheran Church designed the long-demolished Brooklyn Art Association Building on Montague Street in 1869–72. J. C. Cady (1837–1919) was one of the major American architects of his day. Among his well-known works were the Metropolitan Opera House on Broadway and 39th Street (opened in 1883), the south and part of the west façades of the American Museum of Natural History (1888–1908), the Hudson Street Hospital in TriBeCa (1893), and buildings for Yale University, Williams College, Trinity College, and Wesleyan University. Here is a fine Romanesque Revival church in tawny brick. Items of note here are the five arches elegantly receding in reeded brick, and the fine, bold, square tower on the right. At this writing, a sign in front of the building says "Entire building for rent."

William Tubby, who designed distinguished mansions, row houses, and every other conceivable type of building throughout a long Brooklyn-based career, gave us the onetime Brooklyn Public Library branch next door to the east. This, too, is Romanesque Revival, a more austere, cruder variety than the Cady church. Here a rock-faced stone base yields to dark red brick above. The bold arches are outlined in black-painted brick. There are trim and, above the second-floor windows, panels of ornamental patterned brick. The Brooklyn building this most puts me in mind of is nothing by Tubby but William Schickel's St. Peter's Hospital (1888) in Cobble Hill. The building now houses the New York City Board of Education Teen Aid High School Program for Pregnant and Parenting Services. This and the Cady church are fine minor representatives of Brooklyn's Romanesque Revival heyday.

11 *100 Court Street*

11 100 COURT STREET
Between State and Schermerhorn Streets, west side
1998–2000, Hardy Holzman Pfeiffer

This is designed as though it were two buildings. The big Barnes & Noble bookstore at the southwest corner of Court and Schermerhorn Streets is a very tasteful structure of polychrome brick. The entrance and stair "pavilion" of the multiplex cinema at the northwest corner of Court and State Streets is a glass-curtain-wall structure. The auditorium part is, so to speak, cantilevered over the bookstore. The lower half of this part is faced in polychrome tilework in grays and greens, and the upper half is of tilework in bold, jazzy, zigzag patterns in which reds and rusts are introduced to the palette. Hardy Holzman Pfeiffer, a distinguished Manhattan firm, is composed of historically aware architects, and, like Helmut Jahn at his MTA Headquarters nearby, drew on Brooklyn traditions of polychrome masonry and patterned brickwork. The twelve-screen, 2,300-seat multiplex features "stadium seating," the first such in Brooklyn.

12 *Brooklyn Chamber of Commerce Building*

12 BROOKLYN CHAMBER OF COMMERCE BUILDING
75 Livingston Street, northwest corner of Court Street
1927, A. F. Simberg

This thirty-six-story building is one of the most dramatically massed sky-scrapers of the 1920s in New York. It is also among the least known of its brethren, unmentioned, amazingly, in the *AIA Guide.* The north and east façades of this corner building, clad in buff brick, rise from a thirteen-story base in a series of setbacks crested with terra-cotta parapets and pinnacles. At the cor-ner, facing diagonally across Court Street, the setback stages alternate between those coming to a point and those that are straight across, forming a series of diagonal planes up the corner of the building for a faceted and chamfered effect that I believe is quite unlike any other skyscraper in New York. The setbacks rise to a tower crowned by a pyramid. The combination of the complex massing of the setbacks together with the terra-cotta highlights that accentuate that com-plexity makes this a very dramatic building. The obvious comparison is with the

Woolworth Building. This is not nearly so soaring, but the fenestration pattern and some of the ornament are very similar, as is the pyramidal crown. This, however, is post-1916, meaning that the simple base + tower massing of the Woolworth was not an option. Also like Woolworth, which towers over City Hall Park, this towers over what used to be called Borough Hall Park (later absorbed into the much vaster Cadman Plaza).

13 TEMPLE BAR BUILDING
44 Court Street, northwest corner of Joralemon Street
1901, George L. Morse

After the Williamsburgh Savings Bank Tower, this may be the most beautiful skyscraper in Brooklyn. Though it is only thirteen stories, it is said to have once been the tallest building in the borough. The first two floors form a lovely base of rusticated granite. The rustication continues throughout the brick shaft of the building. On the Court Street façade, which reads horizontally in thirds,

13 *Temple Bar Building*

there is a bracketed balcony at the fourth floor in the center section. This center section, comprising three window bays, is framed through the fourth and fifth floors by two-story pilasters, with the center window bay framed by two-story-high Corinthian columns. Above the fifth floor is a cornice. There is a balustraded balcony in the center section of the tenth floor. Above the tenth floor is a massive, modillioned cornice. Two stories rise above that. At the twelfth floor the windows of the flanking sections are topped by beautiful wreathed oculi. Above the end sections are ogee-shaped cupolas of verdigris copper. Projecting from these cupolas are heavily enframed windows with broken pediments framing female heads. These cupolas are as distinctive a skyline feature as Brooklyn possesses. Between the cupolas, along the roofline of the center section, is elaborate cresting. The side of the building on Joralemon Street is deeper than the Court Street front and features much the same treatment, including another cupola at the rear of the building, for a total of three. In a band over the first floor on Court Street are eight carved lion's heads; there are eleven more along Joralemon Street.

This may be its architect's best building. The Maine-born George L. Morse (1836–1924) was a successful practitioner in Brooklyn. He designed the Old First Reformed Church (1893) on Seventh Avenue in Park Slope, among many other Brooklyn buildings. Note that what was true of so many Brooklyn architects was true of Morse. He worked in Romanesque Revival when he designed the Franklin Trust Company Building in 1891 (right around the corner from here on Montague Street), two years before the World's Columbian Exposition in Chicago. Ten years later, when he designed the Temple Bar Building, he was a confirmed classicist. Another way to view Morse's career trajectory is to note that in 1878 he participated, unsuccessfully, in the competition to design the Long Island Historical Society. Fifteen years later, he did not submit a design but rather was asked to be a judge in the competition (won by McKim, Mead & White) for the design of the Brooklyn Museum.

Court Street is Brooklyn's skyscraper row. The row forms a fine wall on the west side of the Civic Center, separating it from Brooklyn Heights. The row is also very distinctive when viewed from across the river in Manhattan. One sees first the bluff of Brooklyn Heights, then, a little distance beyond, the wall of Court Street skyscrapers. It's a very dramatic and underrated sight. Many of these buildings (as the name of the Temple Bar Building suggests) house law offices. The Brooklyn Chamber of Commerce Building, the Municipal Building, and the Temple Bar Building are joined by a couple of others of some distinction. The thirty-story Court-Remsen Building, at the northwest corner of Court and Remsen Streets, was designed by Schwartz & Gross and built in 1926. The developer was Abraham Bricken, known for the many buildings he developed in Manhattan's Garment District in the 1920s, including ones designed by Schwartz & Gross, whose Bricken Broadway Building at Broadway and 38th Street was built in the same year as the Court-Remsen Building. It is 340 feet high and was built to house 2,300 workers in 200,000 square feet of office space. Next door to the south is the forty-story Court-Montague Building, at the northwest corner of Court and Montague Streets. Built in 1927, it was designed by H. Craig Severance and contains 300,000 square feet of office space. At 425 feet, it is the second tallest building in Brooklyn, after the 512-foot Williamsburgh Savings Bank Tower. It is interesting to compare the very straightforward setback massing of this building to the much more complex massing of the Brooklyn Chamber of Commerce Building from the same year. The architect of the Court-Montague Building was one of Manhattan's most prominent skyscraper architects, whose Bank of the Manhattan Building of 1929 on Wall Street was briefly the world's tallest building.

14 CADMAN PLAZA
Bounded by Joralemon Street on the south, Cadman Plaza West on the west, the Brooklyn Bridge approaches (coming in at around the line of Middagh Street to the west) on the north, and Adams Street on the east
1936–1960

It is almost impossible today to imagine what this part of Brooklyn was like before urban renewal. I am too young to have known it. Judging from photographs, I'd say that the transformation was about as total as this sort of thing got. Indeed, this is said to be the largest post–World War II civic-center urban-renewal project in the country. It has been compared to Pittsburgh's Golden Triangle redevelopment, to Philadelphia's Penn Center, and to the rebuilding of the St. Louis riverfront as being among the major transformations of an urban core in the postwar years.

Though most of the Cadman Plaza project dates from the postwar years, it does in a sense go back to 1936, when the approaches to the Brooklyn Bridge were widened. A bit of leftover land from the construction was named after the

14a *New York State Supreme Court Building*

famous Brooklyn preacher S. Parkes Cadman. This original Cadman Plaza included, just to the east of the present corner of Cadman Plaza West and Pineapple Street, the demapped intersection of Fulton and Concord Streets. At the southeast corner of that intersection stood one of Minard Lafever's greatest buildings, the Brooklyn Savings Bank, built in 1846–47. It was among ninety buildings demolished in 1936 for the roadway widenings. The Brooklyn Savings Bank was one of the earliest major examples of the Italian palazzo style, inspired by Sir Charles Barry's London clubhouses, among American commercial buildings. Its influence was enormous, and had it not been felled in 1936, would be one of the revered landmarks of today's Brooklyn.

Fulton Street took its north turn at about Adams Street, skirting the east side of City Hall, and continued north along what is now called Cadman Plaza West, jogging left at Sands Street to the East River, paralleling the Brooklyn Bridge approach. The Fulton Street el followed Fulton until Sands Street and jogged right onto the Brooklyn Bridge. Today, the portion of Fulton Street between Front Street and the East River in the Fulton Ferry District is called Old Fulton Street. The el was taken down in the early 1940s, around the time

Manhattan's els were dismantled. Planning for the new downtown district began right after the war. In the eyes of planners, this was a commercial slum. The southward shift of the heart of downtown had rendered marginal these old streets. In 1944, after the el came down, New York City comptroller Joseph D. McGoldrick spoke of the Civic Center plan as a "program of complete rejuvenation as well as the removal of the blight from this mongrel area." In 1953, as work was just getting under way, Lewis Mumford described the area as "covered by grimy buildings waiting for vandalism or fire or the wrecker's crowbar to level them." Level them the wrecker's crowbar did. Over three hundred buildings were demolished for the project.

Old photographs show how claustrophobic the little plaza in front of City Hall was. Standing there and looking to the north, one's field of vision was dominated by the iron structure of the el, cutting from Adams Street to the west across the front of City Hall. Beyond the el rose buildings of all kinds, tremendously varied in height and bulk and purpose and style—Italianate buildings, Romanesque Revival buildings, buildings that would be landmarks today, other buildings that even the most die-hard preservationist isn't sorry is gone. Some were brick, some cast-iron, some brownstone. Tall signs sprouted from the tops of some buildings; others had large signs painted on their sides. In front of City Hall, Fulton Street, Court Street, Myrtle Avenue, and Washington Street (today's Cadman Plaza East) converged in a dense, tangled mess. One could not see the Manhattan Bridge as one does today. One building that raised its head over the visual jumble was the old Brooklyn Daily Eagle Building, built in 1892 at the southeast corner of Washington and Johnson Streets, across Johnson Street from the General Post Office. Its high cupola-topped tower was a skyline fixture for many years. George L. Morse, architect of the Temple Bar Building, designed it. (The Daily Eagle Building is long gone, but the zinc eagles that once stood on the third-floor entablature can now be seen inside the Brooklyn Public Library at Grand Army Plaza.)

In 1955, Robert Moses said that Cadman Plaza, then taking shape, would be "to Brooklyn what the great cathedral and opera plazas are to European cities." It would, said Moses, "be as much the pride of Brooklyn as the Piazza San Marco is the pride of Venice and the Place de la Concorde the cynosure of Paris." In the Cadman Plaza project, the basic unit of planning was the "superblock." "Redundant streets" were eliminated. Before Cadman Plaza, such streets as Myrtle Avenue, Concord Street, and Nassau Street, which today pull up far to the east of Cadman Plaza West, extended all the way to

Fulton Street. They were eliminated. The two big swaths of Cadman Plaza are superblocks. So, too, are the housing developments, Concord Village and Whitman Close. The later Renaissance Plaza and Metrotech, just to the east of Cadman Plaza, are superblocks, showing that even in the 1980s and 1990s the idea had currency, in spite of its many critics. At the same time, two streets, the north-south Adams and the east-west Tillary, were widened to nearly expressway scale, Adams to serve as an approach road to the Brooklyn Bridge, Tillary to connect the Brooklyn Bridge to the borough's main thoroughfare, Flatbush Avenue.

Among the new government buildings along Cadman Plaza, the most prominent is the **New York State Supreme Court Building** (14a). Its address is 360 Adams Street, which runs along the rear, or east, side of the building. The building fronts on Cadman Plaza and extends from the line of Remsen Street on the south to the line of Pierrepont Street on the north. The main entrance is in the center of the building, opposite Montague Street. It was built in 1957. The architects were Shreve, Lamb & Harmon, whose Empire State Building opened thirty-six years earlier. The State Supreme Court is an unloved building that dominates Cadman Plaza like a beached limestone whale. At its south end are two wonderful bronze lamp standards that once belonged to R. L. Daus's 1905 Hall of Records Building, which was demolished in the 1950s. At this writing a new Federal Courthouse Building is rising at the northeast corner of Cadman Plaza East and Tillary Street and is scheduled for completion in July 2002. The fifteen-story building will seem much taller than that owing to the high ceilings of the courtrooms. With an exterior of limestone, metal, and glass, the building will contain about 630,000 square feet of floor area. The architects are Cesar Pelli & Associates. Pelli is one of the world's most sought-after architects at the turn of the millennium. His Manhattan buildings include the World Financial Center, Museum Tower (next to the Museum of Modern Art on West 53rd Street), and Carnegie Hall Tower (on West 57th Street). Even more impressive, he designed what is for the moment the world's tallest building, the Petronas Towers in Kuala Lumpur, as well as Europe's tallest building, London's Canary Wharf Tower. The new building is located across the street from the northern half of Cadman Plaza, which is bounded by Tillary Street on the south, Cadman Plaza West, the approaches to the Brooklyn Bridge (beginning at the line of Middagh Street) on the north, and Cadman Plaza East (the former Washington Street). The new courthouse building is at the southern end of a large green space called Walt Whitman Park, which was created as part of the Cadman Plaza project. To the east of Walt Whitman Park, across Adams Street, is a housing development called Concord Village, seven fifteen-story red-brick apartment buildings set superblock-style in a staggered pattern within a large green space bounded by Tillary Street on the south, Jay Street on the east, High Street on the north, and Adams Street on the west. A group of Brooklyn savings banks underwrote this middle-income project, of which the first three buildings, designed by Benjamin Braunstein and Albert H. Ryder, were erected in 1953. Four buildings were added in 1958. These later buildings were designed by Rosario Candela, the architect of a number of classy pre-war apartment buildings in the Upper East Side of Manhattan, and by William T. McCarthy, architect in the 1920s of several distinctive houses with driveways along Prospect Park West in Park Slope. The corresponding length on the other side of Cadman Plaza, along the west side of Cadman Plaza West between Clark and Poplar Streets, was developed with several projects that, owing to a variety of delays, came a number of years after Concord Village. Morris Lapidus, architect of flamboyant Miami Beach hotels such as the Fontainebleau, was responsible for the northern part, beginning in 1967 with the Cadman Plaza North apartments on a site bounded by Cadman Plaza West on the east and north, Henry Street on the west, and Middagh Street on the south. A year later Lapidus gave us the Whitman Close town houses and apartments on the large site bounded by Cadman Plaza West on the east, Middagh Street on the north, Henry Street on the west, and Pineapple Street on the south. Cranberry Street and Orange Street terminate at the west side of this project, while Pineapple Street continues east of Henry Street one block to Cadman Plaza West as the pedestrian-only Pineapple Walk. South of Pineapple Walk, extending south one block to Clark Street, is Cadman Towers, completed in 1973 to the designs of the Manhattan architectural firms of Glass & Glass and Conklin & Rossant. Conklin & Rossant would fifteen or so years later carry out the splendid restoration of Borough Hall. These developments were part not only of the makeover of Fulton Street, but of the eastern part of Brooklyn Heights, where they introduced a jarring new scale, new materials, and a new style into the fine old row-house district.

At the midpoint of this northern swath of Cadman Plaza, at about the line of Orange Street, stands the Brooklyn War Memorial. It is a small stone building, the wide south-facing (toward Borough Hall) wall of which features an inscription honoring Brooklynites who fought in World War II. Full-size statues at either end of the wall are of classically gowned figures, one male and one female, appearing solemn with downcast eyes. The architects were Eggers & Higgins. This prolific firm of the 1950s and 1960s was the successor firm to the great John Russell Pope, designer of Washington, D.C.'s National Gallery of Art and of Manhattan's Theodore Roosevelt Memorial Wing of the American Museum of Natural History. Eggers & Higgins designed the Vanderbilt Law School Building of New York University in the same year as the Brooklyn War Memorial. The sculptor, Charles Keck (1875–1951), was an assistant from 1893 to 1898 to Augustus Saint-Gaudens. The Brooklyn War Memorial was dedicated in the year of Keck's death. The statues may be the last classically gowned figures in a work of public sculpture in New York City. Keck's additional works in Manhattan include the granite personifications, classically gowned, of *Letters* (1915) and *Science* (1925) at Columbia University, the statue of Father Francis P. Duffy, dedicated in 1937 at Broadway and 46th Street, and the statue of Alfred E. Smith, dedicated in 1950 at Catharine and Cherry Streets in the Lower East Side. The Brooklyn War Memorial is only partially effective. The figures are fine, but the expanse between is unnecessarily blank. Leslie Katz, writing in the *Nation* in 1962, called it "a billboard made of stone, with two apathetic stone giants doing a television commercial for grief on either side."

To the south, in front of the State Supreme Court Building, is a statue of Christopher Columbus. Emma Stebbins (1815–82) created this marble statue in 1867 for Central Park, where it stood for a number of years. It was removed from the park, lost, found, restored, and, in 1971, installed in its present location atop a high base that A. Ottavino designed. (Jeronimo Suñol designed the statue of Columbus dedicated in 1894 at the south end of the Mall in Central Park.) Emma Stebbins's masterpiece is *Angel of the Waters* atop the Bethesda Fountain in Central Park. There is one way, however, in which the Columbus statue is more representative of her work: it is in marble, where the *Angel of the Waters* is bronze. Stebbins was part of a circle of expatriate American women sculptors living in Rome, where they clustered about the actress Charlotte Cushman. Henry James dubbed this group, which included such important figures as Harriet Hosmer and Edmonia Lewis as well as Stebbins, the "White Marmorean Flock." This, apparently, had a double meaning. They carved marble. They also wore flowing white dresses, so that I suppose they themselves seemed like white marble figures. Stebbins was born in New York City and moved to Rome in the late 1850s.

15 STATUE OF HENRY WARD BEECHER
In Cadman Plaza, roughly on the line of Montague Street
1891, John Quincy Adams Ward
Base: Richard Morris Hunt

The finest piece of sculpture in Cadman Plaza, and one of the finest in Brooklyn, is John Quincy Adams Ward's statue of Henry Ward Beecher (1813–87). The bronze group stands upon and beside a granite pedestal by Richard Morris Hunt. The figure of Beecher stands like a giant in his trademark, flowing Inverness cape (superbly rendered). On the west side of the base, an African American woman reaches up to place a palm branch at the preacher's feet. On the east side of the base, a boy and a girl lift a garland of oak leaves toward Beecher's feet. The African American woman represents Beecher's work as an abolitionist. The boy and the girl on the other side represent Beecher's love of children. These figures are beautifully modeled, as were so many of Ward's figures, and the composition is very interesting. The

15 Statue of Henry Ward Beecher

base is very much a part of the sculpture. Beecher towers over the viewer, as over-life-size figures on high bases do. By Ward's placing the other figures at the sides of the base, they are in the position of the viewer, and Beecher towers over them, too. The viewer is made to identify with them and to become involved in the drama of the sculpture. The statue was originally placed in the small plaza in front of City Hall, facing City Hall. It was moved to its present location as part of the Cadman Plaza project. The art historian Matthew Baigell said the Beecher memorial "may be Ward's greatest achievement."

Beecher, of course, was one of the most famous Brooklynites of his day—probably the most famous. He died only four years before the dedication of this statue. The dedication of a major memorial to the city's most famous resident was bound to be a gala event. The unveiling was on June 24, 1891, before 15,000 people. Members of Beecher's family were there, and a military band played. Spectators crowded the platform of the Fulton Street el, only a few yards to the east, to view the ceremony. Five hundred school children sang "Love Divine, All Love Excelling," Beecher's favorite hymn, while Beecher's granddaughter, assisted by the sculptor Ward, pulled the cord to undrape the statue. Seth Low, the mayor of Brooklyn, delivered a speech. Everyone sang "America," and Rabbi Gottheil bestowed a final blessing.

The art historian Wayne Craven described John Quincy Adams Ward (1830–1910) as "The most celebrated exponent of the galvanized hero . . . who for several decades represented the highest aesthetic standard of undramatic objective naturalism." Ward was born on a farm near Urbana, Ohio, and as a child he modeled figures in clay for fun. His father wanted him to become a physician, but his study of anatomy only strengthened his desire to become a sculptor. His sister lived in Brooklyn and arranged for her brother to meet her neighbor, a sculptor named Henry Kirke Brown. Brooklyn therefore played a crucial role in Ward's career. At nineteen Ward became a paying apprentice in Brown's studio. Before long he was a paid assistant. Brown, a kindly man, and Ward soon became the best of friends. Ward worked on Brown's equestrian statue of George Washington, dedicated in 1856 in Manhattan's Union Square, and Brown saw to it that Ward's name was inscribed on the statue's base along with his own. Brown's naturalistic style, a departure from the neo-classical canons of the day, deeply impressed Ward. He struck out on his own in 1856 and soon established a studio in Manhattan. He traveled among the Indians of the West, observing them closely, whence derived his first major public work, *The Indian Hunter,* dedicated in 1869 in Central Park. In spite of the critical and popular success of this work, Ward would devote the next thirty-five years to portrait statuary. He created celebrated works for Washington, D.C., including the equestrian statue of General George Thomas at Thomas Circle and the James A. Garfield Monument at the U.S. Capitol. Some of Ward's major Manhattan works include the bronze Shakespeare (dedicated 1872), a rare "costume piece," in Central Park; the bronze George Washington (dedicated 1883) at Federal Hall National Memorial on Wall Street; the seated bronze Horace Greeley (dedicated 1890) in City Hall Park; and the bronze Roscoe Conkling (1893) in Madison Square, perhaps Ward's best statue in Manhattan. Ward, said Wayne Craven, "like the painter Thomas Eakins, gave a new vigor and verve to the truthfulness and objectivity that this nation found so desirable in art, especially in portraiture. Ward had practiced his art for twenty-five years when Augustus Saint-Gaudens began his career as a sculptor; these two men, along with Winslow Homer and Thomas Eakins, gave a renewed vitality to American naturalism in the last quarter of the century—before Sargent's English elegance and the French Impressionists sent the art of this country off in other directions."

16 GENERAL POST OFFICE
271–301 Cadman Plaza East (Johnson Street between
Washington and Adams Streets, north side)
1885–91, Mifflin E. Bell
Extended 1930–33, James Wetmore

This is a stately handling of Richardsonian Romanesque inspirations, turreted, towered, mansarded, dormered, and massively arcaded. The polished and rock-faced granite are beautifully handled. It is an enormous, though mannered, building. The post office is a pivotal building in the Cadman Plaza scheme. The open space is vast, and it has been said that the old City Hall, as the southern anchor, is simply too small, that, as Christopher Gray has written, only a building like the Capitol in Washington, D.C., could really work in such a setting. I think this situation was partially rectified by the construction of the Municipal Building, which was carefully designed to be a backdrop to City Hall, and fills the southern vista of Cadman Plaza in a manner that relieves City Hall of some of its difficult responsibility as a visual anchor. To the north from City Hall, the post office, though it is slightly off the axis of the broad sweep of open space leading to the Brooklyn Bridge, is very good as a place for the eye to rest. It is big enough and good enough in the quality of its design that it works as an anchor. Without it, Cadman Plaza would be a disaster. With it, Cadman Plaza almost works. When built, the post office was required to serve no such function as a visual anchor, hemmed in as it was on all sides by other, sometimes quite large, structures. That it was so amply capable of fulfilling its new role must have been a happy surprise for the planners of Cadman Plaza, and it was one of precious few old buildings allowed to remain—in spite of the fact that the post office lobbied for a new, modern facility in the development. In 1953, before it was determined that the post office would remain, Lewis Mumford lobbied for its inclusion, calling it, with none too great enthusiasm, "a decent example of its period." Up close, the post office scores with the strong streetside rhythm of its arcades. Urbanistically the building is splendid—though perhaps more so now than when it was built!

17 RENAISSANCE PLAZA
*Jay Street, opposite Myrtle Avenue, through to Adams Street,
between Willoughby and Johnson Streets
1999, William B. Tabler*

Brooklyn was once known for its hotels. The St. George was the largest hotel in New York City and was famed for its saltwater swimming pool and for its ballroom. The Bossert drew people from across the river to its swank Marine Roof. Before the Marriott was built at Renaissance Plaza, the last major hotel in Brooklyn was Emery Roth's tower addition to the St. George, completed in 1930. The last before that was Starrett & Van Vleck's Leverich Towers in 1928 at Clark and Willow Streets. We are talking almost seventy years between major hotels. What can explain this? It is suggested that as midtown Manhattan developed and took over from lower Manhattan as the focus of visitors and tourists and business travelers, Brooklyn suffered, no longer being a convenient location for hotels. Just so, hotels also left lower Manhattan. In recent years, as "downtown" has become hot, new hotels are springing up all over lower Manhattan. It is unlikely, however, that that is what prompted this new hotel for Brooklyn. Rather, owing partly to the Metrotech development, partly to the revival of nearby brownstone neighborhoods, and partly (perhaps mostly) to the build-up of critical masses of certain immigrant groups, particularly Hasidic and other Orthodox Jews, whose lives and business activities are often focused not on Manhattan but on Brooklyn, it began to seem that downtown could not only support a big new hotel but desperately required one. Enter Marriott. It has, so I understand, proved a resounding success and is looking to expand. In its wake a developer has proposed a new "boutique hotel" in a portion of the old St. George. Brooklyn is hopping. What we call Renaissance Plaza is actually mostly office building, with the Marriott Hotel in its base. William B. Tabler, who designed the building, is known as a hotel architect. He designed the mammoth New York Hilton on the Avenue of the Americas in midtown Manhattan and is working with the London architect David Chipperfield on the conversion of Raymond Hood's wonderful American Radiator Building on West 40th Street into a hotel.

Chapter

3

Brooklyn Heights
North/Fulton
Ferry/DUMBO/
Vinegar Hill

N
W · E
S

MANHATTAN BRIDGE

BROOKLYN BRIDGE

BROOKLYN - QUEENS EXPWY

POPLAR ST

MIDDAGH ST

CRANBERRY ST

ORANGE ST

PINEAPPLE ST

CLARK ST

BROOKLYN HEIGHTS PROMENADE

COLUMBIA HEIGHTS

WILLOW ST

HICKS ST

HENRY ST

MONROE PL

PIERREPONT ST

MONTAGUE ST

CLINTON ST

REMSEN ST

COURT ST

ADAMS ST

CADMAN PLAZA WEST

TILLARY ST

JOHNSON ST

MYRTLE AVE

WILLOUGHBY ST

PIERREPONT PL

ST.

71

1 Long Island Historical Society

Brooklyn Heights North/Fulton Ferry/DUMBO/Vinegar Hill **3**

Brooklyn Heights

**1 LONG ISLAND HISTORICAL SOCIETY
(formerly Brooklyn Historical Society)**
Southwest corner of Pierrepont and Clinton Streets
1878–81, George B. Post

The Long Island Historical Society was an important part of the mid-nineteenth-century development of this part of the Heights as Brooklyn's cultural center. Nearby on Montague Street were Leopold Eidlitz's Brooklyn Academy of Music, Josiah Cleveland Cady's Brooklyn Art Association, and Peter B. Wight's Mercantile Library, all distinguished buildings by distinguished architects. The last of the cultural group to go up was the Historical Society, designed by George B. Post. Post's Williamsburgh Savings Bank on Broadway and Driggs Avenue was still fresh in people's minds when the forty-one-year-old Civil War veteran and onetime assistant to Richard Morris Hunt entered the competition for the Historical Society's design. Post competed against a fascinating array of Victorian architectural talent, including Herman J. Schwarzmann (hot off his success as the principal architect of Philadelphia's Centennial Exposition of 1876), Solon Spencer Beman (soon to design George M. Pullman's model community on the South Side of Chicago), Emlen T. Littel (who shared an office with Henry Hobson Richardson and who designed Manhattan's Church of the Incarnation), Josiah Cleveland Cady (of Brooklyn Art Association fame), the Parfitt Brothers (who would design many Brooklyn Heights buildings in the years to come), J. Pickering Putnam (architect of several noteworthy buildings in Boston's Back Bay), George L. Morse (architect, a few years later, of the Franklin Trust Company Building a block away at Montague and Clinton Streets), twenty-nine-year-old Hugh Lamb (who with his future partner Charles Rich would design Charles Pratt's Astral Apartments), and even seventy-five-year-old Alexander Jackson Davis (architect, some twenty years earlier, of the Edwin Clarke Litchfield house in what is now Prospect Park). In 1898, Russell Sturgis, one of the most influential commentators on nineteenth-century American architecture, said that Post's design for the Long Island Historical Society was an early step in the revival of Classicism that, by the time Sturgis said this, was in full bloom. In fact, Post's slightly earlier Williamsburgh Saving Bank was a much more full-blown forerunner of 1890s Classicism. In comparison, the Long Island Historical Society really seems to belong much more to the Victorian era. Stylistically, I think Post was influenced by the recent design by his mentor Richard Morris Hunt for the Lenox Library of 1870–77 on Fifth Avenue and 70th Street. Probably the Historical Society building's most pioneering aspect is its extensive use of ornamental terra-cotta, designed by Truman Hiram Bartlett.

Post's building is basically a cube of three stories plus an attic. Five bays face Clinton Street and four bays, including the entrance bay, face Pierrepont Street. The entrance is on the far west, or right, as one faces the building. At the first floor, all the bays except the entrance bay feature boldly articulated round-arched windows with heavy keystones, springing from thick, broad piers topped by corbel-like bands of ornament executed in terra-cotta. The window reveals are deep. There is a sense of massiveness and almost a crudeness of detail. The second floor is separated from the first by a course of terra-cotta ornament and a shallowly projecting, though sharply defined, cornice. The second-floor windows are treated in much the same manner as the first floor but with two important differences. The windows are much higher, so that there is less of that Romanesque sense of stubby power that we find in the lower floor, and the spandrels of the arches are filled with exquisite foliate terra-cotta work and, even better, figure heads by the major American sculptor Olin Levi Warner. These heads, for me, strike the purest classical note in the whole building. The attic-like third floor is treated very simply with square-headed windows separated by what I guess one would call dwarf pilasters. Topping the three stories is a bold, somewhat crude cornice, atop which are dormer windows.

Truman Hiram Bartlett was probably more renowned as a teacher and as a father than as a sculptor. He taught for many years at the Massachusetts Institute of Technology, and wrote a biography of the pioneering American neoclassical sculptor William Rimmer. Bartlett's son, Paul Wayland Bartlett, was one of the leading American sculptors of the Beaux-Arts period. (The younger Bartlett did figures for the New York Public Library, was the sculptor of the pediment of the Senate Wing of the Capitol in Washington, D.C., and created the equestrian Lafayette in the courtyard of the Louvre.) Russell Sturgis wrote in 1898 that the Long Island Historical Society was "adorned by, perhaps, the initial attempt to put the work of first-rate sculptors to use for architectural enrichment."

OLIN LEVI WARNER (1844–96)

Olin Levi Warner did the eight spandrel busts on the outside of the Long Island Historical Society. These busts have to be counted among the historical society's greatest treasures. Christopher Columbus and Benjamin Franklin appear on Clinton Street; Shakespeare, Johannes Gutenberg, Beethoven, and Michelangelo on Pierrepont Street. The most prominent are the Viking and the Indian in the spandrels flanking the arch at the entrance on Pierrepont Street. The Viking is said to symbolize sea-faring peoples, while the Indian symbolizes the continuity of indigenous cultures. Be sure to look at these—they are absolutely marvelous pieces of work, better, perhaps, than anything purely architectural that the building has to offer. According to the historian of American sculpture, Wayne Craven, Warner "holds a special place in the history of American sculpture as one of the first to transplant the style of the École des Beaux-Arts to the United States." Born in Connecticut in 1844, the son of a Methodist minister, Warner had to work for six years as a telegrapher to earn enough money to go to the École des Beaux-Arts in 1869, where he befriended Augustus Saint-Gaudens. He studied in the renowned Atelier Jouffroy, and befriended the great French

sculptors Falguière and Mercié, who would later be the teachers of
Brooklyn's Frederick MacMonnies. Warner then worked in Paris as
an assistant to the major French sculptor Jean-Baptiste Carpeaux.
When the Second Empire began to crumble, Warner joined the
French Foreign Legion before returning to America in 1872. In
New York he became friends with the painters J. Alden Weir and
Albert Pinkham Ryder. Warner lived at one time in McKim,
Bigelow & Mead's Benedick bachelor's flats on the east side of
Washington Square, a building that housed Weir, Winslow Homer,
John LaFarge, and other major artists. Early on, Warner's specialty
was portrait busts—a number of them are in the National Portrait
Gallery in Washington, D.C., including his bust of William Crary
Brownell, the fine literary critic who was also Edith Wharton's edi-
tor at Scribner's for many years. (Brownell wrote an appreciation
of Warner, "The Sculpture of Olin Warner," in *Scribner's Magazine*,
in October 1896, following the sculptor's death.) Warner's bust of
J. Alden Weir can be seen in the Brooklyn Museum. Shortly after
working on the Long Island Historical Society, Warner did a statue
of William Lloyd Garrison that stands on Boston's Commonwealth
Avenue. The Metropolitan Museum of Art contains wonderful
medallion portraits of Indian chiefs (for example, *Joseph, Chief of
the Nez Percé*). Warner executed these between 1889 and 1891
while traveling in the West. Warner was hired to do work for the
New York State Pavilion at the Columbian Exposition in Chicago
in 1893. Charles Follen McKim, architect of the Brooklyn
Museum, designed the New York State Pavilion, and Warner executed busts that, very much in the manner of the Long Island
Historical Society, were placed in the spandrels of the building's
entrance arch. His greatest achievement was his work at the
Library of Congress, where he created the great bronze doors. It is
interesting to note that two of the most important contributors to
the Library of Congress, which is one of the greatest of all
American buildings, are represented on this block of Clinton
Street: Elmer Ellsworth Garnsey, a major contributor of all kinds of
work, was responsible for the color scheme in the interior of the
Brooklyn Trust Company, at the northeast corner of Clinton and
Montague Streets. Warner died quite young, in 1896. He was bicy-

cling in Central Park when a carriage struck and killed him. He was only fifty-two. He was at the height of his renown, and certainly numerous major commissions awaited him. Art historians suggest that had he lived, his name today might be as well known as those of Saint-Gaudens and Daniel Chester French. The busts are Warner's only public work in Brooklyn, indeed in all of New York City. One of Warner's students, A. A. Weinman, contributed to the Brooklyn scene by collaborating with Stanford White on the Prison Ship Martyrs' Monument in Fort Greene Park.

At the beginning of 1998, the Brooklyn Historical Society had an endowment of $3.5 million. At the end of 1998, the Society was $16 million dollars richer. Donald and Mildred Othmer made this possible. They were the Brooklyn Heights couple that seemed the quintessence of middle-class thriftiness until they died, when it was revealed that, partly with the help of their old friend Warren Buffett, they had in fact been stupendously wealthy. In their will they donated substantial funds to Brooklyn Polytechnic University, the Brooklyn Historical Society, and others. To renew itself using the funds, the Society closed its building in June 1999 with a projected reopening in fall 2001. Among the changes are a doubling of exhibition space, a new shop and café, and repairs to the leaky roof. The Society also says it believes that the unglazed terra-cotta and redbrick exterior walls of the building had, until this restoration, not been cleaned since the building was erected.

The Long Island Historical Society was founded in 1863. At the time, Brooklyn had a greater identity as part of Long Island; indeed, Brooklyn was by far the most populous part of Long Island. That identity dwindled over the years. Brooklynites uprooting themselves in the suburban exodus of the 1950s and 1960s said they were "moving to Long Island," meaning Nassau and Suffolk Counties, perhaps unaware that they already lived on Long Island. In 1985, the name was changed to Brooklyn Historical Society. It's a bit ironic, perhaps, that an institution dedicated to preserving historical memory should choose to send its historical name down the memory hole. In fairness, it was never truly the Society's purview to cover the histories of (the now extremely populous) Queens, Nassau, and Suffolk Counties as well as Kings County, and it is in fact more accurate that the name refer specifically to Brooklyn. There is now talk of "making the institution more useful," and with the Othmer millions with which to do it, the Society stands at the precipice of change, and only time will tell if the changes shall be salutary.

The library here has for many always been the Society's raison d'être. With 155,000 volumes and such treasures as a copy of the Emancipation Proclamation signed by Abraham Lincoln and the papers of Henry Ward Beecher, the library is one of the major historical research resources in New York City. Its space, too, is magnificent—architecturally by far the finest part of the building. The building enjoys designated landmark status as part of the Brooklyn Heights Historic District. Such status, however, does not extend to building interiors, unless they are separately designated as interior landmarks, as is the case with the library here. The library is eighty feet by fifty feet, galleried, and with a twenty-four-foot-high ceiling. It is closed at the time of this writing, though it should reopen sometime within a few months of this book's publication.

GEORGE BROWNE POST (1837–1913)

George B. Post was a native New Yorker. He studied civil engineering, not architecture, at New York University, an institution barely twenty years old when he enrolled there. He received his degree in 1858. His training in architecture came beginning the same year with his apprenticeship in the office/atelier of Richard Morris Hunt, then still recently returned from the École des Beaux-Arts and determined to train a generation of New York architects in the Beaux-Arts precepts. At the time, Hunt's atelier was in his Studio Building at 15 West 10th Street in Greenwich Village, and Post encountered the numerous artists whose studios were located there, including such titans as Frederic Edwin Church, who in a daring display of artistic entrepreneurship during this time exhibited his painting *Heart of the Andes* there, charging each of the 12,000 people who came to view it twenty-five cents. Frank Furness, who would go on to become Philadelphia's most famous architect, was in Hunt's employ at the same time as Post. In 1861, Post formed a partnership with a fellow Hunt employee/pupil, Charles Dexter Gambrill, and they seemed to have a promising future. The Civil War changed that. Post enlisted and became a captain in the 22nd Regiment of the New York National Guard. He served on the staff of General Ambrose Burnside at the time of the defeat at Fredericksburg in 1862. Post was elevated to Major, Lieutenant Colonel, and Colonel. Unlike many veterans, however, he did not insist after the war on continuing to be addressed as "Colonel Post."

He resumed the practice of architecture on his own in 1867. (Gambrill became the partner of Henry Hobson Richardson from 1867 to 1878. Richardson, though he never designed a building in Brooklyn, would have a profound impact on the evolution of architectural style in Brooklyn.) The Williamsburgh Savings Bank of 1870–75, on Broadway and Driggs Avenue in Williamsburg, was his first commission for a commercial building, and its classical style was enormously influential. It can be said that Post did as much as if not more than any of the architects who had actually been to the École des Beaux-Arts to popularize the new Classicism among rank-and-file architects. Among Post's numerous well-known works still standing in Manhattan and Brooklyn, we may cite his master plan and design of the original buildings of City College in Hamilton Heights in the first decade of the twentieth century, his splendid Beaux-Arts design for the New York Stock Exchange (1901–03), and his New York Times Building of 1888–89 on Park Row. His firm grew to be one of the largest in the world, and it is said that he was responsible for more than four hundred projects.

Yet, as with so many nineteenth-century New York architects (especially Richard Morris Hunt), some of Post's best and best-known works have been knocked down. His Produce Exchange of 1881–84 at 2 Broadway was torn down for a banal office building in 1957. His remarkable fifty-eight-room, château-style house for Cornelius Vanderbilt II, at 58th Street and Fifth Avenue and built in 1882–93, was demolished in 1926 to make way for the Bergdorf-Goodman Department Store. Post also worked with his former mentor, Hunt, on the World's Columbian Exposition in Chicago in 1893, designing the Manufactures and Liberal Arts Building at the fair. A more obscure note about Post is that he served as president of the National Arts Club at the time (1905) the club moved into the former Samuel Tilden house on Gramercy Park. From 1904 to his death in 1913, Post's firm was known as George B. Post & Sons.

2 *Crescent Athletic Club*

2 CRESCENT ATHLETIC CLUB

129 Pierrepont Street, northwest corner of Clinton Street
1906, Frank Freeman

The Crescent Athletic Club was a large and distinguished men's sporting club founded in 1884. At first the club gathered to play football in Prospect Park. By 1912, the club had grown to 2,650 members. Not only did it have a fancy new clubhouse on Pierrepont Street, it operated country-club facilities in Bay Ridge. (In 1929, the club would expand to Huntington, Nassau County.) The Pierrepont Street building was erected in 1906. Frank Freeman, one of the foremost architects of Brooklyn, designed it. Freeman is today admired for his work in the 1880s and 1890s in the Romanesque Revival style, including the Brooklyn Fire Headquarters on Jay Street and the Herman Behr house just to the west of here on Pierrepont Street. Beginning in the 1890s, Freeman also designed in the classical style. One of his few surviving classical buildings is the Brooklyn Union Gas Company Building on Remsen Street. Perhaps his best work in the idiom was his Brooklyn Savings Bank Building, which stood directly across Clinton Street, at the northeast corner of Pierrepont Street, from the Crescent Athletic Club. For the Crescent Athletic Club, Freeman used bold, continuously channeled, rusticated limestone for the base. Up above is light-colored brick, with terra-cotta ornament. The Pierrepont Street façade design at first seems simple enough but is in fact quite complex. It looks like a four- or five-story building, even though it is twelve stories. Freeman used double-height window frames to decrease the apparent height of the building—basically the same technique employed by Charles Follen McKim at his University Club on Fifth Avenue in Manhattan. Above the base is a cornice forming balustraded balconies for the second level of windows. The third-level windows rise in an unusual manner directly out of the round pediments of the second-level windows, creating a sense of vertical compression that also serves to decrease apparent height. Above these third-level windows is another cornice, then another level of high windows, then a row of smaller windows, then a series of even smaller attic windows set within a magnificent terra-cotta frieze below a fine, and final, cornice. Also stuck throughout the façade are small windows that indicate the true number of stories in the building. The treatment of the Clinton Street façade is similar, though since this façade is much wider than the one on Pierrepont Street, there are five rather than three windows across. The central three windows on the second, third, and fourth levels are right next to one another, horizontally compressed. The façades are very busy. Inside, the club had a fantastic variety of spaces, including a swimming pool, basement bowling alleys (Park Slope's Montauk Club had those, too), a double-height dining room, bedrooms, a library, a top-floor gymnasium, squash courts (which with the ones at the Heights Casino on Montague Street had to have made Brooklyn Heights the squash capital of the universe), and so on. All that is gone now. The Crescent Athletic Club moved out of the building and out of Brooklyn Heights in 1956. (The club still exists as the Huntington Crescent Club.) The building was used after that for offices, and the basement bowling alleys were commercially operated in the late 1950s. The building received a new lease on life when in 1966 it became the new home of St. Ann's School.

St. Ann's School opened in September 1965 in the undercroft of St. Ann's Episcopal Church at Clinton and Livingston Streets. The church founded the school for gifted students in the hope of attracting parishioners. The school is grounded in progressive models of education, and has indeed become itself a national model of its approach to education. According to the school, the approach is based on four pillars: psychometric testing of students ("to prevent the tyranny of subjective judgment by authority figures"), no grades, academic rigor, and a "familiar community style." In 1966, the school moved to the old Crescent Athletic Club on Pierrepont Street. This was a harbinger: three years later, St. Ann's Church sold its building to another famous private school, Packer Collegiate Institute, and moved in with Holy Trinity Church on Montague and Clinton Streets, just half a block from where the school had already moved. Affiliated originally with St. Ann's Parish, the school now belonged to the new parish of St. Ann and the Holy Trinity—until 1982, when the school, which had taken on more than a life of its own, severed all formal ties with the church. (The church transferred title to the old Crescent Athletic Club to the school in 1985.) Ranging from preschool through high school, St. Ann's now occupies several buildings, including Nos. 122 and 124 Pierrepont Street and 124 Henry Street, and space in the One Pierrepont Plaza office building. The most architecturally distinguished of St. Ann's buildings is the former Willow Place Chapel, the Russell Sturgis–designed gem at 26 Willow Place, now called the Alfred Tredway White Community Center, housing St. Ann's preschool. St. Ann's is renowned as a school that allows gifted students to work at their own pace in an environment that nonetheless demands the highest academic standards. It is, with Packer Collegiate, Brooklyn Friends, and Poly Prep, one of several Brooklyn preparatory schools of national distinction. St. Ann's is such a fine school that some of its faculty members would do an Ivy League university proud. One such is William R. Everdell, a renowned intellectual historian and the author of *The First Moderns.*

3 CHURCH OF THE SAVIOUR (First Unitarian Church)
Northeast corner of Pierrepont Street and Monroe Place
1842–44, Minard Lafever

This part of Brooklyn Heights was once Minard Lafever country. In addition to Holy Trinity Church and Church of the Saviour, three Lafever churches long demolished were near here as well. His Pierrepont Street Baptist Church was built on the northeast corner of Pierrepont and Clinton Streets in 1843–44 and torn down in 1877 to be replaced by the new First Baptist Church by Lawrence B. Valk. The site was later occupied by Frank Freeman's Brooklyn Savings Bank, itself long gone. Lafever's Church of the Restoration, later known as the Church of the Neighbor, was built at the southeast corner of

Monroe Place and Clark Street in 1848–50. It was among the ninety or so buildings removed for Cadman Plaza in 1964. His Reformed Church on the Heights was built in 1850–51 on Pierrepont Street near the southwest corner of Monroe Place. Unlike the other churches, which were Gothic, this one was in a High Renaissance style. It was one of the buildings replaced in the 1930s by the Appellate Courthouse.

Happily, Church of the Saviour, perhaps better known as the First Unitarian Church, is with us still, and it ranks as one of Lafever's masterpieces. Construction began in December 1842 and the church was consecrated on April 24, 1844. It is of New Jersey brownstone, laid in random ashlar. Polygonal tower/"buttresses," 118 feet high, flank the front entrance. The exterior of King's College Chapel in Cambridge, England, inspired that of Church of the Saviour. The interior is of the "Plaster Gothic" variety that we see in other Lafever churches. As with most old churches, there have been a number of additions and modifications over the years. The present rose window, in the French Rayonnant style, was installed in 1914, replacing Lafever's original window in the English Perpendicular style. The triple-light, Perpendicular-style windows over the aisle doors are original and are similar to what the original center window looked like. The tracery recalls that of King's College Chapel. Around the turn of the century, opalescent windows from the Tiffany Studios replaced Lafever's original Perpendicular-style windows, of colorless leaded glass, on the east and west sides of the church. Originally, the clerestory "windows" were painted on muslin and visible only from inside. Real glass windows replaced these in 1914. The original paintings were, according to Lafever's specifications, to be "executed in the best possible imitation of stained glass." The gatepost lanterns were installed in 1918.

The interior is light and airy, with slender columns and high, wide-arched bays. The chancel is shallow—Unitarians had no use for ecclesiological Gothic. The nave is seventy-five feet long and fifty-seven feet high. The width of the nave plus the aisles is sixty-one feet. The interior is in a combination of Early English and Decorated Gothic.

The chapel beside the church on Pierrepont Street is from 1865–66. The prominent Manhattan architect Ethan Allen Dennison designed the four-story parish house on Monroe Place, built in 1936–37, contemporary with the Appellate Courthouse across the street.

New Englanders founded Brooklyn's first Unitarian congregation in 1833. The architect Robert Meadows beautifully restored the façade in 1995, and today it is just an absolutely splendid presence on Pierrepont Street.

4 GEORGE and P. C. CORNELL HOUSES
108 and 114 Pierrepont Street, opposite Monroe Place
1840

Believe it or not, these two houses were built in 1840 as a unified duo. The stoops of the two two-story painted-brick houses with brownstone basements flank a four-bay-wide center section defined at its ends by brownstone quoins and topped by a pediment and a cupola. Along the attic extended a frieze of small circular windows framed by cast-iron wreaths. The ensemble was, in fact, one of the finest examples of residential Greek Revival architecture in New York. The architectural historian Clay Lancaster called it the "noblest residential building ever to grace Pierrepont Street." The houses look very different today. No. 114 was completely overhauled in 1887 when the publisher Alfred C. Barnes purchased it. As the *AIA Guide* says, "A simple brick building became a Wagnerian stage set." Further alterations were made in 1912 when the house became the Brooklyn Women's Club. Today it has rock-faced brownstone covering the basement and parlor floor. Two floors were added and are of red brick. The stoop was removed and a basement entrance put in. There is a round tower on the left. A gable tops the right side of the house, where a third-floor oriel forms a fourth-floor balcony. There is fine terra-cotta trim and stained glass. In short, nothing could conceivably look less like the Greek Revival. No. 108, by contrast, though sundered from its ensemble, is still identifiably Greek Revival, if only for the fine anthemion-ornamented pediment over its front door. It is of brick with a brownstone basement and brownstone trim. It is quite wide, four bays rather than the customary three, and a third floor was added together with many other alterations in 1907.

5 NEW YORK STATE SUPREME COURT, APPELLATE DIVISION
Northwest corner of Pierrepont Street and Monroe Place
1938, Slee & Bryson

John Bay Slee and Robert Bryson gave us this fine example of "Depression Doric" completed in the year of Bryson's death. They were, from the beginning of their partnership in 1903, one of Brooklyn's most prolific architectural firms. Their works include Albemarle Terrace and Kenmore Terrace in Flatbush (1916–20) and numerous houses in Prospect Park South, Prospect–Lefferts Gardens, and Park Slope. For this rare civic commission,

5 *New York State Supreme Court,*
Appellate Division

they designed a stately limestone courthouse that faces Monroe Place with strong Doric columns flanking a fine pedimented bronze entrance. The building is larger than anything around it, it employs its forms rather grandly, it is white in a sea of reds and browns, and it is elevated from grade level. It sounds like a sure prescription for disaster, yet it is anything but. Somehow the building not only works in its context but enhances it. The scale of the building is impressive, not jarring, and it's hard to imagine this part of Brooklyn Heights without it.

6 161 HENRY STREET (apartments)
Northwest corner of Pierrepont Street
1906, Schneider & Herter

This Beaux-Arts apartment house could not be more different from the same architects' Moorish-style Park East Synagogue (1889–90) on East 67th Street in Manhattan. The nine-story building has a rusticated limestone base above which is red brick with limestone trim, including quoins. Its most distinguishing features are its mansard crown and eight massive limestone brackets at the seventh floor facing Pierrepont Street and seventeen facing Henry

Street. On Henry Street is a huge two-story entrance topped by a colossal broken pediment framing a colossal cartouche. The broken pediment and cartouche composition reappears at the top of the building on Henry Street. This is one of Brooklyn's finest Beaux-Arts apartment houses, kin to Clinton Hill's Mohawk (1904) and Royal Castle (1911–12).

7 HERMAN BEHR HOUSE
84 Pierrepont Street, southwest corner of Henry Street
1888–90, Frank Freeman

This four-story house is one of Frank Freeman's undisputed masterpieces, together with the Brooklyn Fire Headquarters on Jay Street, built two years after this house was completed. It is a powerful essay in the Richardsonian Romanesque. The basement and parlor floor are of rock-faced brownstone with brick above. Flanking the entrance are rounded bays rising through the second story to form third-floor balconies. A large gabled dormer, flanked by high chimneys, projects from a steeply pitched tile roof and crowns the right side of the façade. To the left of the gable is an eyelid dormer. The terra-cotta ornamentation and the stained glass are exquisite, as is the sheer wealth of curving glass panes. The wing-walled stone porch, parallel to the street, rises in three stages to the fine, deeply recessed arched doorway. The house was enlarged in 1919 when it became the Palm Hotel, which became locally notorious as a house of ill repute. It was later, of all things, a residence for Franciscan brothers affiliated with nearby St. Francis College. Since 1977 it has housed apartments. The modern canopy over the porch is a false note.

8 WOODHULL (apartments)
62 Pierrepont Street between Henry and Hicks Streets, south side
1911, George Fred Pelham

Pelham was the architect of several distinguished buildings in Manhattan, including the Hudson View Gardens apartments on Pinehurst Avenue and 183rd Street, built in 1924–25 in a Tudor style very different from this building. The Woodhull is an eight-story Beaux-Arts apartment house featuring a rusticated stone base with light brick above. There is a recessed central section between end pavilions that have curved bays sandwiched by rusticated piers. Cartouches appear over the doorway and over its flanking piers. One does not normally associate Brooklyn Heights with Beaux-Arts design, though with this, the nearby apartment house at 161 Henry Street, and the Hotel Bossert, there are several fine specimens.

9 131 and 135 HICKS STREET
Between Pierrepont and Clark Streets, east side
1848

The Gothic Revival of the 1840s was a style employed mostly for churches, though it was also applied, on occasion, to row houses, such as these superb examples. This pair of three-story brownstones feature Tudor-arched entrances and Gothic-style drip moldings over the windows. Henry C. Bowen built No. 131. He was a prosperous merchant and a founder of Plymouth Church and of the *Independent*, which was the intellectual organ of evangelical Protestantism and which Brooklyn's two most famous Congregational clergymen, Henry Ward Beecher and Richard Salter Storrs, both edited.

Lewis Mumford and his wife, Sophia, moved to No. 135 in 1925. It's where he lived when he published his second book, *Sticks and Stones*. In his autobiography, *Sketches from Life* (1982), he wrote:

> *That September we found just what we wanted in an old brownstone with a slight Gothic touch, at 135 Hicks Street, now deservedly marked as an historic building. There we had a one-and-a-half-room basement apartment, with an open fireplace, and a share in a rear garden which gave on the sandstone Gothic church behind—that tawny Belleville sandstone from New Jersey which has none of the chocolate dinginess of the Hartford variety! The small rear alcove, whose only ventilation came through an airshaft, we dedicated to typing and dressing. (We found later that that airshaft served our upstairs neighbors on the nearer floors, too, for they were amused by overhearing our sometimes bawdy repartee while undressing for bed.)*
>
> *Our new neighborhood was as genial an example of both urbanity and community as Boston's Mt. Vernon Street area. . . . Hicks Street, then so humane and serene with its nearby assortment of restaurants, markets, and shops, at hand but not under one's nose, met our need for esthetic comeliness and social variety. Small wonder many of our younger New York friends had begun to move over to the Heights.*

10 GEORGE HASTINGS HOUSE
36 Pierrepont Street between Hicks and Willow Streets, south side
1846, Richard Upjohn

Richard Upjohn, the great church architect, designed this Gothic Revival house in the year that his Trinity Church and Church of the Pilgrims were completed. The only other known residential design by Upjohn still standing in Brooklyn is his own house in Cobble Hill. His most famous house design was probably the Henry Evelyn Pierrepont house, which stood where the playground now is at the southwest corner of Pierrepont Street and Pierrepont Place. The house was part of a row with Nos. 2 and 3 Pierrepont Place. It was demolished in 1946. Other notable Gothic Revival row houses in Brooklyn Heights include the nearby Nos. 131 and 135 Hicks Street; the brick row at 2 to 8 Willow Place, between Joralemon and State Streets; and the brownstone row at 118 to 122 Willow Street, between Pierrepont and Clark Streets. All were built in the 1840s. The marvelous stoop of the Hastings house, with its trefoil railings, is a recent re-creation.

10 *George Hastings House*   11 *108 to 112 Willow Street*

11 108 to 112 WILLOW STREET
Between Pierrepont and Clark Streets, west side
1883, W. Halsey Wood

The *AIA Guide to New York City* calls these three houses built by the banker Spencer Trask "New York's finest example" of the Queen Anne style inspired by London's Richard Norman Shaw. W. Halsey Wood of Newark was best known for his ecclesiastical works. These beautiful three-story houses, with rock-faced brownstone basements, red brick above, shingled roofs, and superb terra-cotta ornamentation (including images of cherubic nude children), were designed, like William Tubby's Queen Anne row at 272 to 282 Hicks Street (1887–88), in such a way that one cannot easily tell where one house ends and another begins. These houses are a picturesque riot of bay windows, towers, dormers, arches, gables, and balconies, and almost defy description. Inside there must be some eccentric spaces.

12 155 to 159 WILLOW STREET
Between Pierrepont and Clark Streets, east side
1820s

Nothing could be more different from the effusive Queen Anne of Nos. 108 to 112 across the street than this group of three Federal-style houses from the 1820s. Nos. 155 and 157 are each two stories with dormers, while No. 159 is three stories and has no dormers. The houses are red brick laid in Flemish bond, though this can be hard to make out because of the thick coatings of paint. There are low brownstone basements and low brownstone stoops leading to characteristically beautiful Federal-style doorways with leaded transoms and sidelights and flanked by attenuated Ionic columns. The six-over-six windows have lintels of paneled brownstone. This almost picture-perfect trio is one of the best examples of Federal-period design on the Heights.

13 ALEXANDER M. WHITE and ABIEL ABBOT LOW HOUSES
2 and 3 Pierrepont Place between Montague and Pierrepont Streets,
*   west side*
1857, Frederick A. Peterson

The *AIA Guide* calls these twins "the most elegant pair of brownstones remaining in New York." These Italianate mansions are bold and simple,

notable for their superb quoining, strong window enframements, and broad
stoops leading to fine double doors recessed between paired piers with
Corinthian capitals below massive entablatures with dentilated cornices.
Frederick A. Peterson designed both houses. He is also known as the architect
of the Cooper Union Foundation Building (1853–59) at Fourth Avenue and
7th Street in Manhattan. There once was a No. 1 Pierrepont Place, the home
of Henry Evelyn Pierrepont, that Richard Upjohn designed and that was
demolished in 1946 for the present playground.

ABIEL ABBOT LOW AND THE CHINA TRADE

A. A. Low (1811–93) was born in Salem, Massachusetts, the
eldest of the twelve children of Seth Low. The Low family had
been in Massachusetts since the seventeenth century. At a tender
age Abiel got a job as a clerk for a local shipping firm engaged in
the South American trade. Seth Low moved his family to Brooklyn
when Abiel was eighteen. Seth Low was an importer of "drugs and
India wares," and the son went to work for him. In 1833, he sailed
to Canton and worked for Russell & Company, the largest
American firm there. Just imagine what that must have been like.
First of all, it took several months just to get there. One felt one
was far from home in a way that probably no one is able to experience today. Canton must have seemed exotic beyond the most fanciful dreams. In 1840, three years after becoming a partner in
Russell & Company, Low returned to Brooklyn. (Low was in China
at the same time that New Yorker Herman Melville was sailing the
South Seas on a whaler.) He founded A. A. Low & Brother, and
soon was prominent in the importation of China tea and Japanese
silk. The China trade with New York had begun no sooner than
the Revolutionary War had ended. John Jacob Astor was among
those deeply engaged in the trade. Astor transported furs to China,
returning with tea, silk, and porcelain. Abiel's firm was known as
the House of Low, royalty among traders. His ships included the
Houqua, named for the Chinese mandarin who was Low's chief
business contact in China. Low built the *Houqua* for $45,000. The
Houqua and other Low ships were among the new wave of fast,
graceful clipper ships that were developed out of the necessity of

getting tea back from Canton while it was still reasonably fresh. Other Low ships were called the *Samuel Russell* (in honor of the company Low worked for in Canton), *The Contest,* and the *Jacob Bull.* The *Samuel Russell* pioneered a new, more profitable route to China: instead of going around the Cape of Good Hope in Africa, the traditional route of European traders, Low went around Cape Horn in South America. That way the *Samuel Russell* and other ships could stop in San Francisco, depositing those seeking gold, and then continue across the Pacific to China. (Mind you, the transcontinental railroad was still some years in the future.) Soon New York traders such as Low rose in international prominence, serving London as well as New York—an early sign of the rise to world dominance of American capitalism. Low's clipper ship the *Oriental* made the run from Canton to London in a record ninety-seven days in 1850. In Manhattan's South Street Seaport Historic District, one can still see the countinghouse of A. A. Low & Brother (the firm was dissolved in 1887). Built in 1850, it is on John Street between Front and South Streets, and later became the Baltimore Copper Paint Company. Low's clippers took off from right across South Street. It is said that he built his house on Pierrepont Place so he could see his ships from his back windows.

Low helped to finance the Atlantic Cable and was associated with Collis P. Huntington in building the Chesapeake & Ohio Railroad and in founding the towns of Newport News, Virginia, and Huntington, West Virginia. A Unitarian who worshipped at Minard Lafever's Church of the Saviour on Pierrepont Street, Low died in Brooklyn.

SETH LOW (1850–1916)

Seth Low, one of the great New Yorkers of his generation, was the son of Abiel Abbot Low and was born and grew up in the brownstone at 3 Pierrepont Place. Like so many of the eminent Brooklynites of his generation, Seth Low attended Brooklyn Polytechnic Institute, one of the finest secondary schools in the country. (He just overlapped there with his next-door neighbor,

Alfred Tredway White.) From there Low went on to the school with which his name shall forever be closely associated, Columbia College, from which he graduated in 1870. As A. T. White had entered his father's business, so Low entered his father's, becoming a partner in A. A. Low & Brother in 1876. Also like White, however, Seth Low was cut out for bigger things. In 1881, he was elected mayor of Brooklyn, and was reelected in 1883, serving at the time of the opening of the Brooklyn Bridge. As mayor, he is credited with introducing the merit system in civil service appointments, reducing city debt, and reforming the public school system. The die was cast: Seth Low would make his mark as an administrator and as a Progressive reformer. He was a Republican, and his namesake grandfather had founded the Brooklyn Association for Improving the Condition of the Poor. By this time, he had married Anne Curtis of Boston, the daughter of Justice Benjamin R. Curtis of the United States Supreme Court. One might think he could have found a nice Brooklyn girl to marry, but the point cannot be stressed enough: many of these upper-class Brooklynites considered themselves not New Yorkers, but New Englanders. Their lives, their values, their careers, even their very spouses made this plain.

In 1889, Seth Low was named to the presidency of Columbia College, an institution that began as King's College at Park Place and Church Street in New York City in the 1750s. Its early students included Alexander Hamilton, John Jay, Robert R. Livingston, and Gouverneur Morris—about as impressive a roster of Founding Fathers as any school could boast. (Hamilton came to New York from his native Virgin Islands expressly to enroll in King's College.) It is worth noting that Columbia College was an Episcopalian institution. Abiel Abbot Low was a New England Unitarian. Though Seth was raised in the Unitarian church, he converted to the Episcopal—a sign, perhaps, that he was, after all, becoming more of a New Yorker than a New Englander. In any event, Low transformed Columbia College into Columbia University, a full-fledged institution of higher learning based on German models of Ph.D. and professional studies. Low brought Teachers College, Barnard College, and the College of Physicians and Surgeons under the Columbia tent. When he began at Columbia, the college's campus had not long before moved from its original downtown location to a site bounded by Madison and Park Avenues and 48th and 49th Streets. Hemmed in on all sides by booming midtown, there was nowhere for the campus to grow, as grow it would. Low led the search for a new location, and in 1892 purchased seventeen acres of New York Hospital's Bloomingdale Insane Asylum on the Harlem Heights, where he commissioned Charles Follen McKim, later the architect of the Brooklyn Museum, to design a new, expansive and expandable campus. The Morningside Heights (as the neighborhood would be renamed) campus of Columbia is one of America's great university campuses. McKim designed a magnificent library as the centerpiece of the campus. Seth Low donated one million dollars, a third of his personal fortune, toward the library's construction. It is known as Low Library. Its full name is the Abiel Abbot Low Memorial Library—named by Seth Low for his father. (For a thorough and lucid account of Seth Low's tenure at Columbia, read Andrew S. Dolkart's magnificent 1998 book *Morningside Heights*.)

In 1897, as the finishing touches were being put on Low Library, Seth Low ran for mayor of New York City. Robert Van Wyck, the Tammany machine's candidate, defeated Low, and therefore had the privilege of being the first mayor of the newly consolidated Greater New York, including Brooklyn. Four years later, however, Low ran successfully. As he had done as mayor of Brooklyn, he checked patronage. On his watch the first subway trains rolled into Brooklyn. (Earlier, as the Brooklyn mayor at the opening of the Brooklyn Bridge, he had presided over the first elevated trains to connect Manhattan with Brooklyn.) On Low's watch the Pennsylvania Railroad tunnels under the Hudson River were constructed, and the New York Central Railroad was electrified. His was a penny-pinching, clean-slate reform administration of the type New Yorkers turn to whenever the old corrupt practices of swaggering bosses dangling their patronage plums seem just a bit much. In 1903, Tammany Hall pulled out all the stops against him, and he was defeated for reelection.

With thirteen years to go in a life that had been extraordinarily eventful, Seth Low bade politics farewell, though he hardly
sat waiting for the grim reaper. He bought a farm in Bedford Hills,
New York, and became deeply involved in the cooperative-farm-
ing movement. His long interest in improving the conditions of
African Americans led him in 1905 to a membership on the board
of Alabama's Tuskegee Institute. He was chairman of Tuskegee's
board from 1907 until his death in 1916, during which time he
worked closely with Booker T. Washington. (Alfred Tredway
White was a Tuskegee board member as well.) Low was also a
scholar. He penned the chapter on municipal government for the
first edition of Lord Bryce's *American Commonwealth* in 1888. Seth
Low died on his farm in Bedford Hills, at the age of sixty-eight.

---

14 ESPLANADE
Between Remsen and Orange Streets
1950–51, Clarke & Rapuano

When planning for the Brooklyn Heights portion of the Brooklyn-
Queens Expressway began in 1942, it was proposed to run it right through the
heart of the neighborhood, along Hicks Street, on a line with the section to be
constructed south of Atlantic Avenue. When it was later decided to jog the
expressway to the west at Atlantic Avenue and run it closer to the water, the
first plans would have had it run atop the embankment east of Furman Street,
hard behind the houses of Columbia Heights, in much the way it runs behind
the Riverside Apartments. The Brooklyn Heights Association lobbied for a
promenade over the expressway as a way to preserve the gardens behind the
houses of Pierrepont Place and Columbia Heights. Robert Moses, in charge of
the expressway project, was not the most accommodating of men, yet something about the proposal piqued his interest and he expanded the concept into
the Esplanade that we see today, cantilevered over two levels of expressway
and generally regarded as one of the most inspired pieces of urban design of its
period in New York. The Esplanade extends almost the entire length of the
Heights. Some buildings were demolished, including 106 Columbia Heights,
the house from which Washington Roebling directed construction of the
Brooklyn Bridge. Still, in comparison with the destruction wrought by most of

14 *Esplanade*

the expressways built by Moses, one could not have hoped for a happier out-
come. It is worth noting as well that the community in general did not object
to an expressway per se, feeling it was needed to relieve the horrendous traffic
of Henry and Hicks Streets. Brooklyn Heights, alas, was the only neighborhood
spared in this manner. To the south, Cobble Hill and Carroll Gardens were cut
off from the waterfront. To the north, the expressway created desolate nether
regions out of Vinegar Hill and the streets just to the south of the Navy Yard,
cutting it off from Fort Greene.

The Esplanade not only provided the spectacular views of skyline and
harbor that we enjoy today, but it was itself praised for its architectural design.
Lewis Mumford, in particular, thought Clarke & Rapuano's design an architectural masterpiece.

From the Esplanade one can see the disused old docks along Furman
Street. As I write this, controversy rages in Brooklyn Heights over a proposed
plan for an elaborate park at river's edge. Many Heights residents and others feel
that it is time to reclaim that riverfront strip for recreational use. Other Heights
residents, however, object to the park proposal (at least in its current form), fear-
ing the influx of park users and the noise and parking problems they will bring. I
won't comment on the plans that have been published thus far because the park

is still in the early stages of planning, and the design is probably going to change many times over before any construction commences. It is a story, however, that bears following, as any such park will be of the nature of a citywide amenity and not something simply for the pleasure of Heights residents.

15 210 to 220 COLUMBIA HEIGHTS
Between Pierrepont and Clark Streets, west side
1852–60

The architectural historian Andrew Dolkart has said that Brooklyn Heights, though rich in Italianate houses, was so built up by the 1850s and 1860s that there were few opportunities here for those characteristic long rows of Italianate brownstones that we find in such places as Fort Greene and Bedford-Stuyvesant. This is one of the few such rows in the Heights. Though not built all at once, these six houses form a remarkably harmonious streetscape with a stately rhythm of heavily molded window enframements, segmental-arched and square-headed windows, columned doorways with heavy entablatures carried on large foliated brackets, and chunky iron stoop railings. The mansard roofs on some of the houses are later additions. These houses, the rear gardens of which are visible along the Esplanade, are some of the most desirable in Brooklyn.

15 *210 to 220 Columbia Heights*

16 MARGARET (apartments)
97 Columbia Heights, northeast corner of Orange Street
1988, Ehrenkrantz Group & Eckstut

From 1889 to 1980 the Hotel Margaret occupied this site. Frank Freeman designed the ten-story hotel in what at the time was his customary Richardsonian Romanesque style. It was long the highest and most prominent building on the Heights. It burned down as it was being renovated into condominiums, and the present apartment building, now owned by the Jehovah's Witnesses, was completed in 1988.

The Jehovah's Witnesses are a major presence in Brooklyn Heights. It is, in a sense, their Vatican. Architecturally they have been a blessing and a curse to the community. They have erected such modern structures as the residence hall at the southeast corner of Columbia Heights and Orange Street, designed by Frederick G. Frost, Jr., & Associates and built in 1960, and the dormitory and library at the southeast corner of Columbia Heights and Pineapple Street, designed by Ulrich Franzen & Associates and built in 1970. The Jehovah's Witnesses have also splendidly restored some buildings, including the Hotel Bossert on Montague Street. Whether new or rehabilitated, their buildings are immaculately maintained.

17 13 PINEAPPLE STREET
Between Willow Street and Columbia Heights, north side
1830

This three-story shingled frame house is five bays wide, with the entrance in the central bay. It features fourteen six-over-six windows on its Pineapple Street façade. The fine bracketed cornice was added sometime in the late-nineteenth century, and the front-door fanlight and the stoop, parallel to the street, are modern additions.

18 ADRIAN VAN SINDEREN HOUSE
70 Willow Street between Pineapple and Orange Streets, west side
Late 1830s

This is one of the largest Greek Revival houses extant in New York. It is two and a half stories high, and four bays wide, with the entrance in the second

17 *13 Pineapple Street*

bay from the right, up a low stoop with fine iron railings. These railings and the fine iron fence were added sometime in the late-nineteenth century. The stoop, doorway enframement, basement, and trim are of brownstone, while the rest of the house is painted brick. This house was purchased and superbly restored by the well-known stage designer Oliver Smith.

19 20 to 26 WILLOW STREET
Southwest corner of Middagh Street
1846

These four three-story houses are a Greek Revival counterpart to the Federal group at 155 to 159 Willow Street, built about twenty years earlier. The houses are brick with brownstone basements. The front doors are recessed within enframements featuring "Greek ears"—the little projections, or "ears," at the top ends of the enframement—and low-pitched pediments. Henry Ward Beecher lived in No. 22.

20 EUGENE BOISSELET HOUSE
24 Middagh Street, southeast corner of Willow Street
1824

The *AIA Guide to New York City* calls this house the "queen of Brooklyn Heights." Indeed, it is hard to imagine a more perfect specimen of the Federal-style frame house. The clapboarded house is two stories plus an attic, with a basement of Flemish-bond brickwork. Two dormers project from its gambrel roof. The windows are in the six-over-six pattern typical of the time. As with all Federal-style houses, however, the real treat is the doorway. Here a wooden stairway with lovely balustraded railings leads to a paneled door set between elegantly attenuated and fluted Ionic columns. There are leaded sidelights and a leaded transom. The whole composition is surrounded by an elaborately carved enframement including foliated blocks and a foliated panel at the top in the center. At the attic level on the Willow Street side is an arched window flanked by quarter-round windows. A rear garden separates the house from a small structure that was originally a carriage house.

21 56 MIDDAGH STREET
Between Henry and Hicks Streets, south side
1829
Remodeled in 1840s

Records show that this two-and-a-half-story clapboarded house was built in 1829, though its present appearance is largely the result of a remodeling in the 1840s when Greek Revival elements were added. The projecting distyle Doric portico is one such element; so too might be the frieze-like arrangement of the attic windows.

22 PLYMOUTH CHURCH (Congregational)
Orange Street between Henry and Hicks Streets, north side
1849, Joseph C. Wells

Plymouth Church is such an important historical landmark that it is easy to overlook its austere architecture. This would be a mistake. Though the simple Italianate brownstone exterior is relatively unprepossessing (it is not controversial to say that there are several more beautiful churches in Brooklyn

Heights), the interior was enormously influential in certain kinds of Protestant church architecture. The basically square space, with rounded corners, is arranged more like an auditorium or theater than what until then had been considered a church. The pews are arranged semicircularly around the dais. There was already a long tradition of "preaching churches" among some Protestant sects, including the New England Congregationalists with their simple meetinghouses. At Plymouth, however, the preaching principle was taken to a whole new level. Not only was renowned preacher Henry Ward Beecher, who erected the church, the inspiration for this arrangement, he was, we believe, its designer. Joseph C. Wells was a well-known church architect who had designed the fine Gothic Revival First Presbyterian Church on Fifth Avenue and 12th Street in New York City. He apparently deferred to the famous clergyman when it came to the interior design of Plymouth Church. The arrangement allowed the audience—er, congregation—to see and hear the preacher. Not for these Congregationalists what the High Church seminarians call "smells and bells." Beecher was a theatrical preacher; his had to be a theatrical church. Another reason for the arrangement was to accommodate as many people as possible. Beecher's renown was such that his church filled to overflowing on Sundays. One would never guess it by looking at the outside of the building, but the auditorium of Plymouth Church can hold 2,800 people, slightly more than the largest houses for musicals on Broadway can hold. The architectural historian Andrew S. Dolkart, the leading authority on New York church architecture, has said that this is probably the first "theater plan" church ever to be built. Among its progeny we can count Fort Greene's Lafayette Avenue Presbyterian Church of 1860–62 and Hanson Place Baptist Church of 1857–60.

Plymouth Church is a treasure house of stained glass. Frederick Stymetz Lamb (1863–1928), one of the most important American artists of his time, designed nineteen windows for the church. Their theme is the "History of Puritanism and Its Influence Upon the Institutions and People of the Republic." The style of the windows is classical, as befits the setting, and they are executed in the opalescent technique for which Louis Comfort Tiffany was renowned but at which Lamb was every bit as skilled a practitioner. Lamb was the grandson of Joseph Lamb, who founded the J. & R. Lamb stained-glass studio in New York City in 1857. (Lamb Studios is still in operation in Ridgewood, New Jersey, and still producing high-quality stained glass for churches.) Lamb, a muralist as well as a stained-glass artist, founded the National Society of

Mural Painters, and, with his brother Charles Rollinson Lamb, was one of the early movers and shakers of the Municipal Art Society of New York. His masterpiece of stained glass is the window entitled *Religion Enthroned* in the Brooklyn Museum. It is one of the most stunning examples of stained-glass art to be seen in New York City and one of that museum's treasures. In Hillis Hall, the parish social center located behind the church, are several more examples of truly magnificent stained-glass art. When Plymouth merged with the Church of the Pilgrims, that church's windows by Louis Comfort Tiffany were transferred here. The most famous of these windows is the *Ascension,* based on Raphael's painting of the same title. It is in the middle on the north side. Otto Heinigke (1850–1915) did the windows flanking the *Ascension.* Heinigke was a leader in the movement to revive traditional Gothic stained-glass technique and also the creator of the spectacular mosaics in the lobby of the Woolworth Building in Manhattan.

Beecher preached here from its opening until his death in 1887. The Tuscan porch was added after his death. Plymouth Church merged in 1934 with the Church of the Pilgrims to become Plymouth Church of the Pilgrims.

23 PLYMOUTH CHURCH PARISH HOUSE
Northeast corner of Orange and Hicks Streets
1914, Woodruff Leeming

The parish house of Plymouth Church is a large structure of limestone-trimmed red brick. It wraps around the corner of Hicks and Orange Streets and connects to the church on Orange by an enclosed walkway set behind a generous fenced garden. It is a Beaux-Arts design in the Georgian Palladian idiom. In the center of the wall of the connecting wing, facing Orange Street across the garden, is a bronze statue of Henry Ward Beecher. The statue, by Gutzon Borglum (1867–1941), was erected in 1914. It stands against the red-brick wall in a limestone setting between Doric columns supporting a pedimented canopy. Borglum's bronze relief on the wall to the left of the statue shows Abraham Lincoln, who came to Plymouth Church to hear Beecher preach. Borglum is best known as the sculptor of the colossal heads at Mount Rushmore. The parish house has a beautiful Palladian entrance facing the garden. Its architect, Woodruff Leeming (1870–1919), attended Brooklyn Polytechnic Institute, Massachusetts Institute of Technology, and the École des Beaux-Arts, and worked for Heins & LaFarge at the time they were commis-

23 *Plymouth Church Parish House*

sioned to design the Cathedral of St. John the Divine. Leeming started his own practice in Brooklyn, and one of his first works was the rectory (1893) of South Congregational Church in Carroll Gardens—a church the cornerstone of which supposedly was laid by Henry Ward Beecher. John Arbuckle, of coffee fame, funded construction of the Plymouth parish house. Arbuckle lived in a house that Montrose W. Morris designed on Clinton Avenue.

24 **ST. GEORGE HOTEL**
Bounded by Clark, Henry, Pineapple, and Hicks Streets
1885, Augustus Hatfield
Additions: 1890–1923, Montrose W. Morris and others
Tower building: 1929–30, Emery Roth

The St. George Hotel opened with thirty rooms in 1885, and expanded over the years eventually to comprise eight buildings. At the completion of Emery Roth's 400-foot-high tower building, the St. George boasted 2,632 guest rooms, making it the largest hotel in New York City. The grand ballroom and the indoor saltwater ("cleaner than the ocean ever has a chance to be") swimming pool were both located in the tower building and were both famous. The pool, said by some to be the largest indoor swimming pool in the world, was spectacular, with light glinting off its dark glazed tile walls and mirrored ceiling. The ballroom was also said to be the largest in the world. The 11,000-square-foot, thirty-one-foot-high space was designed by Winold Reiss and was the ultimate in jazz-age elegance. Robert A. M. Stern, Gregory F. Gilmartin, and Thomas Mellins, in their *New York 1930*, call it "the single most startling interior public space of the time in New York." Like other Heights hotels—the Bossert, the Leverich Towers—the St. George featured a rooftop restaurant and nightclub. In his spectacularly boosterish 1932 book, *New York: The Wonder City*, W. Parker Chase breathlessly lists some facts and figures about the St. George:

> *Luxurious, up to date and the social mecca of all Brooklyn.*
>
> *Largest and most magnificent swimming pool in the world. Cost $1,264,000.*
>
> *Enormous Banquet Hall—Seats 2,500 and accommodates 3,000 dancers. . . .*
>
> *Largest private incinerator in the world—capacity 26 tons daily.*
>
> *73 ventilating fans—circulating 8,000,000 cubic feet per minute.*
>
> *Over 6,000 windows.*
>
> *7 ¹/₂ miles of corridors and 21 elevators.*
>
> *Over 66,000 electric bulbs.*
>
> *20,000 chairs, 61,000 sheets, 560,000 pillow cases and 655,000 pieces of table linen. . . . .*
>
> *The St. George is a good sized city in itself. It can seat and serve food in its cafes and eating places to 10,000 at one time.*

Room rates in this wonder hotel in 1931 were $2.50 per night for a single room without a bath, $3.50 for a single room with bath, and $5.00 for a double room with bath. (The Leverich Towers began at $3.00. New York City's most expensive hotel at the time was probably the Ritz-Carlton on Madison Avenue and 46th Street, where rooms began at $8.00.) In the 1930s, the St. George pool was open from 9:00 A.M. until midnight. Children were not admitted to the swimming pool after 5:00 P.M. on weekdays or after 12:00 P.M. on weekends and holidays, and a person had to measure at least four feet four inches in height in order to be allowed the pool's use. Hotel guests could use the pool free of charge until noon, and received a reduced rate thereafter.

24 *St. George Hotel*

Others could use the pool for one dollar per day, "including sterilized swim-ming suit." Walter R. Brooks's 1931 book *New York: An Intimate Guide*, alto-gether a more sober affair than W. Parker Chase's book, extols the view from the St. George roof restaurant: "At half past five on a winter evening, when the scrub-women are sweeping out the offices in the downtown skyscrapers, and all the windows are lit, you will have another opportunity to become lyrical and even to philosophize a little on the amazing discrepancy between the prosaic cause and the fantastic effect." In 1964, the St. George still boasted the same exact 2,632 rooms it boasted in 1932. Rates had gone up: four to fourteen dol-lars for a single, ten to seventeen dollars for a double, twelve to twenty-four dollars for a suite, and, something new, two dollars a day to park one's car in the hotel garage. The *Hart's Guide to New York City* (1964), the most com-pendious guidebook published in conjunction with the World's Fair, states of the St. George that "The over-all impression is one of decorative hodgepodge and architectural inconsistency. . . . banal furnishings prevail in most quarters." Though, like all hotels in the metropolitan region, the St. George made a push to cash in on the World's Fair throngs, it is clear that its glory had faded con-siderably—although, to be fair, "decorative hodgepodge and architectural inconsistency" that may have been distinctly unfashionable in the early 1960s might not seem so today. Still, the property was broken up among different owners, and by the 1980s parts of the St. George had been reduced to use as part of the city's network of welfare residences, the most ignominious fate that could befall a once grand hotel, however profitable the arrangement might be for the hotel owner. It got worse: part of the St. George was gutted by fire in 1995. Things may be looking up. On the Clark Street lot where the wing stood that burned, developers are planning a new, eleven-story, 200-room "boutique hotel," designed by the prominent Manhattan architectural firm of Gruzen Samton. Other parts of the St. George have been converted to co-op apartments (including the tower building at 111 Hicks Street) and to student housing. The ballroom has been converted to squash and racquetball courts. The magnificent swimming pool deteriorated over the years and its space has been divided in two, with a smaller pool (making use of the some of the original tilework) and a gymnasium.

Though the tower building was not one of his major designs considered purely from an aesthetic point of view, nonetheless it was a major commission for Emery Roth (1870–1947), one of New York's most prominent architects of hotels and apartment houses in the 1920s and 1930s. The St. George was Roth's only work in Brooklyn. He designed several of the great apartment buildings along Central Park West, including the San Remo (1929–30), the Beresford (1928–29), the Eldorado (1929–30), and the Ardsley (1930–31), all contemporary with his work at the St. George during what must have been a whirlwind couple of years.

Fulton Ferry/DUMBO

When Brooklyn was incorporated as a city in 1834, its entire population of 24,000 people lived within a three-quarters of a mile radius from the Fulton Ferry landing. This was Brooklyn's downtown. The most important commercial buildings, banks, hotels, and mercantile establishments were located along Fulton Street, named in honor of Robert Fulton, who established his steam ferry between Brooklyn and New York City in 1814. Ferry service of one sort or another had existed since the seventeenth century. It was not, however, until the steam ferry that movement back and forth between the two cities became fast and reliable. The Union Ferry Company operated the Fulton ferry, and in 1865 built a new, picturesquely massed, towered and mansarded, French

Second Empire-style ferry house of elaborate woodwork. Leopold Eidlitz, architect of the Brooklyn Academy of Music on Montague Street, may have designed it. In a niche under the central gable of the main section facing Fulton Street stood Caspar Buberl's zinc statue of Robert Fulton, later moved to Fulton Park in Bedford-Stuyvesant. The Union Ferry Company also operated the ferries between Whitehall Street and Atlantic Avenue, Wall Street and Montague Street, Catharine Street and Main Street, and Whitehall Street and Hamilton Avenue. So many Manhattanites came to Brooklyn to attend Plymouth Church on Orange Street—a short walk from the ferry house—that on Sundays the Fulton Ferry was known as "Beecher's Ferry." Ferry service from here ended in 1924. The ferry house was torn down two years later. In 1939, the Federal Writers' Project's *New York City Guide* described Fulton Ferry as "a small isolated sector of musty, dilapidated buildings nestling in the shadows of the Brooklyn Bridge…Fulton Street, in this section, is now a sort of Brooklyn Bowery, with flophouses, small shops, rancid restaurants, haunted by vagabonds and derelicts." A hundred years earlier it was the least isolated part of Brooklyn.

The Fulton Ferry part of the area is easily accessible by foot from Brooklyn Heights. One needs only to walk north on Columbia Heights to Old Fulton Street, where one will be near two renowned eateries. The River Café is one of the swankiest restaurants in New York City. Located on a barge in the river just off Old Fulton Street underneath the Brooklyn Bridge, the River Café is noted both for the quality of its food and for its spectacular views of lower Manhattan. It's rather pricey, which is why I'm a lot likelier to be found at Fulton Ferry's other gastronomical mecca, Patsy Grimaldi's, at No. 19 Old Fulton Street, right across the street from the Eagle Warehouse & Storage Company (see below). Patsy Grimaldi's is an authentic brick-oven pizzeria consistently ranked as one of the best—often as the best—in New York, a city in which pizza is not considered fast food but is taken very, very seriously. Another nearby institution of note is Bargemusic. Olga Bloom founded this, one of America's premier venues for chamber music, in a 102-foot-long barge, once used by the Erie Lackawanna Railroad, in the East River next to the River Café. Bargemusic concerts can often be heard across the country on National Public Radio. Call (718) 624-2083 or check www.bargemusic.org. From the Fulton Ferry District it is easy to continue on into the heart of DUMBO and beyond to Vinegar Hill. The heart of DUMBO can also be reached by taking the F train to York Street station.

25 BROOKLYN CITY RAILROAD COMPANY BUILDING
8 Old Fulton Street
1860–61

The Brooklyn City Railroad Company began in 1853 as a horsecar line providing service to and from the Fulton Ferry terminal. Horsecars were horse-drawn cars running on rails, a huge improvement over the principal form of mass surface transportation until then, which was the horse-drawn omnibus, bouncing violently over cobblestones. The new horsecars ran smoothly and must have seemed to their users like a bit of heaven. The Brooklyn City Railroad replaced omnibus routes with rail lines, and was instrumental in the development of the interior of Brooklyn, including the initial development of the area around the newly constructed Prospect Park. (We are used to thinking of neighborhoods such as Park Slope as having developed only in the wake of the opening of the Brooklyn Bridge, and while the bridge was an enormous

25 Brooklyn City Railroad Company

impetus to these neighborhoods' growth, the truth is that their first waves of development occurred before the bridge, but after the creation of the horsecar lines.) A marvelous color lithograph is reproduced on page 96 of Ellen M. Snyder-Grenier's fine book *Brooklyn: An Illustrated History*, showing one of Brooklyn City Railroad's cars passing by Gamaliel King's old high-domed Kings County Courthouse on Joralemon Street in 1861.

When this building was completed in the year the Civil War broke out, the Fulton Ferry district was in its heyday as the most bustling part of the city. Today, this exceptionally handsome building stands quite alone, its five-story height, already accentuated by the foreshortening of its rising stories, accentuated the more by its freestanding state. The ground floor is cast iron, which had only just come into its own and would become prevalent throughout the 1860s and 1870s, as in the Long Island Safe Deposit Company Building across Fulton Street. What makes the building for me is the manner in which its redbrick mass is sandwiched by granite quoining. Granite is used as well for a variety of devices carried out in the Italianate style of the period, including molded pilasters, window pediments, console brackets and the lintels they carry, and the strong, dentilated cornice. In its rhythms and proportions, in its stately scale and in its sure handling of materials, this is about as handsome a New York office building as its period produced. It later served light manufacturing (it was a factory where toilet-seat covers were manufactured) and in the 1970s the architect David Morton converted it to apartments.

26 EAGLE WAREHOUSE AND STORAGE COMPANY
28 Old Fulton Street, southeast corner of Elizabeth Street
1893, Frank Freeman

Frank Freeman designed this imposing pile of bricks in a style that, while still very much Richardsonian Romanesque, is quite different from such other works of his as the Brooklyn Fire Headquarters (completed one year before this) and the Herman Behr house (completed three years before this). Like H.H. Richardson himself, Freeman chose a more straightforward style for a warehouse than he did for a residence or a civic building. The result is in its way no less interesting. This is Brooklyn's closest kin to Richardson's master-piece of warehouse design, the Marshall Field Wholesale Store (1885-87) in Chicago. The Eagle Warehouse is a fortress of a building, and unlike the architects of many of the other warehouses in the Fulton Ferry/DUMBO area,

26 *Eagle Warehouse and*
Storage Company

Freeman was obviously very concerned to give his building visual interest. It is
seven stories and extremely wide and deep. The entrance is right in the center. It is one of the boldest arches in Brooklyn, a city of bold arches. It is outlined in simple, beautiful bronze lettering spelling out "Eagle Warehouse &
Storage Co." To either side of the entrance are iron-barred windows. Above
the archway is a simple belt course. The building is in a way a "tripartite" skyscraper. Below the belt course is the base. Above is the shaft, rising four stories
and punctuated by twenty identical windows. The center section of four rows
of three windows each is subtly recessed, lending just enough visual interest to
this shaft to inspire the eye to continue upward, to the "capital," or top, to a
series of outsized corbels. Above this, and topping off the building, is another,
plain story, where simple, lovely lettering again appears, this time spelling out
"The Eagle Warehouse & Storage Company of Brooklyn 1805." Between
"Storage" and "Company," in dead center, is a fine clock. The building is
straightforward simplicity itself, yet its scale and its proportions, the lettering
and the clock, and the several small devices Freeman employed to keep the eye

from wearying, give it an undeniable beauty in addition to its power. In 1980, the Brooklyn architect Bernard Rothzeid expertly renovated the building into condominiums. Freeman designed the warehouse extension to the east in 1906. Its subtly convex façade, set back ever so slightly from the lot line of the earlier building, made it a harmonious structure while not destroying the proportions of the original. This building, by the way, dates from after the heyday of the Fulton Ferry area.

27 LONG ISLAND SAFE DEPOSIT COMPANY
1 Front Street, northwest corner of Old Fulton Street
1868–69, William A. Mundell

The Brooklyn-born William A. Mundell (1844-1903) designed this building when he was only twenty-four years old. It may be his most felicitous work, and one of the great cast-iron-fronted palazzi of New York. The building fills an awkward trapezoidal site, and Mundell's solution was to orient the two-story building on a diagonal, with the entrance at the corner, for a chamfered effect. Three-bay wings flare from the corner bay. Each bay contains two floors of three windows each, while the corner bay has a window above the entrance.

27 *Long Island Safe Deposit Company*

All the openings are arched, the seven of the second floor in the Venetian style. Each of the three sections of the façade is framed by diamond-pointed quoins, and a gorgeous cornice carried on heavy brackets tops the building. The scale is almost diminutive, yet the building has great strength, like a bantamweight boxer. Nonetheless, notice how it towers over the even more diminutive Long Island Insurance Company Building next door. The bank closed in 1891, a sign of the flagging fortunes of the ferry area. After years of neglect and abuse, the building is now in a superb state of preservation. Where an earlier owner had painted it black, it is now, appropriately, white—making it stand out rather majestically in this somber-hued precinct. Also, the cornice had been removed, and is now returned.

Across the street from the Long Island Safe Deposit Company, at 2 Front Street at the northeast corner of Fulton Street, stood the Brooklyn-Union Building. Leopold Eidlitz designed it in 1868. The five-story building was in the "Ruskinian Gothic" style, with polychrome stonework, and had a mansard roof with gabled dormers. This was the headquarters of a daily newspaper founded during the Civil War to advance the Union cause. The Brooklyn Bridge Company took offices in the building in 1870.

28 LONG ISLAND INSURANCE COMPANY
5-7 Front Street
1835

This is believed to be the oldest surviving office building in New York City. It is three stories high and three bays wide. The ground floor is faced in granite, the two upper floors in brick, with stone sills and lintels. A low stoop on the left leads to the entrance. Its mien is similar to some of the counting-houses in the South Street Seaport area in Manhattan, from the same period. Today this building houses a restaurant.

29 FRANKLIN HOUSE
1 Old Fulton Street, southeast corner of Water Street
1835, altered 1850s

This four-story building has nine window bays facing Fulton Street. The ground floor has been mutilated. Above is flaking, gray-painted brick. Some of the second-floor window pediments are in place. Others have gone, leaving a

29 *Franklin House*

ghostly triangular outline. These pediments were added in the 1850s when the originally Greek Revival building was given fashionable Italianate flourishes. The Franklin House was a popular hotel and restaurant in the nineteenth century. Today the building again houses a restaurant, with apartments above.

30 TOBACCO INSPECTION WAREHOUSE
25–39 Water Street between New Dock and Dock Streets, north side
Ca. 1860

This mesmerizingly simple two-story brick warehouse has plain arched windows, eight of them on the building's narrow inland side on Water Street, with less dense fenestration on New Dock Street. On the river side, the building, at this writing, is an amazing ruin: a construction crane engaged in— ahem—*stabilizing* the structure accidentally removed a roof joint, causing much of the north wall to collapse. The result is a splendid forty-foot-wide hole in the wall, giving the building an awesome appearance that a part of you kind of wishes it could retain, though the larger part of you knows that it ought to (as it will) be fixed. That then leaves the question of what is to be done with the fixed building, which has been vacant for many a moon. It may be incorporated into the proposed Brooklyn Bridge Park and serve as a café.

31 *Empire Stores*

31 EMPIRE STORES

53–83 Water Street between Dock and Main Streets, north side
Four-story group to west 1870, Nesmith & Sons
Five-story group to east 1884–85, Thomas Stone

There is a quiet, austere majesty to these extremely simple old brick warehouses that form a superb backdrop for Empire-Fulton Ferry State Park. As at the adjacent Tobacco Inspection Warehouse, the fenestration is in the form of simple arched openings. The two groups of Empire Stores are identical but for the one story added to the newer group to the east. The façades are given a little additional interest by the exposed metal tie-rod ends and the metal shutters.

32 GAIR BUILDING (now Clock Tower Building)

1 Main Street
1915
Renovated into apartments 1998–99, Beyer Blinder Belle

This handsome, sixteen-story building, its clock tower the most prominent skyline element between the Brooklyn and Manhattan bridges, is associated with two men who, in different periods and in different ways, were both

113

32 *Gair Building*

bullish on DUMBO. Robert Gair (1839-1927) built this, together with several other nearby buildings that are among the pioneer works of reinforced-concrete construction in America. Part of what we now call DUMBO was once actually known as "Gairville." Gair was a major manufacturer of cardboard boxes, one of the industries for which this area was known in the years between the opening of the Brooklyn Bridge and the recent changes that have overtaken DUMBO (an acronym of recent vintage standing for "Down Under the Manhattan Bridge Overpass"). These recent changes involve the decline of manufacturing in this part of Brooklyn and the relocation to this area of many artists and other creative types who in earlier years might have lived in Manhattan's SoHo or TriBeCa. Along with DUMBO's growing community of artists, we have in the last few years begun to see some of the outward signs of the kind of gentrification that earlier affected those Manhattan neighborhoods. Streetfront galleries and cafés are now found in the streets of DUMBO. Several prominent industrial and commercial buildings have been converted to fairly luxurious apartments, including the Eagle Warehouse & Storage Company, the Brooklyn City Railroad Company Building, and this, which brings me to the other bullish man with whom this building is associated. He is David Walentas, and all New York knows him as the man with a plan for DUMBO, indeed as the man who has been extolling DUMBO's enormous commercial potential for nearly a quarter of a century. (Walentas was involved in some of the early residential conversions in SoHo in the 1970s. He currently owns ten buildings in DUMBO.) It would seem to many outside observers that DUMBO is an area ripe for development, located as it is right on the riverfront, adjacent to swanky Brooklyn Heights, and just across the river from Manhattan, and filled as it is with fine old buildings and atmospheric streets. In 1982 Walentas was involved in a failed plan to create something called Fulton Landing. Designed by Benjamin Thompson & Associates, the architects of Boston's Faneuil Hall Maketplace, Baltimore's Harborplace, and Manhattan's South Street Seaport, Fulton Landing would have been a similar "waterfront festival marketplace." In 1999, Walentas released plans for a major riverfront development on either side of the Manhattan Bridge, to consist of a hotel, a multiplex cinema, stores, and parking. For this development, Walentas engaged no less an architect than the Frenchman Jean Nouvel, more chi-chi than whom one cannot get. Nouvel designed the Institut de Monde Arabe in Paris, one of the most celebrated buildings in the world in the last twenty years. Even many of Walentas's opponents found the Nouvel design striking and even stunning. Whether it will be built or not is an open question. Walentas is a very controversial figure. His opponents in DUMBO include those who feel that the kind of development he promotes will further push manufacturing uses from the area. Others feel his waterfront proposals are too elaborate and too commercial, that the riverfront should be simple, open green space accessible to all Brooklynites. Some DUMBO residents like the remote feeling of the area and fear that further development will cause the streets to be overrun with visitors, not to mention push up rents. It is not my purpose here to take a stand on these issues, but what happens in DUMBO will, one way or the other, be interesting, and, one way or the other, David Walentas will be in the thick of it.

Vinegar Hill

Vinegar Hill is bounded on the north by the East River, on the east by the Navy Yard, on the south by Sands Street, and on the west by Bridge Street. The Vinegar Hill Historic District comprises two small subsections of the larger area, the first mainly along Hudson Avenue between Front and Plymouth

Streets, the second to the west along Front Street between Gold and Bridge Streets. (It is very unusual for a single New York City Historic District to be divided in two in this way.) John Jackson purchased a large tract of land from the Sands family in 1800 and named it Vinegar Hill, after the site in County Wexford, Ireland, where in June 1798 the Irish rebellion was put down by British troops. (The bloody end of that rebellion led several prominent Irishmen to immigrate to New York, where they played a major role in the development of the city. Think particularly of William MacNeven and Thomas Addis Emmet, both conspicuously memorialized in the churchyard of St. Paul's Chapel on Broadway and Fulton Street in Manhattan.) An alternative name for the neighborhood was Irishtown.

Throughout most of the history of Vinegar Hill, the neighborhood was a bustling Irish working-class community comprising a variety of brick row houses and freestanding frame houses interspersed with factories. Local residents worked in the factories, on the nearby docks, and in the Navy Yard. Sands Street, the southern boundary of the neighborhood, named for the prominent landowning family and terminating on its east at the Navy Yard, once was one of the most infamous streets in New York, known for its bars and brothels catering to sailors and waterfront workers, New York's nearest equivalent of San Francisco's Barbary Coast. This is almost impossible to imagine from looking at Sands Street today. The street was truncated at its west end by the Brooklyn-Queens Expressway and, on the east end, irrevocably altered by the Farragut public housing project. After the Second World War, during which the Navy Yard reached its employment peak, Vinegar Hill and other nearby areas declined. The population exodus, which would have been great in any event, was exacerbated by public-works projects. As the Navy Yard became a ghostly relic of its former glory, Vinegar Hill practically fell off the map. When the expressway was built, Vinegar Hill became about as cut off as a neighborhood could be: on the west, the Manhattan Bridge and its approaches; on the south, the BQE; on the east, the shell of the Navy Yard; on the north, the East River.

It is said that at one time the smoke from the Brooklyn Edison Company's plant on Hudson Avenue so permeated the atmosphere of Vinegar Hill that clothes hung out to dry would get dirty with soot. In 1939, the *New York City Guide* of the Federal Writers' Project did not pull its punches, describing Vinegar Hill and vicinity as "a shapeless grotesque neighborhood, its grimy cobblestone thoroughfares filled with flophouses, crumbling tenements, and greasy restaurants.... The area north of Sands Street toward the river is crowded with industrial plants, warehouses, and factories, which charge the air with their mixed aroma of chocolate, spices, and roasting coffee. Scattered among them are ramshackle frame houses—notorious firetraps of squalid appearance." As for the "notorious firetraps," check out Hudson Street between Plymouth and Evans Streets. I am quite sure that the authors of the *New York City Guide* could never have imagined that the "notorious firetraps" about which they wrote would one day be designated New York City landmarks! By the way, the chocolate was that of the Rockwood Chocolate Company, on Park Avenue, once the country's second largest chocolate producer after Hershey.

The Irish maids who worked in the houses of Brooklyn Heights often lived in Vinegar Hill, which was literally on the other side of the tracks—that is, on the other side of the Fulton Street elevated—from the Heights. The el was taken down in 1941.

Today, Vinegar Hill is back on the radar. This is partly to do with the Historic District designation of some of its streets, and the growing interest among historians and preservationists in old working-class neighborhoods, and even more to do with the rise of DUMBO as an artists' quarter, with spillover of artists' studios and homes from the west side of the Manhattan Bridge into Vinegar Hill. To live in Vinegar Hill is now considered very hip, the way it was a few years ago to live in Williamsburg. Vinegar Hill has been many things in its history. Never before, however, was it hip. Much of the area still has a somewhat desolate air, and I recommend that the visitor exercise due caution in walking around here. The streets leading to the Navy Yard can especially seem a tad forbidding.

33 BENJAMIN MOORE & COMPANY FACTORY
231 Front Street between Bridge and Gold Streets, north side
1908, William B. Tubby

To my knowledge, this is the only factory building by Tubby in Brooklyn, where most of his work comprised houses, including Charles Pratt's on Clinton Avenue. It is a handsome and appropriately powerful utilitarian structure that happens to share a block with a lovely row of 1840s Greek Revival row houses, which appear to be in very good condition. Tubby often worked in what we call the Queen Anne style, and some of his works tended to the wild and woolly. Here he is restrained in a way that makes it hard to think he wasn't trying to harmonize with the simple, strong Greek Revival houses. Tubby's forms are tra-beated, as are those of the houses, and his window openings are of about the same proportions as those of the houses. The horizontally banded windows of the factory have continuous stone lintels that may have been suggested by the lintels of the houses. There is much the same feeling here that one gets on a street such as Vandam in Manhattan, where elegant Federal and Greek Revival row houses share the block with massive printing plants.

Tubby's six-story factory is of brick with stone trim. The outer piers are massive, and enclose single-window bays on either side of a center bay with five windows. The arrangement is reminiscent of the work of some turn-of-the-century Chicago architects such as Richard Schmidt and Hugh Mackie Garden. Overall, this block seems to me the quintessence of Vinegar Hill.

33 *Benjamin Moore &*
Company Factory

THE BROOKLYN NAVY YARD

The United States Navy operated the New York Naval Shipyard, better known as the Brooklyn Navy Yard, for one hundred and sixty-five years, from 1801 to 1966.

The Navy Yard is located at Wallabout Bay in the East River, about midway between the Manhattan Bridge and the Williamsburg Bridge. To the north is Williamsburg, to the south is Fort Greene, and to the west is Vinegar Hill. (The neighborhood to the immediate south, though traditionally part of Fort Greene, is sometimes called Navy Hill since the Brooklyn-Queens Expressway cut it off from the rest of Fort Greene.) The street boundaries are Kent Avenue to the north, Flushing Avenue to the south, and Navy Street to the west. The Navy Yard is directly across the East River from Corlear's Hook in the Lower East Side of Manhattan. The site covers 255 acres.

John Jackson, the same man who developed Vinegar Hill, purchased the future Navy Yard site from the Remsen family after the Revolutionary War. Here Jackson built a dock and a shipyard. He built a merchant ship called the *Canton* (shades of Abiel Abbot Low), and a warship called the *John Adams*. Jackson sold the property to the Federal government in 1801 for $40,000. More than a hundred ships were built here for use in the War of 1812. Several famous ships were constructed at the Navy Yard. In 1814-15, the Navy's first oceangoing steamship, the *Fulton*, was built here. The steamship *Niagara*, which helped lay the Atlantic Cable, came from the Brooklyn Navy Yard. The Brooklyn Navy Yard was the center of naval activity for the Union fleet in the Civil War. In the 1880s, the Navy Yard was a major tourist attraction. The U.S.S. *Constitution* docked there and was open to the public, and the Navy Yard featured manicured lawns where proper Victorian ladies would stroll and that provided a favorite subject for the paintings of William Merritt Chase, renowned for his images of park scenes. In 1895, the *Maine*, memorialized in Columbus Circle in Manhattan, was launched from here. Memorialized somewhat farther away, at Pearl Harbor, Hawaii, is the U.S.S. *Arizona*, which though it may have been laid to rest in the Pacific, was born at the Brooklyn Navy Yard.

In 1918, during the First World War, 18,000 people worked at the Navy Yard. The *New York City Guide* of the Federal Writers' Project, published in 1939 before the U.S. entered World War II, stated that the Navy Yard employed 10,000 *men*, of whom perhaps a third were there courtesy of the Works Progress Administration. At the start of World War II, the Wallabout produce market, established in 1890 near Flushing and Clinton Avenues, was demolished for the expansion of the Navy Yard. In 1944, the number of Navy Yard workers had risen to an astonishing 71,000, of whom a substantial percentage, engaged in all facets of ship construction and maintenance, were women—think Rosie the Riveter. (New York City's rent control laws were originally federally mandated to protect against rent gouging as workers poured into the city to work in the wartime industries. Of these industries, the Brooklyn shipyards were paramount.) If American involvement in World War II began on December 7, 1941, in Pearl Harbor, where Brooklyn's *Arizona* was destroyed, the war ended on September 2, 1945, aboard another Brooklyn progeny, the U.S.S. *Missouri*. Activity in the Navy Yard fell off after World War II, but did not die out as precipitously as one might imagine. The Navy Yard remained a major facility through the 1950s. Today it is an industrial park.

Within the Navy Yard are several structures that the New York City Landmarks Preservation Commission has designated as landmarks. Just inside the Navy Yard gate from Evans Street in Vinegar Hill is what once was the commandant's house, built in 1805-06. This is an extraordinarily elegant Federal-style clapboarded house with a front porch the roof of which is carried on extremely slender columns. Above this porch is another, balustraded, roofless porch. Pedimented dormers project from a pitched roof. The front doorway, on the right of the lower porch, is one of those beautiful Federal-period doorways, with a leaded fanlight and leaded sidelights. It is one of the most beautiful houses in New York. Just north of the commandant's house and bordering Vinegar Hill along Little Street in this rather desolate region is something unappetizingly called the "Department of Environmental Protection Sludge Dewatering Facility."

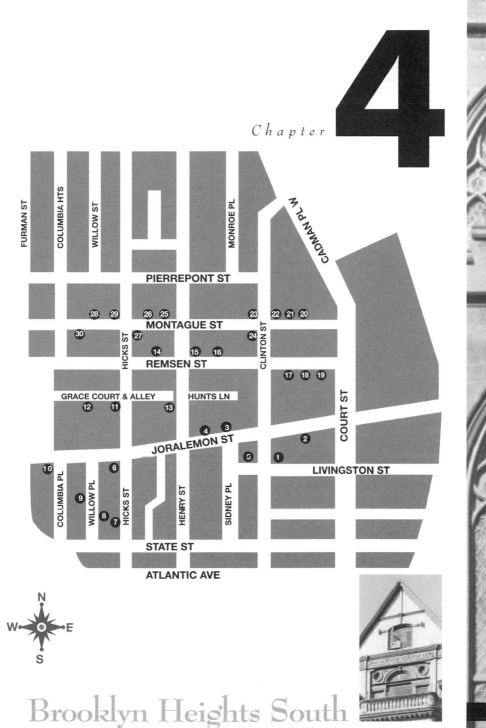

Chapter 4

FURMAN ST

COLUMBIA HTS

WILLOW ST

MONROE PL

CADMAN PL W

PIERREPONT ST

28 29 26 25 23 22 21 20

MONTAGUE ST

HICKS ST

30 27

CLINTON ST

14 15 16 24

REMSEN ST

17 18 19

GRACE COURT & ALLEY   HUNTS LN

COURT ST

12 11 13

4 3

2

JORALEMON ST

5 1

LIVINGSTON ST

10

COLUMBIA PL

6

WILLOW PL

HICKS ST

HENRY ST

SIDNEY PL

9

8 7

STATE ST

ATLANTIC AVE

N
W   E
S

Brooklyn Heights South

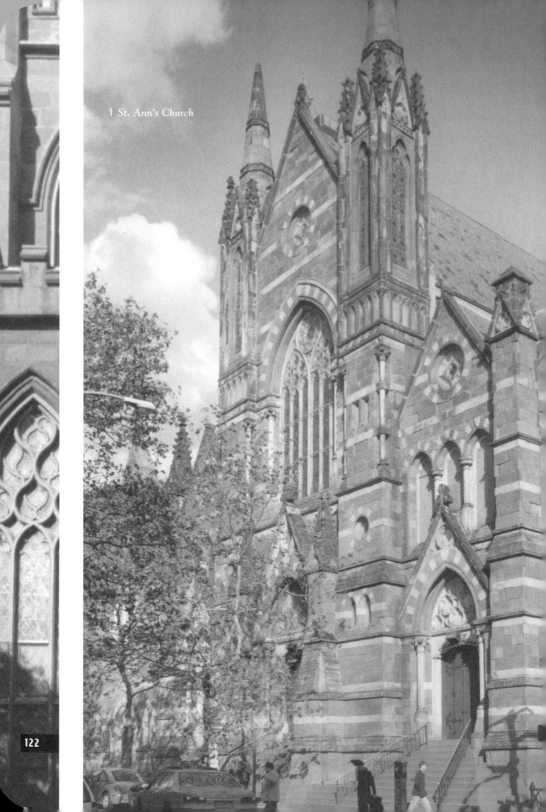

1 *St. Ann's Church*

Chapter
Brooklyn Heights South **4**

This neighborhood, adjacent to the Civic Center, is a hub of subway lines. One can take the 2, 3, 4, or 5 train to the Borough Hall station, the M, N, or R train to the Court Street station, or the A, C, or F train to the Jay Street/Borough Hall station. The closest to St. Ann's Church, the first stop on the Brooklyn Heights South itinerary, is the Borough Hall station, but any of the stations is within a short walk of the starting point.

1 **ST. ANN'S CHURCH (Episcopal)**
Northeast corner of Livingston and Clinton Streets
1867–69, Renwick & Sands

St. Ann's Church, now owned by Packer Collegiate Institute, is one of the finest surviving examples of "Ruskinian Gothic" in New York City. This style is most identifiable by its use of "polychrome" stonework and brickwork. John Ruskin had written in *The Stones of Venice* (1851–53), "I believe it to be one of the essential signs of life in a school of art that it loves colour; and I know it to be one of the first signs of death in the Renaissance schools that they despised colour." Ruskin wrote at a time when the use of color in architecture was a controversial topic among architects in England. Though Ruskin did defend the use of applied color, under strict conditions, his own deepest love was for achieving chromatic effects through the natural colors of stone in surfaces patterned in different colors of stone. In this he was in keeping with the Ecclesiologists' advocacy of the honest use of materials. We see such poly-chrome patterning here in the horizontally banded stonework in which Belleville, New Jersey, brownstone with a hammered surface alternates with smooth, yellowish Ohio sandstone. The same materials alternate in the voussoirs of the pointed arches and in the surrounds of the circular windows. On Clinton Street, the central section soars with extremely narrow twin towers featuring spires, pinnacles, finials, crockets, colonnettes, and leaded lancets. In the center of this section is a high, magnificent stained-glass pointed window. Freestanding gables surmount the central entrance and the flanking entrances. James Renwick, Jr., often employed this type of gable in his churches, as in Grace Church (1843–46) on Broadway and 10th Street, Calvary Church (1846) on Park Avenue South and 21st Street, and St. Patrick's Cathedral (1858–79) on Fifth Avenue and 50th Street. (Note that when Renwick designed St. Ann's he had already designed St. Patrick's; however, St. Patrick's would not be completed for another ten years.) Steep steps lead to the three entrances. The stepped buttresses flanking the central entrance echo the rise of the steps. Everything is up, up, up. The chapel (1866–67) to the north on Clinton Street is also an outstanding work, with its high narrow gable inset with an open pointed arch. On Livingston Street, the pinnacles and gable on the west and the pinnacled and gabled entrance on the east sandwich the aisle arcade and balance the façade.

Renwick's St. Ann's, Richard Upjohn's Church of the Pilgrims and Grace Church, and Minard Lafever's Holy Trinity Church and Church of the Saviour make Brooklyn Heights home to a greater number of masterpieces of ecclesiastical architecture than any comparably sized area within New York City.

James Renwick, Jr. (1818–95), was a native Manhattanite, the son of a renowned professor of natural philosophy at Columbia College. Renwick *père* was a brilliant and worldly man who had to have been one of the first New Yorkers to develop a serious interest in Gothic architecture, an interest he passed to his son. Renwick's mother was Margaret Brevoort, the daughter of Hendrick Brevoort, a prominent landowner. (Renwick *père* and his brother-in-law, Henry Brevoort, were among the closest friends of Washington Irving.) Trained at Columbia College as an engineer, Renwick *fils* had worked for the Erie Railroad and on the Croton Aqueduct System when he received his first professional architectural commission, which was for Grace Church, on Broadway and 10th Street. This was a fashionable society congregation, and the fact that Renwick was only twenty-three years old when he received the commission indicates that family connections had something to do with his getting the job, since the church was built on part of the estate of Hendrick Brevoort. Renwick acquitted himself brilliantly with his design for Grace Church, which was completed in the same year as Richard Upjohn's Trinity Church, and was a very sophisticated exercise in Ecclesiological Gothic. Unlike the devout churchman Upjohn, however, Renwick was philosophically committed to no specific style. His love of the Gothic was a connoisseur's, not a churchman's, love. In this, Renwick was the heir to Minard Lafever, another Gothic architect richly represented in Brooklyn Heights.

St. Ann's is the oldest Episcopal congregation in Brooklyn, founded in the 1780s at Fulton and Middagh Streets, and this was its third home. The church was named in honor of Ann Sands, a prominent parishioner. Its next home, at Washington and Sands Streets, was demolished to make way for the Brooklyn Bridge. One of the Sunday school students at St. Ann's in the 1830s was young Walt Whitman. St. Ann's School, today one of the most prestigious secondary schools in the country, was established in 1965. Four years later, St. Ann's sold its magnificent building to another prestigious school, Packer Collegiate Institute, and merged with Holy Trinity Church on Montague and Clinton Streets to form the Church of St. Ann and the Holy Trinity.

2 PACKER COLLEGIATE INSTITUTE
170 Joralemon Street between Court and Clinton Streets, south side
1853–56, Minard Lafever

When it was built, this must have been one of the most imposing buildings in Brooklyn. The style is Tudor Gothic. The materials are brick, with brownstone for the trim and slate for the roof. The entrance is in the center through a pointed arch topped by a band of corbeling. Atop this, at the second floor, is a square-headed window with a Gothic drip molding. There is then another band of corbeling, then an enormous, stupendous pointed window, fully two stories high. Two-story-high buttresses, rising through the lower corbels, flank the doorway. On either side of the central section are projecting towers. The one on the right is far larger than the one on the left. A revolving dome, removed when the subway was constructed beneath Joralemon Street, originally topped the right, or west, tower. (Lafever did not fare well with the subways he could scarcely have imagined. The tower of his Holy Trinity

Church on Montague Street was also mutilated as a result of the underground construction.) The crenellated parapets of the left tower continue along the entire left side of the façade. On the right, a high gable inset with three two-story-high lancets (answering to the central arch) tops the elevation. This right, or west, section is the Packer Chapel. Flowing ivy covers the upper right portion of this half. There is just enough ivy, and it is so perfectly placed, that it is hard not to think it was part of Lafever's design.

The building is set back in a shallow garden behind a beautiful black iron fence with a trefoil motif. Projecting wings on either side of the main block use a darker palette of rock-faced brownstone and very dark brick. (It is hard to tell whether the brick was originally so dark.) A high stepped gable between crenellated towers tops the left wing. On the right, finialed, polygonal pinnacles flank a stepped gable, slightly different in design from the one on the left, and so buried in ivy that its details are impossible to discern. The renowned firm of Napoleon LeBrun & Sons designed both wings; the east wing, originally known as the gymnasium building and now called the Science Wing, was built in 1886–88, and the west wing, also known as Alumnae Hall, was built in 1907.

The appropriately understated four-story addition on the west, called the Katherine Sloan Pratt House, was built in 1957 on the site of a playground. It contains two gymnasiums, several classrooms, and a theater.

Packer was Lafever's final design, and the building, though not yet complete in every detail, was opened for classes on September 11, 1854, fifteen days before its architect's death.

The Brooklyn Female Academy was founded in 1846. Its original building burned down seven years later. Harriet Putnam Packer (1820–92), the widow of William Satterlee Packer, who had died in 1850 and whose mansion was nearby on the south side of what is now called Grace Court, funded the new Lafever building with a gift of $65,000 (about $1,235,000 today). (Mr. and Mrs. Packer are buried in Green-wood Cemetery, where there is a statue of Mr. Packer, which Mrs. Packer commissioned from the important American sculptor Henry Kirke Brown.) Lafever got the commission through a design competition in which other entrants included Gamaliel King, architect of City Hall, and Thomas Thomas, designer of St. Peter's Roman Catholic Church on Barclay Street in Manhattan. Packer Collegiate, long one of New York's most distinguished private schools, remained all female until 1972.

3 135 JORALEMON STREET

Between Henry and Clinton Streets, north side, opposite Sidney Place
1833

You might think you have never seen a more beautiful house. It is very simple, a twin-dormered, two-story-plus-attic, Federal-style, wood-frame house with a wooden dentilated cornice and an absolutely gorgeous porch with a screen of ornamental cast iron, à la Charleston. The ironwork was added, apparently, sometime after the middle of the nineteenth century. At the spectacular entrance, two full and two half Ionic columns flank the doorway, which has leaded sidelights and a crowning panel of carved vegetation. No period produced doorways more beautiful than the Federal. Though several such houses once stood in Joralemon Street, and nothing built around this house over the years has been particularly sensitive to it, nonetheless the house's stature and charm are undiminished and in certain ways may even be enhanced, which is part of the magic of a neighborhood such as this.

3 *135 Joralemon Street*

4 DANIEL CHAUNCEY HOUSE

129 Joralemon Street between Henry and Clinton Streets, north side
1890, C. P. H. Gilbert

If you think you've seen the most beautiful house in the world when you've seen No. 135, you may change your mind here. Yet no two houses could seem more different! This is one of the most thrilling (near) juxtapositions of houses in the city, from the radiant Georgian humanism of No. 135 to the stony romanticism of No. 129. This is as good as any of the houses Gilbert designed for Park Slope and is a rare example of his work to be found in any Brooklyn neighborhood other than Park Slope. Rock-faced limestone in the lower part of the forty-foot-wide house yields above to yellow Roman brick. It is a lighter palette than Gilbert used in his Park Slope houses of the same period. A broad central section is defined by a high, wide stoop leading to a massive double door of wood with beautiful wrought-iron accents. The doorway is framed in curved chamfering with lush foliate decoration. Above the entrance is a sensuously up-swelling shelf carrying a shallow oriel inset with two beautiful arched stained-glass windows. Surmounting the oriel is a bold, modillioned stone cornice and a balustrade defined at its ends by shields.

4 Daniel Chauncey House

Above and behind the balustrade is a wide Palladian window framed in wood. On the left side of the first floor is a projecting two-sided bay rising to form a second-floor balcony. Old photographs show that originally this two-sided bay was repeated on the right side. The present flat-fronted treatment, with arched windows framed in a fine drip molding terminating in terra-cotta gryphons, was a later alteration, and may trick the viewer into thinking that Gilbert was aiming at the asymmetrical effect often found in his Romanesque work. At the top of the house on either side is a panel of garlands. Crowning the house is a broad gabled dormer projecting from a hipped roof. There is, in the end, a stately quality here (undoubtedly more pronounced before the removal of the projecting bay on the east) and, in spite of the stony masses, a winsomeness that may make this house not so different from No. 135 after all.

5 **ST. CHARLES BORROMEO CHURCH (R. C.)**
Northeast corner of Sidney Place and Aitken Place
1868, P. C. Keely

It is said that this was Keely's 325th church design, and he was only about halfway through his career. It seems to me to be pretty typical of his work. It is of red-painted brick. The front is on Sidney Place, and features a high central tower. A statue of St. Charles stands in a Gothic niche in the tower on a line with the hipped roof of the church. It works very well as a pendant to the more extravagant St. Ann's a block away to the east. Not only is this church contemporary with St. Ann's, but it also opened in the very year that the cornerstone was laid for the Brooklyn cathedral, designed by Keely, that never did get built in Fort Greene.

6 **262 to 272 HICKS STREET**
Southwest corner of Joralemon Street
1887–88, William B. Tubby

Tubby, an architect better known for his work in Clinton Hill and in Park Slope than in Brooklyn Heights, designed this six-house row for Mrs. Packer, who lived around the corner in Grace Court. Its romantic style, part Romanesque Revival and part Queen Anne, is quite restrained in comparison to the row Tubby designed at the same time in Park Slope at 854 to 872 Carroll Street. Rock-faced brownstone bases yield to red brick with stone trim above.

Austere brick arches define the entrances and first-floor windows. The second floors of Nos. 266 and 268 have three-sided oriels with shingled overhangs. Prominent gables top these two houses. Nos. 264 and 270 have tops of round shingles. The house farthest north, at the corner of Joralemon Street, is the most prominent house in the row, as befits its corner siting. Its brick is darker, it has no arches, and it has a superb open parapet with basketweave brickwork. On its Hicks Street front, to the right of the first-floor window, is a small terracotta panel. It is the only piece of applied ornament in the entire row.

6 *262 to 272 Hicks Street*

7 ENGINE COMPANY 224
274 Hicks Street between State and Joralemon Streets, west side
1903, Adams & Warren

Another of the Heights' felicitous juxtapositions is this lovely Beaux-Arts firehouse right next to Tubby's row of houses built fifteen years and a world earlier. The firehouse is red brick with limestone trim. Projecting from its pitched roof are three verdigris copper dormers and, at the corners, acroteria. The firehouse was built in the same year as and is stylistically very similar to its architects' Thatcher Adams house at 63 East 79th Street in Manhattan.

Adding to the felicity of the block is the charming row of five carriage houses, of vaguely Romanesque design, immediately to the south of the firehouse.

8 43 to 49 WILLOW PLACE
Between State and Joralemon Streets, east side
1840s

The "colonnade row" was a popular concept in the Greek Revival 1830s and 1840s. Many people are familiar with Manhattan's LaGrange Terrace on Lafayette Street from the early 1830s. This is simpler than that, though stately still. Thirteen square wooden columns screen four redbrick row houses that have doorways flanked by columns of the same design, though much smaller in scale. There are small front gardens between the colonnade and the sidewalk. Note that right across the street at 46 Willow Place is a single house of exactly the same design, as though it were originally a part of the row but decided it preferred living on its own and moved across the street. Actually, there was once an identical row of four houses on this side of the street, of which two were torn down and one altered beyond recognition, leaving just this one.

9 WILLOW PLACE CHAPEL
26 Willow Place between State and Joralemon Streets
1875 76, Russell Sturgis

Faced in red brick with contrasting sandstone trim, the diminutive chapel has a central pointed-arched projecting porch topped by a gable inset with a two-lancet pointed arch and patterned brick moldings. Pinnacles flank the gable. When the trees surrounding the chapel are in bloom, it is hard to imagine a more charming place. This was a chapel of the Church of the Saviour (First Unitarian Church) on Pierrepont Street and Monroe Place. This modest, charming chapel brought together two titanic personages of nineteenth-century New York. Parishioner Alfred Tredway White (1846–1921), the remarkable philanthropist who among much else built the nearby Riverside Apartments as model housing for the working class, funded the construction of the chapel. Russell Sturgis (1836–1909), who designed it, was one of the leading architectural critics and theorists of the nineteenth century. At the time he designed this chapel, Sturgis was one of the leading American exponents of the ideas of John Ruskin. Shortly after he did this chapel, in 1880, Sturgis felt he had reached a crossroads in his career and he gave up his New York architectural practice and traveled through Europe, shaking off his Ruskinianism. After that, he devoted himself to writing and criticism. His only other work in Brooklyn is the Dean Sage house of 1869 on St. Mark's Avenue in Crown Heights. This chapel closed in 1945 and has since been used for a variety of functions, including, since 1982, St. Ann's preschool.

10 RIVERSIDE (apartments)
4–30 Columbia Place, southwest corner of Joralemon Street
1890, William Field & Son

Alfred Tredway White developed these model tenements as he had earlier done the Tower and Home buildings and the Warren Place cottages in Cobble Hill. The same architects were employed. The Riverside, built to cover only forty-nine percent of its site, is only a couple of blocks south of where White had grown up. (Columbia Place is actually the southern extension of Pierrepont Place, where White's father's house still stands.) The development originally housed 280 families in nine buildings grouped around a courtyard. Each apartment was well lit and well ventilated and had a toilet, none of these being standard features in much of the tenement housing of the period. Bathing, however, was communal and in the basement. The complex appears along Columbia Place as a very long, six-story, redbrick mass. Aesthetic niceties were hardly ignored. There is some lovely patterned brickwork up top, for example the fine stepped corbeling above the top-floor arcaded loggias. The most prominent features of the façade are the four stories of balcony bays recessed within segmental arches with intaglio-patterned brickwork spandrels. The balconies have perforated metal railings with a plain quatrefoil motif. The treatment is similar along Joralemon Street. In his classic 1896 book *How the Other Half Lives*, Jacob Riis called the Riverside "the beau ideal of the model tenement." The Riverside was once twice as deep as it is now, until the western portion was razed for the Brooklyn-Queens Expressway, which runs hard along that side of the building. Four of the nine buildings were felled. The one-time internal courtyard once featured a bandstand where White staged Saturday concerts. The truncated courtyard is now more of a shallow backyard. In 1890, apartments in the Riverside cost eight to eleven dollars a month ($144 to $198 in 1999 currency).

To the south of the Riverside, wrapping around from Columbia Place along State Street to Willow Place, is the Palmetto Playground, created on odds and ends of land left over from the construction of the expressway. In addition to a children's playground, it includes a dog run and a community garden hard by the retaining wall of the roaring expressway above, and seems to me a fine example of otherwise wasted space put to use for the benefit of neighborhood residents. Around here, genteel Brooklyn Heights takes on an altogether different cast. Lovely row-house blocks yield suddenly to the ele-vated structure of the expressway, while across Furman Street to the west are the old riverfront docks. Farther north, of course, the esplanade cantilevers over the expressway. This is, in a way, the private Brooklyn Heights, where one is much less likely than farther north on the Heights to encounter visitors or tourists. Perhaps partly because of that, many people feel that the streets around here are the most delectable on the Heights.

10 *Riverside*

11 GRACE CHURCH (Episcopal)
Southwest corner of Hicks Street and Grace Court
1847–49, Richard Upjohn

Upjohn began work on Grace Church one year after the completion of his two most seminal designs, Trinity Church in Manhattan and Church of the Pilgrims, only two blocks from here. The cornerstone of Grace Church was laid on June 29, 1847, and the church was consecrated on June 26, 1849. It is a superb work in the Ecclesiological Gothic idiom he employed at Trinity Church. The entrance to the church is to the west on the south side of Grace Court. The east end of the church meets Hicks Street with the heavily articulated mass of its chancel, a hallmark of the Ecclesiological school. Here, unlike at Trinity and many other churches, including his own parish church, Christ Church, in Cobble Hill, Upjohn had the freedom to move full-bore down the "High Church" path. The gabled form is inset with an enormous and beautiful traceried window. It and the many vertical projections in the forms of pinnacles and finials and gables and parapets must be among the chief daily delights of the people residing in these close-knit streets and alleys. A low, projecting polygonal corner tower, rising to an ogee-shaped spire, somewhat like those of King's College Chapel, magnificently negotiates the transition from Hicks Street to Grace Court. A southwest tower was planned but never carried out. The brownstone is laid in random ashlar. The forms are largely those of the English Decorated Gothic, the style of the fourteenth century that was prescribed by nineteenth-century Ecclesiological doctrine but often jettisoned in favor of the fifteenth-century Perpendicular style (as at Trinity Church) that, under modern circumstances, proved less expensive. The interior here is characteristic of Upjohn's mature work. Where at Trinity he was forced by a conservative vestry to work in the "plaster Gothic" mode in which lath and plaster simulated the appearance of true stone vaulting (which was too expensive to consider), here at Grace he was allowed to do what he wished to do at Trinity, namely to design an openwork wooden ceiling: he might not be able to do stone vaulting, but at least he could do something that was "structurally honest," another touchstone of Ecclesiological dogma. (This is the principal way in which historians such as Nikolaus Pevsner were able to draw a line connecting the nineteenth-century Gothic Revival to the emergence of the Modern Movement in the twentieth century.)

To the south is a charming cloister-like walkway leading to the door of the parish house, which was not built until 1931. The nearby presence of such undeniable masterpieces as Church of the Pilgrims and St. Ann's Church may somewhat obscure the considerable quality of Grace Church, which, both architecturally and urbanistically, may be the superior work. Indeed, it is close to perfection.

12 GRACE COURT
Between Hicks and Furman Streets

Grace Court is a single block extending west from Hicks Street to a kind of southern chip of the esplanade. There is a mews quality here, with much of the street bordered to the north by the rear gardens of the houses of Remsen Street. On the south, the long side of Upjohn's Grace Church walls the east end of the block. The church and the backyards make for a charming setting, but as one walks west the diversity and the play of scale are beguiling, even with the intrusion of modern structures. There are some superb Italianate row houses here, especially No. 42, which has had its stoop removed but which sports a fine copper oriel, and No. 38, which is of red brick with brownstone trim and which features a beautiful three-sided oriel suspended over the entrance on super-vegetal console brackets. Note also this house's fine, simple Classical window enframements, one of the things the Italianate did best. There are five of these houses on the south side, with a modern, gray brick and glass interloper at No. 36. Farther along on the south, there is an enormous redbrick courtyard apartment house of Tudoresque design with craggy rock-faced stone accents. This apartment house was built after the 1916 demolition of the mansion of William Satterlee Packer, which had a commanding view across the river from this bluff. (Another large house, that of John H. Prentice, stood on the north side of the street.) One would think that such a large building could not exist harmoniously with its more delicately scaled neighbors, yet it does, perhaps because the street gives on the west to the wide-open space of the East River. The larger buildings along here help give definition to the street, and, situated as they are toward the west end of the block, maximize the impact of Grace Court's termination in its own mini-esplanade over the expressway, with the same stunning view as from the esplanade proper just to the north of here.

13 GRACE COURT ALLEY
*East of Hicks Street to a line about midway between
Garden Place and Henry Street*

Across Hicks Street from Grace Court is a real mews. Lovely old carriage houses line the alley, with a particularly fine specimen at the terminal axis. The carriage houses on the north served the houses of Remsen Street, those on the south the houses of Joralemon Street.

14 87 REMSEN STREET
*Between Hicks and Henry Streets, north side
1889, William H. Beers*

The stoop has been removed from this beautiful house that is otherwise in pristine condition. A rock-faced brownstone basement yields to smooth rusticated sandstone at the first floor, which features a prominent segmental-arched window with rusticated voussoirs and a fine console bracket at the keystone. The mood changes at the second floor, which is faced in brick with stone trim. Twisted moldings surround a bowed oriel with stained-glass transoms. An open parapet tops the oriel and encloses a third-floor balcony, the windows behind which are divided by three polished granite columns with composite capitals. Crowning it all is an exuberant Flemish gable.

Beers designed this house one year after his Liebmann Brothers Building that still stands at Fulton and Hoyt Streets.

15 CHURCH OF THE PILGRIMS (Congregational) (now Our Lady of Lebanon Maronite Rite R. C. Church)
*Northeast corner of Remsen and Henry Streets
1844–46, Richard Upjohn
Addition to east: 1869, Leopold Eidlitz*

The Henry Street front is powerfully austere. Stone is laid in random ashlar. The entrance and a high-arched stained-glass window are set within an enormous, slightly recessed blind arch framed within a sweeping gabled façade with a corbeled roofline. On the right at the corner is a prominent projecting, battered square tower plainly inset with narrow round-arched windows. A smaller tower is on the left. The towers are now flat-topped, adding to the general austerity. Both towers, however, have had their original tops removed. Upjohn is equally famous for pioneering two dramatically different approaches to church design in New York (and America). In his designs for Trinity Church on Broadway and Wall Street and for the nearby Grace Church on Hicks Street, Upjohn designed "Ecclesiological" Gothic churches for "High Church" Episcopal congregations for whom the ceremony of the Mass was of the utmost importance. In Brooklyn, the city's oldest Congregational organization, part of the New England wave that washed over nineteenth-century Brooklyn and so affected the city's development, hired Upjohn to design a church that would be in many ways the polar opposite of the High-Church Gothic. The New England Congregationalists were known for their simple meetinghouses. In Brooklyn, Upjohn went back in history for what in effect was the medieval equivalent of the meetinghouse, and designed what is regarded as the first Romanesque Revival church in the United States.

The Eidlitz addition at the end on Remsen Street uses the same random ashlar but with the "Ruskinian" touch of contrasting trim of smoother stone. Here is another tower, rising square to a dormered, hipped roof surmounted by a square, lantern-like form inset with Romanesque arches. This is one of the rare surviving works by Leopold Eidlitz, one of the leading architects of nineteenth-century New York. He was the designer of what once was one of Brooklyn's most famous buildings, the original Brooklyn Academy of Music, which was nearby on Montague Street between Clinton and Court Streets. Probably the best-known surviving work of Eidlitz's, by the way, is his St. George's Episcopal Church at Stuyvesant Square in Manhattan, co-designed with Otto Blesch and built in 1846–48. Upjohn's design for Church of the Pilgrims influenced the Romanesque Revival design of St. George's. Eidlitz, incidentally, had once worked for Upjohn. A Brooklyn church showing the influence of Church of the Pilgrims is Fort Greene's Lafayette Avenue Presbyterian Church, designed by Grimshaw & Morrill and built in 1860–62.

Church of the Pilgrims merged with Plymouth Church on Orange Street, forming Plymouth Church of the Pilgrims in 1934. At that time, this church's Tiffany windows were relocated to Plymouth Church's Hillis Hall. In 1945, this building's new occupants, Our Lady of Lebanon, purchased at auction the bronze doors from the dining room of the French luxury ocean liner *Normandie*. These doors were then installed at the entrance to the church. People seem to be of two opinions about this. Some preservationists abhor the alteration of the pure style of the church. Other people so enjoy these marvelous doors as works in themselves that they don't particularly care about the architectural integrity of Upjohn's church. My feeling is that the new congregation, perhaps not given to the Congregational austerities, found a perfectly appropriate way to put their mark on the church.

RICHARD SALTER STORRS (1821–1900)

On May 24, 1883, the Great East River Bridge was dedicated, marking a new era in the relationship of New York City and Brooklyn. President Chester A. Arthur, a New Yorker, was present. So was Governor Grover Cleveland. Two keynote speeches were delivered, one by a Manhattanite, one by a Brooklynite. The Manhattanite was Abram Stevens Hewitt, industrialist, political reformer, congressman, future mayor of New York City, and son-in-law of the redoubtable Peter Cooper. The Brooklynite was the Rev. Richard Salter Storrs. Hewitt is remembered today, if only in the name of the Cooper-Hewitt Museum. Storrs is little remembered, and that's a shame. The longtime pastor of Church of the Pilgrims was in his day one of the most famous clergymen in the United States, as well as a thinker and writer of high reputation, a sort of more-intellectual counterpart to his fellow Congregationalist from across the Heights, Henry Ward Beecher.

This son of a well-known Congregationalist minister was born in Braintree, Massachusetts. He was one of many New Englanders to leave a mark on nineteenth-century Brooklyn. He was educated at Amherst College and at Andover Theological Seminary, and would receive honorary degrees from Harvard, Princeton, and Columbia. He studied law under the famous Massachusetts trial lawyer Rufus Choate. In 1845, Storrs was ordained a minister in Brookline, Massachusetts, where, some years later, Frederick Law Olmsted would settle. The following year, Storrs took up the pastorate of Church of the Pilgrims. He held it until he died, fifty-four years later. He did not commission Upjohn's epochal design, but he was the congregation's first pastor in its new church.

Storrs was a deeply scholarly and serious man. He was for thirteen years an editor of *The Independent*, an intellectual organ of evangelical Protestantism. (It is well to point out that it is not necessarily the case that "high church" was more intellectual than "low church.") He authored numerous books, including *The Divine Origins of Christianity* and *Bernard of Clairvaux*. The latter was based on lectures Storrs delivered in 1892 in Boston, Princeton, and Baltimore. (His renown was nationwide.) The lectures were formed into a book in 1893. Storrs sided with his hero, Bernard, the twelfth-century monk, against Bernard's enemy, Abelard. Storrs saw in Bernard a proto-Protestant. Many nineteenth-century evangelicals saw in Bernard's Cistercian order a model for their own repudiation of Roman Catholic doctrine, on which Abelard, for all his troubles with the Church, had a profound influence. Some of these nineteenth-century evangelicals went so far as to embrace the architectural style of the twelfth century as a rebuke to the later, doctrinal styles of the thirteenth and fourteenth centuries. The architecture of Church of the Pilgrims can be viewed as a testament in stone to the values of Bernardine Christianity, just as Storrs' lectures and book were a Bernardine testament in words. On these streets of Brooklyn Heights in the nineteenth century, the conflict of Bernard and Abelard, seven centuries distant, was played out in the battle of architectural styles.

Bernard, too, however much he opposed his supernaturalism to Abelard's rationalism, was a man of the world: he who lives in a cave does not found the Knights Templars, after all. Storrs was concerned with how Bernard transmuted his supernaturalism into a vision of the social realm. Here we see the flash of Storrs' mind: his 1883 encomium to the builders of the Brooklyn Bridge reads much like his paean to Bernard. The bridge was a testament of the will. It was, as it were, an exemplar of our modern Crusade. Steel, said Storrs, was "the chiefest of modern instruments." It was "the kingliest of instruments of peoples for subduing the earth." Here, in Storrs' speech, is one of the great expressions of the New England mentality, grown fat in the face of the Roeblings' triumph of the will.

Such was the influence of New Englanders in nineteenth-century Brooklyn that the Reverend Storrs, in opposing consolidation with New York City, expressed his wish that Brooklyn remain "a New England and an American city."

16 CHARLES CONDON HOUSE
(now Brooklyn Bar Association)

123 Remsen Street between Clinton and Henry Streets, north side
Ca. 1875

This picture-perfect French Second Empire–style house has a brownstone basement yielding to three floors sheathed in red brick with light-colored stone trim. The house is extremely wide. A center entrance up a stoop with cast-iron balustraded railings leads to a deeply recessed double door, with a segmental-arched frame, in a projecting porch with a triangular pediment incised with neo-Grec ornament. To either side of the entrance porch are pairs of segmental-arched windows set in heavy, square-headed, molded stone frames. This window treatment is continued on the second and third floors. The windows over the entrance are set between vertically continuous stone quoins, which appear as well at the corners. Atop the third floor is a console-bracketed cornice. A bold, dormered, shingled mansard crowns the house. Several lovely touches make this house a delight, for example the shell forms in round frames in the center of the first-floor lintels, the motif repeated in the round form that rises from the center of the cornice overhanging the central bay of the mansard, and the heavy, carved-stone newel posts.

In his superb, pioneering book *Old Brooklyn Heights* (1961), the architectural historian Clay Lancaster found a listing in an 1856 city directory for a house owned by Charles Condon on this site, and presumed it was this house. Others date the house as 1870s, which is likelier. Perhaps Condon owned an earlier house on the site. The mansard roof made its first American inroads in the 1850s, it is true, though the full-blown mansarded style of this house, replete with its manner of incised ornament, did not really appear until the 1870s.

Brooklyn Heights has long been noted for its private clubs. The Brooklyn Club, founded at the end of the Civil War, was located in the fine Italianate brownstone at 131 Remsen Street, on the north side between Clinton and Henry Streets, built in the 1850s and the home in the 1920s of James H. Post, president of the National Sugar Refining Company. The house is now the Brooklyn Heights Synagogue. The Hamilton Club, one of Brooklyn's most exclusive, was once located at the southwest corner of Remsen and Clinton Streets. The 1884 clubhouse was demolished after the Hamilton Club merged with the Crescent Club at Pierrepont and Clinton Streets. William Ordway

Partridge's fine statue of Alexander Hamilton, now in front of Hamilton Grange at Convent Avenue and 141st Street in Manhattan, was dedicated in 1893 in front of the Remsen Street clubhouse. The statue was moved to its present location in 1936. Partridge was the sculptor of the equestrian statue of Ulysses S. Grant at Grant Square on Bedford Avenue and Dean Street. Two of the best-known Heights clubs, the Rembrandt Club, for men, and Mrs. Field's Club, for women, both date back to the 1880s and have never had a permanent home. Each is limited to one hundred members and is given to cultural pursuits and formal dinners. (William Butler Yeats's first speaking engagement in America was in front of Mrs. Field's Club.) The Crescent Club, whose building is now St. Ann's School, is no more, but the Heights Casino, about which more anon, is still going strong.

17 BROOKLYN UNION GAS COMPANY HEADQUARTERS (now St. Francis College)
176 Remsen Street between Court and Clinton Streets, south side
1914, Frank Freeman

The Brooklyn Union Gas Company had its headquarters here from 1914 to 1962, at which time it became the main building of St. Francis College. This is Freeman in his Classical mood, very different from his earlier Romanesque that we see in his Fire Headquarters on Jay Street or his house for Herman Behr on Pierrepont Street. Here is an eight-story near-skyscraper with a tripartite composition. A fine, wide granite base, in the center of which is a shallowly projecting portico with two Roman Doric columns, rises to an entablature of triglyphs and metopes and a bracketed cornice. The shaft is limestone and very simple in design. The top explodes in a row of six Ionic columns above which is an entablature, with a series of ten blind shields, and a good stone cornice. Nothing too fancy, but the forms are adeptly handled and it is a fine, stately office building demonstrating Freeman's infinite versatility.

St. Francis College has filled in the ground-floor windows with stained-glass in the "Catholic modern" style. What's amazing is that it seems to work. A virtue of a building such as this is its capability of such adaptations.

St. Francis College originated as St. Francis Academy, an elementary and secondary school established at the behest of Bishop John Loughlin on Baltic Street in what is now Boerum Hill in 1859, only six years after the creation of the Diocese of Brooklyn. The student body at first was composed of Irish immigrant boys who at the time had precious few options for a Catholic education. (Keep in mind that at the time the public schools were for all intents and purposes Protestant schools.) It eventually became a college and awarded its first Bachelor of Arts degree in 1885. The secondary school and the college were formally separated, though continued to share quarters, in 1902. The secondary school was renamed St. Francis Preparatory School and in 1953 moved to Greenpoint. As the college expanded, a new building was erected in 1923 on Butler Street, adjacent to the Baltic Street property. In 1960, the college purchased and renovated the old Remsen Street buildings of Brooklyn Union Gas.

18 BROOKLYN GAS LIGHT COMPANY HEADQUARTERS (now McGarry Library, St. Francis College)
180 Remsen Street between Court and Clinton Streets, south side
1857

This was built as the headquarters of the Brooklyn Gas Light Company, which in 1895 became the Brooklyn Union Gas Company. It remained Brooklyn Union's home until the Frank Freeman building next door was built in 1914. This, too, is now part of St. Francis College, which has had its library here since 1962. The lovely two-story building was erected at the same time and in much the same Italianate style as Fort Greene's Hanson Place Baptist Church. The Tuscan-columned arcaded base (answering to the Corinthian porch of the church) features vertically elongated arched windows that are repeated in the floor above. The full-height projecting central block has quoined corners (as does the building as a whole) and is crowned by a triangular pediment. The original sidewalk balustrades have unfortunately been removed. This had to have been one of the most distinctive office buildings of its period in New York.

19 FRANKLIN BUILDING
186 Remsen Street between Court and Clinton Streets, south side
Ca. 1890, Parfitt Brothers

The brothers Parfitt, perhaps best known for their residential and, especially, ecclesiastical work in Park Slope, also contributed a great deal to Brooklyn Heights toward the end of the nineteenth century. Their distinctive and influential apartment houses can be seen along Montague Street (the Grosvenor, the Berkeley, and the Montague, built around the same time as this building), and their craggy, broody Romanesque idiom is evident as well in this six-story office building. This makes, with the two Brooklyn Union buildings to the west, a beguiling row along the south side of Remsen Street. The idiom here is quite familiar: rock-faced brownstone over the first and second floors and deep red brick above, with panels of terra-cotta ornament. There is also the big, bad entrance arch beloved of this romantic style.

MONTAGUE STREET

Montague Street, today the principal commercial strip of Brooklyn Heights, was originally called Constable Street after the family of Mrs. Hezekiah Beers Pierpont. Pierpont's son, Henry Evelyn Pierrepont (note the changed spelling) renamed the street for Lady Mary Wortley Montagu (no *e*), nee Pierrepont. Mary Wortley Montagu (1689–1762) is called the original "bluestocking," and was a poet and, especially, writer of letters that are still read today. She was a friend and patron of Henry Fielding and Alexander Pope, with the latter of whom she had a bitter falling-out that led him to satirize her as "Sappho" in his *Moral Essays* in the 1730s. She is one of two English luminaries from the world of letters to have a Heights street named for her. The other is Sir Philip Sidney, for whom Sidney Place was named.

Montague Street began to take its present form around 1850. When Lafever's Holy Trinity Church was built in 1844–47, Montague Street was still sparsely built up. At that time it extended all the way to the East River and the Wall Street Ferry. Shortly thereafter, the eastern end of the street began to take shape as the young and growing city's cultural center, with a group of structures as impressive as any in the country both in their architectural merit and in the seriousness of the institutions they housed. Today, all these buildings are gone.

Leopold Eidlitz's Brooklyn Academy of Music (BAM) opened on the south side of Montague Street between Court and Clinton Streets in 1861, and immediately established Brooklyn as a city to be reckoned with in the world of music. One of BAM's biggest fans was Walt Whitman, who wrote that it was "so beautiful outside and in, and on a scale commensurate with similar buildings, even in some of the largest and most polished capitals of Europe." BAM was designed in the German Romanesque style, though contemporary commentators tended to call it Gothic, and was Eidlitz's first important secular building. I think its photographs do not do it justice. Montgomery Schuyler, the great architectural critic and a huge fan of Eidlitz, raved about the texture of the materials, the colors, and the fineness of the details—all the things that do not come across in grainy old photographs. BAM was destroyed by fire in 1903, soon after which the new BAM, by Herts & Tallant, was erected in Fort Greene.

In the year BAM opened, Brooklyn was the third largest city in the country (after New York and Philadelphia), with a population of 266,000. At the same time, New York City was growing in a northerly direction, and that city's cultural institutions were leaving their longtime homes in the island's lower part that was so convenient to ferry-commuting Brooklynites. It seemed time for Brooklyn to build its own houses of culture. Among BAM's founders were Henry Evelyn Pierrepont, whose family had owned much of the land that became Brooklyn Heights; Abiel Abbot Low; and Richard Salter Storrs, pastor of Church of the Pilgrims. BAM had 2,250 seats. In 1864, it was home to what in effect was Brooklyn's first and last "world's fair," the Brooklyn and Long Island Sanitary Fair, the purpose of which was to raise funds for the United States Sanitary Commission, which provided medical help for soldiers on the battlefield. (The fair, though headquartered at BAM, also filled three other nearby buildings.) Another event of note that took place at BAM was the official evening reception on the day of the opening of the Brooklyn Bridge in 1883. Guests at the reception included President Chester A. Arthur and Governor Grover Cleveland. Great performers graced the stage of BAM on Montague Street: Edwin Booth (and his kid brother, John Wilkes Booth), Jan Paderewski, John Drew, and Fritz Kreisler. D'Oyly Carte presented *The Pirates of Penzance* and Eleonora Duse appeared, in 1896, as *Camille.*

On the north side of the street, between Court and Clinton

Streets, stood Peter B. Wight's Mercantile Library, built in 1865–68. One of America's masterpieces of the "Ruskinian Gothic," the building was demolished in 1960. Wight, who had designed the National Academy of Design, one of New York City's most important cultural institutions, on Park Avenue South and 23rd Street, was selected as the Mercantile Library's architect in a competition in which other entrants included Richard Morris Hunt, Jacob Wrey Mould, Leopold Eidlitz, and John Kellum—the best architectural talent Greater New York could produce in the Civil War era. The first permanent home of the library that had been founded in 1857, Wight's building was of polychromatic brickwork and featured pointed arches, quatrefoils, and exuberant gables.

In addition to providing books for working people, the Mercantile Library offered courses and lectures, and speakers included Henry Ward Beecher and Ralph Waldo Emerson. The name was changed in 1878 to the Brooklyn Library, and in 1903 to the Brooklyn Public Library. The Wight building served as the Main Branch of the Brooklyn Public Library until the Ingersoll Library was completed at Grand Army Plaza in 1941, at which time the Montague Street building became the Brooklyn Heights Branch.

Following BAM and the Mercantile Library was the Brooklyn Art Association, designed by Josiah Cleveland Cady and built in 1869–72 on the south side of Montague, abutting BAM's west side. This was the first important commission in the career of an architect who would go on to design such notable buildings as the American Museum of Natural History and the Metropolitan Opera House. Gothic in the manner of William Burges, Cady's design, it has been said, was part of a conscious effort to mold Montague Street into the kind of governmental and cultural promenade then taking shape in European cities, such as the Ludwigstrasse in Munich. In his dedicatory speech, Abiel Abbot Low, a founder of the Art Association as well as of BAM, compared Cady's building to Friedrich von Gärtner's Staatsbibliothek of the 1830s.

Just to the west of here, at this writing, is rising a thirty-plus-story luxury apartment building, designed by H. Thomas O'Hara. It is controversial because it is so tall, though also a clear indication of how desirable a neighborhood Brooklyn Heights is at the turn of the twenty-first century. The scale of the thing, as I watch it going up, is a bit jarring, though the architect has clearly attempted to humanize the bulk through his appropriate use of stone-trimmed red brick. Several shades of red brick are employed, and there are areas of exuberantly patterned and chamfered brickwork that seem to call upon a long tradition of that sort of thing in Brooklyn architecture.

20 NATIONAL TITLE GUARANTY BUILDING
185 Montague Street between Cadman Plaza West and
Clinton Street, north side
1930, Corbett, Harrison & MacMurray

This is one of the jazziest little Art Deco skyscrapers in town, its play of projecting piers and receding planes reminiscent of the punching horns of Count Basie's orchestra. Floral and mechanical motifs are mixed in the exuberant traceried relief work. The firm of Corbett, Harrison & MacMurray began work on Rockefeller Center right after designing this building. Harvey Wiley Corbett was mixed up in all sorts of firms. As part of Pell & Corbett, he worked on the Masonic Temple of 1909 on Lafayette Avenue in Fort Greene. As part of Helmle & Corbett, he worked on St. Gregory's Church of 1917 on Brooklyn Avenue and St. John's Place in Crown Heights. (That's the same Helmle who designed the Hotel Bossert a couple of blocks to the west on Montague Street.) Later, as just plain Corbett (and at around the same time he was working on the present building), he designed the Metropolitan Life Insurance Company North Building, the famously unfinished would-be tallest building in the world, on Madison Avenue and 25th Street. Trained at the École des Beaux-Arts in Paris, he began as a confirmed classicist, evolving gradually, as did many members of his generation, toward Art Deco.

21 PEOPLE'S TRUST COMPANY
183 Montague Street between Cadman Plaza West and
Clinton Street, north side
1903, Mowbray & Uffinger
Rear addition: 1929, Shreve, Lamb & Harmon

20 *National Title Guaranty Building*

21 *People's Trust Company*

Mowbray & Uffinger completed this bank four years before their masterpiece, the Dime Savings Bank on DeKalb Avenue and Fleet Street. If this is not quite so fully realized a vision of the Classical bank, it is nonetheless a fine thing. It is also the perfect neighbor to the Brooklyn Trust Company next door to the west. Not only is its style compatible, but also by not being a masterpiece, it does not steal York & Sawyer's thunder. What we have in the People's Trust Company (now a branch of Citibank) is a fine tetrastyle Corinthian portico, the fully modeled, fluted columns set on high bases. The columns rise to a richly decorated entablature below a dentilated cornice. At the top is a full-width, triangular pediment filled with figure sculpture and topped with acroteria. I wish Brooklyn had heard even more from these architects who could so skillfully blend Greek, Roman, and Renaissance elements.

Shreve, Lamb & Harmon completed their rear addition in the year they began work on the Empire State Building.

22 BROOKLYN TRUST COMPANY
177 Montague Street, northeast corner of Clinton Street
1915, York & Sawyer

This is one of New York City's most magnificent banks. At this writing, it is a branch of the Chase Manhattan Bank. Its architects, Edward York and Philip Sawyer, had formed their firm in 1898 after having both worked for McKim, Mead & White. York & Sawyer designed the city's greatest banking buildings. Their works include the Federal Reserve Bank of 1919–24 on Liberty Street, the Greenwich Savings Bank of 1922–24 on Broadway and 36th Street, the Bowery Savings Bank of 1921–23 on East 42nd Street, and the Central Savings Bank of 1926–28 on Broadway and 73rd Street. The Brooklyn Trust Company is older than those others, and if it is not quite so grand in scale, it is their equal in quality.

The exterior was modeled on the seventeenth-century Palazzo della Gran Guardia, by Curtoni, in Verona, the Doric order of which is transformed here into Corinthian. The lower half of the façade on both the Montague and the Clinton Street sides is of vermiculated limestone. The entrance, on Montague Street, is through an exquisite wrought-iron gate set within an arch half the height of the building, with rusticated voussoirs and a shield placed at its keystone. Two stories of square-headed windows flank the entrance. Flanking the steps leading to the entrance is one of the building's most beautiful features, twin bronze lanterns with bases of gryphons and turtles. Over the doorway is a swan's-neck pediment enclosing an American eagle. On the Clinton Street side, a series of arched windows the same height as the entrance arch form a powerful arcade. The upper half of the façade on Montague Street has a central section of windows recessed *in antis,* with two two-story-high Corinthian engaged columns dividing the three windows. Corinthian pilasters flank this window section and also define the corners of the building. On the Clinton Street side is a long Corinthian colonnade. A dentilated cornice tops the whole. Lion's heads project from the cornice above each column and pilaster.

The interior was modeled on the tepidarium of the Baths of Caracalla of third-century Rome. (The concourse of the old Pennsylvania Station, opened five years before this bank, was based on the central hall of the Baths of Caracalla, adjacent to the tepidarium.) The banking hall is an incredible through-block, barrel-vaulted space with one of the most richly coffered ceilings in New York. The ceiling is in several shades of green with gold and buff. The Cosmatesque floor is superb. My favorite things here are the three ornate chandeliers, with their fully modeled female figural statuettes. It doesn't get any better than this building, inside and out.

The beautiful color scheme of the interior was worked out by a man named Elmer Ellsworth Garnsey (1862–1946), a "decorator" who worked with many leading architects to create some of the most distinctive buildings of the Beaux-Arts period. Garnsey was born in Holmdel, New Jersey, and in 1880 joined the crew that painted the Brooklyn Bridge. He attended night classes at Cooper Union, where he studied under the painter George Willoughby Maynard (1843–1923). He soon went to work for the painter Francis Lathrop. Lathrop was well connected, and through him Garnsey was able to meet many of the leading figures in the New York art world. At the Columbian Exposition in Chicago, Garnsey assisted Francis Millet, who was in charge of all the painted decoration. (All three of these painters who played such a large role in Garnsey's development—Maynard, Lathrop, and Millet—had assisted John LaFarge on the murals of H. H. Richardson's Trinity Church in Boston in the

1870s.) At the Chicago fair, Garnsey worked on the Manufactures and Liberal Arts building, designed by George B. Post (architect of the Long Island Historical Society) and on the Electricity and the New York State buildings, designed by Charles Follen McKim (architect of the Brooklyn Museum). Garnsey would work often for McKim on such projects as the Boston Public Library, the Rhode Island State Capitol in Providence, and Low Memorial Library at Columbia University. Garnsey was in charge of decorating Andrew Carnegie's house on Fifth Avenue and 91st Street, designed by Babb, Cook & Willard (architects of the houses of George DuPont Pratt and of Frederic B. Pratt on Clinton Avenue). He worked for Cass Gilbert on the Minnesota State Capitol in St. Paul and on the United States Custom House in New York City, for both of which Garnsey did decorative paintings. He worked on Longfellow, Alden & Harlow's Carnegie Institute in Pittsburgh (on which Brooklyn's J. Monroe Hewlett and Charles Basing also worked). The crowning achievement of Garnsey's career was his role in supervising the decoration of the Library of Congress in Washington, D.C. His specialties were in creating background ornament, designing borders and frames, coordinating decorating projects, and working out color schemes. Everyone knows the names of many architects, painters, and sculptors. Few know the name of Garnsey. Yet by being as good as he was at what he did, he helped make several great American buildings as great as they are.

23 HOLY TRINITY CHURCH (Episcopal)
Northwest corner of Montague and Clinton Streets
1844–47, Minard Lafever

The architectural historian Jacob Landy, the greatest authority on Minard Lafever, said that Holy Trinity was the "outstanding, certainly the most splendid, achievement of Lafever's career." The patron of Holy Trinity was Edgar John Bartow (1809–64). The Bartow name is familiar to enthusiasts of New York City's historic houses. The magnificent Bartow-Pell Mansion, the design of which was once attributed to Minard Lafever, is in Pelham Bay Park in the Bronx. This house was built by Edgar John Bartow's brother, Robert, and was probably designed by John Bolton, the brother of William Jay Bolton, who created the spectacular stained-glass windows of Holy Trinity Church. Bartow dreamt of building the finest church in either New York City or Brooklyn, and he put his money where his dream was: he paid the entire cost of the church

23 *Holy Trinity Church*

himself. This remarkable man also worked closely with Lafever on the church's design and construction. There was no vestry for Lafever to answer to, a rare condition. There was only Bartow. The ecclesiological niceties to be found in the church's design may have come from the influence of Bartow, as such dogma was not known to bind Lafever.

Brooklyn Heights was still fairly sparsely developed when Holy Trinity was built. Bartow purchased the land from the estate of Hezekiah Beers Pierpont. (Bartow was born in Fishkill, New York, and moved to Brooklyn when he was twenty-one, in 1830. He became a wealthy paper manufacturer. He married Harriet Pierpont, daughter of Hezekiah.) Lafever designed the chapel, on Montague Street to the west of the church. The chapel opened for services on June 7, 1846. The church officially opened on April 25, 1847. A contemporary account noted, "It is by far the largest edifice in the city." Not the largest church, mind you, but the largest edifice, presumably of any kind. The tower and spire were unfinished at the time of the church's opening and would not be completed until 1867, after the vestry, which had purchased the church from Bartow in 1856, hired Patrick C. Keely to oversee the work. (This is a rare example of Keely working on a non-Catholic church.) He raised the

height of the tower from Lafever's intended 275 feet to 295 feet, and surmounted it with an eleven-foot-high cross. It was the tallest structure in either
New York City or Brooklyn, overtopping the tower of Upjohn's Trinity Church
by about fifteen feet. The spire was removed about forty years later because of
instability caused by the construction of the subway under Montague Street, as
well as the hassle and expense of maintaining the spire's crumbling sandstone.
Plans were submitted for replacing the spire with one structurally sounder, but
the price wasn't right; instead it was decided to remove the spire and finish the
tower in a crenellated parapet. Even this was not to be, however. John Howard
Melish, rector of Holy Trinity from 1904 to 1949, decided simply to terminate
the tower at its third stage. He said the existence of skyscrapers had made
church spires superfluous since they no longer dominated the skyline as they
were intended to. Thus we have today's rather amputated-looking tower, rising 122 feet.

The exterior is of red sandstone from Haverstraw on the Hudson River
in Rockland County. (Keely employed the same stone for his tower.) The
masonry is more aligned than in Lafever's other churches, where he employed
the random ashlar technique.

Holy Trinity has a shallow chancel. The church, like Upjohn's Trinity, is
nine bays long. Where Trinity's chancel occupied two bays, Holy Trinity's
occupies only one. As Upjohn did at Trinity, however, Lafever raised his chancel a few steps to help set it off from the nave. In both churches, the chancel
is indicated on the exterior by enlarged buttresses and pinnacles. Lafever,
though, treated his chancel, on the exterior, in a very un-Upjohn-like manner
by making it seem almost like a transept, with gables at the levels of the nave
and of the aisle. The gables have pointed-arch windows and, above them, quatrefoil traceried openings. At the street level is a doorway leading to the
chapel, to the west, to the church, and to the south gallery.

The interior of Holy Trinity features elaborate lierne vaulting, not so different from that to be found at Upjohn's Trinity. This type of vaulting derives
from the English Decorated Gothic, which is the dominant style of Holy
Trinity both outside and in. Holy Trinity, as with all Lafever's Gothic churches,
is of the "plaster Gothic" school. That is to say, he employed wood-framed plaster vaults instead of true Gothic construction employing stone vaults. Stone
vaults were very expensive to construct. As a "structurally honest" alternative,
Upjohn, following his use of plaster vaulting at Trinity Church, turned to
exposed wood-truss ceilings. Lafever never followed suit, content to stay with

plaster: he was not hung up, as Upjohn was, with a theologically based concern with transparent construction.

For many people, the greatest treasures of Holy Trinity are its windows by William Jay Bolton (1816–84). Bolton was born into an artistic and ecclesiastical family in England and came to America when he was twenty years old. He studied painting under Samuel F. B. Morse at the National Academy of Design. In 1840, Bolton traveled in Europe, and when he returned he took up stained glass. Holy Trinity was his first major commission. The Ascension is the theme of the chancel window, twenty by forty feet. All sixty stained-glass windows, two thousand square feet in total, in Holy Trinity were designed and produced by Bolton with the assistance of his brother, John—"a remarkable fact," writes stained-glass historian James L. Sturm, "when one realizes the entire project was completed in less than five years." Bolton's windows were executed mainly in the medieval pot-metal tradition, though enamel painting was also frequently employed. While in his use of pot metal Bolton might be seen as a forerunner of the return to medieval glass techniques and styles, his imagery is in fact very much in the Renaissance pictorial tradition. The result is sometimes a little awkward (and not the less interesting for that), the attempt to fit perspective images into the confines of pot-metal leaded windows. This awkwardness was typical of the nineteenth-century Gothic Revival in which artists were drawn to the brilliance, the spiritual luminosity of medieval windows, and yet, after half a millennium of Renaissance linear perspective, could not help thinking that medieval artists were poor draftsmen. Raphael was a particular influence on Bolton. Following his work at Holy Trinity, Bolton worked again for Lafever on the Church of the Holy Apostles (1845–48) on Ninth Avenue and 28th Street in Manhattan. After this, Bolton returned to England, worked on the restoration of the windows of King's College Chapel in Cambridge, and then gave up his career as an artist to become an Anglican priest.

A third major monument of the mature Gothic Revival in New York was erected around the same time as Holy Trinity and Upjohn's Trinity. It was James Renwick, Jr.'s Grace Church, on Broadway and 10th Street in Manhattan. Renwick, who later designed the brilliant St. Ann's Church on Clinton and Livingston Streets, can be considered the true artistic heir of Lafever. Renwick shared with Lafever an undoctrinaire and inventive approach to Gothic, in contrast to Upjohn, whose own theological beliefs led him to embrace a dogmatic ecclesiology. In the 1840s, however, Grace Church, with its raised chancel, was perhaps closer to prescribed ecclesiological practice than either of the other two churches. Still, Renwick's elaborate exterior ornamentation of Grace Church is quite Lafever-like. Lafever excelled both Renwick and Upjohn in the decorative richness of his interior at Holy Trinity.

Holy Trinity has a history of internecine conflicts and financial problems. The church was closed from 1957 to 1962. One reason for the dwindling congregation was parishioners' disdain for the pro-Soviet views of the Rev. Melish. In 1962 the building became the headquarters of an organization called the Church Army, a lay evangelistic group, but in 1967 reverted to the Episcopal Diocese of Long Island and was once again closed. When Jacob Landy published his pioneering book on Minard Lafever in 1970, Holy Trinity was shuttered and seemed dead in the water. The church sprang back to life around that time when it merged with St. Ann's Church, which had vacated its building on Livingston Street. In 1980, under then rector the Rev. Franklin E. Vilas, the church enlisted the support of the New York Landmarks Conservancy and of the architectural firm Mendel Mesick Cohen Waite in restoring the building and its priceless windows, and the Arts at St. Ann's performance programs were inaugurated to help raise funds. The St. Ann Center for Restoration and the Arts, a private, nonprofit, secular organization housed in the church complex, was founded in 1983, an outgrowth of Arts at St. Ann's, and raised over four million dollars for restoration. The center sponsored the stained-glass workshop, under David Fraser, that restored the Holy Trinity windows. The center became an important force on the New York City cultural scene by presenting performances by Elvis Costello, Lou Reed, and Debbie Harry in the church sanctuary. The relationship between the church and the center seemed to be symbiotic and a model for other such partnerships around the country. The resurrection of Holy Trinity was cause for rejoicing among all New Yorkers. Notice the past tense: As I was writing this, and prepared to say how wonderful everything was at Holy Trinity, conflict arose between the church and the center, resulting in the center's moving out and what looks as though it might be the permanent end of a highly productive relationship. In retrospect, the breakup seems inevitable. Twice before, in 1992 and 1995, the church threatened to evict the center unless the church was given greater representation on the center's board. Things came to a head this time over the disposition of a $250,000 grant from New York State, awarded to both the center and the church. The church was concerned that its exact relationship with the center had never been spelled out. In other words, it was a conflict over money. Jane Jacobs, in *The Death and Life of Great American Cities*, wrote of "cataclysmic money" and how it can put a quick end to something good. The church's and the center's interests are very different, except for the one point where they intersect in the matter of restoring the building. Some supporters of the center claim the Episcopal Diocese forced the center out so that the church building could be put up for sale—a claim vociferously denied by the church. If the building is to be sold, one wonders what might become of it. It cannot be torn down, since it is in the Brooklyn Heights Historic District. The uses to which an old church can be put are relatively few. In New York, some have been converted to apartments, and one (Richard Upjohn's wonderful Church of the Holy Communion in Chelsea) has become a discotheque. Don't forget, too, that the current parish of St. Ann and the Holy Trinity was formed when St. Ann's Church sold its magnificent, Renwick-designed building to Packer Collegiate Institute for use as an auditorium. If indeed such a fate were in store for Holy Trinity, it would be a very sad day for New York. One also wonders how the church can continue to restore and maintain its magnificent building without the help of the center. It is all very upsetting, and we shall simply have to wait and see what happens. Meanwhile, about three quarters of the church's windows have been restored. By the way, this is the second time Bolton's windows have been restored. Otto Heinigke (1850–1915) restored them at the beginning of the twentieth century. Heinigke was a Brooklyn artist whose many credits include the ceiling mosaics in the lobby of the Woolworth Building of 1913 as well as stained-glass windows in Hillis Hall of Plymouth Church on Orange Street. The deterioration of the windows over the years was owing neither to a lack of competence on the part of either Bolton or Heinigke. Indeed, Heinigke's work had a reputation for constructional quality. Rather, the problem seems to have been, first, the subway under Montague Street, with the constant vibration, and, second, the neglect of the church building during the times it was closed. In general, if stained-glass windows do not receive regular care and maintenance, they will deteriorate. One therefore worries for the future of this building and its windows.

MINARD LAFEVER (1798–1854)

Minard Lafever was one of the most important Brooklyn architects of the nineteenth century. Calvert Vaux called him "the Sir Christopher Wren of America." The architectural historian Talbot Hamlin said Lafever was "perhaps the greatest designer of architectural decoration of his time in America."

Lafever was born near Morristown, New Jersey. He was Unitarian. Unlike Richard Upjohn, who was Episcopalian and preferred to design Episcopal churches, Lafever would design for any denomination. He designed churches for Unitarians, Episcopalians, Dutch Reformed, Baptists, Presbyterians, and Universalists. Like Richard Upjohn, Lafever became a Brooklynite: throughout his career as an architect he lived on South 7th Street in Williamsburg, and he is buried in Brooklyn's Cypress Hills Cemetery (though he designed memorials in Greenwood Cemetery). His earliest commissions came in the early 1830s, when he worked in the Greek Revival mode that he did so much, through his books, to promote. He later became famous for his works in the Gothic Revival style.

He made his debut as an architect not with a building but rather with a book: he published his *Young Builder's General Instructor* in 1829. Four years later, he published *The Modern Builder's Guide,* two years after that his *Beauties of Modern Architecture,* and, posthumously, in 1856, *The Architectural Instructor.* Though it is believed that he supplied plans for buildings, including New York City houses in the late 1820s and early 1830s (the Seabury Tredwell house, for example, which is now the wonderful Merchant's House Museum on East 4th Street, has much in common with some of Lafever's published designs), his first documented commission came in 1834–35 for the First Reformed Dutch Church in Brooklyn. Odd, given that through his pattern books Lafever did more than perhaps any other man to spread the gospel of the Greek Revival, that this church was the only design in that style that has been definitely attributed to him. It was on the south side of Joralemon Street, between Boerum Place and Court Street, right in back of City Hall (where the Municipal Building now is) and extended through to Livingston Street. The congregation, founded in 1654, was Brooklyn's oldest, and had occupied three previous buildings. Members of the church included several famous Brooklyn families, including Leffertses, Bergens, Schencks, Polhemuses, Johnsons, and Smiths. The building was an austere temple-church with a full octastyle Ionic portico raised from the ground and with a plain pediment. The first such Greek Revival structure in the country was William Strickland's Second Bank of the United States of 1818–23 in Philadelphia. The center portico of Strickland's Philadelphia Naval Asylum of 1827–33 was very similar to Lafever's church. New York City's first Greek Doric temple façade was the Church of the Ascension of 1828 on Canal Street, attributed to Martin Thompson and illustrated in Lafever's *Young Builder's General Instructor* the following year. The most similar New York City building to Lafever's church was St. Peter's Roman Catholic Church, with its Ionic portico, built in 1836–40 and still standing on Barclay Street. Lafever's First Reformed Dutch Church was demolished in 1886. The congregation then built a new church in Park Slope, on Seventh Avenue and Carroll Street, designed by George L. Morse and erected in 1888–91.

Lafever turned with a vengeance to the Gothic Revival with his Washington Square Dutch Reformed Church of 1839–40, on the southeast corner of Washington Square East and Washington Place, just across the latter street from New York University of 1833–36 by Alexander Jackson Davis and Ithiel Town, the first "Collegiate Gothic" building in the country. (While Washington Square was celebrated for its Greek Revival elegance, its east side was heavily Gothic.) Lafever's Washington Square church stood until 1895. The church was twin-towered, and employed a more "archaeological" approach than was customary at that time, when "Gothic" tended to be the bowdlerized variety popularized in the English pattern books of Batty Langley.

It is always interesting to compare the careers and temperaments of the two great Gothic Revival architects who resided in Brooklyn at the same time, Richard Upjohn and Lafever. Upjohn's most famous and influential church (though not necessarily his best) was Trinity Church in Manhattan. This is often regarded as the work that touched off the mature Gothic Revival in New York. He submitted his plans on September 9, 1839. Lafever, however, had been selected to design the Washington Square church on March 17, 1839. Neither architect, apparently, was aware of what the other was up to.

For more information, see Jacob Landy, *The Architecture of Minard Lafever*, New York, 1970. This is not only the authoritative work on Lafever but also one of the best, most thorough, most judicious, and most readable monographs ever written about an American architect. It is also a source of Brooklyniana not to be found elsewhere between hard covers.

---

24 FRANKLIN TRUST COMPANY
164 Montague Street, southwest corner of Clinton Street
1891, George L. Morse

This is a wonderful Romanesque Revival office building, eight stories high and faced in rock-faced granite, limestone, brick, and terra-cotta, with arches, dormers, high chimneys, a mansard roof, and even a "moat." Compare it to the same architect's Temple Bar Building, designed exactly ten years later, around the corner on Court Street. By the later building Morse had moved to a Beaux-Arts classicism.

25 BERKELEY and GROSVENOR (apartments)
111 and 115 Montague Street between Henry
and Hicks Streets, north side
1885–86, Parfitt Brothers

These twin seven-story Queen Anne apartment houses were built in the wake of the same architects' Montague just to the west. They feature round-arched entrance bays in rock-faced brownstone first floors. Above is deep red brick with terra-cotta panels. At the top, dormers sporting swan's-neck pediments define the ends, with a gabled dormer in the middle.

26 MONTAGUE (apartments)
105 Montague Street between Henry and Hicks Streets, north side
1885–86, Parfitt Brothers

At fifty-one feet, this apartment house is not particularly wide. But its 150-foot height, combined with the robust Queen Anne forms, make this a monumental edifice on Montague Street. The first and second floors are of rock-faced limestone, with a round-arched entrance in the center and flanking bowed bays giving great plasticity to the façade. The upper floors are brick and a slightly projecting center section rises to an exuberant gable. There is a lot of lovely terra-cotta work of the same color as the brick. An elevator served the seven floors, which originally contained fourteen apartments, fourteen servants' apartments, and an attic party room for tenants' use. On the partially exposed west side can be seen a faded old painted sign that says "Hotel Montague."

In his excellent book *The City as a Work of Art*, Donald J. Olsen wrote of how in mid-nineteenth-century London the monumental impulse—evident earlier in the Regency era town-planning schemes of John Nash—yielded to what Olsen called the "Victorian Alternative," a sort of privatized monumentality in which buildings "grew more emphatic and assertive, with window dressings, porticoes, and other features more deeply incised, more protruding, bigger, everywhere more visible, more unmistakably themselves." Olsen called it "a rise in intensity." This, rather than, say, the cutting through of grand boulevards, may have answered to something in the English character, perhaps also in the American (certainly in the Brooklynite). The Parfitts were Englishmen, and not for nothing do their apartment houses here have English names. One does not find the Queen Anne or the Ruskinian Gothic or the Richardsonian Romanesque, at least not as such, in Paris with its boulevards or in Vienna with its Ringstrasse. One does find them in Brooklyn Heights.

27 HOTEL DOSSERT

98 Montague Street, southeast corner of Hicks Street
1909, Helmle & Huberty
Addition to south: 1912–13, Helmle & Huberty

Louis Bossert, who had made a fortune in the lumber business and who lived in a mansion on Bushwick Avenue, built this elegant apartment hotel in 1909. As built, the Bossert was a twelve-story Classical building designed in the common tripartite style of its era's skyscrapers. The base was wrapped with a one-story arcade and a two-story Doric colonnade. On Hicks Street is a stately procession of twelve arched bays, each with a lion's-head keystone. The shaft featured balconies at the fourth and tenth floors, with a console-bracketed cornice above the tenth floor. The magnificent cornice sports an acroterion-like shield, emblazoned with the initials "HB," at the building's northwest

27 *Hotel Bossert*

corner, facing diagonally across Montague Street. A large electric sign, announcing the hotel's name, once surmounted the building. The shaft is of cream-colored brick laid in a diamond pattern, enhancing the building's gem-like presence. The ground floor contained a grand lobby and the Palm Room. When the building was enlarged a few years later, a ballroom was added. The Bossert had 375 rooms. The *Brooklyn Daily Eagle* pronounced it "the Waldorf-Astoria of Brooklyn." It was once famous for its Marine Roof, opened in 1916. This two-level restaurant and nightclub with a nautical motif was built atop the building facing west, affording magnificent views of Manhattan. Jimmy Walker and Al Smith were among its patrons. It closed in 1949, twelve years after the Bossert family lost control of the hotel during the depression. (The Marine Roof was apparently briefly revived in the 1960s.) The building's current owners are the Watchtower Bible and Tract Society, the Jehovah's Witnesses who have made their home in the Heights for nearly a century. They have meticulously restored the lobby, a splendid, compact space with marble walls, an exciting, colorful coffered ceiling, and freestanding Corinthian columns. The Marine Roof, alas, shall remain a memory.

One of my favorite books about Brooklyn is *Hattie and the Wild Waves*, a 1990 children's book written and illustrated by Barbara Cooney, the maternal granddaughter of Louis Bossert. Cooney, according to the jacket copy of this book (one of many by the Caldecott Award–winning illustrator), was born in the Hotel Bossert. Her story of an early-twentieth-century Brooklyn girlhood, based on her mother's life, shows us, in splendid illustrations better than any photographs could be, what life was like at the time in Bushwick and at the Hotel Bossert (as well as in Far Rockaway). Not only are no photographs better than these illustrations, but no novel or historical work with which I am familiar provides a more vivid picture of Brooklyn life in its high bourgeois phase.

28 **HEIGHTS CASINO**
75 Montague Street between Hicks Street and Pierrepont Place, north side
1905, Boring & Tilton

29 **CASINO MANSIONS APARTMENTS**
200 Hicks Street, northwest corner of Montague Street
1910, Boring & Tilton

It is hard to imagine two works of architecture built for people at more different stations in life than the Ellis Island Immigration Station and one of the world's most famous private squash clubs. Yet William A. Boring and Edward Lippincott Tilton designed them both. The Heights Casino, a "country club in the city," houses squash and tennis courts, which explains the relative paucity of fenestration on its redbrick mass. A few things keep that mass from being ponderous, however. One is the stone trim, for example in the rusticated voussoirs of the segmental-arched entrance. Another is the elaborate patterning of the brickwork. Another is the iron tie rods on the façade, which are in the shape of squash rackets. Above all is the exuberant Dutch stepped gable crowning the building. It is believed that the Heights Casino was the first building in America designed with indoor tennis courts. More important, the Casino is the epicenter of American squashdom, and has produced so many champions that it is one of the most renowned sites in the international world of squash. ("Casino," by the way, means "little house," and was once often used as a name for clubs and restaurants—think of the Newport Casino, the Central Park Casino, and so on. It has nothing to do with gambling.) Next door to the east is the Casino Mansions apartment building, designed by the same firm and looking as though it is part of the same structure as the club. Originally, this building had only two apartments per floor and was one of the most desirable apartment buildings in Brooklyn.

Boring and Tilton were trained at the École des Beaux-Arts in Paris and worked for McKim, Mead & White before forming their own firm in 1890. They designed the Ellis Island Immigration Station in 1897–1900. They also designed other buildings on Ellis Island. Baltimoreans can tell you that the firm of Tilton & Githens designed the fine Enoch Pratt Free Library, built in their city in 1933. This was Edward Lippincott Tilton and Alfred Githens, the latter of whom later formed a partnership with Francis Keally and designed another great American library, the Brooklyn Public Library.

30 ARLINGTON (apartments)
62 Montague Street between Hicks Street and Montague Terrace,
   south side
1887, Montrose W. Morris

This is Montrose W. Morris just after the Parfitts' Grosvenor, Berkeley, and Montague, and a few years before he designed such apartment masterpieces as the Alhambra of 1889–90 on Nostrand Avenue, the Renaissance of 1892 on Nostrand Avenue, and the Imperial of 1892 on Bedford Avenue and Pacific Street. The Arlington can be viewed both as following the Parfitt lead and as a warm-up for Morris's later works. It can, of course, also be viewed purely as a fine work in its own right. The usual rock-faced stone covers the first floor, with dark red brick above. On the left is a bowed oriel rising from the second through the eighth stories. On the right is a fabulous tower that rises polygonally from the third and fourth floors and round from the fifth to a conical roof hovering over the building's top. Terra-cotta ornaments, arches, gables—the whole shebang—is present here. It originally contained twenty apartments and ten bachelor's apartments. Taller than the Parfitt buildings to the east, the Arlington was once a very noticeable skyline building. This can be seen in old photographs of the pre–Promenade Heights riverfront, with the Arlington prominent in the background.

THE PIERREPONTS

The first family of nineteenth-century Brooklyn Heights was one for whom not one but two neighborhood streets were named (and a third if you count Montague Street). Needless to say, they were New Englanders.

James Pierrepont (1659–1714) was born in Massachusetts, the son of a Londoner. He graduated from Harvard in 1681 and became a pastor in New Haven. He was one of the three ministers who founded Yale College in 1700, and the one who got Elihu Yale to endow it. Jonathan Edwards was Pierrepont's son-in-law. This is called being right in the middle of things.

James Pierrepont's great-grandson was Hezekiah Beers Pierpont (note that he chose to anglicize the spelling of the name), born in New Haven in 1768. A successful financier, in 1793 he co-founded the firm of Effingwell & Pierrepont in New York City, and shipped provisions to France during its revolution. He married Anna Constable, daughter of the rich merchant William Constable, in 1802. Constable had been Alexander Macomb's partner in the purchase of a million acres of land in upstate New York in 1787. Through his marriage to Anna, Hezekiah got half a million of these acres.

In 1804, Hezekiah made a deal for a somewhat smaller parcel of land, purchasing sixty acres in Brooklyn Heights. One might reasonably think that the Pierreponts dated back well in the eighteenth century in Brooklyn, but not so: Hezekiah arrived on the scene a mere thirty years before the incorporation of the City of Brooklyn. In 1819, he retired from all business endeavors save the management of his properties. He died in 1838 in the new City of Brooklyn.

Hezekiah's eldest son was William Constable Pierrepont (1803–85), who lived not in Brooklyn but at Pierrepont Manor in Jefferson County, New York. He managed the family's lands in Jefferson and Oswego Counties.

Hezekiah's other son was Henry Evelyn Pierrepont (1808–88), who was born and died in Brooklyn. Henry was deeply committed to his native city. It is slightly ironic, then, that in the

163

year Brooklyn was incorporated, he was living in Europe. When he returned, he was appointed as a commissioner overseeing the layout of streets and public spaces. Henry was extremely interested in city planning, and is considered one of the pioneer American planners. Part of his plan was the establishment of a large cemetery, realized by Major David B. Douglass in the 1830s as Green-wood Cemetery. In the Heights, Henry spearheaded the excavation of Furman Street and the construction of a 775-foot-long retaining wall to sustain the Heights. He also created five acres of wharf property by building a new bulkhead. He was the founding president of the Brooklyn Academy of Music. He also managed some of the family's upstate lands in Franklin, St. Lawrence, and Lewis Counties.

CLASSON AVE

MYRTLE AVE

WILLOUGHBY AVE

DEKALB AVE

LAFAYETTE AVE

CLIFTON PL

GREENE AVE

GATES AVE

GRAND AVE

RYERSON ST

HALL ST

ST JAMES PL

WAVERLY AVE

CLINTON AVE

VANDERBILT AVE

CLERMONT AVE

ADELPHI ST

WASHINGTON AVE

CARLTON AVE

CUMBERLAND ST

S OXFORD ST

S. PORTLAND AVE

FULTON ST

ATLANTIC AVE

FT GREENE PL

ST FELIX ST

ASHLAND PL

HANSON PL

Fort Greene and Clinton Hill

Fort Greene Park

Fort Greene and Clinton Hill *Chapter* **5**

Fort Greene

1 **FORT GREENE PARK**
   Bounded by DeKalb Avenue, Washington Park Street,
      Myrtle Avenue, and Edwards Street
   1867–69, Olmsted & Vaux

This is the heart of Fort Greene and also the buffer between the relatively genteel blocks of South Portland Avenue, South Oxford Street, and so on, to the south, and the housing projects along the northern border of the park. The hill cuts off visual communication between the two, quite distinct, halves of Fort Greene. The hill of Fort Greene Park is a natural topographical feature and one of the most dramatic sights in any Brooklyn neighborhood. Around the western and northern edges of the park are numerous institutional buildings, most of unprepossessing design. These buildings belong to Long Island University, Brooklyn Hospital, and the aforementioned housing projects (the Ingersoll and the Walt Whitman houses). LIU and Brooklyn Hospital are worthy institutions that have laudably dedicated themselves to Brooklyn, and the housing projects are a cut above the norm, yet the scale of these buildings, which would go unremarked in Manhattan, is overwhelming in Fort Greene. Part of the problem may be the awkward scale of the park itself. At about thirty acres it is neither large enough to be a major metropolitan park (like Prospect

Park) nor small enough to be a residential square or serviceable neighborhood park. The great James S. T. Stranahan, that selfless civic improver who promoted Prospect Park, among much else, sounded a Jane Jacobsean note when the park was proposed: he said the site was too large. Don't get me wrong: the park is a splendid thing; most of its immediate surrounding streets are splendid, too; yet in the end the true heart of Fort Greene is probably to be found away from the park.

Fort Greene Park replaced an earlier park on the site. Washington Park, as the earlier one was called, was built on the site of Fort Greene (named for General Nathaniel Greene), which stood from 1814 to 1850. Brooklyn's first official park, it came into being in part because of the editorial efforts of Walt Whitman at the *Eagle,* and opened in 1850. Its success prompted the creation of the much larger Prospect Park. While Frederick Law Olmsted and Calvert Vaux were designing Prospect Park, the City of Brooklyn engaged them to redesign Washington Park. They created the vault for the remains of the thousands of men who died on British prison ships in Wallabout Bay during the Revolutionary War. These remains had been interred since 1808 at a site near the Navy Yard. Olmsted & Vaux planned a Gothic monument at the crest of the hill to commemorate the war dead, but the monument was never built. The park, which was given its present name in 1897, finally got its monument when, in 1905, McKim, Mead & White were hired (as they'd been hired at Prospect Park) to make alterations. Stanford White designed a new entrance to the vault (which is said to contain the remains of 11,500 men), and a monumental granite stairway leading to the crest of the hill. At the crest he placed the **Prison Ship Martyrs' Monument** (1a), what is said to be the world's tallest Doric column, 143 feet high, surmounted by a bronze lantern designed by the excellent sculptor Adolph Alexander Weinman (1871–1952). Weinman, hailing from Karlsruhe, Germany, had come to New York in 1880 and worked for Olin Levi Warner (who created the façade sculptures of the Long Island Historical Society), Augustus Saint-Gaudens, Daniel Chester French, and Charles Henry Niehaus. Weinman was renowned for his collaborations with McKim, Mead & White, New York's greatest architectural firm. Around the same time that he designed the Prison Ship Martyrs' Monument, he worked with them on the sculptural embellishment of Pennsylvania Station, including its monumental clock. A few years earlier, he had worked with them on the Pierpont Morgan Library, and a few years later he would create *Civic Fame* atop their Municipal Building in Manhattan. As Daniel Chester French's assistant, Weinman contributed to the pediment sculpture of McKim, Mead & White's Brooklyn Museum.

President William Howard Taft attended the dedication of the Prison Ship Martyrs' Monument on November 14, 1908. One person unable to attend was Stanford White. He had been dead for two years, four months, and nineteen days.

North of the park are large public housing projects. The Fort Greene Houses, as they were originally called, are thirty-five brick buildings, ranging from six to fifteen stories, erected in 1941–44 to house wartime workers in the Brooklyn Navy Yard, which is only one block north of the northern boundary of the projects (and which did not seem so cut off from them before the construction of the expressway). In 1957–58, the Fort Greene Houses were renovated and divided into two separate projects, the Walt Whitman Houses to the east and the Raymond V. Ingersoll Houses to the west. In 1959, *Newsweek* magazine made the projects a subject of a scathing indictment of public housing. Fort Greene Houses were cited as "one of the starkest examples" of how public housing had "become million-dollar barracks, in which no one develops a sense of responsibility, or of belonging, or wanting to belong." From a distance, the article said, Fort Greene Houses "has the look of a fine development. Closer inspection reveals windows broken as in an abandoned factory; walls cracking; light fixtures inoperative; doors unhinged; elevators that clearly are used as toilets." A daunting assemblage of big names in New York architecture were involved in the design of the Fort Greene Houses, including Ely Jacques Kahn, Wallace K. Harrison, Rosario Candela, J. André Fouilhoux, Albert Mayer, Ethan Allen Dennison, Charles Butler, Clarence Stein, William I. Hohauser, and Henry Churchill. The boundaries of the thirty-eight-acre projects are Myrtle Avenue on the south, the Brooklyn-Queens Expressway on the north, Carlton Avenue on the east, and Prince Street on the west. A couple of distinguished old structures were retained within the development. In the middle of the projects runs the north-south St. Edward's Street, which is basically the continuation on the north side of the park of Fort Greene Place. On the west side of St. Edward's Street, between Myrtle Avenue and the Brooklyn-Queens Expressway, opposite Auburn Place (which connects St. Edward's Street with North Portland Avenue to the east), stands what was originally the Church of St. Edward and is now the Church of St. Michael and St. Edward. John J. Deery designed this

Roman Catholic church that was built in 1902. It is in a fanciful neo-Romanesque style with twin high round towers, the conical roofs of which are ringed by spiky finials. (Architect Deery had a few years earlier designed the similarly fancifully twin-towered St. Veronica's Church on Christopher Street in Greenwich Village.) In 1972, Carol Dykman O'Connor added a new altar and Robert Zacharian added a new cross, both making use of bits salvaged from the old Myrtle Avenue elevated railway that roared past the corner of the church until 1969. Also left standing, right across the street from the church, on the northeast corner of St. Edward's Street and Auburn Place, is the Walt Whitman Branch of the Brooklyn Public Library, a 1908 building by one of the best of Brooklyn architects, R. L. Daus. Daus designed four of the Brooklyn Public Library's Carnegie branches, three of which still stand. This one is almost identical in design to his Saratoga Branch in Bedford-Stuyvesant, built in the same year. When built, the Walt Whitman Branch fit comfortably in a neighborhood of low-rise houses. Today, it is an anomaly. Originally called the City Park Branch, it is a low-slung building of simple Classical design with a projecting entrance that has foliate carvings in its stone surround topped by a cartouche. The low-angled hipped roof is of asphalt. (The similarly designed roof of the Saratoga Branch is of Spanish tile.)

No longer standing is a building once among the most notorious in Brooklyn, the Raymond Street Jail, which stood on the south side of Willoughby Street between St. Edward's Street and Ashland Place. (Ashland Place used to be called Raymond Street. What is Willoughby Street on the west side of the park becomes Willoughby Avenue on the east side.) William A. Mundell, a prominent Brooklyn architect, designed the prison, which was built in 1880. A somber castellated Gothic affair of rough stone, its main façade seemed almost a parody of the work of Minard Lafever. In 1939, the *New York City Guide* of the Federal Writers' Project said of Raymond Street Jail: "Obsolete, inadequate, and unsanitary, it has been repeatedly condemned by investigating Grand Juries." The site is now partially occupied by Maynard Center, staff housing for Brooklyn Hospital, designed by Walker O. Cain & Associates and built in 1976.

2 WASHINGTON PARK
Between Myrtle and DeKalb Avenues

It is a little confusing that this *street* (which is actually the two blocks of Cumberland Street facing west to the park) should be called the name that Brooklynites once called Fort Greene Park itself. It is a brownstone street. Edith Wharton called brownstone "the most hideous stone ever quarried." For those who agree with her, this street is a vision of hell. While Brooklyn is famous for its brownstones, there is nothing in the city so brownstony as this street. Brownstone was, of course, very fashionable. The *AIA Guide to New York City* says, "These two blocks of brownstones were once the equal in social stature of any in Brooklyn." There are 51 houses on Washington Park between Myrtle and DeKalb Avenues. The houses range in date from 1866 to 1884 and are designed in the typical styles of those years—neo-Grec, French Second Empire, and Italianate (we can call about half the houses Italianate), with a dollop of Queen Anne. We see the couple of examples of Queen Anne at No. 171, an 1884 reworking by Mercein Thomas of the façade of an Italianate house, and at No. 192, the Chester B. Lawrence house from 1881 by Marshall J. Morrill, architect of the nearby Lafayette Avenue Presbyterian Church. It is the ensemble that matters; it is not an architect's street. Besides Thomas and Morrill, probably the only other name architect represented here is George L. Morse, architect of the Franklin Trust Company on Montague Street and of the Old First Reformed Church on Park Slope's Seventh Avenue; he designed the neo-Grec houses at Nos. 195, 195A, and 196, all built in 1879.

Among the solid burghers attracted to this street in its early years we may cite the following: George Wilson (1836–1908), secretary of the New York State Chamber of Commerce, lived in the neo-Grec house at No. 158; William C. Kingsley, Brooklyn's most prominent contractor and the principal early promoter of the Brooklyn Bridge (and later the largest individual stockholder in the bridge company), lived in the Italianate house at No. 176; Albert Keeney, Kingsley's partner in contracting with whom he built Prospect Park, among much else, lived next door at No. 175; Alfred C. Barnes, publisher and son of Alfred S. Barnes (who lived on Pierrepont Street in Brooklyn Heights), lived in the French Second Empire house at No. 182; and Francis W. Goodrich (1833–1906), unsuccessful congressional candidate, Republican Party leader, and justice of the Appellate Division of the New York State Supreme Court, lived in the Italianate house at No. 202.

3 Brooklyn Masonic Temple

3 BROOKLYN MASONIC TEMPLE
317 Clermont Avenue, northeast corner of Lafayette Avenue
1906, Lord & Hewlett and Pell & Corbett

This project engaged quite an assemblage of talent, and it shows. When it was built, *Architecture* magazine said it was "quite the most dignified and impressive piece of architecture which has been done in the past two years." The magazine went on to say that it was "as beautifully thought out in every particular as it is perfect in general conception." And: "the method of using colored terra-cotta . . . is the best of modern times; one is tempted to say the best of all time." The glazed terra-cotta is of course the thing that puts over this otherwise perhaps too stately, almost funereal, building. To imagine this building without its colorful terra-cotta, though, would be like imagining the Parthenon without its columns—a silly exercise. The terra-cotta is this building's raison d'être. White marble and terra-cotta on the ground floor lead to brown brick in the upper stories, with cream-colored Ionic columns, their flutes subtly shaded in an eggier cream. There are verdigris copper antefixae, and ornamental terra-cotta in white, red, green, blue, and yellow. The coloring of the column neckings is particularly wonderful.

Lord & Hewlett comprised Austin Lord (1860–1922) and J. Monroe Hewlett (1868–1941). Lord had worked for McKim, Mead & White, assisted McKim on the Brooklyn Museum and Columbia University designs, and would become director of the School of Architecture at Columbia University. Hewlett was a Brooklynite who studied at Polytechnic Institute and Columbia before attending the École des Beaux-Arts. A muralist as well as an architect, he created the detailed cartoons that served his then partner Charles Basing in the execution of the Sky Ceiling fresco at Grand Central Terminal. (Hewlett was also the father-in-law of the inventor and architect R. Buckminster Fuller.) Pell & Corbett comprised Francis Livingston Pell (1874–1945) and Harvey Wiley Corbett. Corbett was one of the major New York architects of his generation.

4 OUR LADY QUEEN OF ALL SAINTS CHURCH COMPLEX (R.C.)
Northwest corner of Lafayette and Vanderbilt Avenues
1910–15, Gustave Steinback

The *Brooklyn Daily Eagle* of November 28, 1913, said of Bishop Mundelein's church: "It is one of the two or three most beautiful specimens of church architecture in the United States." That was an exaggeration. This is, however, an exciting church. It was dedicated in 1913; the apse and rectory, to the north along Vanderbilt Avenue, weren't completed until two years later. The school, which faces south across Lafayette Avenue and which also serves as the entrance to the church, opened in 1913. The school, the church, and the rectory are interlocking parts of a single, complex structure. The long side of the church faces east across Vanderbilt Avenue. Bishop Mundelein had prescribed something along the lines of Sainte-Chapelle, and he got it. The church complex is of cast-stone, which serves as a very minimal frame for extraordinary expanses of glass. The stained-glass historian James L. Sturm described the windows here as "very unusual pot metal . . . molded like the convoluted surface of some opalescent windows." The Locke Decorative Company produced the windows. This was the company of Alex S. Locke, a

4 *Our Lady Queen of All Saints Church Complex*

prominent turn-of-the-century stained-glass artist whose work in the opalescent manner can also be seen at nearby Lafayette Avenue Presbyterian
Church. Locke lived in a house that C. P. H. Gilbert designed for him at 46
Montgomery Place in Park Slope. On the Vanderbilt Avenue side, the windows are enormous pointed windows; on the Lafayette Avenue, or school,
side, the fenestration has a surprisingly modern feeling to it, with small square
openings not unlike in a modern, curtain-wall office building. (It's similar to a
lot of what was done a few years later in the "Catholic modern" idiom.)
Steinback was one of the best designers of Catholic churches during this
period. In Manhattan, he gave us the beautiful Blessed Sacrament Church of
1921 on West 71st Street. When George Mundelein, who had hired
Steinback to design Our Lady Queen of All Saints, became the archbishop of
Chicago, he brought the New York–based Steinback with him to design that
city's Quigley Seminary of 1918.

5 JOSEPH STEELE HOUSE
200 Lafayette Avenue, southeast corner of Vanderbilt Avenue
Ca. 1850

This lovely, anomalous wood-frame house could not be more felicitously sited, next door to and in the shadow of the much larger (though far from too large), neo-Gothic stone church to the east. No two buildings could be more dissimilar in style, in materials, in color. The church is dour brownstone; the house is painted a pastel yellow. Yet, the juxtaposition is wonderful, an essay in neighborhood scale and in the effective use of traditional architectural forms. In the house, the forms are largely Greek Revival. There is a fine, stately entrance porch and doorway, and a frieze of attic windows beneath a toothy cornice. The pitch of the roof and the crowning cupola suggest the Italian villa style that we see at the Litchfield house of the same decade in Prospect Park. Altogether, the varied Classical elements work together to create as charming a house as Brooklyn can boast. The church, though it appears much older, was

5 Joseph Steele House

built in 1923, replacing its congregation's earlier church of 1853 (around the same time as the house next door) by James Renwick, Jr. It used to be Clinton Congregational Church. In the 1940s it merged with Central Congregational Church and was renamed for that church's onetime minister, the famous S. Parkes Cadman. The man for whom downtown's Cadman Plaza was named was one of the first radio preachers in America. Two things for which he is well-known: he delivered the dedicatory speech at the 1908 unveiling of the Prison Ship Martyrs' Monument in Fort Greene Park and, a few years later, dubbed the Woolworth Building the "Cathedral of Commerce."

6 CATHEDRAL OF THE IMMACULATE CONCEPTION (R.C.)
Bounded by Lafayette, Vanderbilt, Greene, and Clermont Avenues
Unbuilt

The Roman Catholic Diocese of Brooklyn, which had been founded only in 1852, purchased this site in 1860 and projected a great cathedral to be built upon it. The diocese's founding bishop, John Loughlin (1817–91), hired P. C. Keely, the most prolific Catholic architect in America, to design it. Forty thousand people attended the laying of the cornerstone on June 21, 1868. The Brooklyn cathedral would have been the second largest in the country at the time, behind only New York City's St. Patrick's. The entrance facing Lafayette Avenue would have opened to a ninety-eight-foot-high nave. The cathedral, which was to have been built of granite, would have been 354 feet long, with twin 350-foot-high towers. The towers would have been higher than those of St. Patrick's. (The Brooklyn towers would not have matched the extraordinary taper of St. Patrick's, however. The latter's towers rise 330 feet from 32-foot-wide bases; the Brooklyn towers would have risen from 98-foot-wide bases.) But the walls rose to only between ten and twenty feet before funds ran out. Eventually, the Chapel of St. John, one of six chapels planned for the cathedral, was completed to Keely's design in 1878. Keely's residence for the bishop was built in 1883–87 at the northeast corner of Clermont and Greene Avenues. Keely died in 1896. The most important of his several hundred commissions for churches was never built. Two years later, Bishop Charles Edward McDonnell hired John Francis Bentley to resume the project. Bentley's Westminster Roman Catholic Cathedral (1895–1903) was then rising in London. Bentley visited Brooklyn, considered plans for a new cathedral, then died. In 1931, the Chapel of St. John as well as the partial walls were pulled down and replaced by Bishop

Loughlin High School, named for the man who conceived the whole shebang. Eventually, St. James Cathedral (1903, George H. Streeton) downtown would become Brooklyn's cathedral, though architecturally the true successor to this unbuilt project is Our Lady Queen of All Saints.

Across the street from the cathedral site, at the southeast corner of Greene and Clermont Avenues, stood for many years the most prominent church in Fort Greene. The Church of the Messiah (Episcopal) was built in 1865 to the design of James H. Giles (architect of Lord & Taylor at Fifth Avenue and 20th Street in Manhattan) and remodeled in 1888–93 by R. H. Robertson. It was notable for its 130-foot-high Byzantine-style "beehive" spire that was an unmissable neighborhood landmark until the church burned down in 1971.

PATRICK CHARLES KEELY (1816–96)

Keely was the most prolific Roman Catholic church architect of his or any other time in America, designing, it is said, some five hundred churches (some estimates are higher) in the United States and Canada between 1841, when he came to America (Brooklyn, specifically) from his native Kilkenny, Ireland, at the age of twenty-five, until his death fifty-five years later. In the words of the architectural historian William H. Pierson, Jr., Keely "settled in Brooklyn, New York, where he developed a practice which ultimately became a virtual monopoly in Catholic Church building for more than a quarter of a century." This architect's son has often been dismissed as a hack. It is impossible that anyone could be as prolific as he was and produce something fine every time out. His greatest commission, alas, the Cathedral of the Immaculate Conception in Fort Greene, was begun but never realized beyond some walls, one chapel, and the bishop's residence. Had the cathedral been completed, it clearly would have been one of the country's major ecclesiastical monuments, and probably would have made Keely's reputation as something other than simply the man who designed seemingly every other Catholic church in New York City. (He designed Boston's well-known Church of the Immaculate Conception in 1861. I suspect there were many Immaculate Conceptions in Keely's life.) At his best he could be very, very good. In Manhattan, his Church of St. Francis Xavier on

West 16th Street is one of the best Classical churches in the city. It is astonishing that only a few blocks away, on West 14th Street, he could do so creditable a rendition of "Ruskinian Gothic" as the Church of St. Bernard. These aren't hack jobs. Put another architect's name on them and I am sure they would be more applauded than they are. Generally, Keely liked to work in a simple Gothic mode that drew from the ecclesiological Gothic of Episcopal church architecture. As Pierson said of Keely's style, "Related more to the Ecclesiological Gothic of Upjohn than to the erudite eclecticism of Renwick, it set the tone for all Catholic churches of the mid- to late-nineteenth century in this country."

7 ROMAN CATHOLIC BISHOP'S RESIDENCE
367 Clermont Avenue, northeast corner of Greene Avenue
1883–87, P. C. Keely

This austere building, of dark gray Connecticut granite and with a steep copper mansard, is the only surviving element from the great cathedral project that was begun but never finished. The bishop of Brooklyn does not live here. He lives in the former Charles Millard Pratt house on Clinton Avenue (quite some distance from the Catholic cathedral downtown.) This is now diocesan offices and a residence for the brothers who teach at Bishop Loughlin High School. The *AIA Guide* calls it "Dour. Hollywood would cast it as an orphan asylum in a Charlotte Brontë novel." The Landmarks Preservation Commission, however, calls it "a very fine Victorian structure and one of Keely's most notable works in Brooklyn." It is, in fact, an outstanding Victorian Gothic structure, with beautifully worked stone and with a porch that, if we were told it was by Frank Furness, would be famous.

8 LAFAYETTE AVENUE PRESBYTERIAN CHURCH
Southeast corner of Lafayette Avenue and South Oxford Street
1860–62, Grimshaw & Morrill

It was built for a congregation led by the charismatic preacher Theodore Ledyard Cuyler (1822–1909), and was long the parish church of the great poet Marianne Moore, who lived nearby on Cumberland Street. Cuyler was a leader

8 *Lafayette Avenue Presbyterian Church*

of the evangelical revival and of the temperance movement, and was Lafayette Avenue's pastor from 1860 to 1890. One of his first acts as pastor was to hire the firm of Marshall J. Morrill to design a new church. It is built of Belleville, New Jersey, brownstone, and is a preaching church, as opposed to the ceremonial kind of church favored by Catholic and many Episcopalian congregations. Many congregations of the "low" churches, such as the evangelical Presbyterian, the Congregational, the Unitarian, the Methodist, and the Baptist, rejected Gothic, which evolved in relation to the ceremonial liturgy of medieval Catholicism, and took instead to a Germanic Romanesque. Richard Upjohn's Church of the Pilgrims (Congregational) of 1844–46, on Remsen and Henry Streets in Brooklyn Heights, is said to be the earliest Romanesque Revival church in the country, and was enormously influential as an alternative for dissenting, evangelical sects that disdained sacramental pomp and considered preaching to be the point of the worship service. Another famous early example of the tendency is St. George's Church of 1846–48, at Stuyvesant Square in Manhattan, designed by Leopold Eidlitz for a low-church Episcopalian congregation led by a New York City counterpart to Cuyler, the Reverend Stephen Higginson Tyng, whose quest for a preaching church led Eidlitz to the German *hallenkirche,* or "hall church," with its open-hall appearance involving no distinction between nave and aisles or between nave and chancel. Lafayette Avenue is very much in this tradition, and it shares with Church of the Pilgrims and St. George's a brownstone coating. Plymouth Church of 1849, Henry Ward Beecher's church on Orange Street in Brooklyn Heights, designed by Joseph C. Wells, is said to have influenced the internal arrangements here, involving the semicircular arrangement of the rows of pews, focusing on the pulpit. (Nearby Hanson Place Baptist Church was similarly influenced.)

In 1838, the First Presbyterian Church on Henry Street in Brooklyn Heights threw in its lot with the New School Synod, an evangelical group that split from the Old School Synod. The Reverend Cuyler was one of the leading figures of the upstart New School. In addition to its vociferous opposition to slavery, the New School was generally ecumenical and advocated union with Congregationalists. The intellectual heart of the Old School was Princeton Theological Seminary. They opposed revivalism and were not openly opposed to slavery. The principal New York City Presbyterian churches, including First Presbyterian Church of Manhattan, Fifth Avenue Presbyterian Church, and Brick Presbyterian Church, were solidly Old School. The New School, on the other hand, dominated Union Theological Seminary, and found adherents among the churches of Brooklyn. (The Old School was torn asunder when Gardner Spring, pastor of Brick Church, announced his support of the Union cause in the Civil War. From this arose the Southern Presbyterian Church. Later, the Old School faction led by Spring sought rapprochement with the New School.) Cuyler, a standard bearer of the New School, graduated from the Old School Princeton Theological Seminary. During the Civil War, he raised the Union flag above Lafayette Avenue Church.

The tiny triangular park, or "gore" as the Parks Department calls it, bounded by Fulton Street and Carlton and Greene Avenues, three blocks from the church, is named for Cuyler.

Artistically, the most noteworthy things about Lafayette Avenue Presbyterian Church are without question its outstanding opalescent stained-glass windows. According to the Landmarks Preservation Commission, Tiffany

Studios produced nine of the windows. In addition to these are a number of windows executed by Alex S. Locke, Joseph Lauber, and others, dating probably from the 1890s. The juxtaposition of the Art Nouveau windows and the prevailing Presbyterian austerity is quite exciting. A good deal of renovation seems to have gone on here in the 1890s. Montrose W. Morris remodeled the interior of the tower in 1891, and Babb, Cook & Willard remodeled the Sunday school annex in 1899.

Today the interior walls of the church are painted with scenes of Fort Greene life, celebrating the racial diversity of the neighborhood. A 1996 *New York Times* article about the church said that in its commitment to political and cultural activism the church was "a more intimate version of Manhattan's Riverside Church." Every fall, the church hosts a jazz festival, inaugurated almost thirty years ago by a parishioner named Eubie Blake.

Here, at the intersection of Lafayette Avenue and South Oxford Street, and not in the immediate vicinity of the park, is where Fort Greene comes true. The intersection is unplanned, and at least sixty years in the making. And better than this it does not get. On the southeast corner is the church, which makes excellent street walls on South Oxford Street and, especially, Lafayette Avenue. The corner tower, however truncated (its spire was destroyed long ago in a fire), anchors the corner with authority. On the southwest corner is a good Italianate row house, with drippy, vegetal brackets. On the northwest corner is the Griffin, a fine brick apartment house, built in 1931–32, sixteen stories with Romanesque and other flourishes in brilliant glazed terra-cotta, including a fourth-floor-level gryphon standing sentinel from atop a wonderful twisted column at the corner facing diagonally across Lafayette Avenue to the church. (Fred Klie designed the Griffin.) On the northeast corner is a small, altered-beyond-recognition Italianate row house, but just beside it to the north is the broad, beautiful Roanoke of Montrose Morris, about which see below. And to the south and west is a spectacular view of Brooklyn's greatest skyscraper, the Williamsburgh Savings Bank Tower, neither too close nor too far away, just the perfect distance from here. Everything works here to create a scene of surpassing urbanity. The width and depth of the church, the height of the apartment house, the vernacular quality of the Italianate house and the artistic design of the Roanoke, the varied materials, and the generally (though diversely) Romanesque vocabulary make this the happiest spot in Fort Greene and one of the best places in New York City.

MARIANNE MOORE (1887–1972)

The poet Marianne Moore was born in St. Louis, Missouri, on November 15, 1887—ten months and eleven days before T. S. Eliot's birth in the same city. While Eliot expatriated himself to London, Moore expatriated herself to Brooklyn. She graduated from Bryn Mawr College in 1909. In 1918, she moved to New York, and lived with her mother for the next eleven years in the basement apartment of 14 St. Luke's Place in Greenwich Village. From 1921 to 1925 she worked across the street from there at the Hudson Park Branch of the New York Public Library, and from 1926 to 1929 was editor of the *Dial.* An exponent of clear imagery, precise observation, and plain syntax, Moore was witty and unpretentious. As one critic put it, "Her 'predilection'—a favorite word with her and more likely to appear than 'passion'—is for grace and neatness." These qualities made her America's best-loved modern poet. The great critic Randall Jarrell wrote in 1945, "Miss Moore is reviewed not as a poet but as an institution . . . one reviewer calls Miss Moore the greatest living poet . . . ending with the demand that she be placed in Fort Knox for the duration. Certainly she writes better poetry than any other woman alive; but I have used up my small share of superlatives in previous reviews of her—this time let me look through Miss Moore and see neither lies nor Beauty, but some trees. (Whoever you are, I like her as much as you; so don't complain.)" She published her first book of poems in 1921. Her *Collected Poems* appeared in 1951; it was awarded the Bollingen and Pulitzer Prizes and the National Book Award. *The Complete Poems of Marianne Moore* came out in 1967. She died on February 2, 1972.

Moore lived from 1929 to 1965 at 260 Cumberland Street, between DeKalb and Lafayette Avenues. It is a six-story Beaux-Arts–style apartment house, designed by the Brooklyn architects Cohn Brothers and built in 1912. Moore lived on the fifth floor. She moved from here to 35 West 9th Street, between Fifth and Sixth Avenues, in Greenwich Village, where she lived until her death seven years later. She moved from her beloved Brooklyn largely to placate her literary friends, who were afraid she was

unsafe in the increasingly crime-ridden Fort Greene neighborhood. Her funeral, however, was held at Lafayette Avenue
Presbyterian Church, which, when she lived in the neighborhood,
she attended every Sunday morning and Wednesday evening for
services. She also attended many a game of her beloved Dodgers at
Ebbets Field, where she could sometimes be seen in her characteristic tricorn hat and flowing cape. Her service to Brooklyn
included campaigns she led to save the Camperdown elm in
Prospect Park, as well as to save the park's Boathouse.

In 1964, Moore gave directions to her building on
Cumberland Street to George Plimpton, who was coming to visit
her: "am on right, middle of the block, with what look like mothballs on iron stands flanking the entrance." Compare the poet's
marvelous economy with this, from the Landmarks Preservation
Commission's entry on 260 Cumberland Street in their Fort
Greene Historic District Report: "The rusticated limestone first
floor has a central entrance flanked by plaques with carved fruit
forms and topped by brackets that support a large slab lintel with
a parapet ornamented by a cartouche and lion's heads. Flanking
the doorway enframement are limestone brackets that support second story brick plinths on which rest projecting brick piers."

A New York Landmarks Conservancy plaque on the outside
of the building quotes Moore from a 1960 essay: "Brooklyn has
given me pleasure, has helped educate me; has afforded me, in
fact, the kind of tame excitement on which I thrive." Amen.

By the way, the mothballs are gone.

---

9 SOUTH OXFORD STREET
Between Lafayette and DeKalb Avenues

This block comprises sixty-three row houses and an apartment house.
The row houses range from early 1850s Greek Revival to early 1890s Beaux-
Arts. The latter can be seen at No. 26, on the west side of the street. Montrose
W. Morris remodeled two houses (one from the 1850s, the other from the
1870s) with a new Classical façade in 1893, the Columbian Exposition year
after which Morris, renowned for his Romanesque Revival designs, became a

Classicist. This double-width limestone house is like a shaft of light on this otherwise somber-hued street. Just as Morris interrupted the street stylistically and in his choice of materials with No. 26, so, on the other side and farther to the south, he interrupted its scale. Originally called the San Carlos Hotel, and more familiarly known as the Roanoke, No. 69 is one of Morris's several "artistic" apartment houses in Brooklyn. The five-story Roanoke is in a dramatic, beautifully detailed Romanesque Revival idiom, rendered in brick and limestone, and noteworthy for its powerful, rock-faced basement, arched openings, and swelling bays. It was built in 1890, three years before his house across the street. Though it is the largest building on the block, it does not seem intrusive, but seems definitely to belong, even if in a kingly way. Morris's other apartment-house masterpieces include the Alhambra (1889–90) and the Renaissance (1892), both in Bedford-Stuyvesant, and the Imperial (1892) in Crown Heights. In 1987, the Roanoke suffered a disastrous fire of mysterious origin. A developer restored the building, and offered its apartments as co-ops. About half sold before the crippling real-estate recession of the early 1990s. The unsold apartments were then taken over by squatters who, as squatters will do, tried their level best to wreck the building. By the time the community organized to try to get the squatters removed, they had numerous legal protections that made eviction difficult if not impossible. Today, the building still has not recovered from its extraordinary run of bad luck, and it looks, very peculiarly, both restored and rundown at the same time. Except for the two works by Morris, this is a heavily vernacular Italianate row-house street, and typical of these Fort Greene blocks south of the park.

10 HANSON PLACE BAPTIST CHURCH
Southeast corner of Hanson Place and South Portland Avenue
1857–60, George Penchard

Since 1963 this has been the Hanson Place Seventh-Day Adventist Church. Its style is what we call Italianate, or Early Renaissance Revival. Those tall, narrow, round-arched windows belong equally to the Romanesque Revival and to the Italianate (there are many buildings where it is impossible to distinguish the two styles, for the simple reason that the architects often did not so distinguish). The bold, projecting tetrastyle Corinthian portico with a broad (and bare) triangular pediment, the treatment of the entablatures and cornices with tightly spaced dentils and modillions, the tight sandwiching of the portico between end pavilions, the Corinthian pilasters wrapping around the building, and the repetition of the portico pediment on the side of the building are all elements that appear in Joseph Hoxie's Arch Street Presbyterian Church of 1853–55 in Philadelphia. It is quite possible that Hoxie's church was the direct model for this one. If the Hanson Place church doesn't quite match the quality of its Philadelphia counterpart (which sports a magnificent dome, as well as an exciting Classical interior), nonetheless it is of high quality indeed.

11 BROOKLYN ACADEMY OF MUSIC
30 Lafayette Avenue between Ashland Place and St. Felix Street
1905–8, Herts & Tallant

The Brooklyn Academy of Music, or BAM, as it is affectionately known, is one of the great institutions of Brooklyn, and, what is less often noted, one of the borough's great buildings, designed by architects, specialists in theaters, who are perhaps only beginning to receive their due as being among the best architects of New York City. Henry Beaumont Herts (1871–1933) and Hugh Tallant won a competition for the design. The building replaced the old BAM, designed by Leopold Eidlitz and built in 1859 on Montague Street when that was the

11 Brooklyn Academy of Music

cultural heart of the then City of Brooklyn. The Eidlitz building burned down in 1903. Occurring so soon after Consolidation, it seemed symbolic of Brooklyn's declining stature vis-à-vis the borough across the river. The construction of the new BAM, therefore, was an almost Pyrrhic assertion of civic pride.

In respect of its colorful terra-cotta decoration on a boxy brick body, BAM is similar to the Brooklyn Masonic Temple built at the same time—a jeweled box. The new BAM is said to have been the most complexly designed cultural center to be built in Greater New York since Stanford White's Madison Square Garden about fifteen years earlier. BAM contains an opera house, a theater, a lecture hall, and office space, all linked at ground floor by a common lobby and above by a common foyer, convertible into a banquet hall or ballroom. The interior features murals by William DeLeftwich Dodge. It is said that Herts was asked, in conservative old Brooklyn, to clothe the nude plaster putti of the opera house ceiling. He protested, and in compromise only those putti closest to the audience were covered. The opera house, with a seating capacity of 2,200, opened on November 14, 1908, with a production of Gounod's *Faust,* starring Enrico Caruso and Geraldine Farrar. (Gounod's *Faust* was a longtime staple of New York's musical repertory, as we can see from Edith Wharton's *The Age of Innocence,* set in the early 1870s, which opens at the old Academy of Music on East 14th Street. The opera being sung by Christine Nilsson is *Faust.*)

The main entrance of BAM faces south across Lafayette Avenue. A short stair leads to five high, rectangular openings. Above this level is a belt course that wraps around the building; above the belt course and the entrance doors are five fine, high arched windows. Glazed terra-cotta decoration brilliantly outlines the arches and the belt course. Alas, BAM's once crowning cornice and rooftop balustrade have been removed. Twenty or so years later, the Williamsburgh Savings Bank Tower was built adjoining BAM to the south. When BAM is viewed from Lafayette Avenue, the skyscraper looms like a campanile. It is a beautiful juxtaposition of highly disproportionately scaled elements.

Herts & Tallant designed some of the most beautiful theaters in New York. The New Amsterdam Theater of 1903 on West 42nd Street is theirs; though its façade was long ago unconscionably ruined, its auditorium was recently, sparklingly restored as part of the Times Square redevelopment. Many consider Herts & Tallant's Lyceum Theater of 1903, on West 45th Street, to be the most beautiful theater in the city. Their lavish Folies Bergère Theater, later known as the Helen Hayes, of 1911 on West 46th Street, was infamously demolished to make way for the hulking Marriott Marquis Hotel. BAM is not the firm's only work in Brooklyn. They designed the 1907 Liebman house at 375 Clinton Avenue, between Lafayette and DeKalb Avenues.

BAM has hosted a beguiling roster of major talents, including Enrico Caruso, Isadora Duncan, and Arturo Toscanini. (One of the saddest days in New York's musical history occurred in 1920, when Caruso suffered a throat hemorrhage while singing at BAM. He died soon after.) William Jennings Bryan and Winston Churchill delivered speeches here. In recent years, BAM, under the energetic leadership of Harvey Lichtenstein (from 1967 to 1999), has established itself as one of the most important cultural institutions in New York City. As home of the Next Wave Festival (since 1983), BAM is world-famous for its "avant-garde" offerings. Such luminaries as Laurie Anderson, Philip Glass, Robert Wilson, and Mark Morris are closely associated with BAM. More recently, BAM has installed the Rose Cinemas, Brooklyn's show-case for artistic films from around the world, and the BAM Café, which serves highly praised food in addition to presenting serious live music.

The Landmarks Preservation Commission has designated a Brooklyn Academy of Music Historic District, which, though it is within Fort Greene, is separate from the Fort Greene Historic District, which begins a few blocks north of here. BAM, the Central Methodist Church, and the Williamsburgh Savings Bank Tower are all included within the BAM Historic District, as are the wonderfully secluded, handsome brick row houses of the mews-like St. Felix Place running behind the BAM building. (At this writing, the stoops of these houses are all being rebuilt with city funds after years in which they were damaged by sinkage that resulted from the cutting through of the subway tun-nels below. It is, at this writing, a rather bizarre sight, but also an interesting one, for we can sense to some extent what a row like this might have looked like as it was first being built more than a century ago. Construction or no, the charm of the street is still very evident.)

While the BAM district contains so many delectable ingredients that could be whipped up into a savory neighborhood stew, there is little cohesion, and that is largely because of the massive works-in-progress that are the urban-renewal projects begun around here some thirty years ago. The Atlantic Terminal urban renewal area is a 104-acre triangular site bounded roughly by Vanderbilt Avenue on the east, Greene Avenue and Hanson Place on the north, and Atlantic Avenue on the south. The old Flatbush Avenue Terminal of the Long Island Railroad has been knocked down (at this writing much of its site is a gaping hole in the ground), and the Atlantic Center shopping mall has gone up across Hanson Place from the Central Methodist Church. While there are good economic reasons for the redevelopment, the loss of the Flatbush Avenue Terminal is very sad. A great city possesses certain things: a great museum, a great park, a great performing arts space, great universities, great residential neighborhoods, and so on. Brooklyn has all those things. One thing Brooklyn has always lacked is a great cathedral, though this is partially made up for by a plethora of outstanding churches. Another thing a great city should have that Brooklyn doesn't *but once did* is a great railroad station. Flatbush Avenue Terminal was no Grand Central Terminal or Pennsylvania Station. Neither, however, was it anything to scoff at. It was a solid, handsome, large brick building with lovely terra-cotta ornament. Architect H. F. Saxcelbey designed the building for the block bounded by Atlantic and Flatbush Avenues and Fort Greene and Hanson Places. Built in 1902–06, it had a splendid waiting room and was a crucial part of what made the downtown area in its heyday. It should have been but was not designated a landmark by the Landmarks Preservation Commission, which would have prevented the terminal's demolition. It is impossible not to think that the building could have been sparklingly rehabilitated as an anchor for the Atlantic Terminal redevelopment, but it wasn't. In 1919, Flatbush Avenue Terminal handled 263 trains per day, making it the third busiest railroad station in the metropolitan area, busier than the stations in Jersey City and Hoboken and, perhaps surprisingly, about 70 percent as busy as Grand Central Terminal. An earlier phase of the redevelopment project toward the eastern part of the renewal area, displacing the old Fort Greene Meat Market to a site in Sunset Park along First Avenue between 54th and 57th Streets, yielded, among other things, the Atlantic Terminal Houses designed by James Stewart Polshek & Partners and built in 1976 at the northeast corner of Carlton and Atlantic Avenues. This prominent thirty-one-story tower is faced in vertical bands of contrasting dark- and light-colored brick that may have been intended as a bow to the tradition of polychromatic brickwork in nineteenth-century Brooklyn architecture. In 1956, as the Brooklyn Dodgers were considering leaving the city, Brooklyn Borough President John Cashmore unveiled a plan for a 50,000-seat baseball stadium (intended to keep the Dodgers in Brooklyn) for a site bounded by Flatbush, Fourth, and Fifth Avenues and Warren Street, abutting to the south what would later be designated the Atlantic Terminal renewal area. The Dodgers were unpersuaded.

12 CENTRAL METHODIST CHURCH
Northwest corner of Hanson Place and St. Felix Street
1929–31, Halsey, McCormack & Helmer

Modern Gothic, this building is clearly inspired by Giles Gilbert Scott's Liverpool Cathedral (begun 1903) in England. If it lacks the majesty of Scott's cathedral or of the works of New York architect Bertram Goodhue, who was heavily influenced by Scott (Church of St. Vincent Ferrer, Chapel of the Intercession), still it has a powerful presence with its jazzy arrangement of receding and projecting planes (reminiscent, in ways, of Corbett, Harrison & MacMurray's National Title Guaranty Building of 1930 on Montague Street). It was also innovative in the manner in which the southernmost portions of the east and west aisles are in fact shopfronts built right into the church. (The west aisle contains Hanson Pizza.) A pair of short stairs leads to the nave, so that it is lifted high enough to allow space below for a double-height banquet hall and gymnasium. The interior is dark, cool, austere, and in the manner of Goodhue. Halsey, McCormack & Helmer designed the church around the same time as their skyscraper next door, and while the scale is disproportionate, there is a fine ecclesiastical ambience at street level to which the skyscraper, oddly, may add more than the church.

13 WILLIAMSBURGH SAVINGS BANK TOWER
1 Hanson Place, northeast corner of Ashland Place
1927–29, Halsey, McCormack & Helmer

At a mere thirty stories (512 feet), it is the tallest building in Brooklyn and is one of the five to ten greatest skyscrapers in New York City. The building is justly famous in these parts for its profile, its height, its clockfaces, and its dome. Still, where it really comes true is on the ground, where the limestone exterior of the base—with its enormous arched windows, compact elevator lobby (with its beautiful mosaic-covered groin-vaulted ceiling), and the improbably splendid banking hall—possesses an ecclesiastical majesty that the same architects' church next door, fine work though it may be, does not begin to match. Only a couple of the banks of York & Sawyer (such as their Brooklyn Trust Company on Montague and Clinton Streets) come up to the level of this one. It is highly reminiscent in scale, in the sumptuousness of its craftsmanship, and in its Byzantine decoration, of York & Sawyer's magnificent Bowery Savings

13 *Williamsburg Savings Bank Tower*

Bank on East 42nd Street (which has, alas, become a Cipriani catering hall and is closed to the public). The Williamsburgh's hall is 128 feet long, 72 feet wide, and 63 feet high. (The Bowery Savings Bank's hall, for comparison, is 160 feet long, 80 feet wide, and 65 feet high.) The walls are limestone, the counters are red marble (it is said that twenty-two types of marble are employed in this interior), light filters through the aforementioned arched windows, and the Cosmatesque floor is outstanding. The mosaic ceiling featuring signs of the zodiac is by Angelo Magnanti (who also designed the painted ceiling decoration of the Bowery Savings Bank), and Ravenna Mosaics of Berlin created the mosaic panel at the north end, showing an aerial view of Brooklyn. One of the most exciting features is the ironwork of the doors designed by René Chambellan, one of New York's foremost designers of architectural decoration at the time. (He created the bronze fountainhead figures in the Promenade of Rockefeller Center, and the bronze and terra-cotta reliefs of the lower stories of the exterior of the Chanin Building on East 42nd Street, among much else.)

From afar, the building does not so much soar as bore its way skyward to a beautiful tower with what once was the largest four-faced clock in the world. The tower culminates in an octagonal drum and a gilded dome. It is interesting that Halsey, McCormack & Helmer were in many ways far more traditionalist in their office skyscraper than in their church next door.

Clinton Hill

The most convenient subway station to this tour is the Lafayette and Washington Avenues stop on the G line. We are also within hailing distance of the huge subway hub at DeKalb and Flatbush Avenues, where the 2, 3, 4, 5, D, Q, N, and R lines all converge.

14 UNDERWOOD PARK
Lafayette Avenue between Washington and Waverly Avenues, north side

This small park of slightly more than an acre was named for John Thomas Underwood (1857–1937), whose house was on this site. The address of Underwood's large house was 336 Washington Avenue. In 1895, the London-born Underwood bought the patent to the "front stroke" typewriter, the first model to allow the typist to see the letters as they were being typed. Underwood Typewriters set a new standard and came to dominate the industry. Underwood's widow and daughter donated the house to the City of New York so that the house could be torn down and the land made into a neighborhood park, which opened in 1956. The park was renovated in 1997 at a cost of nearly a million dollars. It is said that Underwood's widow and daughter saw that Clinton Hill was deteriorating and did not want their house to be part of the neighborhood's decline. In fact, after some troubled years, and while still a bit rough around the edges, Clinton Hill has hung in there, and today is a vibrant community—and a thriving real-estate market.

Adjacent to Underwood Park to the north is the former Graham Home for Old Ladies on Washington Avenue. Now boarded up and very forlorn-looking, it is still a simple, lovely Italianate building of dark brick with strong four-story pilasters rising to brackets carrying a dentilated cornice below a roof pediment. Classical brackets also carry dentilated window cornices. J. G. Glover designed the building, which was built in 1851. It is stylistically similar to Plymouth Church (1849–50) on Orange Street. The formal name was the

Brooklyn Society for the Relief of Respectable Aged Indigent Females. Manhattan also had its Association for the Relief of Respectable Aged Indigent Females in a building Richard Morris Hunt designed that was built in 1881–83 on Amsterdam Avenue between 103rd and 104th Streets. It is now American Youth Hostels. It seems to me that a youth hostel might be the perfect use for the old Graham Home for Old Ladies.

15 MOHAWK (apartments)
379 Washington Avenue between Greene and Lafayette Avenues
1904, Neville & Bagge

This and the Royal Castle on Gates and Clinton Avenues give Clinton Hill two magnificent early-twentieth-century Beaux-Arts apartment buildings. This is a real piece of work. A limestone first floor yields above to red brick with limestone trim. Two big seven-story wings flank a light court. In the center is a Corinthian-columned entrance. The building is very wide. Each of the two flanking wings is composed of three horizontal parts, with swelling end bays and a recessed center. No holds were barred in the embellishment of the façade. I count twenty-four cartouches and forty console brackets. Note the fine, lacy iron balcony railings. After years of deterioration, the building now looks to be in quite good shape. Apartment buildings just don't get any better than this. Neville & Bagge designed some of the most outstanding Beaux-Arts apartment houses in New York City in the early twentieth century. Examples include the Cornwall (1909–10) on 90th Street and Broadway, and the tenements at 465 to 481 East 140th Street (1901–02) in Mott Haven.

16 EMMANUEL BAPTIST CHURCH
Northwest corner of Lafayette Avenue and St. James Place
1886–87, Francis H. Kimball
Chapel: 1882–83, Ebenezer L. Roberts
School: 1925–27

Charles Pratt was a parishioner of Washington Avenue Baptist Church nearby on the southwest corner of Washington and Gates Avenues. Ebenezer Roberts, an architect Pratt favored, designed it in 1860. Sometime around 1880, however, the pastor, a man of letters, published an antimonopolistic tract. Pratt, who, with his partners in the Standard Oil Trust, felt that monop-

16 *Emmanuel Baptist Church*

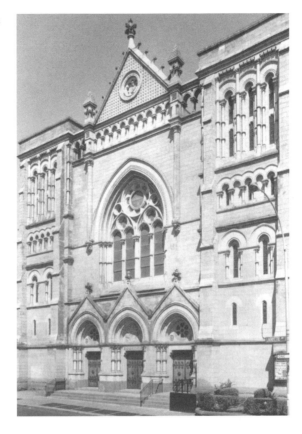

oly was as American as apple pie, was offended, and quit the congregation. He decided to build his own church. Emmanuel Baptist Church was the result. The congregation hired Ebenezer Roberts, who designed the chapel of 1882–83. For the main church, they retained Francis Hatch Kimball. The main church was dedicated April 17, 1887. Photographs always make this church seem much more imposing than it is. Someone who's seen a photograph of it first and then visits the church is likely to be a bit surprised that it does not, in fact, tower over surrounding streets. It is, nonetheless, quite substantial. The style is French Gothic, though there seems to be no exact model for the design. For example, in most twin-towered French Gothic churches, if there were, as there are here, three front doors, there would be one in the base of each of the towers, and one in the center, rather than, as here, all three tightly clustered in the center. What we have here is in fact a blending of twelfth-century French Romanesque, thirteenth-century French Gothic (as at Rheims), and

fifteenth-century French Gothic (the "Rayonnant"). The arrangement of the
various formal elements is fairly original, although in the service mainly of ton-
ing them down a bit from what one might actually see in Gothic France.
Indeed, that is why, in spite of the many specifically Gothic elements, I'm most
put in mind of twelfth-century Romanesque churches, perhaps the Abbaye-
aux-Dames in Caen.

The church is of Ohio sandstone. On Lafayette Avenue is a central
gabled section flanked by massive square towers that rise to a point slightly
lower than the top of the central gable. The towers are of a type clearly meant
to bear spires. The center section is sandwiched by the strong six-stage buttresses of the towers. At the lower level is the triple portal, each doorway surmounted by a freestanding gable. Above the portal is a large pointed window
with elaborate tracery. Separating this window from the crowning gable is an
arcaded band. Though the towers' corner buttresses are in six stages, the towers themselves are in five stages, with increasingly elaborate fenestration in
each succeeding stage. The St. James Place side has five bays each with twin
lancets under a small rose window topped by a freestanding gable. Also on St.
James Place are some of the best gargoyles in Brooklyn. The interior is a dramatic space with a high, barrel-vaulted ceiling and prominent galleries. It is
richly appointed with stained glass, stencil work, woodwork, and brass chandeliers. The pews are arranged in a radial plan of the type that was popular for
Protestant preaching churches. In the end, what may be most impressive
about Emmanuel Church is the manner in which Kimball so skillfully combined a scholarly French Gothic style with the needs of what was, after all, a
Baptist congregation. (About forty years later another Baptist, John D.
Rockefeller, Jr., whose father and Charles Pratt knew each other well, turned
to the French Gothic with a vengeance in his Riverside Church in
Morningside Heights.)

The architect Francis Hatch Kimball (1844–1919) was born in
Kennebunk, Maine, and began his architectural training at the age of fourteen,
when he went to work for a builder. He worked as supervising architect for the
renowned English Gothic Revival architect William Burges on Trinity College
(1875–83) in Hartford, Connecticut. Kimball's New York works, on his own or
in partnership with George Kramer Thompson, include Riverdale Presbyterian
Chapel (1888–89) on Independence Avenue in the Bronx, the Montauk Club
(1889–91) in Park Slope, the New York Architectural Terra Cotta Company
Building (1892) on Vernon Boulevard in Long Island City, the Empire Building

(1895–98) at 71 Broadway, the Gertrude Rhinelander Waldo house (1895–98) on Madison Avenue and 72nd Street, the Trinity and United States Realty buildings (1904–7) at 111 and 115 Broadway, and the J. & W. Seligman & Co. Building (1906–7) at 1 William Street. As this brief listing makes clear, Kimball was one of the most important late-nineteenth- and early-twentieth-century architects in New York.

Right next door at the northeast corner of Lafayette and Washington Avenues is the former Orthodox Friends Meeting House, built in 1868. It is a very simple Romanesque Revival design defined by molded round-arched windows and roof corbeling. The Quakers designed in many different styles but always in those styles' simplest versions. Today this is the Apostolic Faith Church. The building has been painted white with red trim.

17 ADELPHI ACADEMY
St. James Place between Lafayette Avenue and Clifton Place
North building: 1867, Mundell & Teckritz
South building: 1888, Charles C. Haight

The coeducational Adelphi Academy was founded in 1863 on Adelphi Street. Four years later, William A. Mundell and Herman Teckritz designed a new brick Romanesque Revival building for the academy facing St. James Place. No less a personage than Henry Ward Beecher laid its cornerstone. The same architects added wings in 1873 and 1880. In 1888, Charles Pratt, who had become a benefactor of Adelphi Academy, agreed to fund a new building for its collegiate division. Charles Coolidge Haight designed what is now the south wing. A Romanesque Revival design in red brick, it fronted on Clifton Place. Today the north building houses Pratt Institute's School of Architecture. Adelphi Academy was one of Brooklyn's most prestigious schools, as the involvement of figures such as Beecher and Pratt would suggest. The collegiate division became Adelphi University, chartered in 1896 and formally separated from the academy in 1925, moving to its present location in Garden City, New York. Adelphi Academy persists, too, at 8515 Bay Ridge Boulevard in Brooklyn. Both buildings in Clinton Hill exhibit the standard features of the Romanesque Revival, including molded round-arch windows, corbeling, roof gables, high chimneys, and so on. Both buildings are large and handsome. The architects of the north wing, Mundell & Teckritz, were very active in Brooklyn at the time. Mundell designed the cast-iron Long Island

Safe Deposit Company Building (1868–69) on Front Street, the Kings County
Hall of Records Building (1885–87) on Boerum Place, and the Raymond
Street Jail (1880), among other buildings. Herman Teckritz codesigned, with
Gamaliel King, the Kings County Courthouse (1861–65) on Joralemon Street.
Both were architects to whom went prestigious civic commissions. Charles
Coolidge Haight (1841–1917) was born in New York City, the son of the Rev.
Benjamin Haight, assistant rector of Trinity Church and a teacher at General
Theological Seminary. A graduate of Columbia College, he attended Columbia
Law School before deciding on a career as an architect. Among his many
notable works were the buildings of Columbia College (early 1880s) on
Madison Avenue between 49th and 50th Streets, much of General Theological
Seminary (1883–1900) in Chelsea, the New York Cancer Hospital (1884–86)
on Central Park West and 106th Street, and a number of buildings for the cam-
pus of Yale University in New Haven, Connecticut.

18 LINCOLN CLUB
*65 Putnam Avenue, between Irving Place and Classon Avenue,
   north side*
1889, R. L. Daus

This looks almost like a double row-house arrangement akin to Daus's in
Park Slope for William Thallon and Edward Bunker, completed only one year
before this clubhouse. The style is called Queen Anne, which was not so much
a revival of the architecture of the reign of Queen Anne as it was a revival—
and often a crazy-quilt mixing and matching—of elements from all of
pre–Georgian English architecture. There are also touches of Richardsonian
Romanesque. Two things here that one finds often in Queen Anne buildings
around the country are the cylindrical tower that juts out from the third floor
and rises higher than anything else on the building and is capped by a conical
roof, and the several gables, one of which, topping off the left side of the building, is richly embellished with terra-cotta ornamentation, here bearing the
building's name and date. The first floor is of rock-faced stone, with accents of
smooth stone that also trims the upper floors of brick. The tower bisects the
composition. The towers at Ludwig II's castle Neuschwanstein (1869–81), by
Georg von Dollmann and Eduard Riedel, may, as is often noted, have inspired
the tower here. Much the same sort of thing also appears in George Edmund
Street's London Law Courts (1868–82) as well as in some of the Queen Anne

architecture of London. The entrance is up a broad stone porch on the right. On the left is a three-sided oriel rising through the second and third stories to form a fourth-floor balcony. For all the studied variegation and asymmetry, this is actually a fairly simple and tasteful design by an architect who was, after all, trained at the École des Beaux-Arts.

The Lincoln Club was one of several prestigious private clubs in late-nineteenth-century Brooklyn. Formed in 1878, the club's purpose, as it name suggests, was to further Republican Party causes. In this it was similar to the Union League Club at Grant Square, just a few blocks to the south of here. The Lincoln Club folded in 1931. Since the 1940s, however, this has been the clubhouse of the Independent United Order of Mechanics of the Western Hemisphere, and, as Andrew Dolkart points out, this is one of the few nineteenth-century Brooklyn clubhouses still serving in its original function.

19 **ROYAL CASTLE (apartments)**
20–30 Gates Avenue, southwest corner of Clinton Avenue
1911–12, Wortmann & Braun

This big, dramatic apartment complex is worthy of the Upper West Side of Manhattan. Wortmann & Braun designed it in an exuberant Beaux-Arts style. A rusticated stone base yields to brick with lavish stone trim above. It fronts Gates Avenue (the side, with its own entrance, is on Clinton Avenue) with two massive wings flanking a courtyard. The two six-story wings are of identical design, defined through the middle four stories by three-sided oriels that rise from a stone shelf atop the ends of which sit two large console brackets that bracket nothing—they are purely ornamental and seem somewhat like the gestures one finds in certain 1980s postmodernism in which architects took traditional forms and placed them in unexpected contexts. The oriels terminate as well in console brackets, which this time are more conventionally employed, supporting the spring blocks of the wonderful top-floor arches. These arches are in the Venetian style and are surrounded by prominent brick moldings peppered with stone trim. The top floors themselves terminate in unusual shoulder-arched pediments. This building's kin is Janes & Leo's Dorilton on Broadway and 71st Street in Manhattan, built ten years earlier. The Royal Castle is one of Brooklyn's greatest apartment houses.

20 *St. Luke's Church*

20 ST. LUKE'S CHURCH (Episcopal)
520 Clinton Avenue between Fulton Street and Atlantic Avenue, west side
1888–91, John Welch

This is a grand and powerful composition. A massive gabled front with heavily molded corbeling along the top features an enormous rose window set within a receding round arch over a projecting entrance that echoes the gable and arch and is flanked by smaller round-arched openings. On either side of this front are twin polygonal towers rising from round bases springing from fat Romanesque columns. To the left of the front is a two-story corbeled wing that rises to about the level of the top of the round tower bases. This wing connects the church to the smaller gabled chapel, with the same corbeling along the top and with a triple Romanesque window. The composition ends with a high, elaborate bell tower. The materials are contrasting rock-faced and smooth stone with terra-cotta ornamentation. It is one of the city's most thoroughly worked-out Romanesque church designs.

The inspiration seems to be twelfth-century Northern Italian and French Romanesque churches, though so far as I can tell this is a very original adaptation. Indeed, it seems richer than many of its ostensible prototypes. The basic form is that of San Zeno Maggiore in Verona, but Welch's church is a much-embellished rendering of the basic idiom. It may also have been influenced by Henry Hobson Richardson's unbuilt design for All Saints Cathedral in Albany, New York, in 1883. Welch was awarded the commission through a competition in which he defeated Richard Michell Upjohn, R. L. Daus, and J. W. Walter. (The latter was the architect of the beautiful Memorial Presbyterian Church in Park Slope.) St. Luke's Church was also, we are told, one of the first buildings in Brooklyn to be lit by electricity. John W. Welch (1824–94) was a Scotsman who received his architectural training in Europe. Over the same years as St. Luke's, Welch designed the Sands Street Methodist Episcopal Church that once stood on the southwest corner of Clark and Henry Streets in Brooklyn Heights. Photographs of that church show that Welch was, as his career wound down, hitting his stride as a highly original practitioner in a complex and monumental Romanesque Revival mode.

This is now the Episcopal Church of St. Luke and St. Matthew.

Clinton Avenue is one of Brooklyn's grandest residential thoroughfares. It is broad and its freestanding houses give it a feeling altogether different from nearby row-house streets. In many ways Clinton Avenue is similar to Prairie Avenue in Chicago. The merchant George Washington Pine laid out the tree-lined boulevard in 1832. By the Civil War, freestanding wood-frame houses lined the avenue. Charles Pratt's decision in 1874 to build his house on Clinton Avenue changed everything. The avenue became the most fashionable in Brooklyn. Today, with a booming real-estate market that has affected Clinton Hill as it has so many other places, Clinton Avenue is more desirable to more people than it has been in a very long time, and there is the hum of renovation on the avenue. There is a sense of proportion between the sizes of the buildings and the width of the street of the kind planners are always fiddling with zoning codes trying to achieve and never get as perfect as Clinton Avenue. This is an avenue of homely grandeur that is very easy to fall in love with.

21 CHARLES ADOLPH SCHIEREN HOUSE
485 Clinton Avenue between Gates and Greene Avenues, east side
1889, William B. Tubby

William Tubby designed this house for the man who in three years would become mayor of Brooklyn. At first blush, the house seems to be another of the ubiquitous Romanesque Revival houses of its period. The rock-faced stone base, the Roman brick with sandstone trim, the shingled and hipped roof, and the high chimneys are all elements we associate with the Romanesque Revival. This is, in fact, one of those Romanesque/Renaissance hybrids pointing the way to Brooklyn's 1890s Classicism. Note such Classical elements as the balustrade with urns surmounting the distinctive projecting porch, and the Palladian window set within the prominent Flemish gable of the roof. Note also the stately lines, the clean stringcourses of the house. It is thirty-two feet wide and seventy feet deep. It is said that though Tubby had worked for Charles Pratt's architect, E. L. Roberts, it was Tubby's success with this house that led Pratt to sign Tubby to design 241 Clinton Avenue for his son.

Charles Adolph Schieren (1842–1915) was born near Düsseldorf. His father was heavily involved in the goings-on of 1848 and had to beat a hasty retreat. In 1856, the family came to America. Father and son ran a tobacco store in Brooklyn, but the son branched out and started a highly successful leather-goods manufacturing company, Charles A. Schieren & Company. In 1893, he was elected mayor of Brooklyn. During his two-year term, the Williamsburg Bridge was planned. In 1898, President William McKinley appointed Schieren to the chairmanship of the Cuban Relief Committee and as treasurer of the National Red Cross. Governor Theodore Roosevelt made Schieren a member of the Greater New York Chamber of Commerce. He was a founder of the Brooklyn Institute of Arts and Sciences and served as president of the Brooklyn Academy of Music. His widow survived him by twenty-four hours. He is buried in Green-wood Cemetery.

22 CORNELIUS N. HOAGLAND HOUSE
410 Clinton Avenue between Gates and Greene Avenues, west side
1882, Parfitt Brothers

This is the house that put the Parfitt brothers on the map. Their next major works would be their apartment houses for Montague Street. The materials are red brick with light stone trim. The entrance is on the right behind a yard enclosed by an iron fence. The entrance is through a classical arch in brick, and there is a fine double door of iron. The gently projecting second-floor bays are topped by limestone swags. Though this is what we call Queen Anne, which made free use of Classical as well as many other motifs, still there is some Classical decoration here that seems quite unusual for its time. Also in this vein is the panel with the stone urn set in the house's very large gabled top.

Hoagland was the founder of Royal Baking Powder and benefactor of the pioneering Hoagland Laboratory for bacteriological research at Long Island College Hospital in Cobble Hill. His son-in-law, George P. Tangeman of Park Slope, took over the company.

23 JAMES H. LOUNSBERY HOUSE
321 Clinton Avenue between Lafayette and DeKalb Avenues, east side
1875, Ebenezer L. Roberts

This is an enormous brownstone. Its "stoop" leads between paired columns to a double door. This projecting portico forms a second-floor balcony and is flanked by two-sided bays topped by somewhat awkward-looking triangular balconies with balustrades. A gable tops the three-story house, which has neo-Grec flourishes.

Lounsbery was a Pratt associate who died before the house was completed. The design of this house indeed bears similarities to Charles Pratt's house on the next block, which was designed by the same architect at about the same time.

24 JOHN ARBUCKLE HOUSE
315 Clinton Avenue between Lafayette and DeKalb Streets, east side
1887–88, Montrose W. Morris

This thirty-foot-wide house in Morris's early Romanesque Revival style is roughly contemporary with the houses Morris designed on Hancock Street in Bedford-Stuyvesant. Here is a broad porch with the entrance to the left of the stoop. The first floor is faced in brownstone, the second and third in red brick. In the center at the second story is a prominent swelling bay, its top forming a third-floor balcony. A center gable tops the house. There are nice terra-cotta surrounds on the three square-headed first-floor windows.

John Arbuckle and his brother Charles formed the Arbuckle Coffee company in 1865. They patented a special process for preserving roasted coffee beans and basically supplied the Western frontier with their coffee, which became known as "cowboy coffee." It was just as popular among the Indians. Indeed, Arbuckle coffee was among the first mass-marketed products to take advantage of the recently completed transcontinental railroad. In their exploitation of the new technology, the Arbuckles were a sort of nineteenth-century equivalent of today's Internet millionaires. Packages of their coffee contained trade cards that are now much coveted by collectors, judging from the number of web sites devoted to them. The Arbuckles also packaged sugar, tea, spices, canned fruits and vegetables, rolled oats, and "Vesta" laundry soap (what a name!). John Arbuckle held a private competition for the design of his house.

25 CHARLES PRATT HOUSE
232 Clinton Avenue between DeKalb and Willoughby Avenues, west side
1874, Ebenezer L. Roberts

Ebenezer L. Roberts, who designed this house for Pratt *père*, also designed the headquarters of Standard Oil at 26 Broadway in 1884–86. (It was said at the time to be the most famous address in the world.) It is remarkably less of a design statement than any of the sons' houses. The house is red brick with brownstone trim and features a generous covered porch of brownstone, carried on Tuscan columns. There is brownstone quoining and a gabled top. The style is Italianate. The Brooklyn house this most reminds me of is the Charles Condon house at 123 Remsen Street, built (we believe) around the same time. That, however, is a house in what by the 1870s was already a densely developed urban precinct. Pratt's house, by contrast, was much more of the villa type, with a generous surrounding garden.

This house is now, like the George DuPont Pratt house, part of St. Joseph's College.

25 *Charles Pratt House*

CHARLES PRATT (1830–1891)

Charles Pratt was the richest man in Brooklyn. He may have been the richest man ever to live in Brooklyn. New York City's richest man was John Davison Rockefeller. Pratt and Rockefeller were partners. The business was petroleum refining. In recent years, when we think of the oil business we tend to think of Texas. *Dallas*, the big hit of 1980s television, was set among the oil baron families of Texas. If we had had TV a century earlier, however, the hit series might have been *Brooklyn*, perhaps with a family loosely modeled on the Pratts of Clinton Avenue—their lives, their loves, their intrigues, their splendors and miseries. I would have watched.

Charles Pratt was born in New England, as were so many of the prominent Brooklynites of his generation. His was an old New England family, and he was born in Watertown, Massachusetts, just outside of Boston. Old though his family might have been, they were not monied, and he grew up in straitened circumstances, which taught him the virtues of thrift and frugality and also gave him a deep sympathy for the workingman. At the age of thirteen he became a grocery clerk in Boston and later apprenticed as a machinist in Newton. He saved his money and attended Wesleyan Academy in Wilbraham, Massachusetts, for three years. In 1849, at the age of nineteen, he went to work as a clerk in a Boston firm that dealt in paints and oils. Two years later, he moved to New York City and entered a similar firm. His course was set. Paints and oils it would be.

In 1854, he and two others formed their own firm, Reynolds, Devoe & Pratt. Charles was only twenty-four. After thirteen years, he withdrew from this firm and established Charles Pratt & Company, petroleum refiners, in Greenpoint, Brooklyn. The Astral Oil that he produced would become world-famous as very high quality, safe illuminating kerosene. The success of Astral Oil piqued the interest of John D. Rockefeller, then consolidating his holdings in the field. Rockefeller acquired Astral Oil from Pratt in 1874. In the deal, Pratt became a partner in Rockefeller's Standard Oil Company and would become one of the most influential of the company's directors. At the time, fifty or so independent petroleum refineries were ranged along the Brooklyn waterfront in Greenpoint and Williamsburg. Rockefeller and Pratt either bought or drove out of business most of them. Rockefeller appreciated Pratt's extraordinary attention to detail. Both Pratt and Rockefeller were devout Baptists, which probably helped their business partnership.

As Pratt grew rich, his thoughts, like those of many of his contemporaries among the plutocracy of America's cities, turned increasingly to good works. He had sent his children to the nearby Adelphi Academy and became the president of its board of trustees. In 1886, he presented the school with a new building (still standing on St. James Place). A firm believer in the value of higher education, Pratt donated large sums of money to Amherst College and to the University of Rochester. For workers in his petroleum company in Greenpoint, he hired Lamb & Rich to design the Astral Apartments, built in 1885–86 on Franklin Street, model tenements not so different in intention from those erected by Alfred Tredway White in Cobble Hill a few years earlier. Pratt's greatest concern, however, was in providing good manual training for young people to allow them to become self-supporting through the use of their own hands. To this end he made an extensive tour of European technical training schools and, equipped with the most advanced ideas in the field (not least the example of New York's Cooper Union), established Pratt Institute in 1887, enrolling twelve students in its first class. His largess created the Pratt Institute Free Library, Brooklyn's first free public library, open to every Brooklynite over the age of fourteen. In 1888, he created the Thrift, a savings and loan society for working people, modeled on the Birkbeck Building Society of London. (Think of Pratt as a man with the wealth and power of Potter and the heart of George Bailey in *It's a Wonderful Life*.) A devout Baptist, he built one of New York's most beautiful churches, Emmanuel Baptist Church, on Lafayette Avenue in 1886–87. For this he had the sense to hire Francis Hatch Kimball as his architect, a switch from the architects Pratt customarily patronized—Ebenezer Roberts (who designed Standard Oil's headquarters at 26 Broadway in Manhattan as well as Emmanuel's chapel), William Tubby (who designed Pratt's eldest son's house on Clinton Avenue as well as the Pratt Institute Free Library), and Lamb & Rich (who designed the Astral Apartments and the Main Building of Pratt Institute). William Tubby designed Pratt's 800-acre estate in Glen Cove, Nassau County, Long Island.

Pratt was estimated to be worth as much as $20 million when he died. By today's standards that sounds rather low for someone described as Brooklyn's richest man. Inflated to today's currency, Pratt's $20 million comes to $380 million. That, however, does not begin to tell the story. Employing the method worked out by historians Michael Klepper and Robert Gunther for determining the richest Americans of all time, we would first look at what percentage of gross national product Pratt's $20 million was in 1891. By then projecting his fortune as the same percentage of gross national product today, we would arrive at a truer understanding of what his fortune meant in his time. The figure, expressed in today's currency, would come to around $15 *billion* dollars. There have been and are wealthier people. Still, Pratt probably ranks in the top hundred Americans of all time. He was rich.

Pratt had six sons and two daughters by two wives. (The first wife died; Pratt was not the divorcing kind of man.) Three of his sons' houses as well as his own still stand on Clinton Avenue. One son, Harold, led the family's exodus from Brooklyn when he decided to build his house on Manhattan's Park Avenue (it is now the Council on Foreign Relations). Charles Pratt died in his office in the Standard Oil Building at 26 Broadway, supposedly with John D. Rockefeller at his side.

26 GEORGE DUPONT PRATT HOUSE
245 Clinton Avenue between DeKalb and Willoughby Avenues, east side
1901, Babb, Cook & Willard

26 *George DuPont Pratt House*

The house, set behind a circular drive, is of red brick with white lime-stone trim, including limestone quoins, limestone window enframements, and, flanking the doorway, limestone composite columns. There is a limestone car-touche over the second-floor center window. The house is crested with lions' heads. The style is Beaux-Arts/neo-Georgian, stylistically kin to the same firm's house for Andrew Carnegie in Manhattan from 1899–1903. Babb, Cook & Willard must have worked on this house and the Carnegie house at the same time. This is one of the several houses on Clinton Avenue built for sons of Charles Pratt.

It is now part of St. Joseph's College.

27 CHARLES MILLARD PRATT HOUSE
241 Clinton Avenue between DeKalb and Willoughby Avenues, east side
1890–93, William B. Tubby

Built by Charles Pratt *père* as a wedding gift to his eldest son, who was also prominent in the front office of Standard Oil, it is now the residence of the Roman Catholic bishop of the Diocese of Brooklyn. Though completed only eight years before George DuPont Pratt's house next door, it is stylistically a generation earlier. This two-story-plus-attic house is faced in orange Roman brick with matching sandstone trim. The most prominent feature by far, and really one of the loveliest things in Brooklyn, is the magnificent arch of the porte-cochère. The hipped roof of Spanish tile has flared eaves, perhaps a bow to Brooklyn farmhouse tradition. The house features some luscious foliate terra-cotta ornament in the same color as the brick and stone. On the right of the house is a fat (or should I say *tubby?*) round tower with a conical roof. On the house's left, note the terra-cotta panel inscribed with a superimposed C, M, and P, for Charles Millard Pratt. I don't think there is any question that this is William Tubby's finest work. Stern, Mellins, and Fishman's *New York 1880* calls it "the climax of the impact of the Richardsonian Romanesque on urban villa building." The date of its completion is noteworthy. The Columbian Exposition took place that year. After that, the Richardsonian Romanesque, which Brooklyn had practically made its own, would yield to the Beaux-Arts Classicism such as that of the two Babb, Cook & Willard houses flanking this house by Tubby.

28 FREDERIC B. PRATT HOUSE

229 Clinton Avenue between DeKalb and Willoughby Avenues, east side
1895, Babb, Cook & Willard

The most marvelous feature here is the colonnaded and trellised pergola on the left, with a lower level of Ionic columns in polished granite and an upper level of delightful caryatids. Near the sidewalk is a fabulously gnarled wisteria. The pergola is attached on its west side to a row of four very handsome Classical row houses of pinkish buff brick and matching terra-cotta. The pergola leads to the house's front door. The house is of grayish brown brick with limestone trim, and is stylistically kin to Babb, Cook & Willard's house up the street for George DuPont Pratt. The three-story house has a Palladian window at the ground floor behind a generous garden and a second floor with a triple window with two Ionic columns. In the center top is a cartouche with a female head. Another pergola, this one of only one level and with Doric rather than Ionic columns, is visible toward the rear of the house and is parallel to Clinton Avenue. This rear trellis can also be espied through the fence in the back of the house on Waverly Avenue, where the sometimes beautiful carriage houses of these Clinton Avenue mansions can be seen. This is a consummately suave essay in the neo-Georgian vein of Beaux-Arts residential design and may indeed vie with the Charles Millard Pratt house, completed only two years earlier, for title of the Queen of Clinton Avenue.

It's now Pratt Institute's Caroline Ladd Pratt House, a foreign students' residence.

PRATT INSTITUTE

Pratt Institute opened on October 17, 1887. Charles Pratt wished to create a school similar to Peter Cooper's in Manhattan. Pratt died only four years after his Institute opened. His son, Frederic Pratt, took over and guided the school for a number of years. Pratt *père* intended that the school train young people in manual arts, ranging from drawing to bricklaying to sewing to typewriting. From early on the school focused on the subjects for which it has always been renowned: art, architecture, and design. From the very beginning, Pratt admitted both men and women. There was also no discrimination on the basis of race. In 1890, Pratt opened one of the country's first library schools, with the Pratts' Free Library as its laboratory. Pratt Institute did not award the baccalaureate degree until 1936.

Pratt Institute is a superblock bounded by DeKalb Avenue on the south, Classon Avenue on the east, Willoughby Avenue on the north, and Hall Street on the west. Within this superblock are twenty-two buildings grouped around open spaces. Two additional buildings are just outside the superblock. Higgins Hall (the former Adelphi Academy) is one block to the south on the east side of St. James Place (which is the same as Hall Street) between Lafayette Avenue and Clifton Place. Willoughby Hall is opposite the campus on Willoughby Avenue. Note how the buildings are oriented toward north-south walkways. These buildings were erected on city streets (Ryerson Street, Grand Avenue, Steuben Street, and Emerson Place) that were later demapped by 1960s urban renewal to allow Pratt to create a true campus. Today about 3,800 students attend Pratt.

29 MAIN BUILDING
Ryerson Walk between DeKalb and Willoughby Avenues,
east side, south of Memorial Hall
1885–87, Lamb & Rich
Porch: 1894, William B. Tubby

30 SOUTH HALL
1889–91, William B. Tubby

31 MEMORIAL HALL
1926–27, John Mead Howells

Lamb & Rich designed the seven-story Main Building in 1885–87. They were the New York architects Charles Pratt also hired to design his Astral Apartments in Greenpoint. (Lamb & Rich also designed the beautiful house of George Tangeman in Park Slope as well as the original buildings of Barnard College and numerous other noteworthy works.) It looks rather like a TriBeCa warehouse;

29 *Pratt Institute, Main Building*

30 *Pratt Institute, South Hall*

31 *Pratt Institute, Memorial Hall*

in fact, Pratt ordered Lamb & Rich to design it in such a way that if his school should fail, the building could be converted into a factory. The entrance porch, which looks un-warehouse-like, was in fact a later addition, arriving in 1894 and designed, as was South Hall, by William B. Tubby, an architect much favored by Pratt. (Tubby succeeded to the practice of Ebenezer Roberts, who designed Pratt's house on Clinton Avenue.) The Main Building is in the Romanesque Revival warehouse mode, with round-arched and segmental-arched windows, some applied terra-cotta ornamentation, stubby corner towers, and a higher central clocktower. It is handsome in a utilitarian way—what Pratt undoubtedly wanted.

Tubby's three-story South Hall, added in 1889–91, is in much the same vein, and is strikingly similar—for example, in its openwork arcaded parapet and in the discs set into the spandrels of the arches—to Babb & Cook's warehouse at 173 Duane Street in TriBeCa, built in 1879–80. South Hall was originally Pratt Institute High School, which operated from 1888 to 1905. It closed when the public Manual Training High School opened in Park Slope.

John Mead Howells designed Memorial Hall, built in 1926–27 in a Romanesque style. This is not warehouse Romanesque, however, but synagogue Romanesque: an unexpected progeny of Henry Herts's Congregation B'nai Jeshurun Synagogue, built on West 88th Street ten years earlier. Howells was the onetime partner of Isaac Newton Phelps Stokes (they designed St. Paul's Chapel at Columbia University) and later of Raymond Hood (they designed the Daily News Building on East 42nd Street). He was the École des Beaux-Arts–trained son of the novelist, editor, and critic William Dean Howells. Memorial Hall, designed as an assembly hall, memorializes Mary Richardson Pratt, Charles Pratt's second wife. The sculpture of Memorial Hall is by René Chambellan, one of the leading architectural sculptors of the 1920s and 1930s. His work can be seen in such high-profile settings as the Chanin Building on East 42nd Street (where he executed the extravagant reliefs on the base of the building), Rockefeller Center, and Brooklyn's Williamsburgh Savings Bank Tower.

32 **MACHINE SHOP BUILDING**
East of the Main Building
1887, William Windrim

Now called the East Building, and with the Main Building one of the two original Pratt Institute buildings, the Machine Shop Building can be accessed through the gate located between the Main Building and South Hall. This building was the mechanical plant of Pratt Institute and contains three steam engines, installed in 1900, that were manufactured by the Ames Iron Works and that still, remarkably, provide about a third of the power for the campus. From the start the mechanical facilities here were intended not only to power the campus but to be teaching tools, in much the same way that the Free Library was intended to be not only a library for the use of the public but also to provide training for students of Pratt's library school. Today the Machine Shop Building is known as an informal museum of "industrial archaeology." The beautifully main-tained old steam engines can be viewed in action. Also on view are all manner of architectural and industrial odds and ends, including chandeliers from the boardroom of Ernest Flagg's Singer Tower.

33 PRATT INSTITUTE LIBRARY

Hall Street between DeKalb and Willoughby Avenues, east side
1896, William B. Tubby
North porch: 1936, John Mead Howells
Renovation: 1982, Giorgio Cavaglieri

Charles Pratt established this as the first free public library in Brooklyn. (The Mercantile Library on Montague Street, which became the main library of the Brooklyn Public Library system, began as a subscription library.) William Tubby designed it in a Rundbogenstil manner clearly influenced by Manhattan's Astor Library on Lafayette Street. The simple three-story brick structure has a slightly more utilitarian air than its Manhattan counterpart, with slightly projecting end sections, square-headed windows on the first and third floors with round-arched windows between, and a roof balustrade. From the south end projects a two-story wing that housed book stacks. John Mead Howells designed the north porch that was added in 1936. In 1982, Giorgio Cavaglieri and Warren Gran expanded the library underground and created the terrace on the south side of the building, with windows looking down onto the new stacks.

Housed before 1896 in the Main Building, the library originally was open to all Brooklyn residents over the age of fourteen. Since 1940, use of the library has been restricted to Pratt students.

34 THE THRIFT

Northeast corner of Ryerson Walk and DeKalb Avenue
1916, Shampan & Shampan

The Thrift was a savings-and-loan that Charles Pratt founded in 1889 to help working people obtain mortgages. Originally located on the site of Memorial Hall, it was moved twenty-seven years later into this fine two-story building that is now called Thrift Hall. The neo-Georgian building is red brick with limestone trim and has lovely Corinthian pilasters and a strong bracketed cornice. The bank went out of business in the 1940s. Charles Pratt, it seems, combined the roles of Mr. Potter and George Bailey.

---

35 ST. MARY'S CHURCH (Episcopal)
230 Classon Avenue, northwest corner of Willoughby Avenue
1858–59, Richard T. Auchmuty

This is every bit as thoroughly worked out an example of Ecclesiological Gothic as Upjohn's Grace Church in Brooklyn Heights, truly one of the best New York churches of its period, though comparatively little known. It faces west and meets Classon Avenue with its chancel, as well it might, in that this is one of the bravura Gothic chancels in New York, twenty-four feet deep and articulated in every conceivable way. First of all, there is the fact that its roof is significantly lower than that of the nave. Add to that the polygonal bay projecting from the north side that is placed right at the division of nave and chancel. Above all, note the south tower right next to the chancel. On the north side of the tower is a projecting polygonal turret, incised with lancets, rising to a line just above the point of the large chancel window and just below the top of the chancel gable. A broached, verdigris-copper steeple surmounts the tower. The east face of the chancel has on its south side a two-stage buttress with stepped sloping set-offs perpendicular to Classon Avenue. On the north side, an identical buttress is set at a 45-degree angle to the street. The big chancel window is composed of three lancets with quatrefoil spandrels. The stonework is random ashlar in accordance with Ecclesiological precepts. It is all very faithfully done and doesn't fall down when it comes to detail, including the inside. The architect, Auchmuty, was the onetime partner of the famous James Renwick, Jr., architect of St. Ann's Church in Brooklyn Heights.

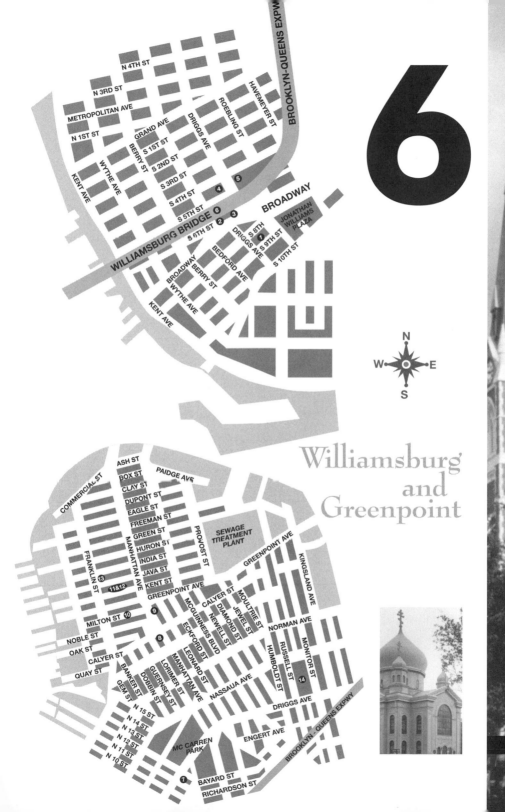

Williamsburg
and
Greenpoint

11 *Reformed Dutch Church of Greenpoint*

Williamsburg and Greenpoint *Chapter* **6**

Williamsburg

Williamsburg was a farming village in the seventeenth and eighteenth cen-
turies. In 1800, Richard M. Woodhull established ferry service between Corlear's
Hook in Manhattan and what is now North 2nd Street in Williamsburg.
Woodhull purchased thirteen acres of land near the ferry landing and hired
Jonathan Williams to survey it. Woodhull named his small development after
Williams, who was a grandnephew of Benjamin Franklin. Woodhull's
Williamsburgh was a notable failure, and in 1806 he went bankrupt.
Nonetheless, the area seemed propitiously sited for development, and others in
Woodhull's wake would make good on the site's promise. In 1818, a steam ferry
was established, and in 1827, the Village of Williamsburgh was incorporated.
Williamsburgh became a city in 1852. Three years later, the City of
Williamsburgh was consolidated into the City of Brooklyn, and the final "h" was
dropped. Around this time, well-to-do Germans and Irish settled in
Williamsburg, which became famous for its beer gardens. In the 1850s, when the
New England Congregational Church was erected on South 9th Street, much of
Williamsburgh still had a genteel air. This air was beginning to wear away some
years before the opening of the Williamsburg Bridge in 1903. Many of the most
famous industrial enterprises of the Williamsburg waterfront began in the nineteenth century, including Hecla Architectural Iron Works, Havemeyer & Elder's
Sugar Refinery, D. Appleton & Company's printing plant, and Pfizer

Pharmaceutical. It is nonetheless true that the bridge sparked a wholesale transformation of Williamsburg into what essentially became an extension of the
Lower East Side of Manhattan. Throughout the early twentieth century, parts of
Williamsburg were heavily built up with tenement housing and became some of
New York's most overcrowded areas, with some of the highest infant-mortality
rates. By 1920, much of Williamsburg had become a "slum." Change never
ceases in Williamsburg, however. In the 1930s, the Williamsburg Houses, one of
the earliest and still one of the most-admired government-subsidized low-income
housing projects in the nation, went up. In the 1940s, ultra-orthodox Hasidic
Jews from eastern Europe, many of the Satmar sect from Hungary and Romania,
began to colonize the southern part of Williamsburg. There are believed to be
fifty thousand Satmar Hasidim in the southern part of Williamsburg, and their
principal language is Yiddish. Many of these Hasidim are relatively poor and are
eligible for public housing. Public-housing projects in southwestern Williamsburg
are filled with Hasidim. These buildings were built with special elevators; on the
Sabbath, they stop on every floor so that no one has to push a button. In the
1950s, Puerto Ricans began filling up large parts of the district. Around the same
time, Robert Moses obtruded his new Brooklyn-Queens Expressway right
through the heart of the district. Williamsburg was a bubbling cauldron of
change. Only Peter Luger's Steak House stayed the same.

1 NEW ENGLAND CONGREGATIONAL CHURCH
179 South 9th Street between Driggs and Roebling Avenues, north side
1852–53, Thomas W. Little

Williamsburgh 1850: New Englanders on the march. Congregationalists
built one of their earliest churches in what would later be Brooklyn.
Williamsburgh would become part of the City of Brooklyn two years after this
church was completed. This was the church of the Rev. Thomas Kinnicut
Beecher. His brother had only slightly earlier (1849) built his own
Congregationalist church on Orange Street in Brooklyn Heights. The Beechers
came to Brooklyn from their native Connecticut, whose eighteenth-century
Congregationalist churches tended to be simple Georgian wood boxes, white-
painted, sometimes with steeples. In the 1820s, Connecticut Congregationalist
churches got a tad flamboyant, though elegantly so, in a late-Georgian idiom
with columned and pedimented porches and sometimes elaborate, multistage
towers and steeples. Still they were white and they were wood. A fine example is

from the Beechers' home of Litchfield, where the First Congregational Church was built on the village green in 1828–29. This is the immediate background to Williamsburg's New England Congregational Church. It is a more elaborate rendering of the simple Italianate style of Plymouth Church, and it could not be more different in feeling from the First Congregational Church of Litchfield. Williamsburgh was growing fast at the time. The Congregationalists became urbanized. This is an urban church. It is an 1850s church. It is brownstone.

It bears similarities as well to Gamaliel King and John Kellum's Quaker Meeting House at Gramercy Park, and to John Street Methodist Church in lower Manhattan. They are all what we call Italianate: gabled boxes with arched windows and simple, Classical moldings. This is the most elaborate of them all, the only one with quoins, console brackets, and pedimented windows. It veers rather hard from the studied simplicity of its brethren, especially in its center section, an elaborate composition featuring an entrance with a triangular pediment, above which is a high, bold arched window flanked at its top by big, bold, beautiful console brackets carrying a heavy cornice on which is set another triangular pediment within the full-width, low-angled pediment that tops off the building. Its architect, Thomas Little, would team ten years hence with Gamaliel King's onetime partner, John Kellum, in codesigning the New York County (aka Tweed) Courthouse on Chambers Street, maybe the most monumental "Italianate" building of its time in New York.

This is now the Light of the World Church.

Four blocks to the west of the New England Congregational Church, on a site bounded by South 9th and 10th Streets and Kent Avenue and the East River, the F. & M. Schaefer Brewery stood for sixty-one years. Frederick and Maximilian Schaefer came to New York City from their native Prussia in the 1830s and in 1842 established the city's first lager brewery. In 1849, they established a large brewery at Fourth Avenue and 51st Street in Manhattan. In 1914, Schaefer Brewery sold the site to St. Bartholomew's Church, and in 1916, Rudolph Schaefer, son of the late Maximilian, opened the new, state-of-the-art brewery in Williamsburg. The timing was poor in that Prohibition was right around the corner, but the brewery stayed afloat producing "near beer." On April 7, 1933, when the Volstead Act was repealed, Schaefer was well positioned and expanded the Williamsburg plant in the 1930s and 1940s. What was state-of-the-art in 1916 was no longer considered to be so by 1972, when Schaefer constructed a new plant in Allentown, Pennsylvania. Schaefer closed the Brooklyn brewery four years later, after 134 years in New York City. For the first time since it became a city, Brooklyn, once one of the great brewing centers of America, was without a brewery. Brewing came back to Brooklyn exactly twenty years later, when the Brooklyn Brewery opened in Williamsburg in a former nineteenth-century iron foundry at 79 North 11th Street, between Berry Street and Wythe Avenue. This is a microbrewery producing a variety of beers of exceptional quality. In its brewing heyday, Brooklyn's German brewers adhered to the *reinheitsgebot,* the German beer purity laws. There were countless breweries offering beers for every palate. It was not until after World War II that American brewing was consolidated among a handful of big players who increasingly produced the thin, pallid, watery swill that most people of my generation grew up thinking of as beer. In the 1980s, however, the microbrewery phenomenon exploded across America, inspired in part by Britain's Campaign for Real Ale. Today, it is easy to find excellent beer, and in New York the products of the Brooklyn Brewery reign supreme. For more information about the brewery's tasting room, tours, and special events, check their Web site at www.brooklynbrewery.com.

2 KINGS COUNTY SAVINGS BANK
135 Broadway, northeast corner of Bedford Avenue
1868, King & Wilcox

Though New York architects had begun attending the École des Beaux-Arts in Paris, their direct influence was still but fitfully felt in the city's environment. Nonetheless, a vogue emerged for the Parisian splendors of Louis Napoleon's Second Empire. The architecture of Haussmann's boulevards often featured the exaggerated use of the sloping roofs invented in the seventeenth century by the great French architect François Mansart. The "mansard," as it was called, is the most defining feature of the Parisian chic that marks New York in the 1860s and 1870s. The so-called Second Empire style, often employed by architects who had never been to France, tended to have a heaped-up, profligate quality that today seems redolent of the Grant era. Think for example of Diamond Jim Brady. He lived in the Gilsey House (1869–71) on West 29th Street, where the barbershop had a floor studded with silver dollars. Diamond Jim, with his folds of flesh and fat jeweled fingers, looked like he himself might have been put together by one of the "Second Empire" architects of New York. The Kings County Savings Bank was built in the year U. S. Grant was elected

2 *King's County Savings Bank*

president. It is probably the finest Second Empire–style building in Brooklyn. Indeed, it is one of the best in all of New York City.

The first of its four floors is fully rusticated, including its projecting porch crowned by a sculptural pediment. The rustication theme is carried through in the second and third stories in the form of quoins. The street level and the windows of the second and third stories sport balustrades, and triangular pediments top the second- and third-floor windows. A heavy cornice surmounts the third story. Above this rises a broad, steep mansard roof. On the Broadway side, a dormer projects, topped by a lovely scrolled pediment. The best thing here, though, is the treatment of the second and third floors in the central section above the projecting porch. The windows here are recessed in antis, with Ionic columns at the second floor, Corinthian above. Overall, there is much detail to savor and a pleasing plasticity and play of shadow over the façade.

This is now the well-preserved home of an enterprising and important organization called the Williamsburg Art and Historical Society.

The former Nassau Trust Company, at the southwest corner of Broadway and Bedford Avenue, was built in 1888. Frank J. Helmle, later of Helmle &

Huberty, designed it. Its stately Ionic columns, rusticated surfaces, and balustraded balconies, executed in limestone and granite, show that Helmle, though not nearly where he would be eighteen years later when he and Ulrich Huberty designed the nearby Williamsburg Trust Company, was nonetheless a leader, not a follower, in Brooklyn's Classical flowering that would not achieve full bloom until after the World's Columbian Exposition, which took place five years after he designed this bank.

On the south side of Broadway at No. 178, between Bedford and Driggs Avenues, is Peter Luger's Steak House. It is a daily anomaly in this part of Williamsburg that limousines pull up, at both lunch and dinner, to deposit Manhattan big shots and Hollywood celebrities at the door of what some consider the finest steak restaurant in the United States. Founded at this site in 1878 as Charles Luger's Café, Billiards, and Bowling Alley, the restaurant has hardly ever waned in popularity in spite of what for its clientele is an out-of-the-way location.

On this stretch of Broadway are two cast-iron buildings worthy of SoHo or Ladies' Mile. On the north side of Broadway at No. 103, between Bedford Avenue and Berry Street, is an 1870s cast-iron-fronted factory, converted to residences, its particularly fine windows with segmental arches carried on Corinthian colonnettes. On the northeast corner of Broadway and Driggs Avenue, across Driggs from the Williamsburgh Savings Bank, is the former Sparrow Shoe Factory Warehouse designed by William B. Ditmars and built in 1882. It is notable for its fluted Corinthian pilasters. These cast-iron factory and warehouse buildings remind us that at around the time the Williamsburgh Savings Bank was built, many years before the Williamsburg Bridge (1903) opened, Broadway was already partly industrial, as Williamsburgh's past as a genteel resort was fading into memory.

3 WILLIAMSBURGH SAVINGS BANK
175 Broadway, northwest corner of Driggs Avenue
1870–75, George B. Post
Addition: 1905, Helmle, Huberty & Hudswell
Addition: 1925, Helmle & Huberty

This may be one of the most important buildings in New York architecture. Few buildings of its time point forward with greater confidence to the coming City Beautiful. George B. Post learned a great deal at the knee of Richard Morris Hunt. The noted critic Russell Sturgis said in 1898 that Post's Long Island

Historical Society in Brooklyn Heights was an important step in the revival of Classicism. That use of the word Classicism is rather imprecise, of course. After all, the Federal of the 1820s, the Greek Revival of the 1830s and 1840s, the Italianate of the 1850s, and the Second Empire of the 1860s were all Classical. New York's architecture has almost always been Classical. Exceptions are the Gothic Revivals of the nineteenth century and the Romanesque and much of the Queen Anne of the 1870s and 1880s. Ninety percent, until after World War II, was Classical in one way or another. Our vernacular traditions, from Georgian to Italianate row houses, are Classical. What Sturgis was getting at, of course, was not Classicism per se, but the City Beautiful Classicism, often marked by monumental forms, that flowered in the 1890s through the 1920s, and that was often produced by architects trained at the École des Beaux-Arts in Paris. In any event, the Long Island Historical Society was built in 1878–81. It is not nearly so full an example of the nascent City Beautiful tendency as this work by Post from a few years earlier. While the Long Island Historical Society is built out of basically Classical forms, its dark palette lends to it the somber, brooding quality

3 *Williamsburgh Savings Bank*

that we associate with Queen Anne. Here, however, a few years earlier, Post engages a light-colored palette of limestone and marble. Also, rather than the essentially boxlike form of the Long Island Historical Society, here we have the kind of complex articulation of building parts that was a hallmark of the later Beaux-Arts style in monumental buildings. Post's portico here, for example, projects to enclose a fine arched entranceway, with the portico topped by a triangular pediment (that might have benefited from sculpture). The attic of the building rises behind and to the sides of the portico pediment, tracing the contours of the projecting block that contains the portico, though cut away to either side of the pediment to leave a shelf at the angle of the portico block. There is thus much play of projecting and receding blocks, making for a very lively, plastic composition. The attic in turn serves as a stage from which rises the building's hallmark, its high, massive Classical dome—one of the most prominent domes in New York City—surmounted by a lantern and weathervane. To the left of the entrance block is a recessed wall featuring a large arched window with circular medallions in its spandrels. This is almost identical to the window treatment of the second floor of the Pierrepont Street façade of the Long Island Historical Society. Actually, this wall was added later by Helmle & Huberty but was replicated from a wall designed by Post on the west side of the building. The additions by Helmle & Huberty actually improved the building. Post, for all the new things he was doing here, created a building that in its original state may have been too compact—it needed to stretch a bit. Also, Post employed the same sort of low-relief, boxy pilasters that he later employed on the Long Island Historical Society, and here, as there, they unfortunately lend a somewhat crabbed quality to the façades, which otherwise are so stately. Flanking the front entrance are ornate bronze lamp standards featuring gryphons. Gryphons also appear in the decoration at York & Sawyer's Brooklyn Trust Company (1915) on Montague Street and at McKenzie, Voorhees & Gmelin's South Brooklyn Savings Institution (1923) in Cobble Hill. Overall, the Williamsburgh Savings Bank building is an imaginative adaptation of largely Palladian prototypes.

The interior is as interesting as the exterior. Peter B. Wight, architect of the Mercantile Library (1865–68) on Montague Street, designed the interior ornament. The main banking room is the rotunda of the dome, and the 100-foot height of the space is truly dazzling. Surprisingly, much is intact here from the building's original appearance. In the dome are small etched-glass panels featuring a superimposed W, S, and B. Note the six-pointed stars in the dome decoration. Note also that there is no figurative imagery in the decoration.

Both these things are part of the original design. It is remarkable that many years later a large number of those using this bank were members of Williamsburg's Hasidic Jewish population. That lack of figurative imagery, by the way, detracts from the artistic value of this otherwise magnificent interior, which cries out for mural painting, particularly in the pendentives.

This was the Williamsburgh's third headquarters (the bank was founded in the independent City of Williamsburgh in 1851), and remained the headquarters until Halsey, McCormack & Helmer's magisterial skyscraper was completed in 1929.

4 WILLIAMSBURG TRUST COMPANY
117–185 South 5th Street, northwest corner of New Street
1906, Helmle & Huberty

Very much in the vein of the same architects' Greenpoint Savings Bank of two years later, this is an extraordinarily refined work of neighborhood bank architecture. Tetrastyle porticoes with triangular pediments and marble Ionic

4 Williamsburg Trust Company

columns face both south, across South 5th Street, and east, toward Continental Army Plaza. The building is faced, except for the marble columns, in glazed white terra-cotta. This was two years after Helmle & Huberty similarly used terra-cotta for the facing of their Boathouse in Prospect Park. The glazed coating of the antefixae of the fine saucer dome, set on a heavily crested octagonal drum, and of the balustrades atop the wings flanking the porticoes, etched against the sky, glisten in the sun. On the south and east façades are beautiful terra-cotta panels showing a woman holding scales, surrounded by cornucopias and fasces. I'm not sure whether she's supposed to be justice or a symbol of balancing one's checkbook, but the other symbols are for abundance and authority. Terra-cotta lions' heads appear on the fully designed west and north façades of the building, which, though they are hemmed in by other construction, are still visible with a little effort. It is rare to find a neighborhood bank designed fully in the round like this, without a single party wall. Williamsburg, though, is such a physical hodgepodge that all kinds of unusual things can be seen here.

The building is now the Holy Trinity Cathedral Orthodox Church.

The Williamsburg Trust Company fronts on an amorphous public open space called Continental Army Plaza. From here, the panorama is both breathtaking and bewildering, and I know nothing else quite like it. The Williamsburg Bridge and its access roads foul the air with the fumes of thousands of automobiles at any given moment, and, with the elevated railway that comes across the bridge and continues east on Broadway, create an almost constant, ear-splitting, heavily metallic cacophony. The tangle of streets and sidewalks is confusing and forbidding. At the same time there is an undeniable majesty to the terrible steel forms thrown across the sky, like a giant steel lizard come to devour Brooklyn. (One recalls Henry James's characterization, in *The Bostonians,* of the Third Avenue el as an "antediluvian monster." The description is far more apt here.) Driving or walking south on Driggs Avenue from Greenpoint, one sees the magnificent dome of the Williamsburgh Savings Bank through the latticed steel framework of the bridge, and there is no sight like it anywhere else in New York. Another thing startles here, and that is the fact that it should have been Rome. The Williamsburg Trust Company, the dome of the Williamsburgh Savings Bank, Shrady's equestrian statue of George Washington—it is given to so few places, not only in New York but in the world, to have individual elements of such beauty in their midst, yet here these elements, so worth seeking out, are buried in steel, soot, chaos, and clangor.

5 *Equestrian Statue of*
  George Washington

5 EQUESTRIAN STATUE OF GEORGE WASHINGTON

In *Washington Plaza, bounded by Broadway, and New, South 4th,*
and Havemeyer Streets
1901–6, Henry Merwin Shrady

New York City is blessed with two bronze equestrian statues of George
Washington, both undisputed masterpieces. The first was Henry Kirke Brown's
(which he worked on in his Brooklyn studio, assisted by J. Q. A. Ward), dedicated in 1856 in Manhattan's Union Square. The second is here, in Continental
Army Plaza, with the Williamsburg Bridge automobile traffic and the elevated
railway roaring by overhead. There may be no more poignant image of
Washington than this statue, showing him as he might have appeared at Valley
Forge in the winter of 1777–78: cold and weary. Washington sits wrapped in a
blanket. His steed, head deeply bowed, is just as weary. This statue, in which the
horse is modeled miraculously well, rivals any image of war's destitution. Placed
more prominently in the city, it would be as famous a statue as New York could

boast. Placed in Continental Army Plaza, it is known only to a few. It shows also how in the right hands a traditional statue can tell us so much more about war and valor than an abstract work such as Maya Lin's Vietnam Veterans Memorial. The sculptor was Henry Merwin Shrady (1871–1922), about whom less is known than many of his contemporaries. He was born in New York City and trained as a lawyer. He attended no school to learn sculpture, but did receive training from the great Karl Bitter. Shrady won a 1901 competition for the statue's design, and it was his first major public work. He is best known for his impressive General Grant Memorial in Washington, D.C. In a much grander setting, the Grant memorial possesses much the same qualities of naturalism and psychological penetration as the Washington statue. Shrady is said to have received that important commission on the strength of his work in Williamsburg. The Grant memorial consumed Shrady's career, taking him twenty-one years to complete, exhausting him totally. He died two weeks before it was dedicated in 1922. Brooklyn architects Austin Lord and J. Monroe Hewlett designed the granite base of the statue here. Where in the 1850s Henry Kirke Brown's bronze equestrian Washington was famous for being only the second public sculpture cast in an American foundry (the Ames Foundry of Chicopee, Massachusetts), fifty years later not only was it common, but Shrady's Washington was cast right here in Brooklyn (at the Roman Bronze Works).

6 WILLIAMSBURG BRIDGE
Connects Broadway in Brooklyn to Delancey Street in Manhattan
1896–1903, Leffert Lefferts Buck, chief engineer

Twenty years after the Brooklyn Bridge opened, the Williamsburg was the second suspension bridge to span the East River. (The Manhattan and the Queensboro Bridges both opened six years after the Williamsburg.) With a maximum span of 1,600 feet, the Williamsburg was the longest suspension bridge in the world, eclipsing the Brooklyn Bridge by 130 feet. (The Verrazano-Narrows Bridge, the world's longest suspension bridge today, has a maximum span of 4,230 feet.) The Williamsburg is part of the ensemble of bridges spanning the East and Hudson Rivers, one of the most exciting sights New York offers to the world, particularly when viewed from an airplane or high up in a skyscraper. That said, I don't think anyone would disagree when I say that the Williamsburg is aesthetically far the least felicitous of the East River spans. Its designer, who had the très Brooklyn name of Leffert Lefferts Buck, had been an assistant to the Roeblings on the Brooklyn Bridge. As the architect Gregory F. Gilmartin has stated, "None of the Roeblings' aesthetic sense had rubbed off on Buck, however." Buck was well connected to the Tammany administration of Mayor Robert Van Wyck, on whose watch Buck was hired to design not only the Williamsburg but the Manhattan and Queensboro Bridges as well. John De Witt Warner, a leader of the Municipal Art Society, said that Buck's designs were a "surrender of the City Beautiful to the City Vulgar." In 1902, a new clause in the city charter granted the city's Art Commission veto power over any municipal project exceeding one million dollars in cost, which of course included the new bridges. Unfortunately, this was too late to stop Buck's design for the Williamsburg Bridge from going through, though it did stop his designs for the other two bridges, which would become among the loveliest bridges in the world. Leffert Buck had headed Mayor Van Wyck's Bridge Department. When Brooklyn's Seth Low became New York City's reform mayor, he dumped Buck and hired Gustav Lindenthal. At the same time, the gifted architect Henry Hornbostel was brought in as a consultant to the Bridge Department. Hornbostel's first job was to provide some decorative relief to Buck's design for the Williamsburg Bridge. It was, however, a self-defeating proposition, given what the architectural critic Montgomery Schuyler in 1909 called the Williamsburg Bridge's "uncouth and bandy-legged aspect which no cleverness in detail could redeem." The Williamsburg Bridge was designed to carry pedestrians, horse-drawn vehicles, trolleys, and elevated trains. Today it carries pedestrians, automobiles, and elevated trains.

One reads and hears much these days about how Williamsburg has become one of the hottest neighborhoods in New York. The *Utne Reader* ranked it the third "hippest" neighborhood in America (after the Garden District of New Orleans and the Mission District of San Francisco). What happened is that as far back as the late 1970s, artists who were priced out of SoHo and TriBeCa began their long march into Brooklyn, settling principally in two areas, Williamsburg and DUMBO (an acronym for "Down Under the Manhattan Bridge Overpass"). Williamsburg was still rather fringey for several years until it exploded in the 1990s. The fashionable part of Williamsburg is what is called Northside. The dividing line between Northside and Southside is Grand Avenue, six blocks north of the intersection of Broadway and Bedford Avenue, where most of Williamsburg's noteworthy architecture is located. Farther south, particularly around Division Avenue, four blocks south of the intersection of Broadway and Bedford Avenue, is the Hasidic Jewish part of Williamsburg, a true world unto itself. Both Hasidic and artistic Williamsburg are in the western part of the district. (I call Williamsburg a "district" rather than a "neighborhood" because, once an independent city, it comprises several distinct neighborhoods, including Northside and Southside.) To the east, Williamsburg is heavily Hispanic. As one walks or drives north on Bedford Avenue, the otherworldly atmosphere of the Williamsburg Bridge area yields to something very different, to cafés and restaurants and bookstores, as one enters fashionable Northside. People who know Bedford Avenue from days of yore still can't quite get over its chic transformation. The closest thing I can think of when it comes to the sheer unexpectedness of it all is Philadelphia's Main Street in Manayunk a few years ago. Yet in that old riverside industrial precinct, big investors (including a former mayor of Philadelphia) were involved from the start in the gentrification. Bedford Avenue, by contrast, still retains a very "indie" feeling, and its denizens wish fiercely to keep it that way. Nonetheless, the restaurants and bars of Northside have become a citywide destination; it may be the first time since the heyday of Brooklyn Heights roof gardens that it has been trendy for Manhattanites to cross the river for nightlife.

HECLA ARCHITECTURAL IRON WORKS

Niels Poulson, the principal founder of Hecla Architectural Iron Works, was born in Denmark in 1843. He apprenticed as a stonemason, entered upon his journeyman years, and, in 1864, at the age of twenty-one, immigrated to America. Many European stonemasons, who had been through the traditional apprenticeship and journeyman years en route to master status, found it rough going in the New World. The reason was that they were too meticulous in their craft, where in America speed of construction was of the essence. Masons such as Poulson could not keep up. Poulson decided to pursue a career as an architect. He could draw, and his knowledge of construction was such that his background suited him for the profession. He took a job as a draftsman in the Office of the Supervising Architect of the United States Treasury in Washington, D.C. While employed there, he became aware of the possibilities of the newfangled iron construction. Smitten with the possibilities of iron, Poulson went to work in New York City for Daniel Badger's Architectural Iron Works, located on the East

River between 13th and 14th Streets. Soon he was in charge of the architectural and engineering department.

Architectural Iron Works, noteworthy for its pioneer work in the construction of cast-iron façades (for example, the Haughwout Store at Broadway and Broome Street in the neighborhood that would later be called SoHo), went out of business in 1876. Poulson then started his own firm with one of his Badger coworkers, a Norwegian-born mason named Charles Michael Eger, whose background was very similar to Poulson's. They called their company Poulson & Eger's Architectural Iron Works, later renaming it Hecla Architectural Iron Works, after a volcano in Iceland. (Perhaps they saw the volcanic heat and lava as symbols for the forging and melting involved in the production of wrought-iron and cast-iron.) Poulson and Eger established Hecla in Williamsburg, near the water between North 10th and North 11th Streets (later extended to North 12th Street) and Wythe and Berry Streets—in the heart of today's fashionable Northside. They set up their showroom in Manhattan on West 23rd Street. At its height, the works would employ one thousand workers. Poulson and Eger created an evening school for training ironworkers and are credited with raising the standard of iron construction in America. These meticulously trained Scandinavian masons, who entered the iron field out of frustration with the lack of careful craftsmanship in masonry construction in America, would get their own back, as it were, by bringing to the new medium of iron as much of a sense of Old World standards as possible under the circumstances.

Hecla produced all manner of ornamental ironwork, and examples abound in the city today. The iron fence surrounding the Dakota apartments on Central Park West—it's a Hecla. The entrance to the St. Regis Hotel on Fifth Avenue and 55th Street, the Temple Bar Building on Brooklyn's Court Street, the original cast-iron entrance kiosks for the Interborough Rapid Transit Company subway stations—all are by Hecla. The iron dome and stair of the old B. Altman & Company department store on Sixth Avenue and 18th Street: Hecla. (This magnificent dome, which is no longer, is illustrated on page 107 of Margot Gayle's indispensable 1974 book *Cast-Iron Architecture in New York*.) The iron

canopies and much else of the new B. Altman store on Fifth
Avenue and 34th Street: Hecla. (Hecla's promotional materials
extolled the company's patented "duplex electro-plate finish" that
made iron look like bronze, "while the cost is considerably less."
Poulson seemed to regard the Altman store as one big advertise-
ment for Hecla.) Lullwater Bridge (1890) in Prospect Park—it's
Hecla, too. Some of Hecla's best work was done for one of New
York's greatest buildings, Grand Central Terminal. From the train
gates to the stair railings, from convector grilles to elevator doors,
from window frames to the famous clock atop the information
booth in the Main Concourse, Hecla produced the bulk of the
bronze- and ironwork of the great building. Alas, its formal opening came two years after Niels Poulson's death.

Poulson designed and built his family's home on Shore Road
and 86th Street in Bay Ridge in 1890. It was famous as the "Copper
House." It is believed to have been the first steel-framed private
house in America, and was sheathed entirely in copper. The house
garnered enormous publicity for its novelty and for the excellence
of its construction, but none of that helped it from being demolished in 1930. Poulson died in 1911 at the age of sixty-eight in his
Brooklyn home. His company hung on until just after World War I,
by which time the great age of ornamental iron had come and gone.

At North 12th Street, one comes to McCarren Park, a thirty-six-acre
recreational park that marks the division between Williamsburg and
Greenpoint. McCarren Park—named for Patrick McCarren, a nineteenth-century Irish immigrant, state legislator of dubious distinction, and promoter of the
Williamsburg Bridge—was originally developed as a city park between 1903 and
1905, though substantially altered in the 1910s and again in the 1930s. This is
no Olmsted and Vaux greensward, intended for contemplation and communion
with nature. From the start McCarren Park has been for active recreation, with
playgrounds, ballfields, running tracks, tennis courts, and such. In 1936, a distinctive swimming pool with a capacity of more than six thousand swimmers
was constructed as a Works Progress Administration project. Aymar Embury II,
whose work can be seen at the Prospect Park Zoo and in the Charles Neergaard
house on Eighth Avenue and 3rd Street in Park Slope, designed the pool, the

structure of which is still quite prominent, though the pool was decommissioned in 1984. Three roads pass right through McCarren Park: Bedford and Driggs Avenues and Lorimer Street. Bedford Avenue, one of the great thoroughfares passing through almost the whole of Brooklyn, begins just on the other side of McCarren Park, near the intersection of Manhattan and Nassau Avenues, the two main shopping streets of Greenpoint. Across the street from the southern border of McCarren Park at North 12th Street, a stone's throw from the hippest part of Williamsburg, is the unexpected sight of a set of onion domes.

7 RUSSIAN ORTHODOX CATHEDRAL OF THE TRANSFIGURATION

228 North 12th Street, southeast corner of Driggs Avenue
1916–21, Louis Allmendinger

Though the form of this church is a Greek cross, as one would expect from a Russian Orthodox congregation, still the one building in Brooklyn this most reminds one of is George B. Post's Williamsburgh Savings Bank in the south part of Williamsburg on Broadway and Driggs Avenue. Each of the four

7 Russian Orthodox Cathedral
of the Transfiguration

arms of the cross is gabled and has a façade featuring a large arched window. Atop the four corners between the arms of the cross rise cupolas topped by copper onion domes and gilded crosses. From the center rises a large, bulbous copper onion dome topped also by a gilded cross. The composition is actually fairly simple. There are some decorative moldings but nothing fancy. The copper domes are a very striking skyline element in these parts. There is not the complexity of Post's building, but the basic form, compact, arched, domed, seems very similar.

The architect, Louis Allmendinger, would later wholeheartedly embrace the modernism of Le Corbusier.

Greenpoint

Greenpoint is bounded on the north and east by Newtown Creek, on the south by the Brooklyn-Queens Expressway and North 7th Street, and on the west by the East River. Williamsburg's "Northside" shades imperceptibly into what has long been recognized as the southern boundary of Greenpoint, though these days people generally regard Northside as extending north to McCarren Park, and Greenpoint really beginning around North 12th Street, at the southern border of the park, which also happens to be around the point where Kent Avenue becomes Franklin Street. In any event, Greenpoint shares a good deal of its history with Williamsburg. Once, Williamsburg, Greenpoint, and Bushwick were called the "Eastern District" of Brooklyn. Heavy industrialization of the East River and Newtown Creek waterfronts began to take place in the 1840s and 1850s. The Eastern District is where Brooklyn's major industrial enterprises were located, including ironworks, sugar refineries, breweries, glassworks, porcelain works, printing houses, pharmaceutical plants, shipyards, and so on. Not least among these industries were oil refineries, of which the most famous was Charles Pratt's Astral Oil Works from 1874, part of Standard Oil. Not to be forgotten either are Eberhard Faber No. 2 pencils, manufactured in Greenpoint. At one time, it is said, the three miles of Newtown Creek carried more traffic than the three thousand miles of the Mississippi River. Greenpoint, so isolated within New York City, long reached out to the world with its industrial wares. The area's shipyards suggested such lovely names for the neighborhood's streets as Java and India. John Ericsson's *Monitor* was built in 1862 at the Continental Iron Works that stood on West and Calyer Streets. Until the 1880s Greenpoint was mostly

English and Irish. In the late-nineteenth century, significant numbers of Italians, Russians, and Poles moved in. Since World War II, Greenpoint has become more and more Polish. On the "high street," Manhattan Avenue, many of the store signs are in Polish, and many of the people converse in Polish. The spiritual home of the Greenpoint Polish is St. Stanislaus Kostka Roman Catholic Church on the southwest corner of Humboldt Street and Driggs Avenue, near Monsignor McGolrick Park. Pope John Paul II visited this church, which was built around 1890. There is a very special quality to the streets of Greenpoint. Historically this has been an industrial area, and perhaps it is because of the industrial noisomeness that the inhabitants of residential Greenpoint have long been noted for keeping their streets so clean and orderly. Waterfront industry has declined, but residential Greenpoint remains an island surrounded by what the *New York Times* calls the "yawning, trash-strewn decrepitude along parts of the East River and Newtown Creek waterfront." Parts of Greenpoint seem a kind of working-class Utopia because of their safety, cleanliness, architectural quality, and liveliness. Maybe that's ladling it on too thick. Still, neighborhoods like Greenpoint are a sine qua non of great cities. In 1982, the New York City Landmarks Preservation Commission designated a Greenpoint Historic District, bounded irregularly by Kent Street on the north, Franklin Street on the west, Calyer Street on the south, and Manhattan Avenue on the east. Everything in the following is within this district, with the exception of the Astral Apartments, which are just outside the district and designated as an individual landmark.

8 GREENPOINT SAVINGS BANK
807 Manhattan Avenue, southwest corner of Calyer Street
1908, Helmle & Huberty

The Greenpoint Savings Bank meets busy, pleasant Manhattan Avenue with four imposing Doric columns, an entablature of triglyphs and metopes, and a broad triangular pediment. From a little farther away, one sees that a splendid saucer dome surmounts the limestone building. Imposing and handsome as it may be on the outside, inside it is extremely fine. One is immediately put in mind of George B. Post's Williamsburgh Saving Bank (1870–75) on Broadway, by the manner in which the main banking room is in the rotunda under a beautiful dome, here of Guastavino structural tile embellished with stained glass. The columns and pilasters are of a lovely aquamarine marble,

8 *Greenpoint Savings Bank*

topped by florid gilded Corinthian capitals. Pilasters separate the windows on the north side. On the south side where the party wall prohibits windows, large mirrors are set between the pilasters, a wonderful effect. This is another of Helmle & Huberty's consummately competent contributions to making Brooklyn the City Beautiful, built two years after their Williamsburg Trust Company on South 5th Street and two years before their Winthrop Park Shelter Pavilion, as they were truly hitting their stride. Greenpoint Savings Bank was founded in 1868. This, the bank's fourth home, opened on November 12, 1908.

9 ST. ANTHONY OF PADUA CHURCH (R.C.)
*862 Manhattan Avenue between Greenpoint Avenue
and Calyer Street, east side opposite Milton Street
1874, P. C. Keely*

This is one of the most dramatically sited churches in New York, superbly commanding the terminal axis of Milton Street at Manhattan Avenue in the heart of Greenpoint. The façade features three entrances,

9 *St. Anthony of Padua Church*

one in each of two gabled wings and one in the center section that they flank. A single, 240-foot-high frontal tower rises to a clock set in a gabled enframement of colorful tilework. The church is faced in Philadelphia pressed brick with extensive white-painted stone trim for a heavily frosted look. Size, color, and height combine for a majestic presence. One of the many joys of living on Milton Street has to be the simple act of leaving the house in the morning, turning east toward Manhattan Avenue, and being greeted by this church. It is sited at a bend in Manhattan Avenue, so although the Milton Street perspective is the more dramatic, the church is also delightfully visible all up and down the "high street," chock-a-block with Polish bakeries and food shops and even Chopin Chemists. It is also fitting that there should be a major church right in the middle of the busiest shopping street of a neighborhood that takes great pride in its houses of worship. The church, which was the congregation's second home, was dedicated June 10, 1874, almost six years after the cornerstone was laid for Keely's ill-fated Cathedral of the Immaculate Conception in Fort Greene. St. Anthony of Padua is one of the best of Keely's five hundred or so church designs.

10 *St. John's Evangelical Lutheran Church*

10 MILTON STREET
Between Manhattan Avenue and Franklin Street

I think Milton Street is one of the most charming streets in all New York. The diversity is beguiling. Styles, scales, setbacks from lot lines, ages of buildings, and kinds of housing all vary enormously in a block that is perhaps a tad too long. Still, a street that terminates in one end at St. Anthony of Padua Church and at the other end at the Greenpoint Terminal Warehouse has got to be good. This street is very, very good, one of the most pleasant and urbane residential streets I know. This one block has housing dating from 1853 to 1909, a stretch of time that saw dramatic changes in Brooklyn architecture. Nonetheless, as if by some kind of urban magic, everything here coheres splendidly, and nothing at all looks like it doesn't belong.

If one approaches from south on Manhattan Avenue and takes a left onto Milton Street, one notices almost immediately the church on the north side of the street. Reminding us that Greenpoint has not always been only

Polish, one reads, inscribed over the entrance, "Evangelische-Lutherische St. Johannes Kirche." This is **St. John's Evangelical Lutheran Church** (10a), designed by Theobald Engelhardt and built in 1891–92. Its Gothic style is rendered in painted red brick. A single tower on the right is balanced on the left by a flying buttress, executed in brownstone. Engelhardt was a prominent Brooklyn architect in the nineteenth century. Among his works was the Bushwick Avenue mansion of hotelier Louis Bossert. He also designed the nearby (worth the detour) Greenpoint Home for the Aged at 137 Oak Street, built in 1886–87 and nicely sited opposite Guernsey Street at a spot with a Commerce Street–like bend.

Across the street is the Greenpoint Reformed Church. If one thinks this looks like it might have once been a house, one is right. The Queen of Milton Street, it might be called. For this was the home of Thomas C. Smith (1815–1900), who designed it himself, as he designed many houses on this street. Smith was the owner of one of Greenpoint's most famous manufacturing firms, the Union Porcelain Works, and a major landowner in the area. His house was built in 1866–67. Smith purchased a good deal of the land on which the houses of Milton Street stand from Samuel J. Tilden, onetime governor of New York and unsuccessful presidential candidate. Tilden had extensive holdings in this area. The house is two stories and freestanding. Its Italianate form is simple, with a projecting center section featuring a Tuscan-columned porch topped by a triangular pediment. The house has been the home of the Greenpoint Reformed Church since 1944, before which the house served as the Greenpoint Branch of the YMCA. Smith moved to New York City from Bridgehampton, Long Island, at the age of sixteen and trained as a builder and architect. He worked successfully in this trade until 1863, when he took an extended vacation in Europe due to ill health. By this time he had acquired a failing porcelain works on Eckford Street in Greenpoint called the Union Porcelain Works. While in Europe he toured the great porcelain works of Sèvres in France and of Staffordshire in England. Upon his return to America, Smith built his house on Milton Street and set about transforming his porcelain works based on what he had learned in Europe. The result was his creation of the first successful hard porcelain manufactory in the United States. In 1874, determined that his decorated wares rank with the best in the world, Smith hired the sculptor Karl Müller (1820?–1887) to design pieces for the firm. Union Porcelain's wares, particularly those designed by Mülller, are much coveted by collectors and are exhibited in a number of museums. The Brooklyn

Museum has a Century Vase that Mülller designed for the Centennial Exposition of 1876 in Philadelphia. After Thomas C. Smith died, his son, C. H. L. Smith, ran the firm, which went out of business in the 1920s following the son's death.

Thomas C. Smith owned more than six hundred feet along the north side of the street between No. 117 on the west and No. 151, the last house before St. John's Evangelical Lutheran Church. All the houses in this stretch are set back twenty-four feet from the lot line, creating a long row of deep, Carroll Gardens–like front yards, some of them quite lushly planted. Smith built (and presumably designed) the eleven houses from Nos. 117 to 137 between 1874 and 1878. He employed Italianate, neo-Grec, and French Second Empire styles for the houses. He built the seven houses from Nos. 139 to 151 in 1894. These picturesque three-story houses use Roman brick at the first floor with Philadelphia pressed brick at the upper floors. Some of the houses have three-sided oriels rising through the second and third floors, and some have second-floor oriels with arched loggias at the third floor. No. 151 has a projecting two-story entrance bay with a covered third-floor balcony. On the other side of the church are three four-story apartment houses built between 1904 and 1909. Of Classical design, they have rusticated limestone first floors and brick upper floors. Above the entrances are limestone balconies carried on large console brackets.

On the south side of the street at Nos. 122 and 124 is a fine four-story Queen Anne double house of red brick, brownstone, and terra-cotta, built in 1889 and designed, like St. John's Evangelical Lutheran Church, by Theobald Engelhardt. Nos. 128 to 134 and 140 to 144 were built in 1909 and designed by the man who has my favorite name of all Brooklyn architects, Philemon Tillion, a local architect with an office on Manhattan Avenue. Nos. 128 to 134 are three four-story apartment houses of Classical design with rusticated rock-faced limestone first floors and brick upper floors. (There is no No. 132 in the street numbering system.) Nos. 128 and 130 were built in 1907 and No. 134 was built in 1909. The Thomas C. Smith house is adjacent to this group to the east. (Smith, for all of Milton Street that he owned, apparently did not own the lots on either side of his own house.) Nos. 140 to 144 are three Classical row houses built in 1909. They are lovely red brick houses with unusual covered porches supported by slender Corinthian columns. Note also their fine arched doorways and fine dentilated and modillioned cornices. Farther west, I like Nos. 110 to 114, three three-story brick row houses in the neo-Grec style, designed by a local architect named Frederick Weber. They were built in 1876, the year that Thomas C. Smith and Karl Mülller were reaping accolades at the Centennial Exposition.

Milton Street's ubiquitous red brick, limestone, terra-cotta, surprising details, and deep-front gardens, all help give the street its cheerful air, so different from the often dour quality of Brooklyn brownstone streets. Brooklyn Heights may have a street named after Sir Philip Sidney. Greenpoint's Milton Street, alas, is not named for the poet but rather, it is believed, for a local sailmaker.

11 ST. ELIAS GREEK RITE ROMAN CATHOLIC CHURCH COMPLEX (formerly Reformed Dutch Church of Greenpoint)

149 Kent Street between Manhattan Avenue and Franklin Street,
  north side
1869–70, William B. Ditmars
Sunday school: 1879, W. Wheeler Smith

The Reformed Dutch Church of Greenpoint was founded in 1848. Its church on Kent Street was dedicated January 30, 1870. They remained in this building until 1943, when they sold it to the St. Elias Greek Rite Roman Catholic Church, and moved to the former Thomas C. Smith house on Milton Street. The façade on Kent Street is quite simple, with a gabled center section containing a projecting gabled entrance above which is a rose window. This section is flanked by projecting square towers of identical design, each with an entrance in its base. An octagonal drum, once surmounted by a sloping octagonal roof, tops the right tower. A mansard roof once topped the left tower, which was always much shorter than the right tower. Though the church has a picturesque profile, it was once more accentuated. The arches are round and there is corbeling. This is one of the Romanesque Revival progeny of Richard Upjohn's Church of the Pilgrims in Brooklyn Heights. As with Henry Dudley's Church of the Ascension down the block, however, William Ditmars introduced "High Victorian" elements, including light stone voussoirs and window surrounds that contrast with the brick, the principal material of the façade. The architect William B. Ditmars is sometimes confused with Isaac Ditmars, who was William Schickel's partner. Apparently little is known about William Ditmars other than that he was an active architect in Brooklyn. He designed the "Ruskinian" Temple Beth Elohim (1876) on Keap Street between Marcy and Division Avenues in Williamsburg. Ditmars collaborated with John

11 *Reformed Dutch Church of Greenpoint*

Mumford on the design of the French Second Empire–style Brooklyn Municipal Building (1876–78) that preceded the present one on Joralemon Street.

Connected to the church on the right is the fine two-story Sunday school by W. Wheeler Smith. It has a three-sided front with round-arched windows. Smith's inspiration was clearly the twelfth-century baptistery at Cremona, Italy. W. Wheeler Smith was a prominent and versatile New York architect around this time. He designed the very prestigious W. & J. Sloane carpet store (1881–82) on Broadway and 19th Street as well as the William J. Syms Operating Theater of Roosevelt Hospital (1890–92) on Ninth Avenue and 59th Street.

12 CHURCH OF THE ASCENSION (Episcopal)
129 Kent Street between Manhattan Avenue and Franklin Street, north side
1865–66, Henry Dudley

This is perhaps more special for who did it than for what it is. Henry Dudley came to America in 1851 from Exeter, not far from where Richard Upjohn was born in the southwestern part of England. Dudley became the partner of Frank Wills, also from Exeter. Together and individually, Dudley and Wills were major figures in the Gothic Revival in America. Wills was recognized as the leader of the New York Ecclesiological Society, founded in 1848 to promote the architectural aims of the Episcopal High Church movement in America. In 1852, the society published its first list of approved architects. Only five names appeared on the list. Wills's was one of them, of course, and so was Dudley's. The others were Richard Upjohn (whose best Brooklyn design along Ecclesiological lines was Grace Church in Brooklyn Heights), John W. Priest, and Philadelphia's John Notman. Of the five, only Priest was American born. Wills, Dudley, and Upjohn were all from southwestern England, and Notman was from Scotland. The Church of the Ascension is significant as one of the four surviving churches designed by Dudley in New York City. It is a small and very simple church in the Early English Gothic style, on a tight, mid-block site. The congregation was founded in 1846. Its church on Kent Street was dedicated September 16, 1866. It is built of rock-faced Hunter's Point granite laid in random ashlar. There are pointed-arch aisle entrances, Early English lancets, stepped buttresses—it really is a study in simplicity. At the

12 *Church of the Ascension*

doors and around the lancets is restrained polychrome banding, perhaps indicating the influence that Ruskin was beginning to have on some who were involved in the Ecclesiological movement. Dudley is particularly renowned for his work in Nashville, Tennessee. In New York he designed St. George's Episcopal Church (1852–54), with Frank Wills, on Main Street in Flushing; St. Mary's Episcopal Church (1853), with Wills, on Castleton and Davis Avenues in the Livingston section of Staten Island (not far from Sailors' Snug Harbor); and St. James Episcopal Church (1864–65) on Jerome Avenue and 190th Street in the Bronx.

13 ASTRAL APARTMENTS
184 Franklin Street between Java and India Streets, east side
1885–86, Lamb & Rich and Ebenezer L. Roberts

A few years after Alfred Tredway White built his model tenements, the Tower and Home buildings, in what is now called Cobble Hill, Charles Pratt, the richest man in Brooklyn, followed suit with this enormous building erected for workers in his nearby Astral Oil Works. In some respects, Pratt went White one better: he hired a more fashionable firm of architects. Above all, he put

13 *Astral Apartments*

bathtubs in the apartments themselves, rather than, as White had done, in communal facilities in the basement. At the Astral, the basement contained a large lecture hall. The apartments included toilets and hot- and cold-running water, and in the hallways were dumbwaiters to facilitate trash removal. Otherwise, the Astral Apartments has much the same presence as White's buildings. Built to house ninety-five families, it occupies a full block, and rises to six stories. Monotony is avoided in its main Franklin Street façade by the projecting three-sided bays at the ends and by the projecting central bay topped by a stepped gable, by the bold arched entrance openings along the street level, and above all, by the manner in which that central bay is defined by a deeply recessed arch rising from the second through the fifth stories. There is also some fine terra-cotta ornament. The stores at the building's corners were originally organized on a cooperative basis as a means of keeping rents low. The building wrapped around a large rear courtyard that ensured light and air to all the apartments. The style has been termed "Queen Anne," and it is pretty clear that Lamb & Rich were familiar with such recent works of Richard Norman Shaw as his Albert Hall Mansions (1879) in London.

Charles Pratt spent a good deal of time traveling through Europe looking at examples of trade schools and of workers' housing before formulating his own plans for the Astral Apartments and for Pratt Institute. In London the housing established by the philanthropic Peabody Trust apparently impressed him. Several examples of this housing can still be seen in that city. (Examples include buildings on Greenman Street in Islington, built in 1865, and ones around Whitecross and Dufferin Streets in Shoreditch, built in 1870.) It is interesting to note that commentators on London architecture tend to deplore the Peabody buildings, where commentators on New York architecture tend to praise works such as the Astral Apartments and the Tower and Home buildings. (The Peabody Trust was established in London in 1864 "to ameliorate the condition of the poor and needy of this great metropolis and to promote their comfort and happiness." The word invariably applied to the architecture of the Peabody estates is "grim.")

Charles Pratt engaged Hugh Lamb (1848–1903) and Charles Alonzo Rich (1855–1943) to design the Main Building of Pratt Institute at the very same time they were working on the Astral Apartments. A few years later, Lamb & Rich designed the superb George Tangeman house in Park Slope. They were known above all as designers of buildings for college campuses. The original buildings on the Barnard College campus in Morningside Heights were built from the 1890s through the 1920s to the designs of Lamb & Rich. In addition, they designed buildings for Dartmouth, Smith, Williams, and Amherst Colleges and Colgate University.

14 MONSIGNOR McGOLRICK PARK (formerly Winthrop Park)

Bounded by Driggs and Nassau Avenues and Russell and Monitor Streets

This park of just fewer than ten acres was laid out in the 1890s and named for a local assemblyman who helped obtain city funds to purchase the site. It was later renamed for a well-known local Roman Catholic pastor. In 1910, Helmle & Huberty's lovely shelter pavilion was added. The curved and colonnaded *pavillon* recalls the structures designed for French formal gardens of the eighteenth century. The park also contains a winged victory World War I memorial from 1923 by Carl Augustus Heber (1874–1956). Heber was the sculptor of the fantastic allegorical groups, *Spirit of Commerce* and *Spirit of Industry,* on the Manhattan piers of the Manhattan Bridge—one can see that he liked wings—and of the figure of Virgil on the west attic of the Brooklyn Museum.

14 *Monsignor McGolrick Park Shelter Pavilion*

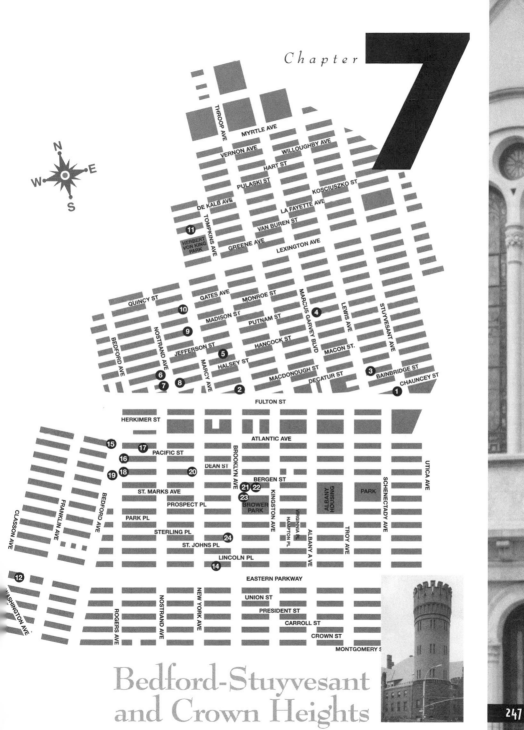

N
W • E
S

MYRTLE AVE
THROOP AVE
VERNON AVE
WILLOUGHBY AVE
HART ST
PULASKI ST
KOSCIUSZKO ST
DE KALB AVE
LA FAYETTE AVE
VAN BUREN ST
TOMPKINS AVE
11
HERBERT VON KING PARK
GREENE AVE
LEXINGTON AVE

QUINCY ST
GATES AVE
MONROE ST
10
MADISON ST
MARCUS GARVEY BLVD
4
LEWIS AVE
PUTNAM ST
9
JEFFERSON ST
HANCOCK ST
STUYVESANT AVE
BEDFORD AVE
NOSTRAND AVE
5
HALSEY ST
MACON ST.
6
MACDONOUGH ST
3
BAINBRIDGE ST
7 **8**
MARCY AVE
DECATUR ST
CHAUNCEY ST
2
1
FULTON ST

HERKIMER ST
ATLANTIC AVE
15
PACIFIC ST
17
16
BROOKLYN AVE
DEAN ST
UTICA AVE
18
19
20
BERGEN ST
21 **22**
KINGSTON AVE
ALBANY HOUSING
PARK
SCHENECTADY AVE
ST. MARKS AVE
23
BROWER PARK
VIRGINIA PL
PROSPECT PL
HAMPTON PL
TROY AVE
CLASSON AVE
FRANKLIN AVE
BEDFORD AVE
PARK PL
ALBANY A AVE
STERLING PL
24
ST. JOHNS PL
LINCOLN PL
14
EASTERN PARKWAY
12
UNION ST
WASHINGTON AVE
ROGERS AVE
NOSTRAND AVE
NEW YORK AVE
PRESIDENT ST
CARROLL ST
CROWN ST
MONTGOMERY S

Bedford-Stuyvesant and Crown Heights

7 Alhambra

Bedford-Stuyvesant and Crown Heights

Bedford-Stuyvesant

The A and C trains penetrate to the heart of Bedford-Stuyvesant. Either can be taken to the Nostrand Avenue or the Kingston-Throop Avenues stations on Fulton Street. Organized walking tours of the area often meet at Restoration Plaza on Fulton Street between New York and Brooklyn Avenues. That is roughly equidistant between the two stations mentioned above. An alternative is to walk over from Clinton Hill. The Magnolia grandiflora and Herbert von King Park are on Lafayette Avenue between Marcy and Tompkins Avenues, a short walk from the Pratt Institute campus. The principal architectural sights of Bedford-Stuyvesant are in the blocks just south of Lafayette Avenue. The G train also stops along Lafayette Avenue, with a station called Bedford-Nostrand Avenues, which is quite close to where you want to be. There is the perception that Bedford-Stuyvesant is a high-crime area. This perception is exaggerated, particularly for the part of the area that concerns us. Nonetheless, do exercise caution here as elsewhere. It is more fun, anyway, to visit new neighborhoods with a companion. If the perception of crime especially troubles you, be advised that there are occasional excellent walking tours of the area. Contact the Brooklyn Public Library, the Brooklyn Historical Society, the Brooklyn Center for the Urban Environment, or the Municipal Art Society of New York to find out if any such outings are scheduled. Finally, the area is quite drivable, if that's your thing.

The colonial village of Bedford was platted for streets in the late 1830s, and several familiar thoroughfares—such as Bedford Avenue and Fulton Street—were soon cut through. Around the same time, the Brooklyn and Jamaica Railroad (forerunner to the Long Island Railroad) constructed a line from the ferry at Atlantic Avenue to Jamaica, Queens, with a station at Bedford Corners, as the most populous part of Bedford, in the northwestern part of the area, was called. (It sounds like a combination of the two famous idealized small towns, Frank Capra's Bedford Falls and Thornton Wilder's Grover's Corners.) Also beginning around this time, only a few years after slavery was abolished in New York State, African American investors purchased farmland in the southeastern portion of Bedford (in the area bounded roughly by Atlantic Avenue, Ralph Avenue, Eastern Parkway, and Albany Avenue) and created the black communities of Weeksville and Carrville. First as slaves and then as freedmen, African Americans have been a part of Bedford-Stuyvesant from its earliest days. Still, Bedford remained mostly rural until the 1860s, when suburban villa development began to take place following the introduction of horsecar service along Fulton Street and Myrtle Avenue. By the mid-1850s, it took a mere thirty minutes to travel from Bedford to the Fulton Ferry. Today the boundaries of Bedford-Stuyvesant, according to *The Encyclopedia of New York City,* are Flushing Avenue on the north, Broadway on the east, Atlantic Avenue on the south, and Classon Avenue on the west. Bedford-Stuyvesant borders on Williamsburg (north), Bushwick (east), Crown Heights (south), and Clinton Hill (west). According to *The Encyclopedia of New York City,* "Before 1977 it extended as far south as Eastern Parkway." Now that's a funny thing to read. Actually, before the early 1900s, the whole area was known simply as Bedford. In the early 1900s, the part to the west was known as Bedford, while the part to the east became known as Stuyvesant. In the 1920s and 1930s, a large part of central Bedford where many blacks had settled became known by the hyphenated name of Bedford-Stuyvesant. By the 1960s, this name was used not only for all of what we now know as Bedford-Stuyvesant but also for much of what we now know as Crown Heights. In 1968, the city established its system of community planning districts and defined Bedford-Stuyvesant as extending south to Eastern Parkway. In 1977, the city changed its mind and decided that the area between Atlantic Avenue and Eastern Parkway was Crown Heights, not Bedford-Stuyvesant. Even so, some community development organizations continued to define Bedford-Stuyvesant as extending to Eastern Parkway. Confused yet?

In the mid-1880s, the Brooklyn Bridge opened and the elevated railway was built along Lexington and Myrtle Avenues and Fulton Street, and the horsecar suburb of detached villas yielded to a district of row houses. The area remained residential and middle-class—indeed what we might call "bourgeois." The physical form of Bedford-Stuyvesant as we know it today was largely created between the 1880s and the 1920s. Prominent residents of Bedford-Stuyvesant in the late-nineteenth century included merchant and philanthropist Abraham Abraham (of Abraham & Straus fame), who lived on elegant St. Mark's Avenue between Brooklyn and New York Avenues in what is now considered, like Grant Square, the northern part of Crown Heights; Frank W. Woolworth, the five-and-dime king, who lived at 209 Jefferson Avenue between Marcy and Nostrand Avenues; and John C. Kelley, manufacturer of water meters, who lived at 247 Hancock Street between Marcy and Tompkins Avenues. Where the Brooklyn Children's Museum now stands were the mansions of L. C. Smith, the typewriter king (Smith-Corona), and of William Newton Adams, the latter the birthplace of the distinguished American historian James Truslow Adams. Bedford-Stuyvesant began to change out of its bourgeois interlude around 1920. Between the wars Bedford-Stuyvesant real estate slumped as the prosperous moved to newer suburbs and families of more modest means bought the row houses, many of which were not that old. The area became a step up the ladder for Jews and Italians from Williamsburg and Brownsville. It was, no less than it had been before, a place that connoted deep respectability. Just as these Jews and Italians had displaced the more affluent, more bourgeois population of Bedford-Stuyvesant, so in their turn would the Jews and Italians be displaced. Bedford-Stuyvesant changed in response to the booming outer areas of Brooklyn, such as Midwood, Bensonhurst, and Canarsie. Blacks, who had been a presence in parts of the area from the very beginning, began to arrive in greater numbers in the interwar years, including a significant number of West Indians. In 1936, the A train (celebrated in song by Billy Strayhorn and Duke Ellington) opened, connecting New York City's two principal black enclaves, Manhattan's Harlem and Brooklyn's Bedford-Stuyvesant. Increasingly through the 1930s and 1940s, the substantial bourgeois brownstones of Bedford-Stuyvesant were carved up into multiple dwellings and rooming houses. A district that once comprised mostly homeowners now comprised mostly renters. Blacks were especially hurt by the depression. Black women from Bedford-Stuyvesant often sought work at "auctions" on Eastern Parkway where they were hired by the day as domestic servants.

By 1940, sixty-five thousand blacks lived in Bedford-Stuyvesant. After World War II, the black population grew to dominate Bedford-Stuyvesant completely, making it second only to Chicago's South Side as the most populous black district of any American city. In the 1960s, Bedford-Stuyvesant became synonymous with the "urban crisis" in America. In July 1964, Bedford-Stuyvesant broke out in four days of rioting after a white policeman shot and killed a black teenager. New York journalist Jack Newfield would write in 1968 that the shooting "signaled the end of the civil-rights movement and the beginning of the long hot summers." In February 1966, Senator Robert F. Kennedy took a walking tour of Bedford-Stuyvesant and met with local leaders. Less than a year later he spearheaded the creation of the Bedford-Stuyvesant Restoration Corporation and of the Development and Services Corporation. These were organizations intended to coordinate various local, state, federal, and private foundation funding programs geared toward social services and the physical rehabilitation of the district, and to bring in consultants to help bolster the business climate of Bedford-Stuyvesant. Senator Kennedy invited the prominent modern architect I. M. Pei to consult on the physical planning needs of the area. Pei said in 1970 that "Like most ghettos, Bedford-Stuyvesant had no focus. There are endless streets leading from nowhere to nowhere." Unfortunately, in spite of the best intentions and the superior minds engaged on the project, the rehabilitation of Bedford-Stuyvesant was ensnared in bureaucracy every step of the way, until changes in federal-level urban-aid programs, together with the city's declining fiscal fortunes in the 1970s, spelled the doom of many of the dreams of the late 1960s. Some things were accomplished nevertheless. The Bedford-Stuyvesant Restoration Corporation rehabilitated a defunct milk-bottling plant on Fulton Street between New York and Brooklyn Avenues as its own headquarters. The architects Fisher/Jackson Associates designed it in 1968–71. Next door at the southeast corner of Fulton Street and New York Avenue, what is called Restoration Plaza was built in 1972–75 to the designs of the Washington, D.C.–based architect Arthur Cotton Moore. Here was an attempt to create the focus that Pei said was lacking in the area. This shopping and entertainment center included thirty-two stores and a large outdoor ice-skating rink. Perhaps the most remarkable fact about Bedford-Stuyvesant today is how so much of the area has remained quite stable throughout all the turmoil of recent decades. Row-house streets, particularly in the Stuyvesant Heights area, have never ceased to be among the most attractive residential streets in Brooklyn. At the turn of the millennium, as nearby Fort Greene and Clinton Hill have boomed, many people unable to afford houses or apartments in those areas are looking to Bedford-Stuyvesant, which is, in the eyes of real-estate brokers, officially hot. This brings us to an important point. It is true that "Bedford-Stuyvesant" has for the past few decades connoted "ghetto" to many people who do not live in the district. Yet I do not know of another "ghetto" where so many homeowners so lovingly tend their vintage row houses, where, indeed, there is such a high degree of close-knit, rooted family stability as one finds in Bedford-Stuyvesant. It would be silly to suggest that Bedford-Stuyvesant does not have serious social and physical problems. It is also true that the center that I. M. Pei lamented the lack of is something that probably cannot emerge without some sort of large-scale replanning of the district. Nonetheless, Bedford-Stuyvesant has, I think, entered into a new "bourgeois interlude."

1 FULTON PARK
Bounded by Fulton and Chauncey Streets and Stuyvesant Avenue

Fulton Park is a two-acre residential square on land set aside in 1904 adjacent to the lovely Stuyvesant Heights Historic District. The square was created between 1904 and 1910, and so named for being on Fulton Street rather than for Robert Fulton (1765–1815), whose steamboat had a profound impact on the development of Brooklyn, though in fact not so much on this neighborhood, which did not begin to take off until the Brooklyn Bridge opened. (Fulton Street

24 *St. Gregory's Church*

was of course named for Robert Fulton.) A curious thing about Fulton Park is
that it post-dates the houses that surround it. This is different from the cases of
most residential squares, which were created to stimulate development. Here,
most of the nearby houses date from the 1880s and 1890s, a decade or two before
the creation of the small park. The park was then insinuated into an already
built-up neighborhood. In 1997–98, the Borough of Brooklyn restored Fulton
Park in a half million dollar capital project.

One might well think the namers of the park had Robert Fulton himself
in mind. After all, there's a statue of Fulton here. The statue is not original to
this space, however. It predates the park by more than thirty years. The sculptor Caspar Buberl (1834–99) made it in 1872 for a niche in the Fulton Ferry
House on the Brooklyn waterfront. The ferry house was torn down in 1926.
The Society of Old Brooklynites salvaged the statue and placed it here in 1930.
The original statue was zinc, but by 1955 it was so badly deteriorated that a
new bronze casting was made, and that is what we see in Fulton Park today.
Buberl, a Bohemian-born sculptor who came to America at the age of twenty
in 1854, is perhaps best known in New York for his figure of Shakespeare's
Puck on the Houston and Mulberry Streets corner of the Puck Building in
Manhattan. Buberl's greatest work, however, is not in New York but in
Washington, D.C., where he created the fantastic relief frieze, thought to be
the longest in the world (it is a quarter of a mile long), on the Old Pension
Building (now the National Building Museum) in the 1880s. Buberl also did
the statuary group *Columbia Protecting Science and Industry* atop Washington,
D.C.'s Arts and Industries Building in the 1870s. Back in New York, his most
famous work no longer exists: he created the figures of the Muses that once
adorned the old Metropolitan Opera House on Broadway and 39th Street.

The New York City Landmarks Preservation Commission has designated
a Stuyvesant Heights Historic District, an irregularly shaped area bounded on
the east by Stuyvesant Avenue, on the south by Chauncey Street, on the west
by Lewis Avenue, and on the north by MacDonough Street, which also
includes MacDonough Street as far west as Tompkins Avenue. The district
provides a good range of Bedford-Stuyvesant architecture, beginning in the
1860s with freestanding villas. Within the historic district, Monique
Greenwood, executive editor of *Essence* magazine, and her husband Glenn
Pogue purchased in 1995 a freestanding, eighteen-room Italianate villa, built in
the 1860s, at 347 MacDonough Street, between Stuyvesant and Lewis
Avenues. They restored it and opened Akwaaba Mansion, an elegant bed-and-

breakfast that has garnered rave reviews. They later opened Akwaaba Café, one of the first fine restaurants in Bedford-Stuyvesant in many a moon. (*Akwaaba* means "welcome" in a Ghanaian dialect.) The district's row houses date mainly from 1880 to 1910. All the row houses were designed by Brooklyn architects—such as George P. Chappell, Magnus Dahlander, and Amzi Hill— in a variety of styles, including neo-Grec, French Second Empire, Romanesque Revival, and Queen Anne.

Within the Stuyvesant Heights Historic District is:

2 TOMPKINS AVENUE CONGREGATIONAL CHURCH (now First African Methodist Episcopal Zion Church)
480 Tompkins Avenue, southwest corner of MacDonough Street
1888–89, George P. Chappell

The 140-foot-high campanile was—like similarly shaped towers at James W. Naughton's Boys' High School (1891) on Marcy Avenue, Mifflin E. Bell's General Post Office (1885–91), John Welch's St. Luke's Episcopal Church (1888–91) on Clinton Avenue, and Frank Freeman's Brooklyn Fire Headquarters (1891–92) on Jay Street—of Richardsonian derivation. There were in Richardson's work two models for such towers. One was at the Albany (N.Y.) City Hall of 1880–83. The other was at the Allegheny County Courthouse and Jail (1883–88) in Pittsburgh. The tower here is clearly of the Albany City Hall type, and it was among the earliest of these Richardsonian towers in Brooklyn. It is a major skyline element in a neighborhood where the sky is thrillingly punctuated by wonderful towers rising over the row-house streets. The Tompkins Avenue congregation was said to be the largest of any Congregational church in the country. The semicircular auditorium, by the late 1880s an architectural feature almost forty years old in Brooklyn (dating back to Plymouth Congregational Church), held 2,100 worshippers. The congregation later merged with that of the Flatbush Congregational Church in Ditmas Park. This is now the First African Methodist Episcopal Zion Church.

Also in the historic district is the fine Our Lady of Victory Roman Catholic Church (1891–95) at the northeast corner of MacDonough Street and Throop Avenue. It is a strong Gothic church of Manhattan schist with highly contrasting limestone trim. Thomas F. Houghton, who designed it, was the son-in-law and former employee of Patrick C. Keely, the nation's most prolific Catholic architect.

Also in the historic district is:

3 MOUNT LEBANON BAPTIST CHURCH (originally Embury Methodist Church)

230 Decatur Street, southeast corner of Lewis Avenue
1894, Parfitt Brothers

This is one of the Parfitts' best, and most restrained, works, a superb Richardsonian Romanesque composition that is not copied from any Richardson work in particular. Looking at it is like taking a bath in Roman bricks. On Decatur Street it is in three parts horizontally. On the left is a gabled section with a high round arch. On the right is a superb projecting corner tower with a conical roof. In between is a porch leading to a massive arch recessed within which is the entrance. The arch is in a wall that projects to meet the corner tower to form a balcony that stretches across the central section to connect with another, smaller conically roofed round tower set between the central section and the gabled section on the left. In the center atop the pitched roof is a flêche. The forms are very simple, yet the building has a presence perhaps greater than any other single building in the historic district. Though it looks like a church, it would take only a minor adjustment here and there to make this look like a house.

4 13th REGIMENT ARMORY

357 Marcus Garvey Boulevard (formerly Sumner Avenue)
between Jefferson and Putnam Avenues, east side
1894, R. L. Daus
1906, Parfitt Brothers

This is one of two great armories near each other in this part of Brooklyn. The other is the 23rd Regiment at Grant Square. The two were erected nearly simultaneously with each other and in very similar neo-medieval styles. Both have massively arched entrances flanked by fat, crenellated towers. Here the flanking towers are much higher. Both armories are vast mounds of bricks. The design here is slightly busier, the façades are more molded, and granite trim is used particularly around the entrance. Something, perhaps that busy-ness or a greater stridency in the machicolations, makes this armory seem more forbidding than the 23rd Regiment's, which is actually rather jolly. This one could almost be mistaken for a prison; the 23rd could not. This is truly a lordly presence in its neighborhood. In 1988, when the armory was being converted into a homeless shelter, Christopher Gray wrote in the *New York Times* that when the State of New York provided the money for the armory in 1890, the *Times,* apparently thinking it a political boondoggle, claimed that the architect was "a young man with but little experience, but a protégé of 'Boss' Hugh McLaughlin." The architect, R. L. Daus, was in fact only thirty-six. He had, however, a string of very successful buildings behind him, including the prestigious Lincoln Club (1889) on Putnam Avenue, as well as several distinguished houses. It is probably true, though, that Daus was politically well connected, seeing as how he later became surveyor of buildings for Brooklyn. Nonetheless, he was more than equal to the task of designing the armory. One thing the *Times* criticized in 1890 was the lavishing of too much money on the exterior and not enough to build an adequately sized drill hall. In fact, the drill hall did have to be expanded, and that appears to be the contribution the Parfitt Brothers made in 1906. This, though, is Daus's building.

MONTROSE W. MORRIS COUNTRY

5 HANCOCK STREET
Between Marcy and Tompkins Avenues

Much of Bedford-Stuyvesant's best architecture is to be found, oddly, not within the historic district but in the streets just outside it, where one will find a heavy concentration of individually designated landmark buildings. Surprisingly, while the Renaissance and Alhambra apartments are designated landmarks, none of the houses of Hancock Street is, yet some of the houses on this street are among the most impressive residences in the district. I speak of the houses designed by one of Brooklyn's greatest architects, Montrose W. Morris (1861–1916). As Robert A. M. Stern, Thomas Mellins, and David Fishman wrote in *New York 1880,* "No architect working in Brooklyn understood the need to establish individuality within the context of the whole better than Montrose W. Morris." He was born in Hempstead, Long Island, and grew up in Brooklyn. He went to work as a teenager in the office of the architect Charles W.

5A *255 Hancock Street*

5B *247 Hancock Street*

Clinton, who had come up in the office of Brooklyn's Richard Upjohn and would later become the partner of William Hamilton Russell (who had worked with James Renwick, Jr.) in the important firm of Clinton & Russell. Morris established his own firm in 1883 at only twenty-two years of age. He purchased land in Stuyvesant Heights, and in 1885 he built his own house at 236 Hancock Street. Morris must have been a real go-getter. We know from the tender age at which he designed these beautiful houses that he was a prodigy of his profession. He was also a shrewd self-marketer. He made his own residence a show house, opening it to prospective clients. As a marketing gambit, it worked. Few other architects would so mark the landscape of Brooklyn. His own house was part of a row that included Nos. 238 to 244 on the south side of Hancock Street between Marcy and Tompkins Avenues. The end houses, Nos. 236 and 244, are flat-roofed. The intermediate three houses face Hancock Street with gabled roofs projecting from steep mansard roofs. The end houses' flat roofs project beyond the roofline

5B *247 Hancock Street*

of the intermediate houses, and so the end houses appear like end pavilions of a single large structure. Morris was a master of designing groups of houses that possessed a unified grandeur. These houses are of red brick with trim of stone and of elaborate terra-cotta work. Their palette is much darker than the four-house row built in 1886 next door to the east at Nos. 246 to 252. Two stoops each serve two houses that have bases of rock-faced limestone and upper floors of Roman brick. The parlor floor features four massive arches of rock-faced limestone. The end arches frame entrances, and the intermediate arches are window bays. Slightly projecting end sections have panels of terra-cotta ornament at the top of the parlor floor featuring Viking heads that look as though they might have been influenced by Olin Levi Warner's Viking head at the entrance to the Long Island Historical Society. The second floors between the pavilions have loggias flanking two window bays, with all four bays having two fluted columns bearing Romanesque capitals. A huge central gable tops the whole, with pairs of dormers on either side of it set in a steep mansard roof. On the other side of Morris's own house at No. 232 at the southeast corner of Marcy Avenue, he designed a house built in 1888 of brick, terra-cotta, and rock-faced stone. A second-story round projecting tower negotiates the corner and leads one to the Marcy Avenue side with a marvelous three-story, three-sided projecting bay on the right, its side walls angled through the first two stories and straight at the third story, over-hanging the lower walls on shelves of receding brickwork. Crowning this bay is a gable and a high chimney. There is a fine bracketed cornice at the top of the second story below a mansard roof. Across the street, Morris designed Nos. 255 to 259, built in 1889—three lovely houses of Roman brick above rock-faced stone parlor floors with twin arches topped by projecting three-sided bays recessed within the plane of the wall. All three houses have third-floor log-gias, that of the center house set within a broad arch, those of the flanking houses square-headed with twin Romanesque columns and enframements of terra-cotta blocks. **No. 255** (7-5a) is in particularly splendid shape. To the west is the Queen of Hancock Street, the eighty-foot-wide, three-story brownstone house at **No. 247** (7-5b). Morris designed this house in the 1880s for water-meter king John C. Kelley. It is very interesting in that it employs a High Renaissance design vocabulary at a time when Romanesque and Queen Anne reigned supreme in Brooklyn, not least in the work of Morris. Yet by this time McKim, Mead & White had rocked the New York archi-tectural world with their Villard Houses on Madison Avenue in Manhattan, and the currents were gaining force that would result in the Columbian Exposition of 1893, following which Brooklyn's architecture would change dramatically. The Kelley house is very stately, with what is less a stoop than a mini-grand stairway leading to the arched doorway centered between two two-story projecting bays. On the parlor level of the end bays are three high, square-headed windows, with the flanking units divided into three lights. The triple windows above these on the second floor are of the Palladian variety, with square-headed windows flanking a higher, arched window. In the center bay of the second floor is an arched window echoing the arched doorway below it.

6 RENAISSANCE (apartments)
488 Nostrand Avenue, southwest corner of Hancock Street
1892

The five-story Renaissance is a massy apartment house that Louis F. Seitz commissioned from Montrose W. Morris to house Bedford-Stuyvesant's burgeoning bourgeoisie. It is only one block north of Morris's Alhambra, and the design of the Renaissance is very similar to that of the Imperial, which Seitz commissioned from Morris in the same year, at Bedford and Pacific Streets in Grant Square. The style is basically French Renaissance, executed here in Roman brick, alternating in vertical bands with terra-cotta, and with a slate mansard roof. There are the standard, powerful round corner towers, capped by conical roofs of slate. The loosely Palladian arrangement of the big, three-story-high center window over the entrance on Nostrand Avenue shows that Morris was tending in the classical direction that would come to define his work later in the 1890s. Coupled with the Alhambra, the Renaissance provides a vision of Nostrand Avenue as once having had the makings of as fine a residential "boulevard" as could be found in Brooklyn. Like the Alhambra, the Renaissance was vacant for many years until Anderson Associates restored it in 1994.

Probably its closest historical antecedent is the Chateau d'Azay-le-Rideau of the early sixteenth century, in the Loire Valley of France. Charles Coolidge Haight's New York Cancer Hospital of 1884–86, on Central Park West and 106th Street, is in like style. It is, however, once again the works of H. H. Richardson to which we should probably turn in seeking an influence for Morris's design. One thinks particularly of the Cincinnati (Ohio) Chamber of Commerce Building (1885–88). There is also a touch of the Ames Memorial Hall (1879–81) in North Easton, Massachusetts. Richardson, who never designed a building in Brooklyn, is nonetheless the one who, through his surrogates, as it were, was indirectly responsible for this city's countless fantastic towers, both square and, as at the Renaissance, round.

7 ALHAMBRA (apartments)

500–518 Nostrand Avenue between Macon and Halsey Streets, west side
1889–90

The Alhambra is 200 feet long on Nostrand Avenue and 70 feet long on Macon and Halsey Streets. At six stories, and set back from the street line by fifteen feet, the building has an awesome presence. Bedford-Stuyvesant's own Montrose W. Morris designed the Alhambra and the nearby Renaissance, along with the Imperial at Grant Square, for the developer Louis F. Seitz. Seitz was only twenty-nine years old in 1889 when he purchased the site directly across Nostrand Avenue from the then newly built Girls' High School. Old photographs show the Alhambra and the Renaissance ranged along Nostrand Avenue, trolleys running down the center of the avenue, in a scene of somber dignity bespeaking the virtues of Brooklyn's long-ago bourgeois interlude, when these buildings were the outward expression of the richly and somberly upholstered interior lives of a nascent mercantile and professional middle class that had claimed Brooklyn neighborhoods such as Bedford-Stuyvesant as their own. (One such photograph from around 1910 is in the collection of the Brooklyn Historical Society and is reproduced on page 901 of *New York 1880*

7 Alhambra

by Robert A. M. Stern, Thomas Mellins, and David Fishman.) Together with Girls' High School, the two apartment houses lent to Nostrand Avenue a monumental aspect that marked it out for high destinies. Much of the Alhambra's majesty is intact, though the building has been truncated. Shop fronts were added at street level in 1923, and today their presence is as unprepossessing as any modernized storefronts on Manhattan's Fifth Avenue. So, look up: at its skyline the building reads much as it did at the turn of the century. There, small projecting gabled dormers enhance the already picturesque conically roofed corner towers. Other gables and other dormers and high chimneys and what is, in fact, a mansard roof, all handled with perfect symmetry, make this skyline an unmitigated delight. The style of the building is Romanesque Revival, and it possesses much the same stately grandeur as Henry Hardenbergh's only slightly earlier Dakota apartments on Central Park West.

The Alhambra is actually two structures occupying the full block front of Nostrand Avenue between Macon and Halsey Streets. Between the two structures is a court screened by beautiful arcaded bridges, which are also fire escapes. The materials are reddish-brown stone below, orange Roman brick above, with trim of often elaborately molded terra-cotta. The apartments were originally six to a floor, featuring eight or nine rooms with sliding doors separating parlor, library, reception room, and dining room. The Alhambra was electrically lit from the beginning. Early residents enjoyed striking amenities, including a croquet lawn and a tennis court. According to Christopher Gray, the 1900 census indicates that half the households had live-in servants. The developer Seitz apparently discovered Morris by visiting the architect's own home, close by at 236 Hancock Street between Marcy and Tompkins Avenues. When Morris built his house there in 1885, he was a little-known architect. He designed his house with the idea of opening it to prospective clients who would see what he was capable of doing. Seitz was one who succumbed to Morris's enterprising marketing gambit. The building's name was probably chosen simply because it sounded good, as the style is not Moorish in the manner of the Alhambra in Granada. Nonetheless, some of this building's loveliest features, the arcaded loggias that appear at the fourth story on all three façades, do give off a faint whiff of, if not the Alhambra, other works of Moorish architecture of the Middle Ages.

The Alhambra was fully occupied until a fire in 1994, then stood empty until Anderson Associates, the same Brooklyn development and architectural firm that rehabilitated the Renaissance, restored it in 1998 in an important sign of the rebirth of Bedford-Stuyvesant.

8 *Girls' High School*

8 GIRLS' HIGH SCHOOL
475 Nostrand Avenue between Halsey and Macon Streets, east side
1885–86, James W. Naughton
Rear addition: 1891, Naughton
Macon Street addition: 1912, C. B. J. Snyder

Though James W. Naughton designed better buildings than this, particularly this one's brother, as it were, Boys' High School, this one seems to me to be the prototypical Naughton school. With its central tower and end pavilions, Girls' High School, the oldest surviving public secondary-school building in Greater New York, helped set the standard for public-school buildings as prominent neighborhood landmarks. The Naughton towers competed with church steeples as skyline elements in Brooklyn neighborhoods. The style combines classical with Gothic elements. The entrance is set within the projecting center-tower section and is defined by a balustrade-topped distyle porch with rather spindly Corinthian columns. Gables with pointed-arch windows top the end pavilions. The important thing here, though, is the pyramidally topped bell tower, which looks very much like it could be on a church.

This was originally called the Girls' Department of Central Grammar School, and beginning in 1891 was known officially as Girls' High School. It is now the New York City Board of Education Adult Training Center. Naughton served from 1879 until 1898 as superintendent of buildings for the Brooklyn Board of Education. During that time he was credited with the design of every public-school building in the city. With the creation of Greater New York in 1898, however, C. B. J. Snyder became the citywide public-school architect. In 1912, Snyder designed the addition to Girls' High School along Macon Street.

Girls' High School alumnae include Lena Horne and Shirley Chisholm, the latter of whom served Bedford-Stuyvesant and Crown Heights as the first African American woman ever elected to the U.S. Congress.

About two blocks north of the Alhambra and Girls' High School, at 209 Jefferson Avenue, between Nostrand and Marcy Avenues, is one among many 1870s brownstones along the street. Here Frank W. Woolworth (1852–1919) lived from 1890 to 1901. He was born in upstate New York, and failed with his first store in Utica, New York, where he priced every item at five cents. Undaunted, he tried again in Lancaster, Pennsylvania, this time pricing items at either five or ten cents. He succeeded. After opening many other stores, he moved his headquarters to New York City in 1886. Oddly, he did not open a store in New York City until ten years later (at 17th Street and Sixth Avenue). He left Bedford-Stuyvesant in 1901 when he hired C. P. H. Gilbert to design a thirty-room house at 990 Fifth Avenue at 80th Street in Manhattan. Gilbert, of course, followed a similar course: his early works were in Park Slope, but with increasing success he shifted his focus to the Upper East Side of Manhattan. (C. P. H. Gilbert, who designed Woolworth's Fifth Avenue house, is not to be confused with the unrelated Cass Gilbert, who designed the Woolworth Building, which opened in 1913.) When Woolworth died, his chain had more than a thousand stores and he was one of the richest men in America. He was buried, alas, not in Green-wood Cemetery, but in Woodlawn Cemetery in the Bronx.

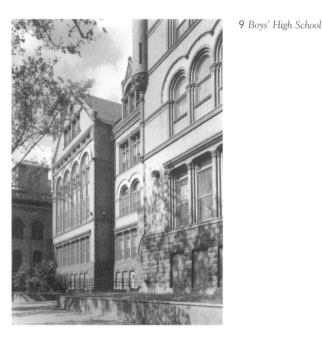

9 Boys' High School

9 BOYS' HIGH SCHOOL

832 Marcy Avenue between Putnam Avenue and Madison Street,
west side
1891–92, James W. Naughton
Additions: ca. 1905–10, C. B. J. Snyder

Prominent corner towers are a Brooklyn tradition, and the one here at the corner of Marcy Avenue and Madison Street is one of the most prominent of them all. Its design is very, very similar to the tower of the nearby Tompkins Avenue Congregational Church built in 1888–89, a couple of years before Boys' High School. It is my feeling that Naughton wished his public schools to have something of the presence of Protestant churches. Rather than being directly inspired by George Chappell's church, however, it is quite likely that both Chappell and Naughton genuflected at the shrine of Henry Hobson Richardson. Both the Chappell and Naughton towers are reminiscent of Richardson's towers at the Albany [New York] City Hall of 1880–83 and at the Allegheny County Courthouse and Jail of 1883–88 in Pittsburgh. Both the Albany and Pittsburgh towers rise to open arcades capped by pyramidal roofs. Where the Albany tower seems more like Naughton's is in the manner of its facing of discrete slit-like openings, reminiscent of bowmen's slots in medieval forts. Complementing the Richardson tower is a smaller but still prominent tower on the other corner, cylindrical and conically roofed like the towers on Montrose Morris apartment houses. Boys' High School has a wonderfully craggy skyline, with towers of varying heights, gables, dormers, and chimneys. The façades are heavily modeled, with pavilions and recesses and lots and lots of bold and minor arches, typically with moldings in the Romanesque style. This is James Naughton's masterpiece.

Boys' High School was founded in 1878 as the Boys' Division of the Central Grammar School. This building originally served 782 boys in twenty-two classrooms, but it had to be enlarged to admit more students after the turn of the century. The additions were the work of Naughton's successor as public-school architect, C. B. J. Snyder. This was once one of the most distinguished public high schools in the country, and its monumental design was intended to reflect the school's prestige.

James W. Naughton was born in Ireland and was educated at the University of Wisconsin and, like so many of his fellow practitioners of the building arts in New York, at Cooper Union. He served as superintendent of buildings for the Board of Education of the City of Brooklyn from 1879 until the Consolidation of Greater New York in 1898, when the new citywide post went to C. B. J. Snyder.

Bertram D. Wolfe, famous as a historian of Soviet communism (*Four Who Made a Revolution*), taught at Boys' High School. Alumni include Norman Mailer, Isaac Asimov, literary critic Clifton Fadiman, philosopher Sidney Hook, real-estate developer William J. Levitt of Levittown fame, and architect Morris Lapidus of Miami Beach fame.

10 ST. GEORGE'S EPISCOPAL CHURCH
800 Marcy Avenue, southwest corner of Gates Avenue
1887–88, Richard Michell Upjohn

This church was designed by the son of Richard Upjohn, architect of some of Brooklyn's most important churches, including Church of the Pilgrims and Grace Church, both in Brooklyn Heights. The son was also a gifted architect, and here worked in what is loosely termed the "Ruskinian Gothic" style, which was the phase of the nineteenth-century Gothic Revival following the Early Gothic Revival, or Ecclesiological Gothic, of which the father was New York's undisputed master. Also known as High Victorian Gothic, the style of

St. George's is similar to that employed by James Renwick, Jr., a master of both the Early and the High Victorian Gothic Revival modes, in his St. Ann's Church (1867–69) in Brooklyn Heights. St. George's, built fully twenty years after St. Ann's, shows the staying power of this style of architecture in nineteenth-century Brooklyn.

High Victorian Gothic emerged in England in the 1850s and 1860s. William Butterfield's All Saints Church on Margaret Street in London is said to have inaugurated the mode. In the United States, Edward Tuckerman Potter (the lone Brooklyn example of whose work can be seen at St. John's Episcopal Church in Park Slope) employed the style at his Nott Memorial Library at Union College in Schenectady, New York, as early as 1856. That's more than thirty years before St. George's. The single most defining characteristic of the style is "polychromy," i.e., the use of different colors. The principle of polychromy was derived from the 1849 book *The Seven Lamps of Architecture* by John Ruskin, which is why the style is often called "Ruskinian." (Ruskin, by the way, came to dislike the directions that much so-called "Ruskinian" architecture came to take.) In *The Seven Lamps,* one of the most influential architectural treatises of the nineteenth century, Ruskin advocated, among other things, for an architecture of color. In a way that was consonant with some of the aesthetic ideology of the Ecclesiological movement (the theological underpinnings of which Ruskin rejected), he insisted that color in buildings be integral, that is to say, that it be a property of the materials themselves, not painted on. Thus, what we call Ruskinian buildings are defined by their use of contrasting stonework, often alternating bands of differently colored and differently textured stone or brick. This is sometimes called "constructional coloration." We see this in the manner in which the red brick of St. George's contrasts with its light-colored stone accents, particularly in the voussoirs of the pointed arches.

Among American architects closely identified with this approach are a couple who are also closely associated with Brooklyn: Peter B. Wight, whose Mercantile Library on Montague Street was once one of Brooklyn's most famous buildings, and Russell Sturgis, whose Willow Place Chapel in Brooklyn Heights was built in 1875–76. St. George's Church may be the last major example of the style to be found in New York City.

As in much of the work of Upjohn *père,* there is in St. George's a careful articulation of masses, with nave, aisles, transepts, chancel, and entrance all clearly marked out on the exterior. The most impressive feature is the small but richly designed polygonal tower to the left of the entrance on Marcy Avenue.

11 *Magnolia Grandiflora*

11 MAGNOLIA GRANDIFLORA
In front of 679 Lafayette Avenue between Marcy and Tompkins Avenues, north side, opposite Herbert von King Park
Planted 1885

There are in New York City two trees that have been designated as landmarks. One was the Weeping Beech in Flushing, Queens, which died. The other is this magnificent Magnolia tree, the Southern Magnolia or, grandiloquently, the grandiflora, in front of 679 Lafayette Avenue. (Two other Brooklyn trees are as famous. One is the humble and ubiquitous ailanthus immortalized in Betty Smith's novel *A Tree Grows in Brooklyn*. The other is the fantastically gnarled Camperdown elm in Prospect Park, which is home to many noble trees.) A man named William Lemken planted Bedford-Stuyvesant's Magnolia grandiflora around 1885 in front of his house. He acquired the seedling in North Carolina. A remarkable neighborhood woman named Hattie Carthan took charge in the early 1950s of protecting the tree, and began the movement that ultimately got it designated a landmark in 1970. It is hard to think that the original Landmarks Commissioners in 1965 ever dreamed they would be in the business of designating trees, yet they did, to the eternal gratitude of Brooklynites.

It is exceptionally rare to see an example of Magnolia grandiflora north of, say, Delaware, and this one may have learned a lesson or two from its ailanthus friends. It is an evergreen, and flowers spectacularly in late spring and summer with extremely large, cup-shaped, white flowers that are fragrant with the scent of lemon. This is the official state flower of both Louisiana and Mississippi.

The surrounding houses, designated as landmarks largely so that the tree would be protected and flourish in its original architectural setting, are nice enough. Nos. 678 and the tree's own 679 are neo-Grec brownstone houses built in 1880–83. No. 677 is a Romanesque Revival house from 1890, designed by Lansing C. Holden, a prominent Bedford-Stuyvesant architect.

Perhaps the most pleasing thing about the tree is that when it was planted, Bedford-Stuyvesant was a white, middle-class neighborhood. Today, the area is largely African American, and many of the residents have roots deep in Magnolia grandiflora country, in the Carolinas, Georgia, Mississippi, and so on. It is as though the tree foretold the profound migrations of the years to come.

Sometimes people think of Bedford-Stuyvesant as being deep in the heart of Brooklyn, difficult of access perhaps, or otherwise uninviting. This is nonsense. The Magnolia grandiflora is a mere *four blocks* from the campus of Pratt Institute—that is, closer to Pratt than Pratt is to Fort Greene Park.

Right across Lafayette Avenue from the Magnolia grandiflora is a small park that used to be called Tompkins Park. The park occupies one full block, about eight acres, bounded by Marcy, Lafayette, Tompkins, and Greene Avenues. Frederick Law Olmsted and Calvert Vaux laid out Tompkins Park in 1870–71. This was their only work in Brooklyn besides Prospect Park, Eastern and Ocean Parkways, and Fort Greene Park. Unlike the other projects, however, this was a small neighborhood park—a residential square, really—and demanded a simple design, one meant more to be seen from the outside than the inside. Alas, literally no trace of Olmsted and Vaux's design remains, so many times has this little park been altered over the years. It isn't even Tompkins Park anymore; it's Herbert von King Park. Actually, in the Olmsted and Vaux scheme of things, the park, however simply handsome, was a minor work indeed. Still, it was a square serving the bourgeois community of Bedford-Stuyvesant at the end of the nineteenth century, and can be seen in its setting of dappled sunlight, billowing white dresses, and urban propriety in paintings made of it by William Merritt Chase. Better known for his paintings of Prospect Park and Central Park, Chase lived for a time on Marcy Avenue near the park, and painted it. One of the best is called *A City Park* and is from 1887. It can be seen at the Art Institute of Chicago.

Crown Heights

The parts of Crown Heights dealt with on the following pages are easy to get to, and so long as you remember where Eastern Parkway is, you won't get lost. You can take the 2 or 3 trains either to the Grand Army Plaza station or to the Eastern Parkway/Brooklyn Museum station, walk east several blocks on Eastern Parkway, and turn left (north) on New York Avenue or Brooklyn Avenue to take in the Brooklyn Children's Museum area. Grant Square at Bedford Avenue is best accessed by the A train to Nostrand Avenue.

The boundaries of Crown Heights are nowadays generally held to be Flatbush Avenue on the west, Atlantic Avenue on the north, Ralph Avenue on the east, and Empire Boulevard on the south. At the borders there is some dispute over the neighborhood's name. The westernmost portion of the area, bounded by Atlantic Avenue on the north, Flatbush Avenue on the west, Eastern Parkway on the south, and Washington Avenue on the east, is often referred to as Prospect Heights, an old name that is being aggressively revived in recent years. Everything north of Eastern Parkway was once considered part of Bedford-Stuyvesant. In the south of Crown Heights, many a Dodgers fan considered Ebbets Field to be in Flatbush, not Crown Heights. Dodgers center fielder Duke Snider was even known as the Duke of Flatbush, not the Duke of Crown Heights. Nonetheless, I am staying with what today are generally considered the boundaries of Crown Heights, and, with apologies to residents of Flatbush, it's in this chapter that I take note of Ebbets Field.

No one seems quite sure how Crown Heights got its name, though we are certain it had nothing to do with English royalty. Some speculate that it derived from "Crow Hill," a derogatory name used for a portion of old Bedford that had a concentration of African American households. Indeed, the earliest settlements in the area were the African American communities of Weeksville and Carrville, established in the 1830s (slavery had only been abolished in New York State in 1827). The only physical remnants of these communities are four simple clapboard houses, known as the Weeksville houses or the Hunterfly Road houses, on Bergen Street between Buffalo and Rochester Avenues. In the 1990s, Li-Saltzman Architects lovingly restored these houses, which were built from the 1840s to the 1880s, as a museum of African American history. The Society for the Preservation of Weeksville and Bedford-Stuyvesant History operates the museum. Later, the area was long one of the great "heights" of Brooklyn, following upon Brooklyn Heights and Clinton Hill as the elevated abode of the affluent. The spine of Crown Heights is Eastern Parkway. Areas both to the north and to the south form some of the most distinctive neighborhood enclaves to be found in New York City. Today Crown Heights is home to a large population of West Indians, with the largest number from Jamaica and Haiti. The annual West Indian parade, held every Labor Day along Eastern Parkway, draws more than a million spectators and revelers. Crown Heights is also famous as the home of the Lubavitch Hasidim, one of the best known of the several ultra-orthodox Hasidic Jewish sects in Brooklyn. The Lubavitch world headquarters is at 770 Eastern Parkway. The Lubavitchers are the largest Hasidic group in the world. They were founded in eastern Europe in the nineteenth century and began moving to Brooklyn after World War II. They are more worldly than most Hasidic groups and are, to my knowledge, the only one that proselytizes. Hasidic men are very easy to identify by their long black suits, beards, and, often, uncut forelocks. There is a bit of a history of tensions between the West Indian and the Hasidic Jewish communities in Crown Heights, tensions that reached a crescendo of sorts in the early 1990s. The fact is, however, that on any given day one can walk or drive around Crown Heights and see people of all kinds just getting on with their lives. While Crown Heights boasts numerous individually designated landmark buildings, parts of the district seem long overdue for designation as historic districts. A casual amble through these areas will leave no doubt about that.

EASTERN PARKWAY

Frederick Law Olmsted and Calvert Vaux conceived of Eastern Parkway in 1866 when they were designing Prospect Park. Two years later, Olmsted coined the term "parkway." This word commonly means one of two things. It can mean a roadway that is landscaped, often with a center mall, in the manner of a park. Or it can mean a roadway that links one park to another. Often, parkways combine both these features. Eastern Parkway was intended to combine these features, but ended up as a parkway only in the first sense. The cutting through of the parkway began in 1870. The parkway was as complete as it would ever be by 1874. It was designed with multiple lanes intended to separate out different forms of traffic, with lanes for carriages, for horseback riding, and for pedestrians. In addition, the center mall was to be lushly

planted, a linear park, with shade trees and benches. Olmsted
believed that the metropolis should be developed along low-den-
sity suburban lines. He envisioned Eastern Parkway bordered by
single-family, suburban villa-type residences. At first, that's how
development took shape along here. But after the turn of the
twentieth century, high-density apartment houses and large institutional buildings began to take over.

Eastern Parkway is generally considered one of the great,
unfulfilled fantasies in Brooklyn's development. It is not, however,
by any means a total failure. Stretches are exceptionally handsome, and some architects, such as Robert J. Reiley and Louis
Allen Abramson, understood exactly what to do with what was
there. The failure, such as it is, is twofold. First, Eastern Parkway
was conceived, along with Ocean Parkway on the other side of
Prospect Park, as part of a metropolitan parkway system that
would link all the parks of Greater New York and fulfill Olmsted
and Vaux's dream of *rus in urbe*. This system was begun but never
completed, and today Eastern Parkway ends—where? It ends at
Ralph Avenue, though a later "Eastern Parkway Extension" takes
a sharp northern turn there and continues to Atlantic Avenue in
the Brownsville section of Brooklyn. Ocean Parkway, on the other
hand, begins, like Eastern Parkway, at Prospect Park but, unlike
Eastern Parkway, has a true terminal point, namely Coney Island
and the ocean.

Olmsted and Vaux carried out something like their full idea
not in Greater New York but in Buffalo. Chicago, also, has a park
and boulevard system along the lines envisioned by Olmsted and
Vaux, though they were not involved in its design.

The other problematic thing about Eastern Parkway is its
appropriateness in the heart of Brooklyn. In her seminal 1961 book
The Death and Life of Great American Cities, Jane Jacobs wither-
ingly criticized the kind of nineteenth-century suburban planning
that created many outlying areas of American cities, including
Brooklyn. Her point, as I take it, is that in city environments the
kind of relaxed and open planning that men like Olmsted advocated often does not work. The space is poorly defined, densities are
too low for proper neighborhood-level informal political organization

and for the all-important "eyes on the street," and safety and the convenience of pedestrians suffer. This is why, as she so eloquently pointed out, the parkways and boulevards and suburban villa developments throughout almost all older American cities have tended to become rundown, dangerous, disreputable areas. There is a major difference when populations are socially and economically homogeneous and the units of municipal administration and governance are small and manageable, as in many independent suburban communities. Within big cities, dense development, high ground coverage, short blocks, and continuous commercial activity are, Jacobs said, among the necessary conditions for vital, successful communities.

I think most of what she had to say on this subject, though occasionally exaggerated for rhetorical emphasis, is generally unassailable. I think this because I have walked and driven through many such areas of cities and wondered why, given that the physical arrangements seem to comport so wholly to the putative values of middle-class Americans, these areas often tend to be economically depressed and physically rundown. The problem, in a nutshell, is that in a city such as Brooklyn, with its extremely diverse population, its variety of aspirations and goals and values, there is, in many parts of the city, too great a legacy of nineteenth-century spatial homogeneity.

What it all comes down to is that when Olmsted visited Paris in 1859 he was charmed by the recently completed (1856) Avenue de l'Impératrice (now called the Avenue Foch), leading from the Arc de Triomphe to the Bois de Boulogne and an integral part of Haussmann's rebuilding of Paris under the Second Empire. The Avenue de l'Impératrice, wrote Paul Cohen-Portheim in 1930, "is a residential street for the very rich, with no hotels or shops or anything else suggestive of work or business in it." In other words, a street not designed for the approbation of Jane Jacobs. It is also not what immediately comes to mind when we think "Parisian boulevard." Rather, we think of broad boulevards like those painted by Pissarro, flanked by massive apartment blocks with shops, cafés, restaurants, and theaters in their bases, and occupied by people of quite varying means—the boulevards of the "flâneurs." American planners, whether Olmsted or Daniel Burnham, tended to think that the commercially barren boulevard was somehow morally superior. This misguided moralism had dire consequences for the American city.

That said, perhaps another kind of boulevard might simply have not worked in this setting. And lest one think Eastern Parkway a dump, it is far from it. Many parts of it, in ways that would surprise Jane Jacobs, are improving, sometimes dramatically, and parts of it are and have always been beautiful. As for the parkway concept, one need only look at these spontaneously regenerating parts of Eastern Parkway to recognize that the concept is hardly altogether wrong.

12 UNION TEMPLE HOUSE
17 Eastern Parkway, northeast corner of Plaza Street
1925, Arnold W. Brunner Associates

The building that sets the tone for the row of high-rise apartment houses along Eastern Parkway is not an apartment house, but the temple house of Union Temple. Union Temple itself was supposed to rise to the west next door to the temple house, and never did, leaving an open lot of venerable vintage that a new apartment building is slated to replace. The temple house, designed by a very distinguished Manhattan firm, has a rusticated stone base with three entrances, each surmounted by a stone balcony and, at the second floor, richly enframed windows. The shaft of the building is faced in brick and is very plain except for the ends, which continue the ground-floor rustication. It rises to a cornice, then to a very high, richly embellished eighth floor, then to another prominent cornice. Except for the height of the eighth floor, which houses a gymnasium and swimming pool (now a health club), the design of the temple house is a pure example of the 1920s neo-Renaissance apartment type found on Eastern Parkway and in Manhattan on Park Avenue. Judging from drawings, the unbuilt temple itself would have been a splendid addition to Grand Army Plaza. Half as high as the temple house, it was fully rusticated in stone and featured an immense hexastyle Corinthian portico topped by a prominent stone entablature with foliate carving and inscriptions. The temple would have earned a place among that handful of exciting Beaux-Arts classical synagogues to be found in New York City, and its style was intended to harmonize with its City Beautiful surroundings, including the Brooklyn Museum, the memorial arch in Grand Army Plaza, and, alas, Raymond Almirall's never-finished Brooklyn Public Library. As magnificent as this stretch of Eastern Parkway, terminating at the plaza, is today, we can only dream of how much more magnificent it came within a hair's breadth of being.

13 CATHOLIC HIGH SCHOOL
Eastern Parkway, southwest corner of Washington Avenue
1929, Robert J. Reiley

Built at the height of the Art Deco period, Catholic High School is a late example of the kind of restrained Beaux-Arts classicism that architects employed for buildings that, though they might house important institutions, nonetheless were intended to defer to preexisting, grander buildings designed in a monumental variety of Beaux-Arts style. For example, the buildings of Manhattan's "Terminal City," erected in the wake of Grand Central Terminal, clearly use a design vocabulary meant to harmonize with the terminal while not in any way upstaging it. (We see how these values were completely jettisoned by the architects of the Pan Am Building!) Just so, Robert J. Reiley designed Catholic High School as part of the setting of the Brooklyn Museum and to relate in an architecturally coherent way to the broad Eastern Parkway running in front of the school. This, like Louis Allen Abramson's Brooklyn Jewish Center just to the east on the parkway, is a long, low building. Here we have twelve three-story-high engaged Corinthian columns that interpret the parkway as a stately, colonnaded corridor. It is a wonderful building, absolutely correct for its site. Reiley was a prominent architect of Catholic churches and institutional buildings. Elsewhere in Brooklyn he designed the fine Our Lady of Solace Church (1925) on Mermaid Avenue. Perhaps his best-known works are Keating Hall (1936) at Fordham University in the Bronx and St. Andrew's Church (1939) near Police Plaza in Manhattan. He was also a onetime partner of Gustave Steinback, one of the nation's foremost architects of Catholic churches, though not at the time Steinback designed Our Lady Queen of All Saints in Fort Greene.

Separating it from the Brooklyn Museum is a fine open space called Dr. Ronald E. McNair Park, formerly known as Joseph A. Guider Park. Guider was a onetime Brooklyn borough president. McNair, an astronaut and only the second African American in outer space, died in the horrendous Challenger explosion in 1986 as he was about to take his second trip into space. A park was created on this site in 1905 and took its present shape, at about an acre and a half, in 1911, as the Brooklyn Museum was also taking its shape. McNair Park was beautifully renovated in 1994 at a cost of about one million dollars. The bronze portrait sculpture of McNair, by Ogundipe Fayomi, was installed at that time.

THE BROOKLYN DODGERS

This part of Crown Heights has the Brooklyn Public Library, the Brooklyn Botanic Garden, and the Brooklyn Museum, a cultural nucleus in the front ranks of American cities. Once upon a time, the nucleus was nicely rounded out by that great American contribution to the culture of the world—major-league baseball. On a site bounded by Bedford Avenue on the east, Sullivan Place on the south, McKeever Place on the west, and Montgomery Street on the north now stands the Ebbets Field Houses, a low-income public housing project built in 1960–62. One twenty-five-story apartment building and seven twenty-story buildings were designed to house 1,317 families. As the project's name indicates, this was once the site of the fabled Ebbets Field, which opened on April 9, 1913, and where the last baseball game was played on September 24, 1957. Charles Ebbets built the ballpark for the Brooklyn Dodgers of the National League. It was their fourth home.

So much has been written about the Dodgers, more, perhaps, than on any other single topic in Brooklyn history, so I will not go on much about them, other than to make a couple of points on matters of interest to me.

First among these points is that Ebbets Field, designed by C. A. Buskirk, was a beautiful structure. Its capacity peaked at 31,497, which is quite small by present-day standards. Indeed, the size kept down the annual number of ticket sales. The all-time single-season attendance record at Ebbets Field was 1,807,526 in 1947, the year Jackie Robinson joined the Dodgers and broke major-league baseball's color barrier. By contrast, the Los Angeles

Dodgers routinely enjoy annual attendance exceeding three million. The outfield at Ebbets was also very shallow, making it a
home-run hitters' park. The only stadium remaining in major-
league baseball with anything like the dimensions of Ebbets Field
is Chicago's Wrigley Field, which opened only one year after
Ebbets. Both Ebbets and Wrigley were among the first wave of
modern ballparks. As Bill James, one of baseball's greatest historians and critics, put it: "[T]he concept of the huge, permanent,
sturdy, fireproof, grand, spacious, elegant thing that we now call a
ballpark sprang into existence rather suddenly in 1907 or 1908."
The first was Philadelphia's Shibe Park (retired in 1970). Ebbets
Field, though, followed close after, and ranks as a pioneer in the
evolution of the modern ballpark. Buskirk designed Ebbets Field in
what was essentially a Beaux-Arts classical style. Long open
arcades were carried on slender Corinthian columns. The brick
façades were patterned with arched and square-headed windows,
blind panels, stringcourses, cornices, and pilasters. It was a fully
realized classical conception that reminds me to some extent of
Stanford White's Herald Building of the 1890s at 35th Street in
Manhattan, with its similarly long Italian Renaissance–inspired
arcades and similar use of a panel motif. Speaking of Beaux-Arts
classicism, Ebbets Field opened exactly two months and one week
after Grand Central Terminal.

Ebbets Field was practically right around the corner from the
Brooklyn Museum, a block from the Brooklyn Botanic Garden, a
few blocks south of Eastern Parkway, and a couple of blocks north
of the handsome residential neighborhood known today as
Prospect–Lefferts Gardens. Except for the botanic garden, all these
elements of Brooklyn's built environment were more or less in
place when Ebbets Field opened, and the ballpark's design did justice to its setting. The ballpark was also just north of Empire
Boulevard and was served, as was the botanic garden, by the
Prospect Park station of the Brooklyn Rapid Transit Company
(later the Brooklyn-Manhattan Transit Company, later the
Independent Subway). For most, though not all, the location
placed Ebbets Field technically within Crown Heights, though
some considered the area part of Flatbush.

As mentioned, the park's small dimensions made it a hitters' paradise. When the Dodgers first moved to Los Angeles they moved to the Memorial Stadium, a minor-league ballpark of small dimensions that was even more of a hitters' park than Ebbets Field. A couple of years later, however, the Dodgers moved to the new stadium, of much loftier dimensions, at Chavez Ravine, one of the greatest pitchers' parks the game has ever known. In the 1960s and 1970s, during a great wave of new stadium construction in which parks of Ebbets vintage were retired, outfields grew to be spacious expanses with plenty of foul territory between the playing field and the stands, and major-league baseball entered into a pitchers' era, which peaked in 1968, the Year of the Pitcher, when Detroit's Denny McLain won thirty-one games and Bob Gibson of St. Louis posted a ridiculously low 1.12 earned-run average. I probably should not stress this point too much since I have not conducted a detailed study, but it seems to me that the dominance of pitching in the 1960s was directly tied to the decay of inner cities. That is, the new parks tended to be built in spacious settings near expressways in suburban areas. The old ballparks tended to be in dense inner-city settings. The outfield dimensions were small because the urban sites were, of necessity, small. The dominance of pitching therefore went hand in hand with team owners and fans deciding they preferred to drive to the suburbs to catch a game rather than take a trolley or subway to Crown Heights. (Parking around Ebbets Field was very limited.) In the 1980s and 1990s, new ballparks in cities such as Baltimore, Cleveland, and Arlington, Texas, were designed to resemble the older ballparks, including smaller outfields, which is a major determinant (much more so than the "live ball") of the recent surge in hitting (for example, Mark McGwire and his seventy home runs). These new stadiums, however, mimic some of the forms and playing-field dimensions of the older parks, but not their seating or parking capacities. The simple fact of the matter is that there are few instances where it is so clear that architecture plays such a determining role in the results of human endeavor. Again, it is Bill James who put it best: "Stadium architecture . . . is the one largest dynamic of change in baseball; if you put the baseball players of today in the parks of the 1920s, with all of the other differences—the racial composition of the players, the schedule differences, the expansion, the different strike zone—with all of those, in three months they would be playing baseball pretty much the way it was played in the 1920s." It has been said, for example, that Brooklyn's favorite son, Sanford Koufax of Bensonhurst, would never have posted the records he did had the Dodgers remained in Brooklyn. The move from Brooklyn to Los Angeles was not only a move from east coast to west but a move from a hitters' park to a stadium described as the "pitcher's best friend." (Mind you, I am not trying to take any-thing away from Sandy Koufax, who is one of my favorite players of all time. He was, indeed, better in that pitchers' park than was any other pitcher. The point, however, is valid: It is almost cer-tainly the case that he would not today be ranked as one of the two greatest left-handed starting pitchers of all time, with Lefty Grove, had his team remained in Ebbets Field.)

The Dodgers' departure from Brooklyn was an enormous blow to civic pride. I know Brooklyn old-timers in my neighbor-hood who still have not gotten over it, and who today root for no team but do make a point of rooting against the Yankees. I cannot imagine the heartbreak so many Brooklynites experienced in 1957. (I was not born yet.) The 1950s, though, was a decade of turmoil in major-league baseball. Attendance declined precipitously throughout all of baseball during that decade (pundits blamed it on television), and one team after another uprooted itself from its native city and headed to where they thought they could survive. The Browns moved from St. Louis to Baltimore (where they became the Orioles). The Braves moved from Boston to Milwaukee. The Athletics moved from Philadelphia to Kansas City. Note that all these teams left cities where there was another major-league franchise (if you can call the Phillies a major-league franchise). Since Brooklyn became part of New York City in 1898, the Dodgers, too, departed a city where there was another team. For all the talk of Brooklynites' love of their Dodgers, why, throughout the 1950s, did Dodgers attendance drop so much? The all-time high in 1947 of about 1.8 million had fallen to just a little over a million by 1957. Mind you, this was a team at the height of its glory, indeed in the midst of one of the mightiest stretches any team in history (other than the Yankees) has ever experienced: From 1947 to 1957, the Dodgers did not post a losing record and won six—count them—six National League pennants in eleven seasons (though, it is true, only one World Series title). Yet at the end of this amazing stretch, attendance was about 56 percent of what it had been at the beginning. That's a number no business could justify. (The New York Giants' attendance in 1957 was only 41 percent of what it had been in 1947!) Walter O'Malley is a dirty name to many Brooklynites. It should not be. He built the Dodgers into the kind of powerhouse franchise every city dreams of, and his reward was declining attendance. Meanwhile, Ebbets Field, for all its beauty, charm, and history, was clearly an obsolescent facility. The City of New York was never seriously interested in helping O'Malley build a new ballpark. This is not the case of the prover-bial greedy owner holding a city hostage. (There are indeed many cases of just that.) I hate the fact that the Dodgers left Brooklyn. If I were Walter O'Malley, however, I probably would have done what he did, and so, too, would most Brooklynites. In 1955, O'Malley even commissioned R. Buckminster Fuller, the son-in-law of Brooklyn architect and muralist J. Monroe Hewlett, to explore the possibility of constructing a geodesic dome baseball stadium in Brooklyn.

The Dodgers' greatest year was 1947. The all-time atten-dance high was reached in that year, and few were quite yet cog-nizant of the wrenching social dislocations that would occur in the 1950s as America abandoned her cities for suburbs along the Federal government-constructed Interstates. In 1947, the Dodgers won the National League pennant with a record of ninety-four wins and sixty losses, five games better than second-place St. Louis. The Dodgers, managed by Burt Shotton, who was at the helm for one season between stints by Leo the Lip Durocher, lost the World Series, four games to three, to their arch-rival Bronx Yankees. If the Dodgers did not win the World Series that year, why, then, do I call it their greatest season? Everyone knows why. Jackie Robinson joined the Dodgers that year. In that year, he did not play second base, but rather played all his 151 games at first base. (Eddie Stanky, one of the players to hurl racial epithets at Robinson, was the second baseman.) He made an immediate impact. The Dodgers' first baseman the season before, Ed Stevens, batted only .242. Robinson in his first year batted .297. (The following year, Robinson moved to second base as the Dodgers added a young first baseman who would become a mainstay of the franchise, Gilbert Raymond Hodges. Eddie Stanky was traded right before the start of the 1948 season to the Boston Braves for outfielder Bama Rowell and first baseman Ray Sanders, neither of whom ever played a day for the Dodgers.) What makes Jackie Robinson so special, of course, was not that he produced a higher batting average than Ed Stevens, but that he broke baseball's color barrier—he was, as every American knows, the first African American player in the major leagues. Robinson endured a great deal of verbal and sometimes physical abuse from fans and other players, though within the next few seasons other African Americans arrived in the major leagues, with the Dodgers continuing to lead the way. Hall-of-Fame catcher Roy Campanella joined the roster in 1948, pitcher Don Newcombe the year after that. Robinson, by the way, not only endured mental and sometimes physical hardship in his ground-breaking role, but he was ignominiously turned away when he attempted to purchase a house near Ebbets Field in what is now called Prospect–Lefferts Gardens. He moved instead to East Flatbush, to 5224 Tilden Avenue, between East 52nd and East 53rd Streets, in an area where there was already an African American population. There he lived during his first three years with the Dodgers. After that he moved to the integrated community of St. Albans, Queens. One final thing that endears Robinson to old Dodgers fans is that his career ended with the team's tenure in Brooklyn. Unlike the beloved native son Koufax and so many others, he did not leave Brooklyn for Los Angeles. To the contrary: having been a standout athlete at UCLA, he went east to where the action was, to Brooklyn. (By the way, another mark of Robinson's superiority of character is that precious few big-league players in his time were college men.) He went from UCLA to the army to the Kansas City Monarchs of the Negro Leagues. Dodgers' general manager Branch Rickey signed Robinson on October 23, 1945. He played the 1946 season for the Dodgers farm club, the Montreal Royals. The rest is history.

The first night game in the history of baseball took place at Ebbets Field on June 15, 1938. The first baseball game ever to be televised took place at Ebbets Field—the Dodgers versus the Cincinnati Reds, August 26, 1939.

---

14 BROOKLYN JEWISH CENTER
667 Eastern Parkway between New York and Brooklyn Avenues, north side
1922, Louis Allen Abramson with Margon & Glasser

In the 1920s, during a period of intensive rebuilding along Eastern Parkway, architects both Jewish, as here, and Catholic, as at Catholic High School down the street, understood exactly how to design for the parkway. Long buildings worked well. So did shallowly modeled walls. The restrained Beaux-Arts detailing was appropriate for buildings that were, in a sense, background for the Brooklyn Museum. Like Catholic High School, the Brooklyn Jewish Center is a wonderfully urbane presence on Eastern Parkway. The lower portion is fully rusticated, as are the end bays of the upper portion. Eleven high, arched windows, filled with stained glass and separated in a very relaxed rhythm by Corinthian pilasters, range along the upper portion, creating exactly the kind of rhythm that is so necessary along a wide, long boulevard. A balustrade tops off the building. As a building tailored to its location, it could hardly be improved.

A few years after he designed this building, architect Abramson worked with Henry Beaumont Herts, the great theater architect who codesigned the Brooklyn Academy of Music, on the Community Center of Congregation B'nai Jeshurun on West 89th Street in Manhattan. Abramson was an architect of great range. He could work in the classical style of the Brooklyn Jewish Center or of his more elaborate Home and Hospital of the Daughters of Jacob, built in 1920 on East 167th Street in the Bronx, or in the very cool modern style of his Countee Cullen Branch for the New York Public Library, built in 1942 on West 136th Street in Harlem.

Grant Square

15 *23rd Regiment Armory*

15 23rd REGIMENT ARMORY
1322 Bedford Avenue between Pacific Street and Atlantic Avenue, west side
1891–95, Fowler & Hough

There is almost a tradition in Brooklyn of prominent, often magnificent, corner towers. Think, for example, of James W. Naughton's Boys' High School (1891) on Marcy Avenue or of the apartment houses by Montrose W. Morris, the Imperial on Bedford Avenue and Pacific Street, and the Renaissance on Nostrand Avenue and Hancock Street, both from 1892. From right around the same time (and across the street from the Imperial) is the 23rd Regiment Armory, with what might be the grandest corner tower of them all. The building features a gabled face with a high, deep arched entrance flanked by twin 70-foot-high crenellated towers. Five more 70-foot-high crenellated towers are disposed about the building. At the corner of Bedford Avenue and Pacific Street is the pièce de résistance, a 136-foot-high crenellated tower, a massive round form with evenly spaced slit-like openings like the bowmen's slots in medieval castles. The brick tower rises from a base of rock-faced sandstone. The whole building, particularly this tower, is among Brooklyn's wonderful examples of the nineteenth-century bricklayer's craft. Sometimes a castellated fantasy such as this does not seem to work as a serious piece of architecture. Yet here the forms—and, even more, the materials—are handled so skillfully and the building is sited so well that it is a major adornment to the Grant Square neighborhood.

Halstead Parker Fowler and William C. Hough were Brooklyn-based architects particularly renowned for churches and hospitals. An example of the former is their Throop Avenue Presbyterian Church (1889–90) at Willoughby Avenue. An example of their work in the latter building type is the Dudley Memorial Pavilion of Long Island College Hospital, on Henry and Amity Streets in Cobble Hill. Built in 1902 in a Beaux-Arts style, it could not be more different from the armory.

16 IMPERIAL (apartments)
1198 Pacific Street, southeast corner of Bedford Avenue
1892, Montrose W. Morris

The Imperial, like the Alhambra and the Renaissance nearby in Bedford-Stuyvesant, is one of the apartment houses Montrose W. Morris designed for the developer Louis F. Seitz. It is a superb example of Morris at his best, both stately and picturesque. The stateliness comes from Morris's general love of balance and symmetry and for very carefully measured compositions. The picturesqueness is in the many skyline projections, the conical towers, high chimneys,

16 Imperial (apartments)

steeply hipped roofs, projecting dormers, as well as in the basically chateauesque mien of the design. Along Bedford Avenue big, bold round towers, rising five stories and topped by conical roofs, flank a powerful five-bay arcade that rises from the second through the fourth stories, and a fifth story treated almost in an aedicular fashion, with a central gabled dormer projecting from a hipped roof over a series of small, attic-like windows. The five big arches spring from blocks supported by paired Corinthian columns. Recessed within these arches, the windows of the individual floors are treated as slightly projecting three-sided oriels. The second-floor windows are decidedly classical in design, with triangular pediments carried on colonnettes. These window bays are framed in metal. The Roman brick and terra-cotta of the façades are used for a striped, polychromatic effect. The roofs are slate.

This is the building that for me most clearly defines the Grant Square neighborhood. It bespeaks the values of Brooklyn's bourgeois interlude, exuding a sense of solidity and longevity that proved rather chimerical, as so often is the case, not only in Brooklyn but in America. In Paris or Vienna or Bucharest, a building such as this might have apartments rented—not owned—by the same families over several generations.

17 **ST. BARTHOLOMEW'S CHURCH (Episcopal)**
1227 Pacific Street between Bedford and Nostrand Avenues,
north side
1886–90, George P. Chappell

This is one of the most unusual churches in Brooklyn. Chappell, an architect who always exhibited a strong romantic streak, perhaps never went further in the direction of a kind of rustic, Arts & Crafts style than he did here. The gabled end of the church, which is constructed with rough-hewn stone at the base and dark brick above, stands next to and is dwarfed by a massive, gently battered square tower that rises to a low-pitched, squatly battered tile-shingled roof. The brick tower has corners of rough stone. On the other side of the tower from the main church is an openwork wooden porch with a shingled, gabled roof and low, rough stone walls. It is a country church through and through, part of the early 1880s effort to promote Bedford as a bucolic suburb. This is the ecclesiastical equivalent of J. Sarsfield Kennedy's house for Howard E. Jones, built in 1916–17 on Narrows Avenue and 83rd Street in Bay Ridge.

The absence of cyclopean masonry may make it so that this does not at first register as Richardsonian Romanesque, but that is indeed what it is. Chappell was a sophisticated practitioner, and it is impossible not to think he was familiar with several designs of Richardson's containing elements that can be found in this church. Such works as the F. L. Ames Gate Lodge of 1880–81 in North Easton, Massachusetts; the Converse Memorial Public Library of 1883–85 in Malden, Massachusetts; the Immanuel Baptist Church of 1884–86 in Newton, Massachusetts; and even some of Richardson's train stations all seem to have contributed to Chappell's design. H. H. Richardson was one of the great form-givers to nineteenth-century American architecture, and nowhere was his influence felt more keenly than in Brooklyn.

About the same time this church was designed, Chappell, an ubiquitous nineteenth-century Brooklyn architect whose row houses can be seen from Park Slope to Bedford-Stuyvesant, also designed the Tompkins Avenue Congregational Church, which was heavily influenced by Richardson as well, at the corner of MacDonough Street in nearby Bedford-Stuyvesant.

18 UNION LEAGUE CLUB OF BROOKLYN
Southeast corner of Bedford Avenue and Dean Street
1889–90, P. J. Lauritzen

The Union League Club was an important and prestigious nineteenth-century organization. It still exists, of course, and is still prestigious, though it no longer has a Brooklyn outpost. In Brooklyn's bourgeois interlude, private clubs, whether the Montauk in Park Slope, the Lincoln in Bedford-Stuyvesant, the Hamilton or the Crescent Athletic in Brooklyn Heights, were very important institutions. Today only a handful hang on. The Union League dates to 1863 and the Civil War. It was an offshoot of the Union Club, one of New York City's oldest and most distinguished gentlemen's clubs. The Union League was formed by supporters of the Union cause in the Civil War. It was founded in Manhattan: onetime Cobble Hill resident Leonard Jerome gave the club the use of his mansion on Madison Avenue and 26th Street. Other Union League Clubs sprang up in other cities. In Philadelphia, the Union League Club on Broad Street is one of that city's architectural adornments. Since 1931, Manhattan's Union League Club, with a large membership, has been housed in an imposing neo-Georgian building on Park Avenue and 37th Street. Brooklyn's Union League Club was here on Grant Square. Club members paid for the fine equestrian statue of Ulysses S. Grant right outside. The clubhouse itself was a distinctive design by

18 *Union League Club of Brooklyn*

Lauritzen & Voss. Rock-faced Belleville, New Jersey, brownstone is coursed with brick, smooth granite, and terra-cotta to create a building of many horizontal parts. On the right along Bedford Avenue is a gently swelling bay rising through the second and third stories to form a fourth-floor loggia. A gabled dormer projects from the hipped roof above the loggia. This part of the design seems quite reminiscent of Park Slope's Montauk Club, which was built at almost exactly the same time as this. At the first floor the left half of the façade features three large arched openings with rock-faced stone voussoirs; the arch on the right is up a stone porch placed parallel to the street and is the main entrance to the clubhouse. Portrait heads of Abraham Lincoln and Ulysses S. Grant appear in the spandrels of the center arch. This half of the first floor carries a balustraded balcony in the center of the building. At the corner of Bedford and Dean Streets is that hallmark of nineteenth-century Brooklyn architecture, the flashy corner tower. It rises as a projection from the second-floor balcony and is crowned four floors above with an octagonal, balustraded balcony beneath a conical tile roof. There were bowling alleys and shooting galleries in the basement (the Montauk, Crescent Athletic, and Knickerbocker Field clubs all had basement bowling alleys), dining and reception rooms on the first floor, library and billiards rooms on the second, private dining rooms and bachelors' apartments on the third, a gymnasium on the fourth, and a rooftop lounge.

It is now the Bhraggs Grant Square Senior Citizens' Center.

19 EQUESTRIAN STATUE OF ULYSSES S. GRANT
Grant Square
Bedford Avenue at Dean Street
1896, William Ordway Partridge

Brooklyn is blessed in having some of America's finest equestrian monuments. Henry Merwin Shrady's George Washington in Williamsburg's Continental Army Plaza is the best. Frederick MacMonnies contributed the excellent equestrian statue of Henry Warner Slocum at Grand Army Plaza. Here in Grant Square, William Ordway Partridge gave us this wonderful bronze equestrian statue of Ulysses Simpson Grant (1822–85). Grant was born in Ohio and graduated from West Point. He fought in the Mexican War in 1845, and in 1852, temperamentally unsuited, even after so many years, to submit to Army discipline, he resigned from the Army and went into business in Missouri and then Illinois. His business exploits were a study in futility, and in 1861 at the outbreak of the Civil War, he rejoined the Army. Because of his background he was made a brigadier general, and led his troops to the first major Union victories of the war. In March 1864, President Lincoln made Grant supreme commander of all Union forces. Robert E. Lee surrendered to General Grant on April 9, 1865, at Appomattox, Virginia. The following year, Grant was made a full general, an honor that had previously been bestowed only on George Washington. In 1868, he was elected president, defeating New York's Democratic governor Horatio Seymour. In spite of an administration marked by scandals and failed Reconstruction policies, Grant was reelected in 1872, defeating another New Yorker, Horace Greeley. The scandals continued, and in 1876, the Republicans refused to renominate Grant. He moved to New York City where, wracked by financial problems and throat cancer, he composed and published the *Personal Memoirs of U. S. Grant* (1885–86), an American literary classic that was also a bestseller, the royalties from which supported his family after his death. He died in Saratoga Springs, New York, the same town in which James S. T. Stranahan would die thirteen years later. Partridge portrays Grant in a naturalistic, unidealized way, portly, rumpled, casual. His horse, by contrast, is a fine specimen, sinewy and alert. Above all, Grant seems alive. One need compare this Grant to the relatively lifeless one that appears in relief (also from 1896) on the Soldiers' and Sailors' Memorial Arch to see how good Partridge's statue is. William Ordway Partridge (1861–1930) was a fascinating figure. Sculptor was but one of the hats worn by

19 *Equestrian Statue of Ulysses S. Grant*

this man who was also a poet, actor, lecturer, author, and critic. He was born in Paris to rich Americans, attended Columbia, and studied in Florence, Rome, and at the École des Beaux-Arts in Paris. In 1889, he established a studio in Milton, Massachusetts. Two years later he created a marble portrait bust of Chief Justice Melville Fuller for the Capitol in Washington, D.C. Partridge exhibited ten works at the Columbian Exposition in 1893, including a model of the bronze statue of Alexander Hamilton placed that year on Remsen Street in Brooklyn Heights, where it stood for forty-three years in front of the prestigious Hamilton Club before being moved to its present location at Hamilton Grange on Convent Avenue and 141st Street in Manhattan. At Columbia University, Partridge's alma mater, he did another Hamilton (1908) as well as a fine bronze Thomas Jefferson (1914). Late in his career Partridge did the bronze statue of Samuel J. Tilden (1926) on Riverside Drive and 112th Street. Partridge's marble Pietà from 1906 can be seen in the ambulatory of St. Patrick's Cathedral.

The two most famous Civil War generals associated with Brooklyn, by the way, were both Confederates. In the 1850s, Robert E. Lee and Thomas "Stonewall" Jackson were both stationed at Fort Hamilton in Bay Ridge, and were well known to members of the greater community. Indeed, Jackson was baptized at the age of thirty in St. John's Episcopal Church in Bay Ridge.

The St. Mark's Avenue Corridor

20 **FIRST CHURCH OF CHRIST, SCIENTIST**
Southwest corner of New York Avenue and Dean Street
1909, Henry Ives Cobb

The entrance of this remarkable limestone church is on New York Avenue, where one finds a three-part design with end pavilions flanking a convex center section. Broad arches with mini-rose windows top the doorways in the end pavilions. The convex section features seven elaborate arched windows separated by slender stone columns in the Romanesque style. Above and behind this convex section is the unusual octagonal form of the church itself. The church has a pyramidal tile roof with a prominent gabled dormer on each of its eight sides. The south-facing dormer is pointed right into the light court of the apartment building at 110 New York Avenue. The church features lots of arches and fine stained glass. Henry Ives Cobb (1859–1931) was born in Brookline, Massachusetts. He attended the Massachusetts Institute of Technology and Harvard and worked for the Boston firm of Peabody & Stearns before moving in 1882 to Chicago, the city with which he is most closely associated. Cobb designed several major landmarks in that city, most notably the Newberry Library (1890–93) and the original parts

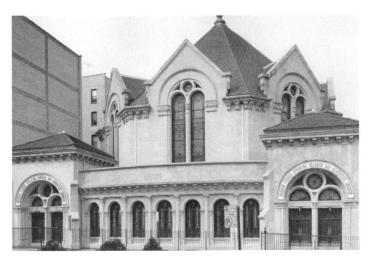

20 *First Church of Christ, Scientist*

of the University of Chicago campus in the 1890s. He also designed the monumental old Federal Building and Court House, which was torn down in the 1960s. In 1902, Cobb moved his practice to New York City. He designed the Sinclair Oil Building (1909–10) on Liberty Street in Manhattan, which he must have been working on at the same time as this church.

It is now the Hebron French-Speaking Seventh-Day Adventist Church. Across New York Avenue is another church of interest. Originally the New York Avenue Methodist Church, it is now the Union United Methodist Church. It was built in 1892, and its red brick and red sandstone make it chromatically as different as can be from the First Church of Christ, Scientist. J. C. Cady & Co. designed it. This was the firm of Josiah Cleveland Cady, who designed the Brooklyn Art Association Building (1869–72; demolished) on Montague Street and the German Evangelical Lutheran Church (1888) on Schermerhorn Street. The New York Avenue Methodist Church is in the Romanesque Revival style, including some elements stylistically similar to the church across the street though the effect is very different. The entrance is through a fine receding arch in the base of the high, bold tower that has slit-like openings, a turret on the left, and a Romanesque-style arch composition at the top. Note the excellent stepped corbeling.

21 DEAN SAGE HOUSE
839 St. Mark's Avenue, northeast corner of Brooklyn Avenue
1869, Russell Sturgis

We can see from this house that Crown Heights became a fashionable area at around the same time as Fort Greene and Clinton Hill. Grand houses appeared in the St. Mark's Avenue area after the Civil War, as on Clinton Avenue, and gradually yielded to substantial row houses as the century drew to a close. The Dean Sage house is an excellent example of the kind of solid, comfortable villas built in the northern part of Crown Heights after the Civil War. The style is Romanesque Revival, and the dominant material is rock-faced brownstone laid in random ashlar. The design is deceptively simple. A two-stage stepped walkway of stone leads from the street across a slightly elevated front garden to a broad stone porch and an arched entrance framed in terra-cotta ornament. The willowy, almost Art Nouveau–seeming ironwork of the transom is especially fine—maybe the single finest thing about the house. A fine black iron fence encloses the garden. The house's windows are square-headed with smooth stone surrounds and

21 *Dean Sage House*

are topped by segmental-arched moldings of smooth stone. In the rear on Brooklyn Avenue is a fine polygonal tower. Three dormers project from the tower's steep, pointy pyramidal roof, making for a lively silhouette. The tower has pointed-arch windows. Above the cornice, which is carried on wood beams, is a hipped roof with broad, hipped dormers and high chimneys. The Sage house exhibits very well the qualities described by the architectural historian Leland M. Roth in his discussion of the lessons Sturgis learned from his study of John Ruskin: "Planning should be simple and straightforward, with boldly irregular masses expressive of human use." One can see much in the Sage house that appeared in 1869–70 in Sturgis's most celebrated design, Farnam Hall at Yale University.

RUSSELL STURGIS (1836–1909)

Russell Sturgis was only thirty-three years old when his house for Dean Sage was built on St. Mark's Avenue. He was born in Baltimore in 1836 and graduated from the College of the City of New York in 1856. The year after the Dean Sage house was built, Sturgis received an M.A. degree from Yale, which awarded him the Ph.D. degree in 1893. He maintained a New York City practice from 1863 to 1880. He left New York City in 1880 for an extended trip through Europe. As a writer for the *New Path*, Sturgis was one of the foremost American exponents of the ideas of John Ruskin (1819–1900). Another contributor to the *New Path* was Peter B. Wight, who designed the Mercantile Library on Montague Street and the interior of the Williamsburgh Savings Bank on Broadway and Driggs Avenue. Sturgis and Wight became close friends while students together at the College of the City of New York in the 1850s. Together they discovered Jacob Wrey Mould's All Souls' Unitarian Church on Fourth Avenue and 20th Street. Sturgis and Wight got to know Mould and credited his works with inspiring their desire to become architects. Sturgis and Wight together read Ruskin's *Seven Lamps of Architecture* (1849) and *Stones of Venice* (1851–53). In 1863, the two friends helped found the Society for the Advancement of Truth in Art. The society's journal, which appeared from 1863 to 1865, was the *New Path.* Sturgis worked briefly for Leopold Eidlitz, architect of the Brooklyn Academy of Music on Montague Street, and through him acquired a taste for the German *Rundbogenstil.* Sturgis was more significant as a writer than as a designer. He was an art critic for the *Nation,* wrote for the *North American Review* and *Architectural Record,* and was arts editor of *Scribner's* magazine. He was editor-in-chief of the very important *Dictionary of Architecture and Building* (1901–2). Both as a designer and as a critic, Sturgis mentored a generation of New York architects, whose work in the end turned out to be much different from what Sturgis prescribed. In 1867, two years before the Dean Sage house, Charles Follen McKim, architect of the Brooklyn Museum, worked in Russell Sturgis's office before heading to the École des Beaux-Arts. At the time of the Dean Sage house, William Rutherford Mead worked as a paying pupil in Sturgis's office, under the supervision of George Fletcher Babb who, as part of Babb, Cook & Willard, would contribute a good deal to Brooklyn's architectural scene. Mead worked for Sturgis from 1868 to 1871 before touring Europe for a year. Sturgis's office at this time was at 57 Broadway. In the same building were the offices of Gambrill & Richardson. When in 1872 Mead returned to New York, he went to Sturgis's office to inquire about work. Sturgis was out of town, so Mead went to the Gambrill & Richardson office. There he met a Gambrill & Richardson employee, Charles Follen McKim. Such was the genesis of McKim, Mead & White, much of whose output would meet with Sturgis's stern disapproval.

22 *855-857 St. Mark's Avenue*

22 855–857 ST. MARK'S AVENUE
Between Brooklyn and Kingston Avenues, north side
1892, Montrose W. Morris

Montrose Morris designed this double house one year before the Columbian Exposition and three to seven years after his houses on Hancock Street in Bedford-Stuyvesant. I think we see Morris here in a transitional phase from his Romanesque Revival of the 1880s to his later classicism. This three-story, light-colored double house has a first story faced in rough stone and second and third stories faced in Roman brick trimmed with stone. There are two stoops. The houses have a shared gabled top with a Palladianesque arrangement. On the right of the house is a prominent three-story round tower, reminiscent of the towers of the Renaissance Apartments on Nostrand Avenue and Hancock Street, built in the same year as this double house. On the left of the house is a second-floor balcony behind a stone balustrade. In the center over the double doorway is a loggia-like balcony framed by two stone columns in the Romanesque style. A band of wonderfully intricate terra-cotta ornament tops this balcony. The mansardish roof is of shingle tiles.

23 BROOKLYN CHILDREN'S MUSEUM
Southeast corner of Brooklyn and St. Mark's Avenues
1972–77, Hardy Holzman Pfeiffer

The Brooklyn Children's Museum, which recently celebrated its one-hundredth birthday, is entered at the northwest corner of Brower Park. Most of the museum exists below the park. The Brower Park site has had a complicated history. The City of Brooklyn acquired the southern half of the site fronting on Park Place in 1892. The northern half of the site was at that time occupied by a pair of mansions of the kind that made St. Mark's Avenue famous. One was the William Newton Adams house, built in 1867 and the birthplace of the distinguished American historian James Truslow Adams. The house was taken over by the then new Brooklyn Children's Museum, a branch of the Brooklyn Institute of Arts and Sciences, in 1899. In the late 1920s, the museum expanded into the 1890 mansion next door, the L. C. Smith house. The Brooklyn Children's Museum is said to have been the first museum in the world dedicated exclusively to children, and pioneered hands-on, or what we might call "interactive," exhibits, as a way of engaging the interest of children. Many of the museological methods pioneered here have become standard not only in other children's museums, where they make a great deal of pedagogical sense, but in all kinds of other, "adult" museums as well, where the implication is that adult attention spans have become shorter and shorter as the twentieth century has progressed. Be that as it may, the Brooklyn Children's Museum is justly renowned. Among the items displayed in the museum are numerous ethnographic and natural history objects, some of which were once housed in the Brooklyn Museum but eventually spun off as that institution felt the need to refine its focus. After about seven decades in the Adams house and five in the Smith house, the Brooklyn Children's Museum decided that in order to carry out its mission more effectively, both houses had to be torn down and a new, purpose-built facility erected in their place. The houses came down in 1967. As a result of the city's fiscal crisis, the new museum's opening was delayed until 1977. It is a complex structure, most of it subterranean, designed by the renowned Manhattan firm of Hardy Holzman Pfeiffer, and making playful use of all manner of architectural and industrial detritus. One enters the museum, for example, through a trolley kiosk dating from around 1910, which once stood at the Queensboro Bridge. When the museum opened, Paul Goldberger, architectural critic for the *New York Times,* praised it effusively, calling it "a sort of learned funhouse—a collection of educational exhibitions housed in a wildly exuberant structure that is itself the best exhibition of all."

Brower Park was named for George V. Brower (1839? –1921), who succeeded the great James S. T. Stranahan as Brooklyn Parks Commissioner, serving from 1889 to 1894 and earning M. M. Graff's accolade as the most competent of Brooklyn's parks administrators after Stranahan. ("The excellent, capable George Brower," she called him.) Brower also served as New York City Parks Commissioner from 1898 to 1901. He lived nearby at 1084 Park Place, where he died in 1921.

St. Mark's Avenue is still pretty grand, though only a shadow of what it once was, as several of its mansions have been wantonly demolished. The Adams and Smith houses went for the new Brooklyn Children's Museum. The Marcus Garvey Nursing Home on the south side of St. Mark's Avenue between New York and Brooklyn Avenues, one block to the west of the Brooklyn Children's Museum, replaced several houses in 1977, including what had been the home of Abraham Abraham, the founder of Abraham & Straus.

24 ST. GREGORY'S CHURCH (R. C.)
224 Brooklyn Avenue, northwest corner of St. John's Place
1917, Helmle & Corbett

In his definitive monograph on McKim, Mead & White, the architectural historian Leland M. Roth wrote of Stanford White's Judson Memorial Baptist Church (1888–93) that it "had little immediate influence, for Gothic still conveyed an image preferred by Roman Catholics and most Protestant denominations; indeed, within less than a decade the successful efforts of

24 *St. Gregory's Church*

Henry Vaughan and Ralph Adams Cram to reinvest Gothic with formal, icono-
graphical, and structural meaning were to limit the influence of McKim, Mead
& White in developing a Renaissance ecclesiastical style." That is generally
true. No one, however, told Frank J. Helmle (1869–1929).

Helmle & Huberty, Brooklyn's leading firm of classical architects had, many
years before, worked closely with Stanford White on the introduction of classical
elements into Prospect Park. Helmle & Huberty designed the Boathouse (1904),
among other things. Between the Boathouse, completed two years before
Stanford White's death, and St. Gregory's Church, Helmle & Huberty gave
Brooklyn the Williamsburg Trust Company (1906) in Williamsburg, the
Greenpoint Savings Bank (1908) in Greenpoint, the Hotel Bossert (1909) in
Brooklyn Heights, and St. Barbara's Church (1910) in Bushwick. Ulrich Huberty
died in 1910 at the age of only thirty-three. After Huberty's death, Helmle teamed
up with a young architect named Harvey Wiley Corbett. At around the same time
they were working on St. Gregory's Church, they were designing the Bush Tower
(for Brooklyn's Irving Bush) on West 42nd Street. Bush Tower was mainly Harvey
Wiley Corbett's job. St. Gregory's was mainly Frank Helmle's.

It is one of the most beautiful churches in Brooklyn. The plan is basilican
in the manner of Early Christian churches in Rome of the fourth and fifth centuries. The portico features six polished granite columns. The body of the church
is light-colored brick with trim of limestone and light-colored terra-cotta. The
three front doors have elaborate terra-cotta enframements in floral, bead, and
astragal patterns. A terra-cotta angel tops the center door. Past the columns on
the porch, look up and note the porch roof of polychromed wood beams. The
upper part of the Brooklyn Avenue façade above the columned portico features
a fine rose window designed by J. Gordon Guthrie (1874–1961), one of the leading American stained-glass artists of the time. The rose window is flanked by two
niches on either side containing fully modeled statues of the four Evangelists
(from left to right, Mark, John, Matthew, and Luke) above panels containing
their symbols. Toward the back on St. John's Place is the high, seven-stage, brick
and terra-cotta bell tower. The basic form of St. Gregory's clearly derives from
the fourth-century San Paolo fuori le mura in Rome. The exact relationship of
church, tower, and rounded apse, however, may be closer to the seventh-century
Santa Agnese fuori le mura in Rome. In the base of the tower is a doorway with
an arched hood in the fifteenth-century Italian Renaissance manner. The tower
and this doorway are derived from the same sources as and are distinctly reminiscent of Stanford White's Judson Memorial Baptist Church.

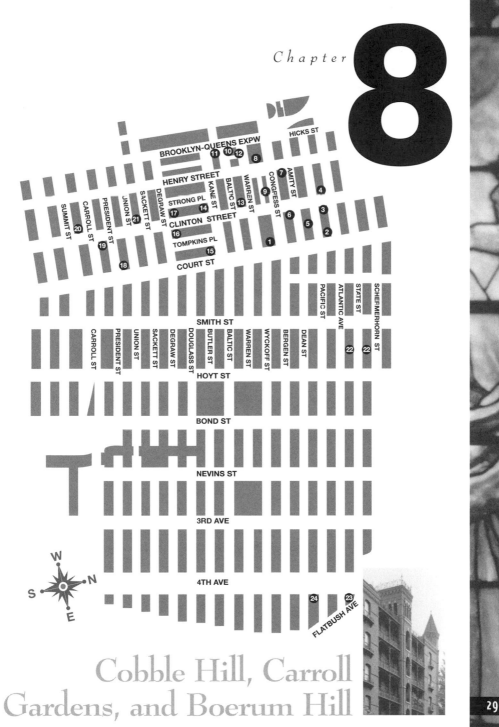

Cobble Hill, Carroll Gardens, and Boerum Hill

14 *Sanctuary,*
Christ Church

Cobble Hill, Carroll Gardens, and Boerum Hill

The nearest subway station to our starting point is the Bergen Street stop on the F and G lines at Smith Street. Walk west on Bergen Street for two blocks to Court Street. On the west side of Court Street, Bergen Street changes its name to Congress Street. St. Paul's Church is right at the corner of Court and Congress Streets.

Cobble Hill

Cobble Hill is bounded to the north by Atlantic Avenue, to the west by the Brooklyn-Queens Expressway, to the south by Degraw Street, and to the east by Court Street. In 1969, the New York City Landmarks Preservation Commission designated a Cobble Hill Historic District with basically the same boundaries, except for a few blocks in the northwest corner of the neighborhood where the buildings of Long Island College Hospital are concentrated.

"Cobble Hill" is a coinage of 1950s real-estate brokers. The area seemed poised for a comeback after years of declining property values. It had always been considered South Brooklyn. In the 1960s and 1970s, young professionals found in certain South Brooklyn neighborhoods much of what they admired in adjacent Brooklyn Heights but for less money. "Cobble Hill" was itself an indication of growing historical interest in the area, for the name comes from "Cobleshill," which appeared first on a 1766 map. When ferry service began in 1836 from the foot of Atlantic Avenue, the area boomed.

301

Farms that had been here since the seventeenth century were subdivided and the streets were lined with brick and then with brownstone row houses. Cobble Hill is only slightly less old than most of Brooklyn Heights and exhibits the same progression of residential architectural styles, from Greek Revival to Italianate to Romanesque Revival and Queen Anne. Cobble Hill is a major urban success story. It is a close-knit, low-crime, family-oriented neighborhood, though one that is increasingly expensive (many houses cost more than a million dollars). Court Street, the "high street," is filled with interesting restaurants, cafés, and shops, all of them, in contrast to Montague Street in Brooklyn Heights, of the independent, mom-and-pop variety. As one walks farther south along Court Street toward the contiguous neighborhood of Carroll Gardens, Italian specialty stores and restaurants and bakeries begin, deliciously, to dominate.

1 **ST. PAUL'S CHURCH (R. C.)**
Southwest corner of Court and Congress Streets
1838, Gamaliel King
Steeple: early 1860s
Brownstone veneer: 1888
New sanctuary and sacristy: 1906
Rectory: 1936, Henry J. McGill (234 Congress Street
between Clinton and Court Streets, south side)

It's now St. Paul's, St. Peter's, Our Lady of Pilar Church—the ungainly name the result of successive mergers of congregations as the number of Sunday churchgoers has declined. Gamaliel King designed this church around the same time he designed Brooklyn City Hall. While City Hall is still recognizably his building, however, this one is not. The original style was, believe it or not, Greek Revival, as at City Hall. Remodelings and accretions over the years have almost completely obscured King's design. The verdigris copper steeple was added about twenty-five years after the church opened, and the brownstone veneer about twenty-five years after that. What was modest Greek Revival became Victorian Gothic, its high steeple visible up and down Court Street.

Most interesting of all, St. Paul's Church was built on land that was part of the estate of Cornelius Heeney (1754–1848), who is buried in the churchyard. Heeney was a Catholic emigrant from, as fate would have it,

Kings County, Ireland. At the age of thirty he came to America—first to Philadelphia, then to New York City. In New York he took a job as a book-keeper for the furrier William Backhouse of Little Dock Street. Another of Backhouse's employees was John Jacob Astor. Eventually Heeney made his fortune in the fur trade. He devoted his life to charitable causes and is considered by some a candidate for sainthood. William Harper Bennett, in *Catholic Footsteps in Old New York* (1909), said of Heeney that "Wealth flowed in upon him, and his disposition of it entitles him to be described as New York and Brooklyn's greatest philanthropist." He was a trustee of St. Peter's Church, New York City's oldest Roman Catholic congregation, and was the donor of pews and gallery fittings to its new church of the 1830s on Barclay Street. That building, which is still standing, was one of New York's most important in the Greek Revival style. When Heeney donated the site of St. Paul's Church on Court Street, he stipulated "that it should architecturally conform to St. Peter's," and so it did. One wonders what, from his vantage point at the back of the church, he thought of all the alterations over the years. In 1828, the trustees of St. Peter's, including Heeney, purchased a block on Manhattan's Fifth Avenue with a view toward establishing a Catholic cemetery. The site eventually was used for St. Patrick's Cathedral. He helped establish the Sisters of Charity in New York and personally appealed to Mother Seton to send some of her nuns from Emmitsburg to open an orphanage on Prince Street. In 1806, he purchased a seventeen-acre site, bounded by the present Court, Congress, and Amity Streets and the East River, for his estate. His large wood-frame house looked across the river to lower Manhattan. Heeney donated the land bounded by Court, Congress, Clinton, and Warren Streets for a seminary after the one in Nyack burned down in 1833. In a manner oddly typical for Brooklyn, foundations were dug and walls began to rise for the seminary, then work halted. Heeney and Bishop Dubois were unable to come to terms with each other on the issue of the role of laymen in running the seminary. Heeney withdrew his offer of the land, and the site was then used for St. Paul's Church. Heeney became guardian to a fatherless ten-year-old Brooklyn boy named John McCloskey, who would become New York's second archbishop and the country's first cardinal. It is impossible to calculate the contribution of Heeney to the growth of the New York Catholic Church. One can see his grave by entering the small garden on the Congress Street side, then passing through the small chapel into the churchyard.

2 SOUTH BROOKLYN SAVINGS INSTITUTION
130 Court Street, southwest corner of Atlantic Avenue
1922, McKenzie, Voorhees & Gmelin
Addition: 1936, Charles A. Holmes

This is a splendid classical bank by architects who would become known as masters of the Art Deco skyscraper. The façade is fully rusticated, and the entrance arch is in the Tuscan style of the early Renaissance. Best of all is the wonderful row of carved eagles serving as brackets under the cornice. Note also the figure sculpture in the tympanum of the entrance arch and the fine iron fence with its gryphons. (Gryphons, which symbolize strength and vigilance, can also be found at York & Sawyer's Brooklyn Trust Company on Montague and Clinton Streets.) On the north half of the Court Street façade is a bronze plaque with an equestrian relief of George Washington. John DeCesare was the sculptor. The inscription reads:

> *Near this place during the Revolutionary War stood the Ponkiesberg fortification from which General George Washington is said to have observed the fighting at Gowanus during the Battle of Long Island, August 27, 1776, erected in 1926 by the South Brooklyn Savings Institution.*

The South Brooklyn Savings Institution became Independence Savings Bank, which continues to maintain its headquarters in this building. "South Brooklyn" once referred to such neighborhoods as Cobble Hill, Carroll Gardens, and Red Hook when they were the southernmost of the developed communities of the old City of Brooklyn. I suppose the bank changed its name because "South Brooklyn" became geographically inaccurate.

Around the corner on Atlantic Avenue, which separates Cobble Hill from Brooklyn Heights, is New York City's principal commercial strip of the Arabic-speaking population from Lebanon, Morocco, Yemen, Syria, and other countries of the Middle East. Arabs had long been concentrated in the lower West Side of Manhattan in the Washington Market vicinity. Postwar urban-renewal projects, however, of which the biggest was the World Trade Center, caused the Arab population to migrate across the East River to Cobble Hill. In the late-nineteenth and early-twentieth centuries, prior to the immigration restrictions of 1924, most Arabs in New York City were Christians. Near this Arab shopping district is Richard Upjohn's Congregational Church of the Pilgrims on Remsen and Henry Streets, which is now Our Lady of Lebanon Maronite Rite Roman Catholic Church. These local Arab Christians may have a thing for old Congregational churches, because they also took over the Park Congregational Church on Eighth Avenue in Park Slope, now called Virgin Mary Byzantine Melkite Catholic Church. After immigration restrictions were lifted in 1965, new waves of Arab immigrants in New York have as often been Muslim as Christian. Cobble Hill is now home to many Muslim as well as Christian Arabs. Of great renown is the Sahadi Importing Company at 187 Atlantic Avenue, between Court and Clinton Streets on the north side. It is said to be the largest Middle Eastern food store in New York City. On the same block at No. 195 is Damascus Bakery, renowned for its many varieties of pita bread. On a slightly different note, at the intersection of Atlantic Avenue and Court Street is a utility hole leading to the Atlantic Avenue Subway Tunnel. This tunnel was built for a subterranean railway in 1861 and abandoned in 1884. A local transportation history buff named Robert Diamond rediscovered the tunnel, had it reopened, successfully campaigned to have it placed on the National Register of Historic Places, and leads occasional tours of it.

3 SOUTH BROOKLYN SAVINGS BANK
191 Clinton Street, southeast corner of Atlantic Avenue
1871, E. L. Roberts

Crisp execution in Tuckahoe marble of deep window reveals, segmental arches, a strong cornice, and the lovely incised ornament make this a picture-perfect neo-Grec commercial building. Now used as apartments, this was the headquarters of the bank that later moved around the corner and became Independence Savings Bank. The architect, Ebenezer L. Roberts, designed Charles Pratt's Clinton Avenue house three years after this bank. Pratt may have been responsible for the selection of Roberts to design Standard Oil's headquarters at 26 Broadway in Manhattan in the 1880s. William B. Tubby, who designed the nearby apartments at 194–200 Court Street (1898) between Congress and Warren Streets, worked for Roberts and succeeded to his practice.

4 214 CLINTON STREET (apartments)
Northwest corner of Pacific Street
1892, H. W. Billard

The romantic materials are rock-faced brownstone and heavily textured brick. The doorway on Clinton Street has a Romanesque-feeling arch. The heavy pediment has cornices of rock-faced stone that look like logs. It is hard to tell if this was intentional or the result of excessive weathering. Either way, it is strikingly unusual. In the tympanum is a human face. The same treatment can be seen at the Pacific Street entrance, though the human face has completely worn away.

5 197 AMITY STREET
Between Court and Clinton Streets, north side
1849

With, at this writing, its façade heavily weathered, this house is not physically prepossessing. It is, however, of enormous historical interest. This was the birthplace on January 9, 1854, of Jennie Jerome (d. 1921), the daughter of the lawyer, financier, and society figure Leonard Jerome (1817–91). As though a character in a Henry James novel, Jennie married British nobleman Lord Randolph Churchill in 1874. That same year, their son, Winston, was born. Jennie's father was a fascinating man. The onetime American consul in Trieste, he was nineteenth-century New York's quintessential sporting gentleman. His great love was racing horses, and in 1866 he established the Jerome Park Racetrack in the Bronx. This fashionable course is where the Belmont Stakes was held every year until 1890, when the Jerome Park Reservoir replaced the track. Jerome laid out his eponymous Boulevard, which still exists, as a route to his racetrack. (Several institutional buildings, including those of Bronx High School of Science and Lehman College, also stand on land that was part of the racetrack complex.) The Jeromes moved in 1859 from Amity Street to a mansion (since demolished) on Madison Avenue at 26th Street in the then-fashionable Madison Square neighborhood.

See Anita Leslie, *The Remarkable Mr. Jerome* (New York, 1954), and Ralph G. Martin, *Jennie* (New York, 1971).

6 219 CLINTON STREET
Southeast corner of Amity Street
1844
Remodeled: 1891, D'Oench & Simon

The stoop, which is parallel to the street, and the base are of brownstone with brick above. Originally the house of Abraham DeGraw, the local landowner remembered in the name of Degraw Street, the Greek Revival house was substantially remodeled and enlarged for Ralph L. Cutter almost fifty years after it was built. Among the additions were the stepped gable in front and the picturesque stepped profile of the south side leading to a tile-topped tower of medieval mien. It is said that the house originally had a view of the harbor that was later blocked by larger structures built in the neighborhood. The new tower restored the view. Large and freestanding, this corner house is the Queen of Cobble Hill. And it has grounds: surrounding the house is what appears to be a large and extraordinarily lush private garden. On the south side the garden takes up an entire building lot. Note that I write "appears to be": the garden fence is so thick with ivy that one can only surmise what lies beyond. The house is highly unusual in its context, yet so designed that it does not stand out sorely, but rather seems an appropriate step up in scale. Albert D'Oench (1858–1919) was the codesigner a few years later of the Germania Life Insurance Company Building on Park Avenue South and 17th Street, one of the period's most beautiful Manhattan skyscrapers.

7 DUDLEY MEMORIAL, LONG ISLAND COLLEGE HOSPITAL
Southeast corner of Amity and Henry Streets
1902, William C. Hough

This elegant and modestly scaled building, originally a nurses' residence, is of stone-trimmed red brick and is festooned with notable console brackets and garlands. Note especially the garland-framed second-floor bay in the center over the entrance. The style is French Renaissance of the Henri IV period, late-sixteenth and early-seventeenth centuries. It is a particularly appropriate style for a hospital, since it was the style of the Hôpital Saint-Louis in Paris, built by Henri IV in 1607–11. A Brooklyn building of similar mien is Babb, Cook & Willard's house at 45 Montgomery Place (1898–99) in Park Slope, which recalls Henri IV's Place des Vosges. This is another example of Brooklyn architects going in a different direction at the turn of the century. William C. Hough was the onetime partner of Halstead Parker Fowler. Together they designed such buildings as the Throop Avenue Presbyterian Church (1889–90) and the 23rd Regiment Armory (1891–95), works in the rich Romanesque Revival vein mined so successfully by Brooklyn architects of the 1880s and early 1890s. Hough's building for Long Island College Hospital shows his turn to the classical, one taken by countless Brooklyn architects in the wake of the Columbian Exposition. This is but one of many nearby buildings of Long Island College

Hospital, which was founded by German immigrants in 1857. It is today the sixth largest hospital in Brooklyn and is a major employer in Cobble Hill; the hospital's modern buildings dominate this northwestern part of the neighborhood. Examples are the buildings to the north of the Dudley Memorial, along the east side of Hicks Street between Amity Street and Atlantic Avenue (the E. M. Fuller Pavilion, 1974, at the northeast corner of Hicks Street and Atlantic Avenue, and, to the south, the Polak Pavilion, 1984 with a 1988 addition), and, one block to the east of the Dudley Memorial, at the northeast corner of Henry and Amity Streets (the Prospect Heights Pavilion, 1963, named following Long Island College Hospital's merger that year with Prospect Heights Hospital). In his *Guide to the Architecture of Paris,* architect Norval White, in discussing a 1980s annex to the Hôpital Saint-Louis, asks, "Why are most hospitals usually so afflicted with mediocre architecture and then divorced from the urban design of the surrounding city? This is particularly galling at a site where the parent building is a seventeenth-century gem of both architecture and urbanism." Granted that the Dudley Memorial is no Hôpital Saint-Louis, a similar question might be asked of the hospital here as well as of many others in New York.

At the southeast corner of Pacific and Henry Streets once stood the Hoagland Laboratory of Long Island College Hospital. Cornelius Hoagland, founder of Royal Baking Powder and resident of Clinton Avenue, funded this pioneering bacteriological research laboratory. John Mumford designed its 1888 building in the Romanesque Revival style. The building burned down some years ago. The "Necrology" in the third edition of the *AIA Guide* said, "Its early Art Nouveau copper signs were glorious." Besides the Dudley Memorial, probably the best of the hospital's remaining buildings is the Polhemus Pavilion (1897) at the southwest corner of Henry and Amity Streets. M. L. Emery, who designed it, later designed the chapel (1911–12) of St. George's Episcopal Church at Stuyvesant Square in Manhattan.

8 ST. PETER'S HOSPITAL
274 Henry Street between Congress and Warren Streets, west side
1888–89, William Schickel & Company

This is an enormous, full-blockfront, Romanesque Revival powerhouse. It is austere: only some drip moldings and a little stone trim relieve its redbrick massiveness. The base is rock-faced granite, which yields to acre upon acre of red brick. There is an enormous round-arched entrance in the projecting cen-

8 *St. Peter's Hospital*

ter bay. Once a Roman Catholic hospital associated with St. Peter's Church around the corner, the building now houses the Cobble Hill Health Center, a facility for the elderly. According to Christopher Gray in the *New York Times,* when the hospital opened in 1889, it had three hundred beds, of which two hundred and fifty were set aside for charity patients. People were treated here for such afflictions as tuberculosis, rheumatism, alcoholism, and bronchitis. The Sisters of St. Francis, who had operated the hospital since its founding, were forced to close it in 1962, largely because of declining admissions of pay-ing patients. Two years later the building's interiors were gutted when it was converted into a nursing home. Numerous exterior alterations were also made, foremost among them the removal of the projecting center bay. In 1976, at a time of nursing-home scandals in New York City, the facility was taken away from its owner for mismanagement of patients. A community group saved the nursing home and in 1989 hired the local architect Stanley Maurer to renovate the building, including restoring its projecting center bay. According to Christopher Gray, it is "nearly but not exactly" a replica of Schickel's original.

William Schickel, who had once worked for Richard Morris Hunt, designed some of the most distinctive buildings of late-nineteenth-century New York, including the Century Building of 1880–81 across 17th Street from

Union Square, the Ottendorfer Branch of the New York Free Circulating Library and its neighboring Deutsches Dispensary (Stuyvesant Polyclinic) in 1883–84 on Second Avenue near St. Mark's Place, and the Church of Saint Ignatius Loyola of 1895–1900 on Park Avenue and 84th Street. His 1880s works are all in Romanesque Revival or Queen Anne, while the Church of Saint Ignatius Loyola in the late 1890s is in a Beaux-Arts Baroque style.

9 COBBLE HILL PARK
Bounded by Clinton and Congress Streets and Verandah Place
1965
Renovation: 1989

Cobble Hill, for all its leafy, human-scale streets, is relatively lacking in open space. Even this small park did not exist before the 1960s. Two large houses and one of Brooklyn's most remarkable churches occupied the site. The church was the Second Unitarian Church, designed by Jacob Wrey Mould and built in 1857–58. Mould was one of the most imaginative and eccentric designers in New York in his time. He created, with Calvert Vaux, Bethesda Terrace in Central Park and also worked on the Concert Grove in Prospect Park. His All Souls Unitarian Church (1853–55) on Fourth Avenue and 20th Street in Manhattan inspired Russell Sturgis and Peter B. Wight to become architects. Because of its alternating horizontal bands of dark and light stone, that church was called the "Church of the Holy Zebra." Mould's church in Cobble Hill had a nickname, too. It was called the "Church of the Holy Turtle." Its domed roof was pulled down over the building in a way that made people think of a turtle's shell. Samuel Longfellow, brother of Henry Wadsworth Longfellow, was its first pastor. The church lasted about a century before being abandoned. In the 1940s, the two large houses were torn down, and in 1962, the church met the same fate. Developers planned a supermarket for the site. Neighborhood residents had other ideas, though, and campaigned hard for the creation of a park. They were successful, and the park was dedicated in 1965. A thorough renovation of the park in 1989 greatly enhanced its appearance and won awards from the Municipal Art Society and from the Parks Council. The pleasant park, with its bluestone paving, many trees, playground equipment, and benches, is an indispensable neighborhood amenity.

Along the south side of the park runs a mews called Verandah Place, built in the 1840s and 1850s for the carriage houses and stables of the people living in the neighborhood's fine houses. The novelist Thomas Wolfe (1900–38) lived at No. 40 in 1930–31, in between living in Greenwich Village and Brooklyn Heights. His Verandah Place apartment apparently made such an impression on him that he described it in two works. In his novel *You Can't Go Home Again*, Wolfe wrote:

> *The place may seem to you more like a dungeon than a room that a man would voluntarily elect to live in. It is long and narrow, running parallel to the hall from front to rear, and the only natural light that enters it comes through two small windows rather high up in the wall, facing each other at the opposite ends, and these are heavily guarded with iron bars.*

In his novella *No Door*, Wolfe described the apartment this way:

> *The place is shaped like a Pullman car, except that it is not so long and has only one window at each end. There are bars over the window that your landlady has put there to keep the thugs in that sweet neighborhood from breaking in; in winter the place is cold and dark, and sweats with clammy water; in the summer you do all the sweating yourself.*

It seems that Cobble Hill (which Wolfe would not have called his neighborhood), or at least part of it, was a rough and rundown place around 1930. That is not the case today, and apartments such as Wolfe's are much sought after. The park, which was not there in Wolfe's day, gives to Verandah Place something of the feeling of a more modest Gramercy Park.

At the northeast corner of Hicks and Warren Streets is St. Peter's Church (R. C.), built in 1859–60. Patrick C. Keely designed the large, but simple, redbrick Romanesque Revival church with a single, central, frontal tower. It was one of his five hundred or so Catholic churches. The church was part of a complex of buildings that included St. Peter's Hospital, which is directly in back, and St. Peter's Academy (1866) to the north of the church. All the buildings are of red brick, and with the Tower and Home buildings just to the south gave to this part of Cobble Hill a scale very different from that of the rest of the area. Today the church looks out over the Brooklyn-Queens Expressway, which runs in a depression on the west side of Hicks Street. The expressway was cut through in the 1950s. A little to the north, in Brooklyn Heights, the expressway resulted in the Brooklyn Heights Promenade. There was no such luck for Cobble Hill, however. Once the neighborhood extended to the west, to the waterfront piers where thousands of longshoremen worked. The expressway divided the neighborhood in two, and the new designation "Cobble Hill" did not apply to the area west of the expressway, which continued to be called South Brooklyn or Red Hook. Beginning with the expressway, then the decline of waterfront business as shipping lines moved to new containerized facilities in New Jersey, then a disastrous sewer project that caused buildings to fall down, this area suffered one setback after another from the 1950s on. In the 1960s, the city announced it was going to level the area for a new containerport to compete with New Jersey. The containerport was never built, but the announcement caused families and businesses to flee. Each setback helped to depopulate the area until it earned a reputation as a no-man's-land. The area began to turn around in the 1980s as the city used its powers of condemnation to aid developers in erecting subsidized housing—for example, Columbia Street Terrace, built in 1985–89 on Columbia Street between President and Carroll Streets. (Columbia Street is actually continuous with well-known Brooklyn Heights streets, namely Columbia Heights, Pierrepont Place, Montague Terrace, and Columbia Place.) Today, real-estate brokers are marketing the area as "Cobble Hill West," though when the *New York Times* profiled the area for its "If You're Thinking of Living in . . ." series, it called it, rather prosaically, the "Columbia Street Area." In any event, housing prices are skyrocketing. Where once young families desiring to live in the city came to Cobble Hill because they could not afford Brooklyn Heights, so now they are going to the Columbia Street Area because they cannot afford Cobble Hill. Where next?

10 **TOWER BUILDINGS**
Hicks Street between Warren and Baltic Streets, east side
1878–79, William Field & Son

11 **HOME BUILDINGS**
Southeast corner of Hicks and Baltic Streets
1876–77, William Field & Son

Alfred Tredway White had seen the model tenements put up in London by Sidney Waterlow's Industrial Dwelling Company. Walt Whitman had reported on them in the *Brooklyn Times* in 1857. Whitman had encouraged New York developers to follow the London example and provide decent housing for the working classes. It need not be an entirely philanthropic gesture, either. White did not believe one should provide homes for the poor without seeking profit: "philanthropy plus five percent" was his famous motto. He

10 *Tower Buildings*

seems genuinely to have believed that the poor family would be better in spirit knowing they were contributing to another's profit. And who's to say he was wrong? Certainly his buildings never experienced the social problems that we associate with government-subsidized housing for the poor. Maybe it's time for a new Whitman and a new White to bring back "philanthropy plus five percent." Brooklyn could use a little of that about now as people of modest means are forced from fast-gentrifying neighborhoods.

The Home Buildings to the south consist of two apartment houses and came first. The Tower Buildings, three in number, were built along with the tiny row houses (see below). In all, White built 218 units. The Tower and Home Buildings were a pioneering attempt at tenement reform and were designed to provide tenants with, if not much in the way of space, at least well-lit and well-ventilated apartments and their own toilets, which were very rare at the time in working people's housing. (Bathing, however, was in common, in the basement.) The three six-story Tower Buildings were in a U-shaped arrangement around a large internal courtyard. (The backs of White's row houses enclosed the courtyard on the east.) The two Home Buildings formed an L-shaped arrangement around an internal courtyard. The most distinctive exterior visual features of the buildings are their open stair towers leading to apartments that open onto loggia-like balconies. White wished to do away with the often dark, dank, and fetid stairs and corridors to be found in many tenement houses. The balconies here have perforated metal railings decorated with a simple Greek cross form. At White's later Riverside houses in Brooklyn Heights, the similar railings have quatrefoil cutouts instead. Here as in the Riverside project, the general style is Romanesque, evidenced principally in the extensive corbeling along the buildings' attics as well as by a vague feeling engendered by the brick massiveness of it all; note though that the round-arched windows of the stair towers are more classical in design, with their keystones, molded voussoirs, and stone sills. Before the Brooklyn-Queens Expressway, which these buildings overlook to the west, was built, Hicks Street was a shopping street, and there were stores in the bases of the Hicks Street side of the buildings.

When the Tower Buildings opened in 1879, the two- to five-room apartments rented for $7.20 to $14.00 per month ($125 to $235 today). It did cost tenants an additional thirty cents (about five dollars today) to take a bath in the basement. Still, A. T. White was able to make his 5-percent profit, which only goes to show the extent of unconscionable rent-gouging that goes on in New York City at the dawn of the twenty-first century.

12 WARREN PLACE
Entered from Warren and Baltic Streets
between Hicks and Henry Streets
1878, William Field & Son

Alfred Tredway White built this, as charming an ensemble of tiny houses as one will ever see, as part of his experiment in working-class housing that also included the Tower and Home Buildings. Here are twenty-six houses, sometimes called the Workingmen's Cottages, facing across a narrow garden at one another. Each two-story house is only eleven and a half feet wide and thirty-two feet deep. At the ends of each row are larger houses facing onto the east-west streets (Warren and Baltic); they are three stories and sixteen feet wide (which is still narrower than the conventional twenty-foot-wide Brooklyn row house). In the court is a strong visual rhythm of round-arched entrances topped by gables of patterned brick, and of windows with brick moldings in the form of segmental arches. It is narrow, tight, dense, with a lot of black iron. Lilliputian stairs lead into the houses. It is beautifully kempt and there is nothing in the city more charming, not even the celebrated Grove Court in Greenwich Village.

An 11½-foot-wide house on Warren Place rented in 1878 for eighteen dollars a month, which is $300 or so in current dollars.

12 *Warren Place*

ALFRED TREDWAY WHITE (1846–1921)

Alfred Tredway White was born in Brooklyn. His father was Alexander Moss White of the importing firm of W. M. & A. M. White. A. M. White was born in Connecticut of old Massachusetts stock and came to Brooklyn among the waves of settlers from New England in the nineteenth century. Exceptionally successful in business, he built a commodious brownstone house for his family, still standing at 2 Pierrepont Place. (His neighbors on the short block were Abiel Abbot Low and Henry Evelyn Pierrepont. It is safe to say that from the social point of view there was no more distinguished block in Brooklyn.)

A. T. White received his secondary education at the Brooklyn Collegiate and Polytechnic Institute, then on Livingston Street. (The name was changed to Brooklyn Polytechnic Institute in 1889 and the secondary division moved in 1917 to Bay Ridge, where it is known today as Poly Prep.) In the late nineteenth century, this was one of the most distinguished secondary schools in the United States. After graduating from Polytechnic, White went up to Rensselaer Polytechnic Institute in Troy, New York, to study civil engineering. Following this, he became a partner in his father's importing company. His thoughts tended to wander away from importing, however. He had an improving streak, to say the least, and with his background as a civil engineer, he concentrated his energies on the physical improvement of his native city.

He built model tenements: the Tower and Home buildings, the Warren Place houses, the Riverside apartments. His motto was "Philanthropy Plus Five Percent." It is easy nowadays to scoff at this, to think that White was profiteering in low-cost housing. He wasn't. He believed that the dignity of those he helped to house would be better served if they did not feel they were the recipients of charity. Such thinking has become passé. That is not to say it was wrong (or would be wrong if resurrected). White did much more than build low-cost, model housing. He was a student of the field, and through his several books he tried to inspire others along the same line. (White himself had been inspired by another son of Brooklyn, Walt Whitman, who as a journalist was the first in New York to write about Sidney Waterlow's similar endeavors in London, which White went to check out.) White's books included *Improved Dwellings for the Laboring Classes* (1879), *Better Homes for Workingmen* (1885), and *Sun-Lighted Tenements: Thirty-five Years Experience as an Owner* (1912). He did inspire: his efforts are credited in part with the Tenement House Law of 1901, authored largely by Lawrence Veiller, which the historian Roy Lubove said was "among the most significant municipal reforms of the Progressive era." White's model tenements also inspired the City and Suburban Homes developments in Manhattan.

In 1893, Brooklyn Mayor Charles Adolph Schieren appointed White to the post of Commissioner of City Works, the second most powerful position in Brooklyn government after the mayoralty. His concern for racial justice made him a patron of Tuskegee Institute in Alabama and of Hampton Institute in Virginia, universities founded to serve African-American students, and still going strong. He endowed Harvard's department of social ethics. He was a trustee of the Russell Sage Foundation, was involved in the planning of the model community of Forest Hills Gardens in Queens, and was a patron of the planner Charles Dyer Norton and of the Regional Plan of New York and Its Environs. (Frederic B. Pratt, son of Charles Pratt and a resident of Clinton Avenue, was also a backer of this project.)

Finally, White was the principal figure behind the founding of one of his city's most magnificent embellishments, the Brooklyn Botanic Garden.

White was a still-vigorous seventy-five years old when he died in a very unfortunate manner. He was ice skating on a lake at Harriman State Park in Orange County, New York, when the ice cracked. He was pulled under and drowned.

---

13 RICHARD UPJOHN HOUSE

296 Clinton Street, northwest corner of Baltic Street
1842–43, Richard Upjohn
Addition at 203 Baltic Street: 1893, Richard Michell Upjohn

It is a simple brick house with a gently swelling, somewhat Bostonian front. (Upjohn had, indeed, come to New York from Boston.) The house was quite large even before the addition by Upjohn *fils* on Baltic Street. It was of course the home of the great architect and his family. Upjohn purchased the land from Nicholas Luquer on August 8, 1842, eleven days after Christ Church was consecrated. When the Upjohns moved into the house in 1843, Trinity Church at Broadway and Wall Street was under construction.

13 Richard Upjohn House

14A *Christ Church*

14B *Sanctuary, Christ Church*

14 CHRIST CHURCH (Episcopal)
Southwest corner of Clinton and Kane Streets
1841–42, Richard Upjohn

Though this lovely church was completed long before Upjohn's Trinity Church on Broadway and Wall Street, Trinity's cornerstone was laid June 3, 1841, and Christ Church's was laid June 26, 1841. Upjohn was engaged on the Trinity commission before this one, so Christ Church cannot be considered a forerunner of Trinity. The design resembles that of Trinity, with its brownstone facing and single, central, frontal tower. It is closer, however, to Upjohn's Church of the Ascension (1840–41) on Fifth Avenue and 10th Street in Greenwich Village. Upjohn did not charge a fee for his design of Christ Church, and was rewarded with a life deed to a pew. This was his parish church from the time of its opening in 1842 until his death thirty-six years later. He was a vestryman here from 1843 to 1847.

The style is a mix of Early English Gothic, such as one finds nearby at

14C *Sanctuary, Christ Church*

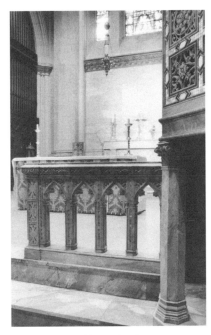

14D *Sanctuary, Christ Church*

Minard Lafever's Strong Place Baptist Church (1851–52), and Perpendicular Gothic, which is the dominant style of Trinity Church. The 117-foot-high tower has three pointed windows above the pointed doorway, and three pointed openings just below the tower's crenellated top. The tower buttresses are five stages plus a pinnacle. Four stages are topped by stepped sloping setoffs, and the top stage has a simple cap molding. The pinnacles have gabled terminations and are surmounted by conical finials. The brownstone is laid in random ashlar. On Kane Street are seven bays with pointed windows separated by two-stage buttresses with stepped sloping setoffs. The chancel is not articulated.

Inside, the three-aisled church has a hammerbeam ceiling of the kind Upjohn might have wished to employ at Trinity but was not allowed to by a vestry that desired the appearance of stone vaulting, which resulted in a ceiling of lath and plaster. The chancel here is rather shallow and, although this was Upjohn's own parish church, it is not so fully an example as some other Upjohn churches of the Ecclesiological Gothic he strongly advocated.

14E *Sanctuary, Christ Church*

Louis Comfort Tiffany designed the altar, altar railing, reredos, lectern, pulpit, and chairs in 1917. He also designed a number of windows; a 1939 fire destroyed most but not all of them, and those that remain are a treat.

RICHARD UPJOHN (1802–78)

Richard Upjohn was one of the most important architects ever to work in New York. He was born in Shaftsbury, Dorset, England, in a region with a very strong Gothic heritage, replete with churches and castles of the Middle Ages. His birthplace was only twenty miles from Salisbury Cathedral. He was trained as a carpenter, cabinetmaker, surveyor, and draftsman. With this training and with a deep, inborn appreciation of the Gothic, he came to America in 1829 at the age of twenty-seven. (Thomas Hardy would not be born in Dorset until eleven years after Upjohn's departure.) He was also a devout Anglican. To some extent, his life paralleled that of the painter Thomas Cole, born in Lancashire a year before Upjohn and already trained as an engraver when his family went to America when he was seventeen. Like Upjohn, Cole was a devout Anglican.

Upjohn's background fitted him for his role as the leader of the American Gothic Revival in a way that no native-born architect could hope to match. He settled in Boston in 1834 and worked for the neoclassical architect Alexander Parris. Two years later Upjohn received the commission to design St. John's Church in Bangor, Maine. The church, completed in 1839, was not as advanced a Gothic design as he would soon be producing. Nonetheless, it introduced Gothic details that clearly pointed the way to a mature Gothic Revival for America, and led the Rev. Jonathan Wainwright, an enthusiast of Gothic, to ask Upjohn to New York to consult on needed repairs to Trinity Church. The first Trinity Church had been built in 1698 and was destroyed in the Great Fire of 1776. The second Trinity was built in 1788–90. It was decorated in the Gothic manner but in the style that is called "Georgian Gothic," that is, a Georgian body with some Gothic appliqué, the only sort of Gothic to be found in America when Upjohn came over. When Upjohn was called to Trinity, his analysis concluded that the church was structurally unsound and should be replaced altogether. He submitted his first drawings for the new Trinity in September 1839, the cornerstone was laid on June 3, 1841, and the church was dedicated on May 21, 1846. The decorative richness of the church, and its adherence to Ecclesiological dogma, marked it as the most mature work in the Gothic style yet erected in America. Though controversy within the vestry resulted in numerous compromises in the Ecclesiological purity of the design, nonetheless Upjohn was set on his course, and several of his later churches would better fulfill his "high church" vision of American Gothic. In 1842, he bought a plot of land on Clinton Street in the neighborhood we now call Cobble Hill, and there he lived out his years.

By 1850, he began to let his son and trusted assistant, Richard Michell Upjohn (1828–1903), run the office. People are sometimes confused as to which Upjohn designed what, and in fact for a number of years the two worked practically as one. Upjohn *fils* was also born in Shaftsbury, Dorset, and was one year old when he came with his parents to America. At eighteen he entered his father's employ. Some of the New York works, all Episcopal unless otherwise indicated, of Upjohn *père* include Church of the Ascension (1840–41) on Fifth Avenue and 10th Street in Greenwich Village; Congregational Church of the Pilgrims (1844–46) on Remsen and Henry Streets in Brooklyn Heights, as much a pioneer of the Romanesque Revival as Trinity Church was of the Gothic Revival, and now Our Lady of Lebanon Maronite Rite Roman Catholic Church; Church of the Holy Communion (1844–46) on Sixth Avenue and

20th Street, now the Limelight Discothèque; Grace Church (1847–49) on Hicks Street and Grace Court in Brooklyn Heights; and Trinity Chapel (1850–55) on West 25th Street, site of the marriage on April 29, 1885, of Edith Newbold Jones and Edward Wharton, and now the Serbian Orthodox Cathedral of St. Sava. Works by Upjohn *père* outside New York City include First Parish Congregational Church (1845–46) in Brunswick, Maine; St. Mary's Church (1846–48) in Burlington, New Jersey; St. Thomas Church (1849–51) in Amenia Union, New York; St. Paul's Cathedral (1850–51) in Buffalo, New York; Church of St. John in the Wilderness (1851–52) in Copake Falls, New York; St. Paul's Church (1851–52) in Brookline, Massachusetts; St. John Chrysostom Church (1851–53) in Delafield, Wisconsin; St. Luke's Church (1857) in Clermont, New York; and the Chapel of St. Mary the Virgin (1859–60) in Nashotah, Wisconsin. Works credited to Richard Upjohn & Son or to R. & R. M. Upjohn include the transepts (1858) added to Minard Lafever's Church of the Holy Apostles on Ninth Avenue and 28th Street in Chelsea; the Green-wood Cemetery Gate (1861–65) on Fifth Avenue and 25th Street in Sunset Park; Christ Church (1865–66) on Riverdale Avenue in the Bronx; and the clergy house of Trinity Chapel on West 25th Street (1866). Works credited to Richard Michell Upjohn include St. Alban's Church (1865) on Staten Island; St. Paul's Church (1867–84) on Clinton and Carroll Streets in Carroll Gardens; and St. George's Church (1887–88) on Marcy Avenue in Bedford-Stuyvesant.

15 KANE STREET SYNAGOGUE (Congregation Baith Israel Anshei Emes; originally Middle Dutch Reformed Church)
Southeast corner of Kane Street and Tompkins Place
1856

Originally a Dutch Reformed Church, it became Trinity German Lutheran Church in 1887 until that congregation built itself a new, smaller home in 1905 (see below). Since then this has been Kane Street Synagogue. It was originally of brick and brownstone but now has an all-over smooth stuccoed surface, painted brown. The style is Romanesque, and though it wasn't built as a synagogue, many Jewish congregations were opting for Romanesque in the late-nineteenth century. There's a prominent corner tower at Kane and Tompkins. In the front are three rather stately, vertically elongated, round-arched entrance openings, with three corresponding round-arched windows above, then a corbel series linking the west (corner) tower to the smaller east tower. The towers have blind arches. It is a lovely setting, as Tompkins terminates at Kane, which has a fine long row of brownstone-trimmed red-brick Greek Revival houses across the street from the synagogue. Around the corner on Tompkins is a lovely street, particularly noteworthy for its profusion of iron railings.

Congregation Baith Israel Anshei Emes, the proud steward of this fine building, is a conservative synagogue that Dutch and Bavarian Jews founded in 1856, as fate would have it, in the very year this building was erected.

16 TRINITY GERMAN LUTHERAN CHURCH
Degraw Street between Clinton Street and Tompkins Place, north side
1905, Theobald Engelhardt

This diminutive white-brick church, built by the congregation that had once worshipped in what is now the Kane Street Synagogue, is in a simple-as-can-be Gothic style. It's a charming, tiny church—it seems like it must have served the people who lived in Warren Place. Five sets of stained-glass windows, in splendid shape, are visible on the east side, as is a lovely, beautifully tended garden. A recent residential conversion, it has a just-scrubbed look. Look at it closely. It may mesmerize you.

This is a late design by Engelhardt, whose major works were in the 1880s and early 1890s. He designed St. John's Lutheran Church of 1891–92 on Milton Street in Greenpoint, the Mason Au & Magenheimer Candy Company of 1885 on Henry and Middagh Streets, and the home of Louis Bossert of 1887 on Bushwick Avenue. Bossert was the developer of the Hotel Bossert on Montague Street. (Barbara Cooney charmingly illustrated Engelhardt's Bossert house in her 1990 children's book of old Brooklyn, *Hattie and the Wild Waves*.)

17 STRONG PLACE BAPTIST CHURCH
Northwest corner of Degraw Street and Strong Place
1851–52, Minard Lafever
Chapel
56 Strong Place between Degraw and Kane Streets, west side
1849, Minard Lafever

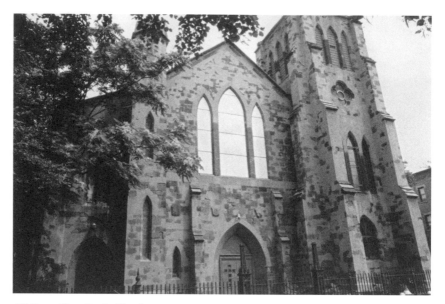

17 *Strong Place Baptist Church*

This was Lafever's own favorite among all the churches he designed. The style is Early English Gothic. Jacob Landy, the great authority on Lafever, wrote that Strong Place was his "closest approximation to the spirit of an English parish church design." Lafever often visited Strong Place, especially in his declining years, finding some sort of solace here.

The corner tower at Degraw Street and Strong Place is a massive anchor. Thirty feet square and sixty-four feet high, it was intended to have a spire, which was never built. Angle buttresses rise in four diminishing stages with stepped sloping setoffs. The large quatrefoil in the third stage of the tower is reminiscent of Early English and geometric-decorated belfry windows. At the west corner of the Degraw Street façade is a diagonal buttress in two stages with stepped sloping setoffs. Pinnacles originally surmounted this buttress and the small tower to the left of the entrance, and today the composition seems oddly truncated. Other missing features are the drip moldings and molded dividing shafts of the Early English–style triple lancet over the entrance. In a remodeling somewhere along the way, moldings, stringcourses, and dripstones were removed, and the present broad stone bands were added. There once was a much greater plasticity to the façade.

Carroll Gardens

Carroll Gardens is bounded on the north by Degraw Street, on the west by the Gowanus and Brooklyn-Queens Expressways, on the south by 9th Street, and on the east by Hoyt Street. In 1973, the New York City Landmarks Preservation Commission designated a Carroll Gardens Historic District, though it takes in a much smaller part of the area than anyone would guess. The historic district covers only the blocks of President and Carroll Streets between Smith and Hoyt Streets—only eight blockfronts. These blocks were singled out for their interesting layout. Richard Butts, a surveyor, planned the area in 1846, including not only the blocks in today's historic district but also the many blocks to the south bounded by 1st Place, Henry Street, 4th Place, and Smith Street. The row houses in the historic district were built from 1869 to 1884 and are mostly Italianate brownstones. Butts's cleverness is apparent in two ways. First, the houses are so sited on their lots that they have unusually deep front yards—the "gardens" of Carroll Gardens. Second, he fiddled with the grid in a way one wishes many more developers had done: the east-west streets jog slightly so that houses terminate the vistas along these streets. It seems such a small thing yet it makes all the difference between ho-hum and exciting.

"Carroll Gardens," like "Cobble Hill," is a real-estate coinage, this time from the 1960s. Again, South Brooklyn and even Red Hook is what the area used to be called. In the early- and mid-nineteenth century the area was mainly Irish. From the late-nineteenth century on it has been predominantly Italian. In the 1960s, when young professional families were moving into Cobble Hill, they came to Carroll Gardens as well. Because of its location contiguous to Cobble Hill and because of Cobble Hill's contiguity to Brooklyn Heights, Carroll Gardens got lucky at a time when many similar ethnic enclaves experienced wrenching changes. Property values not only remained stable, they increased at a time when they weren't supposed to increase, according to the experts. The location and the fine old row houses attracted young people to Carroll Gardens in the 1960s and 1970s, as did the Italian ambience, the food stores, the restaurants, the cafés, and the rest, not least the safe, clean streets. Of course, with property values shooting through the roof at the turn of the millennium, one may wonder how much longer before Carroll Gardens becomes fully deracinated. It hasn't happened yet, however, and shows no signs of doing so in the near future, and the neighborhood remains, for the visitor, an unmitigated delight.

18 *South Congregational Church*

18 SOUTH CONGREGATIONAL CHURCH COMPLEX
Northwest corner of Court and President Streets
Church: 1857, architect unknown
Chapel: 1851, architect unknown
Ladies' Parlor

257 President Street between Court and Clinton Streets, north side
1889, Frederick Carles Merry
Rectory

255 President Street between Court and Clinton Streets, north side
1893, Woodruff Leeming

It is both odd and somehow fitting that the architectural heart of the heavily Italian-American community of Carroll Gardens should be a Congregational church. It is odd because one might well expect a Catholic church, and it is somehow appropriate because New England Congregationalists built so much of nineteenth-century Brooklyn. The church here is from the 1850s—the decade in which the Congregationalist brothers Beecher were setting up their churches (New England Congregational Church in Williamsburg, Plymouth Church in Brooklyn Heights). It is said, indeed, that the idea for this church was that of Henry Ward Beecher himself. That may be, but the style employed here is more that of the Rev. Storrs's Pilgrims than the Italianate seemingly favored by the brothers Beecher. A decade or so before this complex began to rise, the Rankin mansion, two blocks away on Clinton and Carroll Streets, was erected amid fields. Carroll Gardens (that name was still far in the future), however, soon began its explosive growth.

We do not know the architect of the church or the chapel, yet he was quite knowledgeable about what he was doing. Richard Upjohn had introduced the Romanesque Revival to New York church design in his Church of the Pilgrims in Brooklyn Heights, about ten years before the main church here began to go up. The church here is a splendid example of the genre, and unlike so many of its brethren, retains its original towers. The gabled front of the church features a fine receding round arch. To either side of this gabled front are the twin towers, which are marvelous. Built with four stages featuring stepped sloping setoffs, the towers terminate in corbels and merlons and, pointing high in the sky and visible all up and down Court Street, finials that rise from pinnacles at the four corners of the square towers.

The church and chapel are now apartments. The congregation worships in the former Ladies' Parlor behind the church and chapel on President Street. It is a wonderful building, also Romanesque Revival though of the 1880s Richardsonian variety. It is faced in brick with extensive terra-cotta trim, all in rusty red. There is "Ruskinian" polychromy in the voussoirs of the entrance arch, an asymmetrically placed and vertically accentuated projecting bay rising a story above the rest of the building, and lush bands of terra-cotta ornament along the top of the building. It is somewhat reminiscent of Frank Freeman's Brooklyn Fire Headquarters on Jay Street, built three years after this. The architect, F. Carles Merry, designed in the same year as this Ladies' Parlor a group of wonderful row houses on Lenox Avenue (Nos. 220 to 228) between 121st and 122nd Streets in Harlem. Two years earlier he had designed the House for the Relief of the Destitute Blind on Tenth Avenue and 104th Street. Merry had worked for George B. Post in the 1870s, at the time the Williamsburg Savings Bank Building on Broadway and Driggs Avenue was erected. He had also once worked for H. H. Richardson.

The rectory, just to the west of the Ladies' Parlor, is yet another fine work, built thirty-six years after the main church and in a different style. The architect was Woodruff Leeming, who twenty-one years later would design the parish house of Plymouth Church on Orange Street. Leeming was born in Illinois but came to Brooklyn as a lad to attend the prestigious Polytechnic

Institute, following which he went on to the Massachusetts Institute of Technology and the École des Beaux-Arts in Paris. He worked for Heins & LaFarge at the time they won the competition to design the Cathedral of St. John the Divine, and struck out on his own, establishing his office in Brooklyn, in the very year he designed the rectory here. It may have been Leeming's first work on his own. It is in a Gothic style with a basement and parlor floor of rock-faced brownstone; above is red brick with brownstone trim. The stoop is on the left and leads to a doorway set within a pointed-arch molding. On the right is a round bay. Two gables, both set with pointed arches, top the house. Twenty-one years later, Leeming designed the very large parish house of Plymouth Church on Orange Street, in a way bringing the story of the relationship of South Congregational Church and Plymouth Church full circle.

19 ST. PAUL'S CHURCH (Episcopal)
Northeast corner of Clinton and Carroll Streets
1867–84, Richard Upjohn & Son

This brownstone Gothic church was designed largely by Upjohn *fils*. Its best feature by far is its projecting triple portal of light sandstone, with clustered columns and trefoil arches. The arches are of polychrome stonework, possibly once more-pronounced than now. The portal is sandwiched by three-stage buttresses with gabled and stepped sloping setoffs. To the south of the portal, at the corner, is a massive square base for a tower that was never built. The corner tower base has a fine entrance recessed behind a trefoil arch on Carroll Street, and anchors the corner well. The Carroll Street façade has three aisle bays with a series of clerestory windows above and behind them, followed by a shallow transept and then a five-sided apse that expresses the well-defined space of the chancel. Upjohn *fils* designed St. George's Episcopal Church on Marcy Avenue in Bedford-Stuyvesant in 1887–88 in a style similar to St. Paul's. He was still mining that "Ruskinian" vein of Gothic long after most other architects had moved on to other things. It is not as though Richard Michell Upjohn were some provincial designer several years behind the trends. As the son of one of America's most important architects, and as a very active practitioner in New York, he was quite aware of everything that was going on. One gets the feeling that he might have found in Ruskinism a kind of fulfillment or refinement of his father's type of Gothic architecture, and felt that he'd found, perhaps, a true style that went beyond mere fashion.

20 John Rankin House

20 JOHN RANKIN HOUSE
440 Clinton Street, southwest corner of Carroll Street
1840

The Greek Revival went in for austere effects. For example, Greek Revival town houses dispensed with the effete embellishments of the Federal style. Greek Revival was manlier. The merchant John Rankin built himself a Greek Revival mansion in a sparsely developed part of South Brooklyn, commanding a fine view of the harbor. When one hears "Greek Revival mansion," perhaps something on the order of a southern plantation house comes to mind. This is in some ways the South Brooklyn equivalent of that. There is no columned porch, no air of mint juleps on the verandah, such as one may find in the Greek Revival South. There is, rather, an air of stolidity, sobriety and, indeed, mercantile austerity in this plain and imposing brick house. It is as close as any rich man's house of the era, perhaps anywhere in the country, came to being an unadorned box. Yet interest is sustained by the very simple molding of the façades, in the form of the strong end pilasters, the ever-so-slightly projecting center bay, and the fine Greek Revival entrance. This is a Brooklyn country mansion from about fifteen years and one stylistic generation before the Litchfield house in what is now Prospect Park.

The Rankin house is exceptionally well preserved as the F. G. Guido Funeral Home.

21 BROOKLYN PUBLIC LIBRARY, CARROLL PARK BRANCH
396 Clinton Street between Union and Sackett Streets, west side
1905, William B. Tubby

Brooklyn architects who came of age in the Romanesque Revival and Queen Anne 1880s and early 1890s tended to turn to the classical after the Columbian Exposition of 1893. Montrose Morris, R. L. Daus, and Frank Freeman all produced classical work every bit as good as their work in the earlier styles. William Tubby (1858–1944), among top Brooklyn architects, is the one who most seemed to have been dragged kicking and screaming into the classical nineties. Born in Iowa, Tubby came to Brooklyn to attend Brooklyn Friends School and then Polytechnic Institute, following which he went to work for Ebenezer Roberts, architect of Charles Pratt's house on Clinton Avenue. Tubby succeeded to the Roberts practice and designed some of the most distinctive Brooklyn buildings of the 1880s and 1890s, including the Queen Anne row houses at 864 to 872 Carroll Street (1887) in Park Slope, the row houses at 262 to 272 Hicks Street (1887–88) in Brooklyn Heights, the Charles Adolph Schieren house (1889) on Clinton Avenue, the magnificent Charles Millard Pratt house (1890–93) on Clinton Avenue, and the 20th Precinct Police Station House (1894–95) on Wilson Avenue in Bushwick. This last is an extraordinary castellated affair that one cannot help thinking was Tubby's in-your-face reaction to the City Beautiful. It is not that Tubby disdained classical elements altogether. Indeed, as early as 1889 in his Schieren house we see that combination of Romanesque and Renaissance features that seems to herald the coming Classicism of the 1890s. Nonetheless, the Beaux-Arts Classicism that we associate with turn-of-the-century Brooklyn is something we do not associate with Tubby. This redbrick and limestone Carnegie branch library is one of Tubby's fullest exercises in a kind of Beaux-Arts Classicism. With its Ionic columns, pediment, arches, roof balustrade, pilasters, and dentilated cornice, this is a stately presence in the Carroll Gardens neighborhood. Many of these branch libraries, modest structures though they may be, nonetheless have a kind of monumentality in the neighborhood setting, and the best of them, such as this one, are among the buildings that make neighborhoods great. It is rather startling, by the way, to think that William Tubby lived until 1944.

Boerum Hill

Boerum Hill is bounded to the north by State Street, to the west by Court Street, to the south by Warren Street, and to the east by Fourth Avenue. It was developed out of farmland owned by the Boerum family. The mostly three-story brick and brownstone row houses of Boerum Hill were built between the mid-1840s and the early 1870s, mostly in the Greek Revival and Italianate styles. In 1973, the New York City Landmarks Preservation Commission designated a Boerum Hill Historic District. It is irregularly bounded by Nevins Street on the east, Wyckoff Street on the south, Hoyt Street on the west, and Pacific Street on the north. "Boerum Hill," like "Cobble Hill" and "Carroll Gardens," is a name of recent vintage, this time from the 1960s, when the same kinds of people who were moving to Cobble Hill began moving to Boerum Hill as well, just as Boerum Hill had developed in tandem with Cobble Hill beginning in the 1840s after ferry service began from Atlantic Avenue. Boerum Hill, though, was slightly lower on the social ladder than Brooklyn Heights or Cobble Hill. It has been said that the people living in Boerum Hill today are the richest residents the area has ever known, which is probably not the case in other Brooklyn brownstone neighborhoods. Sometimes called South Brooklyn, the more common name for what is now Boerum Hill was for about a century North Gowanus. In the nineteenth century, middle-class merchants and their families populated the area. By the 1920s, many Irish lived here. In the 1940s and 1950s, however, large numbers of Puerto Ricans moved in, and brownstone after brownstone was converted to a rooming house. By 1960, the neighborhood was predominantly Puerto Rican and African American. By the early 1960s, Boerum Hill was one of the poorest neighborhoods in New York City, a textbook study in urban decline. This trend was reversed by "urban pioneers" in the 1960s, who were attracted by the quality of the housing stock and the excellent location of the neighborhood. Boerum Hill went from being a textbook study in urban decline to a textbook study in the perils of "gentrification," as journalists, activists, and others focused attention on the problem of displacement of the poor. Boerum Hill today is more racially and economically mixed than Cobble Hill, Carroll Gardens, or Park Slope. This is in part because, as the writer and longtime Boerum Hill resident L. J. Davis pointed out, the young professionals who have moved into Boerum Hill from the 1960s on have been less affluent than those moving to Brooklyn Heights or Cobble Hill. Boerum Hill is also home, as

Brooklyn Heights, Cobble Hill, and Park Slope are not, to public housing projects. Nonetheless, Boerum Hill today is about as expensive a place to buy or rent a home as Carroll Gardens, though slightly less expensive than Cobble Hill. Smith Street in Boerum Hill has become, to just about everyone's amazement, one of the hottest places for new restaurants in the city.

As I was writing this book on the evening of Tuesday, July 11, 2000, a tragic event occurred in Boerum Hill. The home of a couple, Leonard and Harriet Walit, a row house at 420 State Street, between Nevins and Bond Streets, blew up as a result of a gas leak. The Walits arrived home from a day trip to Connecticut. Upon reentering their house, they smelled gas. Mr. Walit called for his next-door neighbor and good friend, Khay Cochran, to come over to help. The house exploded, killing the Walits and Mr. Cochran. At first it sounded like the kind of disaster that is reported in the news every day. This one, however, touched many people, and it had a lot to do with what was revealed about the urban values and the history of the people who lived in this Boerum Hill community. The Walits, it turned out, were not simply well-liked neighbors. They were esteemed members of the community who had selflessly dedicated themselves to making Boerum Hill a better place to live. Mrs. Walit, sixty-six years old, was a retired social worker. Mr. Walit, seventy-two years old, was a retired accountant and a history buff. A childless couple, they volunteered for charitable organizations and were heavily involved in their block association and in the Boerum Hill Association, a community group. Neighbors described Mrs. Walit as the "den mother" of State Street. They had purchased their Boerum Hill home in 1970, an early enough date to qualify them as "pioneers." It was, said the *New York Times,* "a time when anyone moving in had to be willing to inhabit a treeless street filled with dilapidated buildings and to rebuild, restore and make their places livable." Mr. Cochran lived next door at 418 State Street with his partner of fifty-three years, Julian Jackson. Mr. Cochran and Mr. Jackson's house was also destroyed, along with Mr. Jackson's collection of art and antiques. Mr. Jackson had purchased his State Street house in 1963. A lawyer, he was at that time an assistant corporation counsel for New York City. He had met Mr. Cochran in 1946 when the two appeared as extras in a production of the Metropolitan Opera Company. They kept an apartment in Manhattan, but spent much of their time on State Street in what Mr. Jackson called their "country home." Mr. Cochran and Mr. Jackson had long been close friends of the Walits. Together they worked for and experienced the rejuvenation of Boerum Hill. Their block, outside the historic district, nonetheless had great character and great diversity of architecture and uses. Along with elegantly restored row houses, the block contained distinctive nineteenth-century apartment houses, a public school, a drug rehabilitation center, an 1889 firehouse, and houses of worship serving Eastern Orthodox and Spanish-speaking Pentecostalist congregations. These are just a few facts about these people that I culled from news reports at the time. I did not know any of them, though I know many people who, at least outwardly, are like them. What affected me, and many others, in reading the accounts of these people's lives was not how gratuitously unjust that the lives of these people who had lived thirty and thirty-seven years in Boerum Hill should end so abruptly and absurdly. Rather, it sometimes takes a disaster like this to make people remember that others all over the city are making lives for themselves and also contributing to making their communities better places to live. In the end, for most of us on the outside looking in, it was not the deaths that moved us, it was the lives.

22 STATE STREET HOUSES
290–324 State Street between Smith and Hoyt Streets, south side
291–299 State Street between Smith and Hoyt Streets, north side
1847–74

This is a superb, and superbly preserved, row of twenty-three row houses just a couple of blocks outside the formal Boerum Hill Historic District. Yet as much as anything within the Historic District, these houses encapsulate the development of this section of Brooklyn. When the wealthy merchant John Rankin built his large Greek Revival country house not so far from here on Clinton and Carroll Streets, this was still largely farmland. In short order, however, the fields were developed. This street was built up throughout the period of explosive growth in these parts. It is a textbook illustration of the classical vernacular that made so much of Brooklyn what it is. Cities are defined by the vernacular architecture of their neighborhoods. What we call "vernacular" are those buildings erected by developers or builders without the aid of professional architects. These are the forms and styles that are in the air, that have become codified in standard usages. We do not look to such works for masterpieces or showpieces. We look to them as designs for living, for qualities they impart to everyday lives of everyday people who call them home. Here on State Street we see an ensemble that in spite of having been built in pieces over nearly a quarter of a century nonetheless exhibits a remarkable stylistic cohesion. Details differ enough to create variety for the eye, though never at the expense of harmony. We start with 1840s Greek Revival and move through Italianate, all handled expertly, and demonstrating above all that classical forms are a fully worked-out language of design that can be mastered by local builders to create urbane streetscapes.

23 TIMES PLAZA CONTROL HOUSE
Intersection of Flatbush, Atlantic, and Fourth Avenues
1908, Heins & LaFarge

On one side of Flatbush Avenue is Boerum Hill. On the other is Fort Greene. Boerum Hill is that strange, slithery sort of neighborhood that seems to share a border with every other neighborhood. At some point Boerum Hill borders Brooklyn Heights, the Civic Center area, downtown, Fort Greene, Park Slope, Gowanus, and Cobble Hill. That's pretty impressive for an area that covers about a quarter of a square mile. The Times Plaza Control House was originally the entrance kiosk for the Atlantic Avenue station of the IRT subway. The architects George Lewis Heins and Christopher Grant LaFarge became partners in 1886. (Christopher LaFarge was the son of the great painter John LaFarge.) Five years later they were hired to design the Cathedral of St. John the Divine in Morningside Heights, a job at which they toiled for twenty years before Ralph Adams Cram unceremoniously replaced them. In 1892, Heins & LaFarge designed a beautiful group of three houses at Nos. 488 to 492 4th Street, between Seventh and Eighth Avenues in Park Slope. In the first decade of the twentieth century, Heins & LaFarge designed numerous stations and station entrances for the new IRT subway. Most of the station entrances have been destroyed, and the stations mutilated or poorly maintained. Their Brooklyn Borough Hall station is among those that retains much of its original beauty, and even has a new entrance kiosk just to the north of Borough Hall, modeled after some of the Heins & LaFarge originals. The Times Plaza Control House is an original, though it is no longer used as a subway entrance. When it was built in 1908, this intersection was called Times Plaza, after the nearby offices of the Brooklyn *Daily Times.* Here converged the elevated railway, the subway, and trolley lines in what was one of the busiest transportational hubs in the city. Heins & LaFarge's lovely little structure of glazed-white terra-cotta with its Flemish gable helped make sense of the chaotic scene by clearly announcing by its color, shape, and siting that it was the entrance to the subway. The el came down in the 1940s and the trolleys ceased operating in the 1950s. Today this intersection is choked with automobiles. In 1971, the kiosk ceased to function as a subway entrance and was converted into a newsstand and fast-food stand. In 1977, in an entirely ill-conceived attempt to update the appearance of Times Plaza, a modern superstructure with superscaled lettering was placed over the old control house. This wrapping was happily later removed. In the 1990s, however, the control house was boarded up. At this writing, new uses are being considered for the structure. Some in the surrounding neighborhoods would like to see it returned to use as a newsstand, while others hope for a tourist information booth. Stay tuned.

24 BROOKLYN PUBLIC LIBRARY, PACIFIC BRANCH
Southeast corner of Pacific Street and Fourth Avenue
1903, Raymond F. Almirall

Raymond Almirall (1869–1939) designed this Carnegie branch library on the eastern edge of Boerum Hill. Many outstanding architects lived and worked in Brooklyn. Almirall may be the best architect actually to have been born in Brooklyn. He attended Brooklyn Polytechnic Institute and then the École des Beaux-Arts in Paris, from which he received a diploma in 1896. This was the first of four Carnegie libraries Almirall designed for Brooklyn between 1903 and 1914. He was also, of course, the architect of the great, unfinished main library at Grand Army Plaza. Probably his two finest buildings in New York City are the Emigrant Industrial Savings Bank (1908–12) on Chambers Street in Manhattan, and St. Michael's Roman Catholic Church (1905) on Fourth Avenue and 42nd Street in the Sunset Park section of Brooklyn. Almirall graced Fourth Avenue not only with this library and with St. Michael's Church but also with Public Bath No. 7 (1906–10), not far from here at the northeast corner of President Street in Gowanus. That building is notable for its magnificent glazed terra-cotta decoration, especially the blue water pouring from the attic. The library is a more sober affair. Something apparent in many of Almirall's works is his concern for how his buildings stand against the sky. His tops are often bold or unusual. We see this in the "beehive" spire of St. Michael's Church, in the elaborate pedimented forms atop the high-rise Emigrant Industrial Savings Bank, and in the domical vault of his

Brooklyn Public Library. Here we see another unusual top, in the low pyramidal form surmounted by an unusual dormer with a segmental-arch window
with a prominent keystone. This crowning window echoes the design of the
much larger first-floor windows and the central doorway they flank. The building is of red brick trimmed with limestone. Four two-story brick pilasters separating the openings terminate in heavy stone brackets beneath a cornice that
was simplified in 1951. This was the first Carnegie library to open in Brooklyn.
Almirall had to restore it in 1914 when it was damaged by subway construction, and in 1917 when it was damaged by fire. The community saved the
building from being torn down after a fire in 1973, and it was rehabilitated two
years later. Seemingly simple, it is a minor masterpiece by one of Brooklyn's
best architects.

Diagonally across Fourth Avenue is the Church of the Redeemer, built
in 1870, about as different a building from the library as one can imagine.
Patrick C. Keely, who designed more Gothic Revival churches than any man
in America, was responsible for this brownstone church for an Episcopal congregation, though he mostly designed Catholic churches.

PARK PL

2

STERLING PL

3   5

ST. JOHNS PL

4   1

LINCOLN PL

BERKELEY PL

9   8

UNION ST

10

11

PRESIDENT ST

7   6

CARROLL ST

12-14   23   24-25

15-16   17-22   26

33-37

MONTGOMERY PL

38   27

28-32

39   40   41-42

GARFIELD PL

POLHEMUS PL

FISKE PL

1ST ST

2ND ST

43-44

3RD ST

46   45

4TH ST

5TH AVE

6TH AVE

7TH AVE

8TH AVE

PROSPECT PARK WEST

5TH ST

48   47

6TH ST

7TH ST

8TH ST

49

9TH ST

10TH ST

11TH ST

12TH ST

N
W   E
S

Park Slope

2 St. Augustine's
Church

Chapter Park Slope **9**

A good starting point for an amble in Park Slope is around Eighth Avenue and St. John's Place. This is quite near the Grand Army Plaza station of the 2, 3, and 4 trains, and the Seventh Avenue station of the D and Q trains.

New York City Mayor **William Jay Gaynor** (1849–1913) lived at 22 Eighth Avenue, one in a row of four neo-Grec brownstones (Nos. 20 to 26) that the developer-architect William Flanagan built in 1883 between St. John's Place and Lincoln Place. Gaynor was one of the most remarkable mayors in New York City's history. Of Irish Catholic descent, he grew up in poverty in Oneida County, New York. He trained for the priesthood but decided against taking orders and instead became a member of the Christian Brothers (he was Brother Hadrian Mary). He served as a missionary in Panama and Mexico. Then, at the age of twenty-one, he renounced the Church and became a journalist and a lawyer. In the late 1870s he moved to a then still sparsely settled Flatbush and practiced law in its small-town atmosphere. He moved to Brooklyn in 1885. (Flatbush would not become part of Brooklyn until four years before Brooklyn became part of New York City.) In 1893, he was elected a judge of the New York State Supreme Court. He sent the corrupt Coney Island political boss John Y. McKane to prison for election fraud. In 1905, he was appointed a judge of the Appellate Division. Four years later he was elected the ninety-fourth mayor of New York City. Oddly for a man whose reputation was that of incorruptibility and high principle, he was the candidate of the Tammany Hall Democratic machine. It was one of those times when Tammany Hall, feeling the heat, had to put someone clean at the head of the ticket and hope that out of gratitude at being helped to the mayoralty he would fall in line. Gaynor did not fall in line. He became the scourge of Tammany Hall. He worked to curb patronage and to reform the civil service, striking right at the heart of Tammany operations. One of the things for which he is best known today was his strongly expressed view that the subways should be owned and operated by the city and not private businesses. Gaynor, local lore has it, often walked from his home on Eighth Avenue to his office in City Hall via the Brooklyn Bridge. In 1910, while he was on the deck of an ocean liner about to leave for Europe, a disgruntled city employee shot him. Gaynor survived, but the bullet lodged in his throat never was removed. This strong-willed mayor proved popular and was naturally considered for higher office. He refused to run for governor because he believed the only office higher than that of mayor of New York City was president of the United States. Interestingly, no New York City mayor has ever gone on to the White House, though a New York City police commissioner (Theodore Roosevelt) did. He was mayor when Grand Central Terminal opened on February 2, 1913, and when Ebbets Field opened on April 9, 1913. On September 10, 1913, while aboard a steamship six hundred miles off the Irish coast, Gaynor suddenly died. He was still mayor of New York City and he still lived at 22 Eighth Avenue. The lingering effects of the bullet in his throat caused his death; although it was three years since he had been shot, his assassin had succeeded. Gaynor was known as a scholarly man who particularly favored Epictetus and Cervantes. Following the shooting in 1910, he was also known as hot tempered, brusque, pitiless, and one who did not suffer fools.

Alfred P. Sloan, a tea and coffee importer, lived at 117 St. John's Place, between Sixth and Seventh Avenues, one in a row of twelve neo-Grec brownstones (Nos. 115 to 137) built in 1887. His son, **Alfred P. Sloan, Jr.** (1875–1966), who grew up in this house, would become chairman of the board of General Motors. Young Sloan attended Brooklyn Polytechnic Institute and went on to the Massachusetts Institute of Technology. He got a job as a draftsman for the Hyatt Roller Bearing Company of Newark, New Jersey. This company produced bearings for automobiles. In 1899, at the age of twenty-four, he became president of the company, and in 1916 merged it with the United Motors Company, of which he became president. In 1918 General Motors (ten years old at the time) purchased United Motors, and Sloan became vice president of General Motors. Five years later he succeeded Pierre S. du Pont as president. Sloan was chairman of the board from 1937 to 1956.

1 MONTAUK CLUB

25 Eighth Avenue, northeast corner of Lincoln Place
1889–91, Francis H. Kimball

Toward the end of the nineteenth century, bourgeois Brooklyn boasted many private clubs. The Lincoln Club built its clubhouse on Putnam Avenue in Bedford-Stuyvesant in 1889, the Union League built its clubhouse on Bedford Avenue and Dean Street in 1889-90. After the turn of the century, the Crescent Athletic Club and the Heights Casino opened in Brooklyn Heights. There were many others—on the Heights, in Williamsburg, in Bedford-Stuyvesant and Bushwick, in Fort Greene and Clinton Hill—some forgotten, their buildings long demolished. Park Slope's Montauk Club was incorporated on March 11, 1889. The cornerstone was laid on December 14 of that year, and the club opened on May 23, 1891. Architect Francis H. Kimball (1845–1919) won a competition for the club's design. (It is said that C. P. H. Gilbert, an entrant in the competition, fully expected to be awarded the commission.) Kimball's many noteworthy works include the Gertrude Rhinelander Waldo house of 1895–98 on Madison Avenue and 72nd Street in Manhattan and Clinton Hill's Emmanuel Baptist Church of 1886–87.

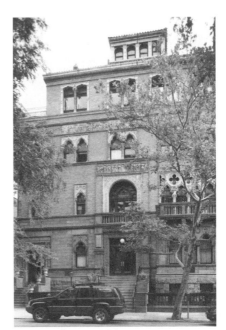

1 *Montauk Club*

Kimball had worked for the London architect William Burges on Trinity College in Hartford, Connecticut. Burges was an exponent of the Victorian Gothic precepts that devolved from the writings of John Ruskin. Ruskin's love of the Venetian Gothic, filtered through such nineteenth-century architects as Burges, informed the style of the Montauk Club. Charles T. Wills, the most prestigious stonemason and building contractor in New York, was in charge of construction. Though not as well known as the architects for whom he worked, Wills built many of the most beautifully crafted buildings in New York City, including Charles Follen McKim's University Club of 1896–1900 on Fifth Avenue and 54th Street, C. P. H. Gilbert's DeLamar house of 1902–5 on Madison Avenue and 37th Street, McKim's Pierpont Morgan Library (with its ancient Greek method of anathyrosis stone construction) of 1902–7 on East 36th Street, and Stanford White's sadly demolished Madison Square Presbyterian Church of 1903–6 on Madison Avenue and 25th Street. Not for nothing does this roster comprise some of the most legendarily well-constructed buildings in New York.

The materials of the Montauk Club are brownstone and brick, the latter in shades of brown, orange, and red. Skillfully combined, they yield a soft, golden hue. Among the most noteworthy features of the building is its superb terra-cotta ornamentation, much of it depicting Native American subjects, particularly having to do with the Montauk people. The building has the rare distinction of three full exposures, on Eighth Avenue, Lincoln Place, and Plaza Street. The entrance is up the high stoop on Eighth Avenue. Traceried openings are grouped asymmetrically to the right of the entrance; the similar traceried fenestration of the Lincoln Place and Plaza Street sides is arranged more symmetrically. To the left of the entrance is a separate, smaller doorway that was originally the ladies' entrance. The Montauk was one of New York's first gentlemen's clubs to offer its facilities to members' wives, who by entering through their own entrance could ascend to the third-floor dining room while bypassing the lobby, thus preserving its atmosphere of male sanctuary. Above the main—the male—entrance is a carved stone band of Indian heads. At the second floor is a round-arched window set in a panel of terra-cotta ornament combining classical forms with American Indian content. Resting upon the arch is a terra-cotta frieze depicting the club's founders and builders laying the cornerstone in 1889. It is a marvelous vignette of Victorian gentlemen in top hats and frock coats. At this level, leaded-glass windows are set within pointed arches with quatrefoil spandrels. Above the third floor on all three exposed sides of the building is a continuous terra-cotta frieze depicting the history of the Montauk Indians of Long Island. On the Lincoln Place side is a first-floor projecting bay, screened by ten pointed arches. (On the Eighth Avenue side, a similar projecting bay, three arches wide, is located to the right of the entrance.) A second-floor balustraded balcony, carried on lion's-head brackets, deeply overhangs this bay. Above and behind the balcony is a loggia screened by pointed arches with quatrefoil spandrels identical to those on the Eighth Avenue side. The arches spring from dwarf columns surfaced in a basket-weave pattern. Note how Kimball sets his wall openings in deep reveals to create striking contrasts of solids and voids, a device we associate with designers influenced by Ruskin. Above the second-story is a terra-cotta panel illustrating the inscription: "1659 Wyandance Sachame of Pamanack, his wife and his son Wiankabone giving a deed to Lion Gardiner of Saybrook, Easthampton, Long Island, July 14, 1659." On the Plaza Street side is a swelling two-story bay that forms a balcony for the third-floor dining room. Note the picturesque effect (so pronounced in all of Kimball's works) of the high chimneys, the copper dormers, and the steep, tiled roof crowned by American eagles. Note also the fine iron fence surrounding the property. The posts feature bas-reliefs of Indian heads. At the corners of the fence are winged lions holding shields bearing the crest of the Montauk Club.

Venice's Ca' d'Oro (1424–36) is often said to have been a model for the design of the Montauk Club. Indeed, the club's traceried openings, its quatrefoil motif, and its balustraded balconies are similar to those of the Venetian masterpiece. Other Venetian buildings of the fifteenth century have these features as well, and also have features in common with the Montauk Club that are not found at the Ca' d'Oro. The club's hipped roof, for example, is of a type that is more pronounced on the Palazzo Pisani Moretta than on the Ca' d'Oro. Indeed, the Palazzo Pisani Moretta seems to me to be slightly the closer model for the Montauk Club. One feature that the Montauk Club originally possessed and that has been removed was a fine modillioned cornice above the frieze over the third-floor windows. A balustrade surmounted this cornice and wrapped around the building. The cornice was very close to that of the Palazzo Pisani Moretta.

The first, second, and third floors were originally for dining and entertaining. The top two floors contained bedrooms. In the basement was a bowling alley. Timothy L. Woodruff, who had been Theodore Roosevelt's lieutenant governor, lived in the building after being elected club president in 1904.

Today, the old bedroom floors have been converted into cooperative apartments, while the club continues to occupy the lower floors.

On the north side of Lincoln Place between Seventh and Eighth Avenues is the Berkeley-Carroll School, a prestigious private school and a bastion of the new Park Slope gentry. Richard A. Walker of the firm Walker & Morris designed the 1896 building for what at the time was the all-girls **Berkeley Institute,** founded nine years earlier by David Augustus Boody, who would later be mayor of Brooklyn. Walker designed several Carnegie branch libraries in Brooklyn. In 1912, he joined the great Manhattan firm of Warren & Wetmore, architects of Grand Central Terminal. The style is Jacobean in red brick with stone trim. John Burke designed the utilitarian but handsome gymnasium building to the east, built in 1937–38. The large Manhattan firm of Fox & Fowle designed the superb addition, built in 1992, located at the north end of the small courtyard between the two earlier structures.

On the north side of Lincoln Place between Sixth and Seventh Avenues, at No. 153, is a large Romanesque Revival house of brick with brownstone and terra-cotta trim. Lamb & Rich, architects of the George P. Tangeman house (see below) on Berkeley Place, designed it for **Frank Lusk Babbott** (1854–1933) in 1886–87 (expanded to the rear in 1896). Babbott had been an Amherst classmate of Charles Millard Pratt and married Lydia Pratt, Charles Millard's sister and one of Charles Pratt's two children by his first wife. Babbott operated the Chelsea Jute Mills in New York City, was a director of the Atlantic Avenue Elevated Railroad Company and of the Long Island Railroad, and was a trustee of the Brooklyn Trust Company and of the Brooklyn Savings Bank. Next door, the large austere house of red brick with brownstone and terra-cotta trim at the northwest corner of Seventh Avenue and Lincoln Place was built in 1881. S. F. Evelette designed the house for William M. Brasher. The house later became the Park Slope Masonic Club and is now the Brooklyn Conservatory of Music, a music school that also offers excellent concerts.

On the south side of Berkeley Place between Seventh and Eighth Avenues, note No. 204. J. W. Walter designed this 1885 house for **David Augustus Boody** (1837–1930). Boody was a lawyer elected to the U.S. Congress in 1891, resigning after only a few months to become mayor of Brooklyn, serving until 1893. He was the founding president of the nearby Berkeley Institute from 1886 to 1922, one of the founding members of the Montauk Club in 1889, and president of the Board of Trustees of the Brooklyn Public Library from 1897 to 1930. He is buried in Green-wood Cemetery.

SOME PARK SLOPE CHURCHES

Park Slope is famous for its churches. Here are six clustered close together—two Roman Catholic, one Episcopal, one Methodist, one Presbyterian, one Dutch Reform, and all six Gothic.

2 ST. AUGUSTINE'S CHURCH (R. C.)
Sixth Avenue between Park Place and Sterling Place, west side
1897, Parfitt Brothers

The first thing that strikes one about St. Augustine's is its monumentality, conveyed through size and massing. The next thing is its use of color. The principal material is brownstone laid in random ashlar. The roofs are of red tile, and numerous forms rising from the roofs are of verdigris copper. The church meets Sixth Avenue with a massive and very high tower on the right. To the left of this is a powerfully swelling center section, expressing the nave, with six high stained-glass lancets. The red-tiled, half-conical end of the pitched roof of the nave tops this swelled front. The

2 St. Augustine's Church

tower on the left, about half as high as the one on the right, has a pyramidal roof of red tile. Both towers have entrances in their bases. The right tower rises to a conical roof of red tile, topped by a verdigris copper cross. Above the tower's pointed-arch entrance is a series of empty niches for sculptures. A bit above these are open lancets. Atop the four corners of the tower are verdigris copper pinnacles with finials. Atop the conical roof of the center section is the trumpet-blowing angel Gabriel, rendered in verdigris copper. This center section has a crenellated parapet along the base of its roof. The transept on Sterling Place has an enormous pointed-arch stained-glass window. St. Augustine's Academy next door is of dark brick and has crenellated parapets and a wonderful high brick tower of its own. The church has a high flèche of verdigris copper topped by a weathervane. The play of forms—conical and pyramidal, flat and swelled—and the play of colors make this one of the most powerful church designs in Brooklyn and indisputably the Parfitt Brothers' masterpiece. Though this church is built of Gothic forms, the skillful use of color and the sheer force of the massing make this more reminiscent than any other church in Brooklyn of H. H. Richardson's Trinity Church in Boston. The church's opalescent stained-glass windows are believed to come from Tiffany Studios, though no documentation exists.

3 ST. JOHN'S EPISCOPAL CHURCH COMPLEX
*St. John's Place between Sixth and Seventh Avenues, north side
Chapel and Rectory: 1869–70, Edward Tuckerman Potter
Church: 1885, John R. Thomas*

Quite different from, though equal in quality to, St. Augustine's is this marvelous complex that has been likened to an English country church. The chapel is the part that fronts on St. John's Place. It was built simultaneously with the rectory next door to the west. The cornerstone was laid on June 15, 1869, and the chapel opened the following year. The church is the long portion, parallel to the street behind a generous fenced garden, and was ingeniously appended to the chapel fifteen years later. The style of all three structures is "Ruskinian Gothic." The principal material of the whole complex is Belleville, New Jersey, brownstone laid in random ashlar. The polychrome contrast is provided by light-colored Ohio sandstone. The chapel meets St. John's Place with a gabled form featuring seven elegantly attenuated lancets arranged to a point echoing the form of the gable. All the openings are pointed arches, and all have polychrome voussoirs. The chapel is topped by a gabled bellcote, resting on colonnettes, with an open pointed arch. The church to the right hails the street with the broad sloping plane of the pitched roof of the nave. Below this are bays with pointed-arch windows and polychrome voussoirs. From the roof project simple dormers with trefoil stained-glass windows. The garden inevitably leads to comparisons with the Church of the Transfiguration on East 21st Street in Manhattan. The rectory to the left of the chapel is a simple, boxy form with mansard roof, dormers, and pointed-arch windows.

The chapel is similar to Russell Sturgis's Willow Place Chapel in Brooklyn Heights, built a few years after this. Well might they be similar, given that Russell Sturgis and the architect of St. John's, Edward Tuckerman Potter (1831–1904), were among the American architects most influenced by John Ruskin. Potter was born in Schenectady, New York. He was the brother of Henry Codman Potter (1834–1908), who as bishop of the Episcopal Diocese of New York from 1888 to 1908 initiated the construction of the Cathedral of St. John the Divine. Edward T. Potter was also the half-brother and sometime partner of William Appleton Potter, another leading ecclesiastical architect, whose works include St. Martin's Church (1887–89) on Lenox Avenue in Harlem. Edward T. Potter's most famous works are the Nott Memorial Library (1872) of Union College in Schenectady, New York, and his house for Mark Twain (1874) in Hartford, Connecticut. In New York City he designed St. Paul's Memorial Episcopal Church (1866–70) in the Stapleton Heights section of Staten Island. He had apprenticed in the office of Richard Upjohn.

The architect of the church was John Rochester Thomas. He designed the Reformed Low Dutch Church of Harlem (1885–87, the church where the Boys' Choir of Harlem was founded) on Lenox Avenue and 123rd Street and the New York

Presbyterian Church (1884–85) on West 128th Street, also in
Harlem. Thomas was known as a church architect when he
entered the 1893 competition for the design of a new city hall for
New York City. The city hall was never built, but Thomas's design
was resurrected a few years later for the Hall of
Records/Surrogate's Court building (1899–1907). Here Thomas
switched gears from the Gothic and Romanesque styles of his
churches to a Beaux-Arts classicism that ultimately resulted in one
of the city's most interesting buildings. The story of Thomas's
design and the problems encountered in the construction of his
building is one of the most complicated and fascinating in New
York architecture and is recounted with admirable clarity by
Gregory F. Gilmartin in his 1995 book *Shaping the City: New York
and the Municipal Art Society.*

Right across the street, notice the double house at Nos. 176
and 178. These are the William M. Thallon and Edward Bunker
houses built in 1887–88. R. L. Daus designed these wonderful
Queen Anne houses of brownstone and red brick—gabled, arched,
dormered, and towered—for a pair of physicians. Note the
caduceus, symbol of the medical profession, in the gable of No. 178.

The corner of Seventh Avenue and St. John's Place has these
two brownstone Gothic churches catercorner to each other, forming
a richly towered gateway to the bustling "high street" of Park Slope.

4 MEMORIAL PRESBYTERIAN CHURCH
*Southwest corner of Seventh Avenue and St. John's Place
1881–82, Pugin & Walter
Chapel on St. John's Place: 1888, Marshall & Walter*

Built of Belleville, New Jersey, brownstone laid in random ashlar, this church meets Seventh Avenue with a gabled section that
connects to the north via a wall with an open quatrefoil parapet to
the corner tower at St. John's Place. The tower rises to a marvelous
broached spire, one of surprisingly few such spires in Brooklyn. On
St. John's Place is a series of gabled forms connected by walls with
open quatrefoil parapets. The gable to the right of the tower has a

large pointed-arch stained-glass window. The chapel to the west on St. John's Place is carefully integrated with the church. The church's greatest treasures are its windows by Tiffany Studios. It is possible that all the church's windows are from Tiffany, and many of them, unlike those at St. Augustine's, are well documented.

5 GRACE UNITED METHODIST CHURCH
Northeast corner of Seventh Avenue and St. John's Place
1882, Parfitt Brothers
Parsonage: 1887, Parfitt Brothers

This is another of the Parfitt Brothers' best outings. The main material is a light brown sandstone trimmed in terra-cotta and in a darker sandstone. The church meets Seventh Avenue with the gabled end of the nave, set with an enormous pointed-arch stained-glass window. To the right is a fine corner tower, crenellated and pinnacled though missing its original spire. The best part of the church is its St. John's Place side, six bays long with double lancets for aisle windows. The bays are separated by flying buttresses. The clerestory windows, between the buttresses, are round with an eight-foil design. The windows are set on a beautiful diaper-work background of foliated terra-cotta tiles.

These next two churches have extremely high white towers that are impossible to miss from the F train when it rises over the Gowanus Canal.

6 OLD FIRST REFORMED CHURCH
Northwest corner of Seventh Avenue and Carroll Street
1893, George L. Morse

Here, a little south on Seventh Avenue in the bustling heart of the "high street," we come to a church not of brownstone but faced entirely in white limestone. The corner tower at Carroll Street rises high to a pointed spire. To its right on Seventh Avenue is a gabled front with the entrance, a fine composition of a vast receding pointed arch topped by a freestanding gable. Above the entrance is a large rose window. Apparently no records exist concerning this window. To the right of the gabled section is a driveway entered through a pointed-arch opening and overhung by two flying buttresses, the easternmost of which balances the tower on the south end. Around the corner on Carroll Street is another gabled section featuring a large rose window by Otto Heinigke and Owen Bowen.

This is the congregation's fifth home, succeeding the church that Minard Lafever designed in 1834–35 on the site of the Municipal Building on Joralemon Street. That church was the only Greek Revival design in Brooklyn ever positively attributed to Lafever. The architect of the present church, George L. Morse (1836–1924), was a prominent Brooklyn architect whose works include the Franklin Trust Company (1891) on Montague Street and the Temple Bar Building (1901) on Court Street.

7 ST. FRANCIS XAVIER CHURCH (R. C.)
Northeast corner of Sixth Avenue and Carroll Street
1900–1904, Thomas F. Houghton

A block to the west on Carroll Street is this imposing Roman Catholic church with a 156-foot-high tower. The cornerstone was laid on December 19, 1900, and the church was dedicated on May 15, 1904. The style is basically Early English Gothic. By far the best things here are the beautifully laid granite ashlar walls, trimmed in Indiana limestone. The palette is similar to that of the Old First Reformed Church. The architect, Thomas F. Houghton, came up in the office of his father-in-law, Patrick C. Keely, the most prolific architect of Catholic churches in America. The design here is similar to that of Houghton's slightly larger St. Agnes Church (1905) on Sackett and Hoyt Streets. Houghton also designed the fine Our Lady of Victory Roman Catholic Church (1891–95) on Throop and MacDonough Streets in the Stuyvesant Heights Historic District. For a look at some non-ecclesiastical work by the same architect, walk north a little on Seventh Avenue. On the east side of the avenue at Nos. 13 to 19 between Sterling and Park Places are four speculatively built neo-Grec row houses Houghton designed in 1882.

8 GEORGE P. TANGEMAN HOUSE
274–276 Berkeley Place, between Eighth Avenue and Plaza Street,
south side
1890–91, Lamb & Rich

Tangeman ran the Royal Baking Powder Company, founded by his father-in-law, Dr. Cornelius N. Hoagland of Clinton Avenue. Hoagland, a surgeon who made good in business, was also the founder of Cobble Hill's Hoagland Laboratory of Long Island College Hospital, built with the baking powder fortune and one of the country's first bacteriological research laboratories. (Its very distinctive 1888 building on Henry and Pacific Streets is, alas, no more.) Tangeman served as a trustee of Hoagland Laboratory. He also inherited his father-in-law's house in Glen Cove, Long Island, which C. P. H. Gilbert had designed.

Lamb & Rich's house for Tangeman was completed in the same year as the nearby Montauk Club and was published in *American Architect & Building News* for February 27, 1892.

The house is entered on the right via a "stoop" that is more like a stone porch across two-thirds of the front, basically forming the base of the house. Its light-colored, rock-faced stone yields at the first floor to stone of the same color but with a smooth finish. The third floor is faced in Roman brick. The steps of the porch lead to a square-headed doorway with a square-headed window to its right. In arch-happy Park Slope, one of its most famous houses is arch-less. Above this section is a trio of second-floor windows separated by Ionic colonnettes and topped by ornamental panels. The left side of the façade employs the same materials as the right but is a large, two-story, swelling bay, three windows on each floor, capped by an elegant balustrade. From the center of the steeply pitched tile roof projects a large, gabled dormer that extends in equal measure over both the flat and swelling halves of the lower façade. Cherubs delightfully bracket the dormer. Within the dormer are three windows. This dormer story is faced in brick, though the tile of the massive gable dominates. The east and west façades are defined by stepped gables into which are worked high, vertically paneled chimney stacks that seem to bookend the house. We normally identify as Romanesque Revival such elements as the contrasting use of rock-faced masonry with Roman brick and the broad, tiled roof planes. Closer inspection, however, shows classical details, especially in the doorway, which has an egg-and-dart frame and an entablature carved in an anthemion motif. The second-story Ionic colonnettes were already noted. It has been said that the introduction here of classical elements presaged the classical period of Park Slope architecture that would arrive in the wake of the World's Columbian Exposition of 1893.

Some sense of Park Slope's skyrocketing property values at the turn of the millennium is indicated by the fact that this house was purchased in 1991 for $550,000 and was on the market in 2000 for four million dollars.

9 64 and 66 EIGHTH AVENUE
Between Berkeley Place and Union Street, west side
1889, Parfitt Brothers

These are two beautiful houses showing the Parfitts at their residential best. Both houses have light-colored, rock-faced sandstone bases. The parlor floors are faced in smooth stone, with the rock-faced treatment returning in the second and third floors. No. 64, the northernmost of the pair, has a bowed oriel at the second floor, while No. 66 has a three-sided projecting bay at the parlor and second floors. The houses' ornamental carving is extraordinarily lush. Note the beautiful gables set with Romanesque arches. We normally associate the Parfitts with dark-colored buildings.

9 64 and 66 Eighth Avenue

10 *Mrs. M. V. Phillips House*

10 MRS. M. V. PHILLIPS HOUSE
70–72 Eighth Avenue, northwest corner of Union Street
1887, Lansing C. Holden

This large, picturesque, and wonderful Queen Anne house has two full exposures. On the forty-foot-wide Eighth Avenue side, the base and parlor floor are of rock-faced stone, with brick, stone, and terra-cotta above. The arched entrance is on the right. This east façade is dominated by a massive gabled dormer and by the corner tower that provides a superb transition to the Union Street side. The tower is topped in a tiled thimble and has terra-cotta panels bearing the sunflower motif that was a staple of the Queen Anne. On Union Street is a high, gabled bay to the left of the tower. The gable is in the Jacobean style, a typical borrowing of the Queen Anne, and has patterned brickwork expressing the chimney flues it conceals. Between the tower and the high-gabled bay is a high chimney. To the left of this bay is a second-floor porch overhung by a shingled roof. This is followed to the west by another, recessed, gabled bay. This is a powerfully picturesque composition that commands its corner site on two wide streets as few houses do. Note that the materials are similar to those of the Tangeman house, yet the feeling is very different.

Mrs. Phillips, for whom the house was built, moved here from 251 Washington Avenue in Clinton Hill. That may tell us something about residential mobility in late-nineteenth-century Brooklyn. (Stewart Woodford had also just moved from Clinton Hill to Park Slope.) The house became a restaurant and bridge club in the early 1930s. It has in recent years been sparklingly cleaned and restored and probably looks as good as it did when it was just built.

11 STEWART LYNDON WOODFORD HOUSE
869 President Street between Seventh and Eighth Avenues,
*   north side*
1885, Henry Ogden Avery

Stewart Lyndon Woodford (1835–1913) was born in New York City and graduated from Columbia College in 1854. A lawyer, he served as Assistant United States Attorney in New York City from 1861 to 1862, when he joined the Union Army. By the end of the war he was a brigadier general. He was the first Union military commander in both Charleston and Savannah. After the war he was elected lieutenant governor of New York but was unsuccessful in his gubernatorial campaign of 1870. He was a U.S. congressman from Brooklyn

11 *Stewart Lyndon Woodford House*

from 1873 to 1874, and was U.S. Attorney for the Southern District of New York (the same job Rudolph Giuliani would hold) from 1877 to 1883. His illustrious public career was topped off when he was named U.S. ambassador to Spain, serving from 1897 to 1898. He delivered one of the official speeches at the opening ceremonies of the World's Columbian Exposition in Chicago in 1893. Woodford, who was also a prominent member of the Montauk Club, moved to President Street from 67 Cambridge Place in Clinton Hill.

Henry Ogden Avery (1852–90) was Woodford's architect. Avery was the Brooklyn-born son of the noted art collector Samuel Putnam Avery (1822–1904). Young Avery studied at Cooper Union, worked for Russell Sturgis, and attended the École des Beaux-Arts. Returning to New York in 1879, Avery went to work for Richard Morris Hunt, the city's leading architect, and contributed to the design of the base of the Statue of Liberty. Avery established his own practice in 1883, but it was short-lived. He died when he was only thirty-eight. In his memory his father endowed Columbia University's Avery Architectural Library.

At thirty-six feet, the Woodford house is unusually wide, and Avery seemed to wish to accentuate this width. The three-story house has a perfectly symmetrical façade of red brick with very sparing stone trim. In the dead center of the first floor is a stoopless arched entrance, approached by a couple of steps, with a beautiful iron-and-glass doorway. Patterned brickwork forms voussoirs for the entry arch as well as for the arched leaded-glass windows on either side of the doorway. Above the entrance and separated from it by a large expanse of unornamented brick is a small square window of leaded glass. To its sides are the dominating features of the façade, two two-sided projecting bay windows framed in wood and supported by wooden struts that reach down from the bottom points of the oriels to the center tops of the first-floor arched windows flanking the doorway. These struts are reminiscent (it is often remarked) of the designs of the French Gothic Revival theorist Viollet-le-Duc. The third floor has three sets of two windows bordered on the top and bottom by continuous stone bands. The sides of the doorway and of the first- and third-floor windows are defined by alternating square-edged and chamfered bricks. The house is topped by a deep cornice carried on four evenly spaced brackets extending from discreet bits of corbeled brickwork. Original features now missing are the somewhat odd coxcombs that crested the oriels, actually the only elements of true applied decoration on the façade. The general feeling may be very vaguely Romanesque, with the round arches and hints of corbeling, but in fact the design is strikingly original.

This stands in the front rank of the "artistic houses" of the 1880s. It is safe to say that Avery would have gone on to become one of New York's most significant architects.

Since 1964, this has been the residence of the Missionary Servants of the Most Holy Trinity, a Roman Catholic organization headquartered in Washington, D.C., and dedicated to helping the poor.

12 JOHN W. WEBER HOUSE
101 Eighth Avenue, southeast corner of President Street
1909, Daus & Otto

Like Montrose W. Morris over the same years, R. L. Daus traveled a course from picturesque Romanesque Revival to an elegant Classicism, with the latter tendency finding a fine expression in this exceptionally large neo-Georgian house for John Weber, president of the Ulmer Brewery in Bushwick. The base is stone, but the dominant material is heavily mortared red brick laid in Flemish bond, creating a kind of speckled appearance. The Doric-columned entrance, with a beautiful wrought-iron canopy and iron-and-glass doors, is set dead center on the Eighth Avenue side. Flanking the entrance are windows with round pediments with carved swags. Up top, animal heads project from a cornice over an entablature featuring triglyphs and metopes; an elegant balustrade tops the house. It is of the same genre as Mowbray & Uffinger's 1 Montgomery Place of one year later.

13 M. and J. TRACY HOUSE
105 Eighth Avenue between President and Carroll Streets, east side
1912, Frank Helmle

The limestone house is set back from the street behind a small garden to leave room for a remarkable two-story, boldly bowed, tetrastyle Corinthian portico that looks like it belongs in a William Kent garden. If the portico were flat across the house, it would devour the whole façade. It is an attempt at a winking monumentality in the tight confines of a Park Slope block. What's amazing is that it works—completely. Other stops are pulled, too. The same two stories over which that portico lords are fully rusticated. The third floor is a frieze-like band of small windows, above which is a palmette frieze under a

13 *105 Eighth Avenue*

bracketed cornice topped by a very elegant balustrade. Back on the first floor, triangular-pedimented windows set within partially blind arches with rusticated voussoirs flank the portico, which has magnificent bronze-and-glass doors. Balustrades run across the bottoms of the windows. I have always adored this house and fully accept its regality, even as I know it is make-believe.

The Tracys were involved in the lighterage business in New York Harbor. As a partner in Helmle & Huberty and later in Helmle & Corbett, Frank Helmle was one of the major Brooklyn architects of his time. The Montessori School now occupies the house.

Thomas Bennett designed the fine Beaux-Arts-style limestone houses on the west side of Eighth Avenue, at Nos. 106 and 108, between President and Carroll Streets. They were built in 1900. Bennett is best known for his Park Slope apartment houses. These are his northernmost works in the neighborhood. This prolific architect is probably more responsible than any other for creating the classical fabric of turn-of-the-century Park Slope.

14 THOMAS ADAMS, JR., HOUSE

115–119 Eighth Avenue, northeast corner of Carroll Street
1888, C. P. H. Gilbert

This is Gilbert's laureate essay in the Richardsonian Romanesque, a round-arched style immediately identifiable by its rock-faced masonry (often accented by contrasting materials) and by a sense of massiveness and solidity (achieved through such means as deep window reveals and broad roof planes). The style is named for Henry Hobson Richardson (1838–86), who worked mainly out of the Boston area. A product of the training at the École des Beaux-Arts, Richardson mentored a generation of American architects, including Louis Sullivan, Charles Follen McKim, and Stanford White. The house was designed as a double residence for Thomas Adams, Jr., inventor of Chiclets chewing gum and of the automatic vending machines that dispensed it, and for his son, John Dunbar Adams.

Note how the rock-faced brownstone plays off of the smooth Roman brick and how the materials work with the massing of the building to communicate strength and power. Yet note also how this strength and power exist harmoniously with the most delicate bits of ornament. The entrance arch on

14 *Thomas Adams, Jr., House*

Carroll Street may be the finest thing here, with its extravagant foliate decoration in terra-cotta.

The main, or Carroll Street, façade plays with notions of symmetry and
has a somewhat stately presence. The first floor is of rock-faced brownstone laid
in random ashlar. The upper floors are faced in Roman brick. A central section,
occupying about a third of the façade, projects from the body of the house. The
main entrance, that of Adams *père,* is in the center of this section's first floor.
Curved wing-walls sweep one up to the deeply recessed front door under a
Romanesque arch springing from clustered dwarf columns. Lush, naturalistic
foliate ornament in terra-cotta defines the arch. Symmetrically disposed on
either side of this section are arched windows with rock-faced, rusticated voussoirs. Flanking these window sections are polygonal corner towers, each with a
polygonal, conical crown of red tile. In the second floor of the central section is
a series of three small windows separated by Romanesque columns. Bands of
ornamental terra-cotta richly frame this series. The floor above features a pair
of arched windows springing from Romanesque columns and topped by a double-arched drip molding. The top floor of the central section forms a large gable
inset with four slit-like windows and topped with a triangular panel of lush,
flowing terra-cotta ornament. At the third floor, a bracketed balcony connects
the projecting central section to the projecting corner tower to the west. No
such balcony appears on the other side. The house's steeply hipped tile roof
strikes a note of asymmetry. The west half is higher than the east. Both halves
have gabled dormers. The west half also has, between the gabled dormer and
the gable of the central section, an eyelid dormer.

The west, or Eighth Avenue, side is almost symmetrical. The corner
tower on the right is round in its first story and polygonal in its second and
third stories. Balancing it on the north end of the house is a two-story bowed
bay that rises to an openwork parapet enclosing a balcony. A hipped dormer
tops this side of the house. Two massive arches define the center of the façade.
The one on the left is the entrance to what was originally the home of Adams
fils. The arch on the right is a window. Both arches have rock-faced voussoirs
contrasting with the smooth Roman brick that surrounds them.

The house was built with an elevator. There is an often-told neighborhood story that the Adamses once went away, leaving their servants to look
after the house. Some of the servants got trapped in the elevator when it
stalled and were not found until they had died. The house, it is said, has been
haunted ever since.

CHARLES PIERREPONT HENRY GILBERT (1863–1952)

C. P. H. Gilbert was one of New York City's great turn-of-the-century architects. His numerous significant works in Manhattan include the Otto Kahn house (now the Convent of the Sacred Heart) of 1913–18 on Fifth Avenue and 91st Street, the Felix M. Warburg house (now the Jewish Museum) of 1906–8 on Fifth Avenue and 92nd Street, and the Joseph Raphael DeLamar house (now the Consulate of the Republic of Poland) of 1902–5 on Madison Avenue and 37th Street. Note three things. First, in working for Kahn and Warburg, it appears that Gilbert was a favored architect among "Our Crowd," the German-Jewish financiers and philanthropists who left such a mark on turn-of-the-century New York City. Second, these great Manhattan houses were built some years after Gilbert's great Park Slope houses. The Brooklyn houses tend to be late 1880s and early 1890s. The Manhattan houses tend to be early-twentieth century. Third, the Kahn and DeLamar houses are consummate essays in Beaux-Arts Classicism at its grandest. Though trained at the École des Beaux-Arts, Gilbert at first mined, like Henry Hobson Richardson (also Beaux-Arts–trained), the Romanesque Revival before turning, like so many others (not Richardson, who was dead by the time), to the classical in the 1890s.

Gilbert was born in New York City and educated at Columbia College and in Paris at the École des Beaux-Arts. He began his architectural career in mining towns in Arizona and Colorado before returning to New York around 1885. His first important commissions were in Park Slope, and there is no other neighborhood in which his works so abound. When he started designing houses in Park Slope in 1887, he was only twenty-four years old, which was, as it still is, amazingly young for an architect. Yet establish his reputation he did, such that by the turn of the century he was becoming one of the most prolific residential architects in the burgeoning Upper East Side of Manhattan. He lived long enough to see the United Nations Headquarters rise on the east side of Manhattan, the distance between its International Style and the style of Gilbert's houses being incalculable.

15 **121 EIGHTH AVENUE**
Southeast corner of Carroll Street
1894, Montrose W. Morris

Montrose Morris broke out of his Romanesque Revival straitjacket when he designed this elegant neo-Renaissance house that may not get as much attention as it deserves, being right across Carroll Street from the powerful Adams house by Gilbert. Here, in the greatest of all possible contrasts to the Adams house, are white brick, white limestone, and white terra-cotta. The house is four stories. The doorway entablature is carried on slender Corinthian columns and topped by a round pediment fabulously encrusted with terra-cotta decoration. The three third-floor windows are topped by cartouches.

16 **123 and 125 EIGHTH AVENUE**
Between Montgomery Place and Carroll Street, east side
1902, Peter Collins

Eight years after the Morris house next door, the speculative builder-architect Peter Collins put up these two houses that form a beautiful row with the other house and that are among the finest Beaux-Arts–inspired house designs in Park Slope. The two four-story houses are all limestone, and both have rusticated parlor floors. At No. 123, the rustication is carried through the upper stories as quoins that are designed like banded pilasters, rising to Ionic capitals at the top of the third floor. A wonderfully complex scrolled form with a shell tops the three-sided second-floor oriel. A dormer window topped by a round pediment projects from the mansard roof. At No. 125, the entrance is up the stoop to the right. To the left a giant cartouche tops the parlor window. The two second-floor windows are set in deep arches with curved chamfering. Scrolled and foliated decorations top these windows. These are wonderful houses.

**CARROLL STREET BETWEEN EIGHTH AVENUE
AND PROSPECT PARK WEST**

Unlike neighboring Montgomery Place (see below), the park block of Carroll Street is not credited to a single developer with a vision. Still, it is almost as good as its neighbor. The remarkably diverse houses, some by notable architects, work beautifully

361

together to create one of the most dazzling blocks in Brooklyn. There's a lot of C. P. H. Gilbert here, too. Here are some highlights.

South side:

17 JAMES H. REMINGTON HOUSE
838 Carroll Street
1887, C. P. H. Gilbert

An unusual feature of this three-story-plus-attic house is its full facing of rock-faced brownstone laid in random ashlar. There is no brick. Low stone walls sweep up to form the wing-walls of the stoop leading to the deeply recessed front door, which is most surprisingly right in the center of the house. The perception of this is thrown off by the dominant feature here, which is the full-height round tower to the right, occupying a third of the front elevation. The doorway is part of a double-arched composition in the Romanesque style, with the window to the left. At the second floor is a projecting three-sided bay faced in smooth stone. The parapet of this bay encloses a balcony at the third floor, behind which are four windows defined by a continuous drip molding of Romanesque arches. The attic story features a three-windowed, gabled dormer projecting from a steeply pitched, tiled roof. The bold corner tower is encircled at each floor by square-headed windows trimmed in smooth stone. The conical roof is of the same tile as the pitched roof.

The use of the smooth stone for framing the windows adds a somewhat genteel note to what otherwise might appear the high rock wall of a medieval rampart. This is a powerful essay in the Romanesque Revival that, because it is in the shadow of the stupendous Adams house across Carroll Street, may tend to receive less attention than it otherwise would.

18 GEORGE W. KENYON HOUSE
842 Carroll Street
1887, C. P. H. Gilbert

This is second only to the Harvey Murdock house (see below) in its feeling of medieval ruggedness, and in some ways may even surpass the Murdock house in this quality. The base is of rock-faced brownstone; above is Roman brick with stone trim. The Romanesque-arched entrance is up the stoop on the left, with a window to its left that is divided into four lights by "Latin cross" mullioning similar to that of the Murdock house. Above the doorway at the second floor is a window divided horizontally in two and topped by a band of rock-faced stone. To the left of this is a rounded projecting bay of three windows, each treated in the same manner as the window to the right, including the surmounting band of rock-faced stone. At the third floor are three more such windows. They are placed centrally in their half of the façade. On the right side of the front at the first floor is another such trio of windows, a bit wider than the others. Above these are four windows so treated, and above those three more, identical in placement to the ones on the left side. The house is topped on the right by a gable with four close-spaced, slit-like windows, like bowmen's slots in medieval forts. In the point of the gable is a triangular panel of patterned brickwork. On the top to the left is visible the house's steeply pitched roof set with a small dormer.

There is not a trace of applied ornament. Even the archway of the front door, where often in this Romanesque Revival idiom one will find terra-cotta ornament, there is only patterning of rock-faced stone. The house is quite austere.

19 CHARLES ROBINSON SMITH HOUSE
846 Carroll Street
1887, C. P. H. Gilbert

Compared to the preceding Remington and Kenyon houses, this seems decidedly Italianate. The front entrance, on the right up a wing-walled stoop, is recessed within a wide arch with rock-faced stone voussoirs coming to a Tuscan point. To the left is a four-part window with Gilbert's trademark "Latin cross" mullioning, the only instance here, really, in which this house seems to work toward the same effect as many of Gilbert's other nearby houses.

The basement and parlor floor are of light-colored, rock-faced stone. Above is orange-colored brick. The palette is very different from the preceding houses. This house gets downright genteel above the parlor floor. At the second and third floors, there are four evenly spaced windows on the right with full enframements of molded brickwork. On the left are six windows, treated as a single unit and framed in molded brickwork with a trio of blind panels separating the second from the third floors. It's simple and rather elegant. A bold modillioned cornice with prominent end brackets that terminate in animal heads marvelously tops the whole. Below the cornice is a frieze of patterned brickwork in a fretwork design.

20 850 CARROLL STREET
1922, Mott B. Schmidt

This is one of Park Slope's last great houses (if not its last great house). Mott B. Schmidt, one of his era's best architects, designed it in the neo-Federal style at which he was so adept. (See, for example, his house for Vincent Astor, built in 1927–28 at 130 East 80th Street.) It is a very wide house with a full facing of buff brick laid in Flemish bond. The English basement entrance, with leaded fanlight and fluted columns, forms an elegant arcade with the three windows to its left. The windows on the other three stories are all square-headed. The corners of the house are of brickwork patterned to emulate rustication.

21 864 to 872 CARROLL STREET
1887, William B. Tubby

Tubby designed this picturesque, wonderfully rambling group of five houses under the influence of the Queen Anne style that London's Richard Norman Shaw pioneered in the 1870s. What we call the Queen Anne style was a picturesque hodgepodge. Queen Anne herself reigned in the early eighteenth century, the last British monarch before George I. The Queen Anne movement of the late nineteenth century was not so much a going back to the style of Queen Anne's reign as it was a return to the varied forms of English architecture between the Middle Ages and the Georgian era. We find, for example, hearty doses of Tudor, Elizabethan, and Jacobean in what we call Queen Anne, as well as Renaissance elements of the kind Inigo Jones imported from Italy. The appeal of the Queen Anne (generally more marked among the public than the critics) in London and in New York was its varied profiles and textures, answering to the Victorian taste for picturesque romanticism. (We so often think the Victorians were paragons of probity and rectitude, and though in many respects they were, their taste in design was often what can only be called wild and woolly.) Tubby's Carroll Street row is one of Park Slope's finest Queen Anne essays.

At first it appears there are only three houses since there are three entrance arches. Two of the arches, however, each conceal two entrances. These arches have bold, rock-faced voussoirs. The parlor and second floors are faced in brick, but the third floor is heavily shingled and designed to seem as one with the roof. The two arches to the east have deeply recessed doorways, while the westernmost arch has a flush doorway. The whole is treated as a single composition without clear expression of the individual units. Projecting bays, patterned brickwork, eyelid dormers, and more are employed to intensify the picturesque impact. Note how the upper sash of many of the windows is divided into several small lights, while the lower sash is a single pane. This Tudoresque element was characteristic of the Queen Anne. Several years after he did this row, Tubby employed Jacobean forms in a much more "proper" way in his house for William Childs on Prospect Park West and 2nd Street.

22 LOUIS M. MOWBRAY HOUSE
874 Carroll Street
1904, Mowbray & Uffinger

Mowbray & Uffinger designed this house for one of their own. Louis Mowbray was a senior partner in the distinguished firm that designed the Dime Savings Bank and the People's Trust Company. They also designed the enormous neo-Georgian house at No. 1 Montgomery Place. Like the house at No. 850, designed some years later by Mott B. Schmidt, we have here an excellent essay in the neo-Georgian, with red brick laid in Flemish bond, an English basement entrance, and a Palladian window.

North side:

23 WILLIAM R. WEBSTER HOUSE
863 Carroll Street
1890, Napoleon LeBrun & Sons

At this writing, climbing foliage has all but swallowed this lovely house; the foliage is so dense it is hard to believe the house's residents could see out the front windows. I think this unfortunate. This is a very rare example of a residential work by one of America's leading architectural firms of the time. The house is of brownstone and Roman brick. The first-floor stonework is rusticated, as are the voussoirs of the arched doorway. The brownstone has a hammered surface. Note the elegant roof balustrade. LeBrun & Sons was the firm begun by Napoleon LeBrun (1821–1901) of Philadelphia, an architect who had trained under the great Thomas Ustick Walter (architect of the U.S. Capitol dome, of Philadelphia's Girard College, and of much else) and rose to prominence in his native city. (LeBrun's father was a French immigrant.) LeBrun, well before his sons entered the business, designed some of Philadelphia's best-known nineteenth-century buildings, including the Academy of Music on Broad Street and (in conjunction with John Notman) the Cathedral of Saints Peter and Paul at Logan Circle. Later, LeBrun's eldest son, Pierre, took charge and moved the firm to New York City. He was the principal designer of the firm's several outstanding Manhattan buildings, including the Home Life Insurance Company Building of 1892–94 on Broadway and Murray Street, the Church of St. Mary the Virgin of 1894–95 on West 46th Street, and, most famous of all, the Metropolitan Life Insurance Company Tower of 1907–9, once the world's tallest building, on Madison Avenue and 24th Street. In Brooklyn, the LeBruns designed the east wing (1886–88) and the west wing (1907) of Minard Lafever's Packer Collegiate Institute on Joralemon Street. These, not houses, were the sorts of buildings for which the firm was known. In Park Slope, they made an exception for the engineer William Webster.

---

24 **13 and 15 PROSPECT PARK WEST**
Between President and Carroll Streets
1919, W. T. McCarthy

Around the turn of the third decade of the twentieth century, Brooklyn architect W. T. McCarthy designed several lovely houses in neo-Tudor or neo-Georgian along Prospect Park West. They were among the last of the single-family residences to be built in the neighborhood and their design reflected a major transformation then beginning to overcome Brooklyn. I speak of these houses' driveways, the first in the neighborhood. (They are still, I think, the only driveways in the neighborhood built as original parts of houses.) The driveways, the date, and the Tudor style of these houses cannot fail to make one think of one of New York's (and America's) most beautiful suburban developments, Forest Hills Gardens, then taking shape in Queens. In this period before the highway-induced sprawl of the post–World War II years, "suburban" immediately evoked images of gracious living. McCarthy was obviously trying to move Park Slope into the brave new world with his driveway houses, as quaintly charming today as they must have seemed progressive in the 1920s.

25 **16 and 17 PROSPECT PARK WEST**
Northwest corner of Carroll Street
1899, Montrose W. Morris

Here is the redoubtable Montrose W. Morris in high classical mood, with a pair of sumptuous limestone palazzi that would not be out of place in the Upper East Side of Manhattan. No. 16, with its entrance on the right, has a bowed parlor bay on the left. On the second floor, Ionic colonnettes separate the windows, and there is a lovely console-bracketed cornice. No. 17 shows that Morris might never have lost his love of the Romanesque; though this has much the same classical feeling as its neighbor, note the Romanesque arches of the parlor floor and the Romanesque treatment of the second floor. Between the floors is a classical balustrade repeated between the second and third floors, where it encloses a balcony serving a loggia. Ionic columns beautifully screen the loggia.

The parents of actress and congresswoman Helen Gahagan (who allegedly coined the term "Tricky Dick" to refer to Richard Nixon) once owned No. 17, in the garden of which she married actor Melvyn Douglas.

26 **18 and 19 PROSPECT PARK WEST**
Southwest corner of Carroll Street
1898, Montrose W. Morris

Here is more Morris in Italian Renaissance mood. No. 18 has a superb rusticated parlor floor. The entrance, on the left, has a spectacular bronze-and-glass canopy with anthemion cresting. To its right is a Palladian window with Ionic colonnettes. The second and third floors are bookended by two-story-high Ionic pilasters and have beautifully framed windows. No. 19 is essentially identical, save for the canopy.

Morris received the commissions for the two pairs of houses at this corner from two different clients. Designed within a year of each other, they create an almost monumental gateway from Prospect Park West to Carroll Street. This is an outstanding example of a gifted and successful architect making a beautiful urban-design statement that, in its much smaller compass, is as significant an insinuation into the cityscape of City Beautiful ideals as the arch and its surroundings a couple of blocks away at Grand Army Plaza. Morris also designed the fine limestone classical house at 22 Prospect Park West (1899).

27 **28 PROSPECT PARK WEST**
Southwest corner of Montgomery Place
1901, Charles Brigham

Boston's Charles Brigham designed this impressive mansion in a basically Renaissance style with Romanesque touches (as in some of the window arches). The walls are Indiana limestone with a hammered surface. Note the wealth of sculptural embellishment, including human masks and animal forms. On the right is a big, two-story bowed bay rising to a parapet, with carved-stone designs, enclosing a balcony behind which raises a prominent gable set with a beautiful Palladian window topped by a gryphon finial. The entrance, on the left, has a deeply recessed doorway and is topped by an entablature on which lions sit. A polygonal dormer tops this side of the house.

Brigham was one of Boston's major architects of this period. Every visitor to Boston has seen his splendid Christian Science Mother Church (1903–6). He also designed the impressive Albert C. Burrage mansion of 1899 on Commonwealth Avenue. In New York City Brigham also designed the Messiah Home for Children (1908) on West Tremont Avenue in the University Heights section of the Bronx.

MONTGOMERY PLACE

Harvey Murdock developed most of Montgomery Place. He hired Charles Pierrepont Henry Gilbert to design no fewer than twenty houses on the one-block street. Other outstanding architects contributed, as noted. This is one of New York City's most celebrated blocks. The *AIA Guide to New York City* calls it "One of the truly great blocks in the world of urbane row housing. . . . a symphony of materials and textures." In *New York 1880*, Robert A. M. Stern, Thomas Mellins, and David Fishman call Montgomery Place "one of the period's great urban ensembles." No one who walks along it will disagree.

Since 1889, the street has been named for General Richard Montgomery, felled in the Battle of Quebec in 1775. This is the selfsame Montgomery who is memorialized by Jean-Jacques Caffiéri on the porch of St. Paul's Chapel on Broadway and Fulton Street in Manhattan.

Gilbert designed, on the south side, Nos. 14, 16, 18, 36, 38, 40, 42, 44, 46, 48, 50, 54, 56, 58, and 60. On the north side he designed Nos. 11, 17, 19, 21, and 25.

This is a street where every house deserves to be treated, but with space constraints in mind I shall point out the ones that strike me most.

South side:

28 14 MONTGOMERY PLACE
1887–88, C. P. H. Gilbert

The basement and most of the parlor floor are of rock-faced brownstone while red brick is used above. The second floor has a bowed oriel across almost the entire front. The third floor has a trio of Romanesque-arched windows. Above these is a band of foliate terra-cotta, above which is an attic story marked by four vertically slit windows beneath a prominent, almost full-width gable.

29 16 MONTGOMERY PLACE
1887–88, C. P. H. Gilbert

The entrance is on the left, unlike the house next door to the west, where the entrance is on the right. The materials and many of the forms are the same as the neighbor to the west, though the feeling is much more compacted. At the second floor is a three-sided oriel, its parapet forming the enclosure of a third-floor balcony deeply recessed within a broad arch. A gable similar to, though smaller than, the one to the west tops off the house.

30 18 MONTGOMERY PLACE
1887–88, C. P. H. Gilbert

Of these three houses at Nos. 14 to 18, all built at the same time, this seems the most imposing. As is typical in these parts, the basement and parlor floor are faced in rock-faced brownstone, while the upper floors (three in this case) are of light-colored brick. The entrance is on the right. The second floor has a three-sided oriel that stretches across almost the entire front, in the manner of the curved oriel of No. 14. The parapet encloses a balcony in front of a broad, segmental-arched window at the third floor. The fourth floor has three windows grouped by a Romanesque-arched drip molding. The crowning gable here is of the stepped Dutch variety, echoing that of the Murdock house right across the street. Near the top of the gable are three vertically slit windows over a narrow shelf of corbeled brickwork.

31 42 and 44 MONTGOMERY PLACE
1888–89, C. P. H. Gilbert

This three-story double house uses the same materials and some of the same details and was built in the same years as the three houses by Gilbert at Nos. 36 to 40 to the west. The two entrances are in the center, up low stoops, and are flanked by two-story swelling bays. The parlor floors are faced in rock-faced sandstone, and the upper floors are of orange-colored brick. Along the tops of the second and third floors is "intaglio" brickwork, and across the top of the houses is a band of elaborate diamond-patterned brickwork under a stupendous wood cornice carried on long beams.

31 *42 and 44 Montgomery Place*

32 A. S. LOCKE HOUSE
46 Montgomery Place
1888–89, C. P. H. Gilbert

This house is a symphony in Roman brick, including the voussoirs of the segmental-arched parlor window on the right and of the doorway, up a low, broad stoop, on the left. Almost the whole second floor projects. It is shingled, and is carried on a sensuously upswelling shelf of Roman brick. Its sloping roof is of tile. There is fine terra-cotta ornament at the top of the house, and a stained-glass transom over the parlor window. It's really one of the most felicitous houses in Park Slope.

Gilbert designed this house for Alex S. Locke, a renowned stained-glass artist whose works can be seen in two churches in Fort Greene—Lafayette Avenue Presbyterian Church and Our Lady Queen of All Saints Roman Catholic Church.

North side:

33 1 MONTGOMERY PLACE
1910, Mowbray & Uffinger

The architects of the People's Trust Company on Montague Street designed this enormous neo-Federal house at the northeast corner of Eighth Avenue. Louis Mowbray of Mowbray & Uffinger lived a block away on Carroll Street. Red brick is laid in Flemish bond above a low marble basement and marble steps.

34 HARVEY MURDOCK HOUSE
11 Montgomery Place
1887–88, C. P. H. Gilbert

Gilbert designed this house for the principal developer of Montgomery Place, and it may have been the first of the street's houses to be built. There is a powerful, primitive feeling to this house, its Romanesque forms unrelieved by any delicate terra-cotta ornamentation or such. The façade reads vertically in thirds, with the entrance in the far left third reached by a broad stone stoop and topped by a stone transom bar and a transom. The transom is inset with a heavy iron screen. This first floor, as well as the base below it, is of boldly rock-faced brownstone. The upper floors are Roman brick with rock-faced brownstone trim. The second-floor window above the front entrance is divided into four lights by rock-faced stone mullions forming a Latin cross and imparting a strange, primitively religious feeling. The same sort of fenestration occurs in the first and second floors in the right two-thirds. These floors form a broad and boldly swelling bay. In the left third of the third floor is a double window with a big block of rock-faced stone above it and a shelf of corbeled brickwork below it. The right side features a trio of round-arched windows that are defined as Romanesque by their surmounting triple-arched drip molding. The fourth or attic story features a hipped, tiled dormer in the left third, projecting from the steeply pitched tile roof. On the right is a high, Dutch stepped-gable inset with, of all things, a Palladian window.

There may be no house in Park Slope that is more rugged than this or that imparts so primitive an air.

35 17 and 19 MONTGOMERY PLACE
1887–88, C. P. H. Gilbert
*(Note that Nos. 13 and 15 are omitted from
the street numbering system.)*

These houses directly to the east of the Harvey Murdock house possess much the same feeling as that house. They are not quite of the grand scale of the Murdock house but otherwise clearly form an ensemble with it. Instead of the swelling bay, No. 17 has a three-sided bay, and No. 19 is flat across the first floor, with a three-sided bay projecting from the second floor and carried on large, rugged brackets over the first floor's broad, heavy-mullioned arched window.

George P. Chappell designed the four limestone, brick, and terra-cotta houses at Nos. 37 to 43 in 1890–91.

36 45 MONTGOMERY PLACE
1898–99, Babb, Cook & Willard

This French Renaissance–style house features a rusticated granite base with a broad porch, a limestone parlor floor, and limestone-trimmed red brick above. It seems almost a miniature version of the same architects' Andrew Carnegie mansion on Fifth Avenue and 91st Street, begun right after this house. There is a bowed parlor bay on the left. The second and third floors

36 45 Montgomery Place

each sport four square-headed windows with rusticated limestone surrounds. A balustrade crowns the whole. The most beautiful thing here is the entrance, with its elaborate consoles and superb central cartouche. This is the French Renaissance of the late sixteenth and early seventeenth centuries that we associate with the hôtels of the *places* of Paris, such as the Place des Vosges. Babb, Cook & Willard, one of the great New York firms of their period, also designed a couple of the Pratt family houses on Clinton Avenue.

37 47 MONTGOMERY PLACE
1890, R. L. Daus

Daus designed this rather exotic house in the French Renaissance manner with a full front of red sandstone. White limestone could not stand out more among brownstones than does this sandstone. Everything looks like it was molded from a single piece of clay. The Francophilic decoration is graceful around the beautiful segmental-arched entrance, and especially the fleurs-de-lys in the gabled dormer of the steep, pyramidal, tiled roof. To the left is a two-story three-sided bay rising to form a third-floor balcony. Though this and the house next door at No. 45 are both called "French Renaissance," this is the early-sixteenth-century version of the style, the one we associate with the great châteaus of the Loire Valley. Daus was trained at the École des Beaux-Arts, and also, after living for many years in Brooklyn, died in Paris. Note that this was built nineteen years before the house for John Weber that Daus designed for the southeast corner of Eighth Avenue and President Street.

Martyn N. Weinstein designed the apartment house at 140 Eighth Avenue, opposite Montgomery Place, built in 1935–36. This elegant Art Deco building, though stylistically a world apart from the houses of Montgomery Place, nonetheless provides the perfect, handsome, non-attention-grabbing closure that lends the wonderful mews-like quality to Park Slope's most beautiful street.

38 143 EIGHTH AVENUE and
10 MONTGOMERY PLACE (apartments)
Southeast corner of Montgomery Place and Eighth Avenue
1910–11, Montrose W. Morris

These two buildings may be Park Slope's most beautiful purpose-built apartment houses. Here is late Morris, who had moved from Romanesque

Revival through a relatively chaste Classicism to the Beaux-Arts effulgence of buildings such as this. It is hard to imagine a more urbane street wall for a broad avenue than this building, the scale of which is restrained without giving away anything of an appropriate grandeur. Together with Simon Eisendrath's beautifully designed classical synagogue next door to the south, this east blockfront of Eighth Avenue between Montgomery Place and Garfield Place ranks as an object lesson in Beaux-Arts urbanism. It is exceptionally wide, the width accentuated by the banded rustication of the limestone first floor. The entrance is in the dead center of a perfectly symmetrical composition with flanking pairs of arched windows. The second and third floors are faced in red brick trimmed in cream-colored brick with cream-colored terracotta ornament. Consoles top the windows on these floors. The fourth floor is the same except that the windows bear segmental arches. Topping it all is a cornice with console brackets and modillions. Other fine features are the second-floor balconies, carried on console brackets and enclosed by beautiful wrought-iron railings. The forms and materials add up to a work of melting sensuousness, like a piece of exquisite French pastry. Morris was never better.

39 TEMPLE BETH ELOHIM
Northeast corner of Eighth Avenue and Garfield Place
1908–10, Eisendrath & Horowitz

Here is casual grandeur, one of the most difficult qualities for an architect to pull off. The synagogue is a truly grand building, but skillfully sited and scaled so as not to bear too hard upon what is, after all, a quiet neighborhood corner. It is a measure of great cities that they can manage this sort of thing. New York does it in spots; London does it all over the place. Park Slope does it here. The synagogue is oriented diagonally toward the corner, with a not-too-grand, not-too-small flight of steps leading to its round-pedimented entrance between two stately Corinthian columns. This diagonal orientation of the entrance is not only a splendid urbanistic gesture but also signalizes that the building is pentagonal in plan, symbolizing the Pentateuch. There is nothing better than when urbanism and symbolism are so seamlessly mated. On the Eighth Avenue side is an enormous arched window; smaller arched windows flank it. A triangular pediment crowns this elevation. The building manages the rare feat of seeming larger the farther from it one is. From a distance, the saucer dome is imposing. Close up, it is concealed from view. The whole thing

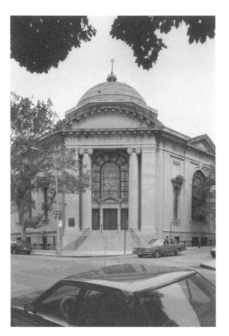

39 *Temple Beth Elohim*

is beautifully designed. With the Morris apartments next door to the north, and the Henry Pohlman apartment house (the Belvedere) across Eighth Avenue, here is an easy urbanity of a sort that, as much as grand effects, defines great cities.

Across Garfield Place from the synagogue is the Temple House of Congregation Beth Elohim. Built in 1928, it was designed by Mortimer Freehof and David Levy of cast stone with a yellowish hue. Its decorative forms combine Romanesque and Art Deco in what at the time was a style frequently used in Jewish architecture ("Jewish Deco").

Across Eighth Avenue from the temple, at the northwest corner of Garfield Place, note the elegant apartment house called the Belvedere. Step around the corner to the block of Garfield Place between Eighth Avenue and Fiske Place; note that the Belvedere is one in a group of four identical buildings. Their names, from east to west, are the Belvedere, the Ontrinue, the Lillian, and the Serine. Henry Pohlman designed them and they were built in 1903. Like the apartment houses of Thomas Bennett, Pohlman's works help form the fabric of Park Slope, the handsomely crafted structures that provide the urbane backdrop for the occasional masterpieces by such architects as Gilbert and Morris, or, in this case, for a really grand building such as the temple across the street.

40 RODNEY ALLEN WARD HOUSE

*319 Garfield Place, between Eighth Avenue
and Prospect Park West, north side
1889, C. P. H. Gilbert*

Robert A. M. Stern, Thomas Mellins, and David Fishman, in their *New York 1880*, call this house "one of Gilbert's best." Indeed it is. Ward was the brother-in-law of Timothy L. Woodruff, Theodore Roosevelt's lieutenant governor and fellow Park Sloper.

Though this house was built around the same time as Gilbert's houses on Montgomery Place for Harvey Murdock, and on Carroll Street for Thomas Adams, Jr., and though it uses essentially the same formal vocabulary as those other houses, the feeling is very different. This lovely house is more like a well-tailored suit. The façade is of rock-faced limestone laid in random ashlar on the base and most of the first floor, and orange-colored brick above with some stone and terra-cotta trim. The front is divided in half. On the left is the front door with a broad window to its left. Above this is a triple window—

40 Rodney Allen Ward House

almost a "Chicago window," with a wide central pane and narrower flanking panes—set among four slender Romanesque colonnettes. Above this and extending across the full façade is a plain band of stone. Rising over this is a molded brick panel inset with a kind of rectangular garland of terra-cotta. A third-floor Palladian window surmounts this and is in turn topped by a high, sharp gable. This gable is divided vertically in half by a line of molded brick-work rising from the top of the keystone of the Palladian arch. On either side of this line of brickwork is a vertically elongated oval window. On the right half of the front is a two-story swelling bay. The first floor of this bay has three windows with stained-glass transoms. On the second floor is a curving varia-tion of the triple window on the left. The curved bay is surmounted above the second floor by a classical cornice and a rather delicate classical balustrade, behind which is visible the high, steeply sloping roof of tile. (The roof is obscured on the left by the gable.) Projecting from the tiled roof toward the balustrade is a dormer with a conical tiled roof rising about half the height of its neighboring gable. The first-floor windows on both sides, as well as the doorway, are framed by rock-faced limestone arches that are more Tuscan than Romanesque. The front stoop, or porch, is placed dead center, extend-ing over half of both halves of the front.

Like Lamb & Rich's house for George P. Tangeman and Gilbert's house at 846 Carroll Street, it is one of the neighborhood's transitional works from the formal vocabulary of the Romanesque to the Renaissance Revival.

Gilbert also designed No. 313 (1889) to the west.

Around the corner from Garfield Place to the south on Prospect Park West are:

41   29 and 31 PROSPECT PARK WEST
Between Montgomery Place and Garfield Place
1919, W. T. McCarthy

W. T. McCarthy designed these three houses, with his characteristic driveways, in a neo-Federal style with red brick laid in Flemish bond. Note the mullioned windows, the stone panels with swags, the arched dormer windows in the steeply pitched roofs, and the splayed lintels of the second-story win-dows. McCarthy's styles, neo-Tudor and neo-Georgian, were those of well-heeled 1920s suburbia.

42 FRANK SQUIER HOUSE
32 Prospect Park West, between Montgomery Place and Garfield Place
1888, George P. Chappell

The base and parlor floor of this Romanesque Revival house are of rock-faced Belleville, New Jersey, brownstone, which also faces the second story of the two-story three-sided bay on the right. The remainder of the surface is brick. The entrance, on the left, is topped by lovely terra-cotta foliate ornament. In the brick wall above this is an oval window of classical feeling, and above this is a brick gable rising to a pointed, picturesque finial and set with two arched windows and, above them, a single slit window.

Chappell designed this house for Frank Squier, who in the early 1890s was Brooklyn's parks commissioner. He oversaw a good part of the City Beautiful phase in Prospect Park's development. His accomplishments included commissioning Frederick MacMonnies to design the quadriga atop the Soldiers' and Sailors' Memorial Arch, the *Horse Tamers* at the Park Circle entrance, and the equestrian statue of Henry Warner Slocum; commissioning Stanford White to redesign the north entrance to the park; and moving the Parks Department headquarters from City Hall into the Litchfield house. Squier was perhaps Brooklyn's most capable parks commissioner after the great James S. T. Stranahan. Considering that Squier was one of the men who brought the City Beautiful to Prospect Park, it is interesting to see that he lived not in one of Prospect Park West's City Beautiful palazzi but in a house that Olmsted and Vaux might have considered suitable for its site right across from the park. The house would not be at all out of place on any number of Park Slope streets, but on Prospect Park West its somber palette stands out indeed.

43 HENRY CARLTON HULBERT HOUSE
48–51 Prospect Park West, southwest corner of 1st Street
1889, Montrose W. Morris

Henry Carlton Hulbert (1831–1912) was a financier and industrialist in the paper-supply business and sat on the boards of the New York Life Insurance Company and Chicago's Pullman Palace Car Company. The house was a double house. Hulbert's residence was at the corner, and his daughter Susie and son-in-law Joseph H. Sutphin occupied the slightly smaller residence to the

43 *Henry Carlton Hulbert House*

south. Sutphin was a partner in H. C. Hulbert & Company. The house became the Brooklyn Ethical Culture School, then the Woodward Park School, and is now Poly Prep Lower School.

Like C. P. H. Gilbert's house on Carroll Street for Thomas Adams, Jr., the Hulbert house is in bravura Romanesque Revival style. This is Montrose Morris at the apogee of his Romanesque Revival phase. Here, however, the whole feeling is different, largely because of the use throughout of light-colored limestone, laid mountainously in random ashlar, instead of brownstone and brick. The principal east elevation faces Prospect Park. Boldly articulated corner towers, round on the left (rising from a hexagonal base) and hexagonal on the right (rising from a round base), connect via a bracketed balustrade across the central section at the second-floor level. The entrance is reached from a large limestone porch. To the left are two large Romanesque arches; to the right is a round-arched window. Above the balustrade are two four-light, mullioned windows. At the third floor is a shelf of stepped corbeling surmounted by a loggia screened by a trio of Romanesque columns. Two attic-dormers project from the hipped, gray-slate roof. The round tower on the left culminates in

a round conical roof of gray slate; the tower on the right has a six-sided conical roof. This east front of the house plays with stately notions of symmetry.
Not so the fully exposed north face. Here the tower-connecting second-floor
balustrade wraps around to connect the north tower with a full-height projecting bay to the west. Rising high from the third-story level of the area
between is a group of clustered chimney-stacks. An identical group rises from
the projecting bay to the west and a third such group rises from the south side
of the building. Farther west, a wing of the house faces north, with a pitched,
gabled roof perpendicular to the hipped roof of the rest of the house. This has
a two-story bowed bay topped by a balustrade enclosing a third-floor balcony
and loggia screened by Romanesque columns. A modified Palladian window is
set within the gable atop the loggia.

Three things, I think, most impress the viewer here. First is the size. This
has to be one of the largest houses in Park Slope, if not the largest. Second is
the robust, rock-faced ashlar. Third is the exuberant skyline, marked by the conical towers, the gables, and above all by the high chimney stacks. Closer inspection, however, reveals that all these size-accentuating elements are humanized
by the extensive incorporation of stone carving, often of a delicate nature. Of
particular note are the capital of the single column separating the two arched
entrance doors on the east front, as well as the spring blocks of those arches,
and the enframement of the third-story loggia, also on the east front.

It is good to keep a couple of things in mind here. One is that the
Hulbert house predates its neighbor to the south, the Childs house, by more
than a decade, and was indeed quite isolated when built on what was still
called Ninth Avenue. Imposing as it is now, it must have had a downright
châteauesque aspect back then. Another is that this is the earliest extant work
by Morris in the neighborhood and his only remaining Park Slope work in
Romanesque Revival. His main contribution to the Park Slope of today is in
his classical houses farther up Prospect Park West and his apartment houses on
Eighth Avenue. He designed the Hulbert house at the same time that he did
the Alhambra apartments on Nostrand Avenue and his several houses on
Hancock Street, all in Bedford-Stuyvesant where he resided.

At the northeast corner of Eighth Avenue and 1st Street, note the four-
story apartment house called "The Aster." Built in 1906, it is among the most
felicitous of Thomas Bennett's many designs for living, with its Ionic porch (a
Bennett trademark) and excellent use of materials, with limestone at the
ground floor and banded Roman brick above.

43a *Park Congregational Church*

At the southwest corner of Eighth Avenue and 2nd Street is the former **Park Congregational Church** (43a), once the principal Congregational church in Park Slope. (There were never as many Congregationalists in Park Slope as in Brooklyn Heights nor, it would seem, as in Bedford-Stuyvesant.) This has been since 1952 the Byzantine Melkite Catholic Church of the Virgin Mary. George W. Kramer and C. C. Hamilton designed it in 1903–4 in the Romanesque Revival style. The random ashlar walls of rock-faced granite are superbly crafted. Kramer designed buildings for Oberlin College and for Ohio University.

44 WILLIAM H. CHILDS HOUSE
53 Prospect Park West
1900–1901, William B. Tubby

The materials of this fine neo-Jacobean house are red brick laid in Flemish bond, with limestone for trim and red tile for the roof. The most noteworthy features are the stepped and curved gable crowning the house, and the second-floor projecting bay, which forms a balustraded third-floor balcony. There was in New York City little of a Jacobean Revival to speak of, though

44 *William H. Childs House*

there was strong Jacobean influence in the architectural style we call the Queen Anne, of which Tubby was a master. (See his row at 864 to 872 Carroll Street, built in 1887 and exhibiting Jacobean influences.) Also noteworthy here is the extensive garden to the south of the house, enclosed by an iron fence. Tubby added the sun porch jutting from the south side of the house in 1907. William Childs, for whom the house was built, was the founder of Bon Ami Cleansing Powder and a friend of Theodore Roosevelt, who was, we are told, a guest in this house. If so, T. R. might well have taken the occasion to walk a block south to 3rd Street to look at the mountain lions at the 3rd Street entrance to the park. Their sculptor, Alexander Phimister Proctor, was a good friend of T. R.

Since 1947, this has been the meetinghouse of the Brooklyn Society for Ethical Culture. The house's library can be seen in Spike Lee's film *Malcolm X* as the office of Elijah Muhammad.

Across 2nd Street, the house at 61 Prospect Park West was built by Childs for his daughter and son-in-law, Mr. and Mrs. Ernest G. Draper, in 1910. Tubby was again the architect, turning this time to a Northern Italian Renaissance design vocabulary for the dark brick house, which features a tile roof and a bracketed copper cornice.

45   63 and 65 PROSPECT PARK WEST
Between 2nd and 3rd Streets
1919–20, W. T. McCarthy

These three lovely neo-Georgian houses have driveways, as do all of McCarthy's houses along Prospect Park West. At the turn of the third decade of the twentieth century, Park Slope entered the automotive age.

46   CHARLES F. NEERGAARD HOUSE
234 Eighth Avenue, northwest corner of 3rd Street
1913, Aymar Embury II

In many ways, this is the most unusual house in Park Slope and has a slight air of unreality. It is probably the single most suburban-seeming house in the district. The style is neo-Georgian. The simple, handsome house is of dark red brick with white-painted wood trim. A shallow lawn, a very unusual thing to see in Park Slope, surrounds it. The house was built for the son of John W. Neergaard, founder of the New York College of Pharmacy. The family's name is well known to Park Slopers from Neergaard Pharmacy, one of the long-established businesses on the Seventh Avenue "high street." The architect, Aymar Embury II, designed the buildings of the Prospect Park Zoo (1935) and the McCarren Park Play Center (1936) in Greenpoint. He was a specialist in the design of structures for parks and beaches, working under Robert Moses, with whom Embury's name will always be linked. He also helped design Orchard Beach (1936) in the Bronx and Jacob Riis Park (1937) in Queens, as well as structures for Central Park (including the present Boathouse, the Kerbs Model Boathouse, and buildings for the Central Park Zoo).

The two blocks of 3rd Street between Seventh Avenue and Prospect Park West compose one of Park Slopers' most beloved streets. I suspect that many a Park Sloper would say he likes it as much as he does Montgomery Place. It is partly its stately width, partly its shady trees, and partly its houses. As for the last, it is well to note that none of 3rd Street's houses is in itself exceptional. No name architects are represented here except for Slee & Bryson, who designed the four neo-Tudor houses between Seventh and Eighth Avenues on the south side of the street at Nos. 516 to 522. Built in 1929, they were part of the Tudor vogue that in the 1920s defined American suburbia. These houses are probably as close as Park Slope comes to the sort of picturesque Garden City design of Slee & Bryson's houses in the Albemarle-Kenmore Terraces Historic District in Flatbush of a few years earlier. Workaday builders and architects, not caring to be original, but skillful in exploiting the superb taste of the day, dominate the remainder of the street. We may cite a couple of these architects. Eisenla & Carlson were responsible for the eight limestone houses built in 1909 between Seventh and Eighth Avenues on the south side of the street at Nos. 546 to 560, houses slightly more picturesque than their work on 1st and 2nd Streets, as befits the more romantic 3rd Street. On the same side of the street, Brooklyn architect Axel Hedman designed the eleven neo-Renaissance limestone houses at Nos. 524 to 544. No discussion of the weavers of the Park Slope fabric can leave out Axel Hedman, who designed numerous fine (and sometimes better than fine) row houses and apartment houses in the neighborhood. Between Eighth Avenue and Prospect Park West, we encounter Eisenla & Carlson and Axel Hedman again. The former designed the eleven neo-Renaissance limestone houses at Nos. 581 to 601 on the north side, built in 1911. Hedman designed the fine row of eight neo-Renaissance houses, built in 1910, at the east end of the north side of the street. Third Street terminates beautifully at its park end. Elegantly modeled bronze **pumas** (6c), set on high granite pedestals, flank the park's entrance drive. Alexander Phimister Proctor, one of the best animal sculptors of his time, created the pumas, erected in 1898. (Proctor worked with Augustus Saint-Gaudens on the General Sherman equestrian statue in Manhattan's Grand Army Plaza, arguably the finest piece of public sculpture in New York City.) Stanford White designed the pedestals, his deepest insinuation into the immediate fabric of Park Slope.

Farther south we enter what I like to call Thomas Bennett Country. The "South Slope" comprises many of his fine, modest, classical apartment houses, as well as a few surprises from other architects.

47 488 to 492 FOURTH STREET
Between Seventh and Eighth Avenues, south side
1892, Heins & LaFarge

Here are three three-story houses designed as a unit. The basements and stoops are stone and the rest is Roman brick. The composition is basically symmetrical. There are two-story projecting end bays framing a center section that has doorways at either end. Between are three window bays, though closer inspection reveals that the "window bay" farthest to the right is in fact a third doorway. Slender Ionic columns flank the end doorways, which have leaded-glass fanlights. The projecting bay on the right is curved, while the left projecting bay is three-sided. Dormers with Palladian windows top the end bays. Between, dormers with scrolled pediments project from a pitched roof of red tile. In the center of it all is a large Palladian window at the second floor. The style is the neo-Georgian that McKim, Mead & White had recently introduced into American architecture. If these do not at first strike one as neo-Georgian, that is probably because of the use of Roman rather than red brick. These are in fact among the most beautiful houses in Park Slope. The architects, George Lewis Heins and Christopher Grant LaFarge, had only the year before been awarded the commission to design the Cathedral of St. John the Divine. (Bishop Henry Codman Potter, who awarded the commission, was the brother of Edward Tuckerman Potter, who designed St. John's Episcopal Church on St. John's Place between Sixth and Seventh Avenues.) Brooklyn architect Woodruff Leeming worked for Heins & LaFarge at the time these houses were designed.

48 Former MANUAL TRAINING HIGH SCHOOL (now John Jay High School)

Seventh Avenue between 4th and 5th Streets, east side
1902, C. B. J. Snyder

This massive high school is a beautiful building. It is five stories, faced in red brick and in limestone, and stretches across the entire blockfront on Seventh Avenue, with sides extending very deep on the side streets. Its land coverage is among the highest of any building in Park Slope. The first floor is of rusticated limestone. There are projecting end bays. The windows of the first and fourth floors are segmental-arched. Scrolled brackets range along the top of the fourth floor. Topping the entrance in the center of the first floor is a scrolled pediment framing the bust of a boy. The pediment itself is filled with books and is carried on large brackets on either side of the doorway. The segmental arch of the doorway is outlined in wonderful, lush foliate stone carving. The building's original mansard roof has disappeared. Even so, this building stands out for its quality.

Alumni of Manual Training High School include the Nobel Prize–winning physicist Isidor Isaac Rabi (1898–1988), Henny Youngman, Alexander Scourby, Thelma Ritter, and Yankees first baseman Joe Pepitone. Any school that can produce both Rabi and Youngman can't be bad.

The park block of 9th Street is extremely interesting, the first real whiff of classical urban planning south of Grand Army Plaza. Limestone dominates in the rows of neo-Renaissance houses along this unusually wide street. We may cite Nos. 519 to 543 on the north side. Thomas Bennett designed these houses built in 1908–9. The most special thing here, though, is that the street was given a bit of civic grandeur, rather than merely terminating at its east end in Prospect Park. At the 9th Street entrance to the park we find the Lafayette Memorial. Henry Bacon designed the elegant granite stele, and Daniel Chester French created the bronze figures. The foreground figure of Lafayette is in such high relief that it is practically a freestanding statue. French, a consummately gifted sculptor, captures both the nobility and the foppishness of the French aristocrat. Behind Lafayette is his horse in profile, facing north, almost filling the frame of the stele. Behind the horse's head and holding its bridle is a black man, presumably a slave. Rising behind the horse's tail and arching over its back is a beautifully rendered leafy tree, cut off by the stele frame. It is an exceptional piece of sculpture, monumental and intimate at once, heroic and at the same time a genre piece. It is much underrated, and shows French at his best. No less a personage than Marshal Joffre came to Park Slope to unveil the memorial in 1917. The same architect-sculptor team also produced the Lincoln Memorial in Washington, D.C., dedicated five years after the Lafayette group.

49 PROSPECT BRANCH, BROOKLYN PUBLIC LIBRARY
431 Sixth Avenue, northeast corner of 9th Street
1906, Raymond F. Almirall

Raymond F. Almirall designed four Carnegie branch libraries for Brooklyn (Bushwick, Eastern Parkway, Pacific, and Prospect), and designed the main library at Grand Army Plaza that was never completed and eventually replaced by the present Githens & Keally structure. Like fellow Brooklyn architects Woodruff Leeming and J. Monroe Hewlett, Almirall was a product of both Brooklyn Polytechnic Institute and the École des Beaux-Arts, and eventually left Brooklyn for Paris, where he assisted Welles Bosworth on the Versailles restoration and was made a chevalier of the Legion of Honor. He was one of Brooklyn's most interesting architects. His Prospect Branch is one of the Brooklyn Public Library's finest branch libraries. The main Sixth Avenue façade of this building is of red brick with limestone trim. Pediments with deep raking cornices top the fully exposed north and south sides, which are faced entirely in limestone. Blocky pinnacles rise from the points of these pediments and might be of Viennese Secessionist inspiration. Paired Tuscan columns flank the front entrance and carry a heavy entablature, which features some fine foliate carving. Over the entablature is a cornice carried on large stone dentils. Above the cornice is an attic inscribed with "Brooklyn Public Library." Garlanded torches appear as keystones over all windows and over the main doorway, which has a rich enframement of foliate-carved limestone reminiscent of the carving at the entrance to Manual Training High School on Seventh Avenue. The entrance is up a fairly broad flight of stairs. The building is set back in a generous garden behind a black iron fence. It has a monumentality appropriate for a branch library in its neighborhood setting. No branch library in Brooklyn has a more celebrated interior. Here are stained glass, tiled fireplaces, elaborate wood paneling, and marble mosaic flooring.

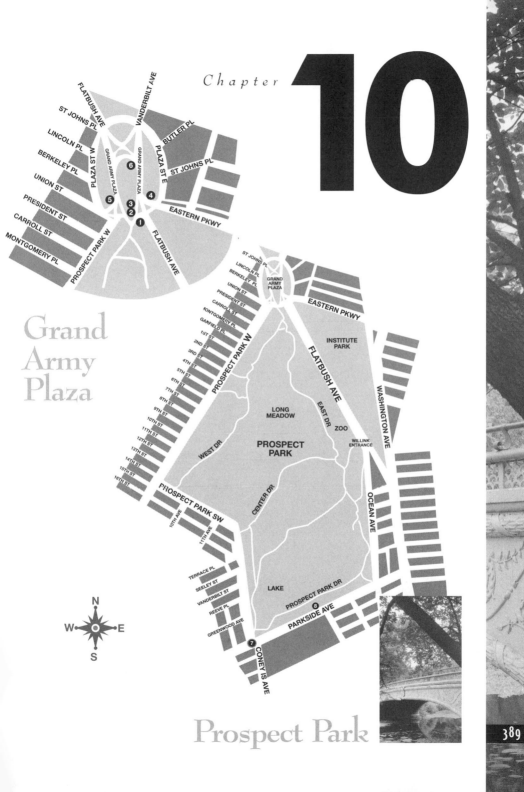

Chapter

10

Grand
Army
Plaza

Prospect Park

7 Horse
Tamer

Chapter *Chapter* **10**
Prospect Park

Prospect Park has, unlike its sister park in Manhattan, irregular boundaries, though it is actually almost diamond-shaped. The northern point of the diamond is Grand Army Plaza at the confluence of Flatbush and Vanderbilt Avenues and Eastern Parkway. The southern point is Park Circle at the intersection of Prospect Park Southwest, Fort Hamilton Parkway, Coney Island Avenue, and Parkside Avenue. The western point is Bartel-Pritchard Square at the intersection of Prospect Park West, Prospect Park Southwest, and 15th Street. The eastern point is the Willink Entrance at the intersection of Flatbush and Ocean Avenues and Empire Boulevard. The park defines the neighborhoods that border it, and each of these points marks the division between neighborhoods. The north point is where Crown Heights meets Park Slope, the west point is where Park Slope meets Windsor Terrace, the south point is where Windsor Terrace meets Flatbush, and the east point is where Flatbush meets Crown Heights. The streets that border the park are Prospect Park West in Park Slope, Prospect Park Southwest in Windsor Terrace, Parkside and Ocean Avenues in Flatbush, and Flatbush Avenue in Crown Heights. The neighborhood that enjoys the most frontage along the park is the only one with "park" in its name, Park Slope.

In 1860, two years after construction commenced across the river on Frederick Law Olmsted and Calvert Vaux's Greensward Plan, the City of Brooklyn purchased a tract of land—including what would later become the northern half of Prospect Park together with what would later be termed the

391

"East Side Lands" (today's Institute Park)—in the sparsely developed southern part of the city at Mount Prospect, near the border between Brooklyn and the Town of Flatbush. One thing that appealed to some people about putting a park at this location was its association with the Battle of Long Island, which took place on the site in August 1776. To lay out the new park, the city hired Egbert Viele, the same engineer New York had previously hired to design Central Park (and whom Olmsted and Vaux replaced). Viele proposed a design, but before construction could begin, the hand of God intervened in the form of the Civil War, postponing any further work on the park. This gave James S.T. Stranahan and his Board of Park Commissioners the occasion to review Viele's scheme, which was clearly inadequate. In 1865, Stranahan hired Calvert Vaux to review the situation and make suggestions for improving Viele's plan. At this stage, Olmsted was to be found nowhere near Brooklyn. It was Vaux's gig.

Viele had designed the park to straddle the already existing Flatbush Avenue, but no one liked this. Vaux suggested that the East Side Lands be eliminated from the park so that Flatbush Avenue would not bisect it. (Though the East Side Lands were eliminated from the park proper, the city retained control of them in order to prevent development around the Mount Prospect reservoir.) In order to keep the park as large as originally envisioned, Vaux suggested that the city acquire additional land to the south and west. Thus, Vaux was involved in the very process of acquiring land and fixing the park boundaries. In New York, Vaux and Olmsted had had no say in this process, and had had to fit their design into the bounds of the perfect rectangle that the city had mapped out of the gridiron of streets. Stranahan clearly respected Vaux enormously, and whenever Vaux expressed his wishes, Stranahan did his level best to make them a reality. Again, this was different from the situation across the river, where Stranahan's opposite number, Andrew Haswell Green, had made Vaux's and Olmsted's lives miserable. When Vaux first attempted to lure Olmsted to Brooklyn from the Frémont estate in California, he had to convince Olmsted that Stranahan was no Green.

FREDERICK LAW OLMSTED (1822–1903)

Olmsted's is one of the greatest names from nineteenth-century America. He is regarded as the father of American landscape architecture (though the title perhaps belongs more rightly to Calvert Vaux), and his works, first in collaboration with Vaux and later on his own, transformed one American city after another. He also led a remarkable, varied life that intersected with so much of what was most interesting and significant in nineteenth-century America.

Olmsted was born in 1822 into a prosperous and cultured Hartford, Connecticut, family. (He can be considered yet another of the multitude of New Englanders to have had a profound influence on the development of Brooklyn.) He was a student of modest attainments and did not, as his brother did, attend Yale College. Instead, young Olmsted indulged a romantic taste for adventure and went to sea. His reformer's zeal came out of his reflections on his experience of the degraded life of a merchant seaman. He exemplified the New England combination of Puritanism, yeomanry, and scientific rationalism. His next career was that of gentleman scientific farmer, on Staten Island. He fell in with his brother's Yale set, including the reformer Charles Loring Brace. While attempting to farm on Staten Island, Olmsted became a devotee of a magazine called the *Horticulturist* that landscape gardener Andrew Jackson Downing published. Olmsted also read Ruskin and Emerson. Not exactly a roaring success as a farmer, Olmsted turned to journalism. In 1850, he traveled in England, where his visit yielded his first book, *Walks and Talks of an American Farmer in England*. His introduction to the beauties and verities of the English countryside and to the English romantic landscape design tradition appear to have produced in him a crystallization of romantic feeling and aesthetic response that would bear heavily upon his future life. Back in America, Olmsted's writings were well received, and he got a job as an editor at *Putnam's Monthly,* the most distinguished periodical in the country, publishing Emerson, Thoreau, Melville, and Longfellow, as well as his own work. He borrowed money from his father to purchase the publishing firm that owned *Putnam's Monthly,* but when the firm failed, the thirty-five-year-old Olmsted felt himself at a career crossroads. He was nearing middle age, unmarried, a failed gentleman farmer, and an impecunious writer whose résumé did not exactly tell of singleness of purpose. Yet somehow, fortuitously and circuitously, he got himself hired in 1857 to the position of superintendent of New York City's Central Park project.

No one, not Olmsted nor anyone, could have foreseen at the time he was hired that he would actually end up helping to design the park. Though he had admired Downing's writings and had desultorily engaged in some arranging of plantings on his Staten Island farm, nothing in Olmsted's background suggested that he might become a landscape architect. Even so, Olmsted would not have undertaken to work on the design of the park, as opposed to supervising its construction, had not a young English architect named Calvert Vaux knocked on his door and asked him to be his collaborator in an entry in the competition for the park's design.

While working on Central Park, Olmsted took time off to visit Europe to study its parks. In Paris he met Adolphe Alphand and looked at Haussmann's boulevards. Olmsted was most impressed by the Avenue de l'Impératrice (now Avenue Foch), which would inform his and Vaux's later plans for Eastern Parkway and Ocean Parkway.

Following his work on Central Park, Olmsted served as chairman of the United States Sanitary Commission, forerunner of the Red Cross, during the Civil War. (Brooklyn's only "world's fair," so to speak, the Brooklyn and Long Island Sanitary Fair of 1864, was organized to raise money for the Sanitary Commission.) After that, he got a job managing John C. Frémont's Mariposa estate in California. It was then that Calvert Vaux called Olmsted back east to work on the design (already largely worked out by Vaux) for Prospect Park.

CALVERT VAUX (1824–95)

Calvert Bowyer Vaux was born in London in 1824. Following grammar school, he apprenticed with a Gothic Revival architect in London named Lewis Nockalls Cottingham. In 1850, the American landscape gardener Andrew Jackson Downing (1815–52) went to London in search of a sympathetic young architect to join him in his new practice in Newburgh, New York, and recruited Vaux. (Frederick Law Olmsted, already a devotee of Downing's writings, also visited England in 1850, though Vaux, who at this time had never heard of Olmsted, would not have known this.) Downing, however, died two years later (in the sinking of the steamer *Henry Clay* in the Hudson River).

Vaux moved from Newburgh to Manhattan in 1857, and immediately became involved in the controversy over the design of the new Central Park. Downing had been, along with William Cullen Bryant, one of the two principal advocates for the creation of the park. Had Downing lived, he probably would have designed the park (with Vaux assisting him). In his absence, the commission was awarded to an engineer named Egbert Viele, whose proposed design of 1856 pleased no one. It was unfortunate for Viele that, although he was immensely gifted in his field of civil engineering (his hydrological and topographical map of Manhattan is still used by some city agencies), he will always be remembered as the man whose designs for both Central Park and Prospect Park Calvert Vaux came along and displaced. Vaux was among those who clamored for the rejection of Viele's plan and for holding an open competition for the park's design. At this stage Vaux and Olmsted barely knew each other. When the competition was announced, Vaux went to Olmsted, the itinerant journalist and gentleman farmer who had, by fortuitous means, been hired as superintendent of construction for the park. Vaux evidently felt that Olmsted's knowledge of the terrain and of the administrative and political problems involved in the project made him the ideal partner. It is very important to understand that Vaux was a skilled architect who had worked for the leading landscape gardener in America, and that Olmsted had no design background whatsoever. This is important because even today too many people refer to "Olmsted's Central Park" or "Olmsted's Prospect Park" as though Vaux either didn't exist or was somehow second fiddle. It is closer to the truth that, at least in these two projects, Olmsted was second fiddle to Vaux. As the architectural historian George B. Tatum succinctly put it, without Vaux, "Olmsted would be remembered—when he was remembered at all—as a journalist and author." In any event, Vaux and Olmsted's Greensward Plan of 1858 won the competition, and construction of the park began almost immediately.

Vaux and Olmsted's partnership lasted from 1858 to 1872, during which they collaborated on Central Park and Prospect Park and also on the impressive park and parkway system of Buffalo, New York, which was, in many ways, the fulfillment of their only fitfully realized vision for Greater New York, and on the town plan of Riverside, Illinois. Vaux and Olmsted also collaborated on some other Brooklyn projects. They redesigned Fort Greene Park and laid out Eastern Parkway and Ocean Parkway. They also designed Tompkins Park in Bedford-Stuyvesant. Vaux typically worked with partners through out his career. After Olmsted, he formed partnerships with Jacob Wrey Mould, Frederick Clarke Withers, and George K. Radford. Vaux and his family lived in Richard Morris Hunt's Stuyvesant Apartments, one of the city's pioneer apartment houses, on East 18th Street. Vaux was committed to the design style we now call "Victorian Gothic." From his apprenticeship with Cottingham forward, Vaux attempted in his architectural works to apply the principles of John Ruskin. As an exponent of "Ruskinian Gothic," as it came to be known, Vaux was in league with the likes of Peter B. Wight, designer of Montague Street's Mercantile Library, and of Russell Sturgis, designer of Willow Place Chapel in Brooklyn Heights. While Brooklyn is exceedingly rich in works of Victorian Gothic, it is interesting to note that there are no building designs of Vaux's outside of Prospect Park in Brooklyn. Vaux did design one house, with Withers, and one school, with Radford, in Brooklyn, but both buildings are gone. In Manhattan, several interesting examples of Vaux's building designs remain today. Portions of his and Jacob Wrey Mould's designs for the original buildings of the Metropolitan Museum of Art and of the American Museum of Natural History may still be espied, though the manner in which these have been built around by other architects yields an inadequate picture of Vaux's accomplishments. Vaux and Withers designed the Third Judicial District Courthouse in Greenwich Village, one of New York's principal landmarks of Victorian Gothic, built in 1874–77. Vaux and Radford remodeled a couple of standard-issue brownstone houses on the south side of Gramercy Park into a Victorian Gothic extravaganza of a single house in 1881–84 for Samuel J. Tilden.

Vaux's most beguiling structures, however, were ones he designed for Central Park and Prospect Park. In Central Park, the

Dairy, Bow Bridge, Belvedere Castle, and others survive to remind us of Vaux's rich imagination and expert sense of how to design appropriately for the romantic landscape. Vaux worked with Jacob Wrey Mould on the design of Central Park's Bethesda Terrace, one of the most thrilling structures in the United States. (Many of Vaux's other Central Park structures have vanished, mostly during the tenure of Robert Moses as parks commissioner.) So it is with Vaux's structures in Prospect Park, about which more anon.

The circumstances of Vaux's death are murky. On November 19, 1895, while visiting his son in the still-new development called Bensonhurst-by-the-Sea (the area had been annexed by the City of Brooklyn only in the previous year), Calvert Vaux disappeared. Two days later his body washed up from Gravesend Bay. Some have speculated that the seventy-year-old Vaux may have committed suicide. As an architect he was considered a has-been. The Victorian Gothic that he did so much to promote had been completely superseded by Beaux-Arts classicism. The parks that he created were being overrun by "improvements." It is likelier, though, that his death was, as it was officially reckoned to be, accidental. The coroner's report noted that the morning of November 19 was dense with fog. An elderly man, in an environment with which he was not familiar, might have well walked off the end of a pier. I suppose we will never know for sure, though all indications were that his personal if not his professional life was quite happy at the time. He was buried in Kingston, New York. Both Calvert Vaux's greatest work and his death happened in Brooklyn.

JAMES S. T. STRANAHAN (1808–1898)

"The truth is, that Mr. Stranahan is one of the very few men who have creative genius. In the not remote future, the question will be asked by intelligent writers, who were the real architects of Brooklyn? who were the men who lifted her out of the cowpaths of village advance and put her on the road track of Metropolitan importance? When that question is answered, the name named with greatest honor will be that of James S. T. Stranahan."

So said the *Brooklyn Daily Eagle* in 1882. James Samuel Thomas Stranahan was born in Peterboro, in Madison County, New York. He may not have been a New Englander, as were so many of the nineteenth-century builders of Brooklyn, but his family could trace itself to early-eighteenth-century New England. Stranahan's parents were Scotch-Irish, and he grew up on a farm. At the age of twenty-one he became a schoolmaster. That, as he entered adulthood, he would one day be the grandest public figure of one of the world's largest cities—a city not yet founded—would have been utterly inconceivable to him.

He made strides in the direction of his later career when he became a land surveyor. He then worked as a wool merchant in Albany. There were opportunities for a bright, industrious young man who had learned to save his money. He got into real estate and building, and in 1832, many years before he changed the face of Brooklyn, he helped to develop the manufacturing town of Florence in Oneida County, New York. (It would be another sixteen years before John Humphrey Noyes would establish his utopian community nearby.) At the tender age of thirty Stranahan was elected to the state assembly. When he entered the legislature, the City of Brooklyn was all of four years old.

In 1840, he moved to Newark, New Jersey, a city then booming as a port and transportational hub. He was now seizing his opportunities in the burgeoning railroad field. For his work as a railroad contractor, he often astutely took his payment in the form of stock. In 1844, he moved his contracting business to the young city of Brooklyn.

Spreading his wings, he developed port facilities, the Atlantic Basin and Docks. He invested in East River ferries. He had a vested interest in the growth of the city. Unsuccessful in his bid to become mayor of Brooklyn, he was elected to the United States Congress, as a Whig, in 1854. From 1860 to 1882, he was, as is well known, president of the Brooklyn Park Board, and promoted and oversaw the creation of Prospect Park. His expertise in civic affairs, his appreciation of aesthetics (his second wife was an art historian), his command of the details of construction, and his warm personal manner endeared him to the park's designers,

Frederick Law Olmsted and Calvert Vaux. Seldom has an American city been blessed with so diligent, so intelligent, and so effective a public administrator as Stranahan.

Stranahan also was among the principal promoters of the Brooklyn Bridge and, fatefully, of consolidation with New York City. He died in his vacation home in Saratoga Springs, New York, in the year the MacMonnies quadriga was installed atop the Soldiers' and Sailors' Monument in Grand Army Plaza. His body was transported back to Brooklyn and he was buried in Green-wood Cemetery.

---

1 STATUE OF JAMES S. T. STRANAHAN
Grand Army Plaza entrance to Prospect Park,
to the east of the entrance drives
1891, Frederick W. MacMonnies

Around Prospect Park are works by MacMonnies of high drama, such as *The Army, The Navy, The Triumphal Progress of Columbia, The Horse Tamers,* and the equestrian statue of General Slocum. In contrast, this statue is a simple standing figure of a balding, frock-coated bourgeois *gentilhomme,* as pacific in appearance as the other works are violent. Yet this simple statue is as moving as any of the other works and must be ranked among MacMonnies's finest accomplishments. Three years before the statue was dedicated, the Reverend Richard Salter Storrs, pastor of Church of the Pilgrims, spoke at the Hamilton Club on Remsen Street: "People say not infrequently; 'By and by we must put up a statue to Mr. Stranahan in Prospect Park,' of course we must. But why wait?" The bronze figure of Stranahan was dedicated on June 6, 1891, with Stranahan himself in attendance. It was typical of him that when asked to pull the cord to unveil the statue, he declined the honor and handed the cord to the young sculptor MacMonnies. The statue had, together with his statue of Nathan Hale, earned MacMonnies second place at the Paris Salon of 1891, an unprecedented achievement for an American sculptor. It was the first of MacMonnies's public works in either New York City or Brooklyn. Stranahan stands with his left foot forward. His right arm hangs at his side as he holds his top hat. Draped across his cocked left arm is his topcoat, as he holds a walking stick. He is shown in the typical bourgeois dress of his time, baggy trousers, frock coat, waistcoat, bow tie. He looks ahead to greet the visitor to the park.

Inscribed on Stanford White's elegant pedestal are the words "Lector Si Monumentum/Requiris Circumspice." These are the same words that appear on the tomb of Sir Christopher Wren in London's St. Paul's Cathedral: "Reader, if you seek my monument, look about you."

2 GRAND ARMY PLAZA
Intersection of Flatbush Avenue, Plaza Street, Union Street, Prospect Park West, and Eastern Parkway

Calvert Vaux laid out the plaza in its present elliptical form as part of his design for Prospect Park. It was clear that this would be the park's main entrance, since it was the point of the park nearest the major roads and nearest the most built-up sections of Brooklyn. Vaux had two main goals in mind: he wanted a gracefully curved entrance to the park, and he also wanted to block out the traffic of the several roads converging at this point. The main entrance to the park, stretching between Flatbush Avenue and Prospect Park West, is concave, forming the southern arc of the plaza's oval. The rest of the plaza was designed with thickly planted mounds that block the sight of the traffic and absorb its roaring boom. In these ways, Vaux's plaza is a very important element in Prospect Park's design. The problem turned out to be what, exactly, to put in the plaza. Most of the plaza was of but not in the park. How should it be planted, if at all? It obviously could not be an extension of the park, nor would it do to landscape it formally in a manner bound to conflict with the park. Leave it a stony expanse, and that would conflict with the park, too. Very early on, in 1869, the plaza was adorned with the Henry Kirke Brown statue of Lincoln that now stands in the park's Concert Grove. There was also a simple fountain and a pair of flagpoles. As for the rest, it was a stony expanse. In 1873, a strange and elaborate Victorian Gothic fountain with colored jets of water replaced the simple fountain. The rest remained a stony expanse, and apparently most people considered the plaza an aesthetic failure. One Brooklynite with a desire to see something special made of the plaza was Seth Low. In 1889, he sponsored a competition for the design of a memorial to the Union dead. Manhattan architect John Hemenway Duncan, later to be famous for his design of Grant's Tomb, won with his design for an eighty-foot by eighty-foot granite arch. In that year, William Tecumseh Sherman laid the cornerstone of the arch. President Grover Cleveland was on hand for the memorial's dedication in 1892. Duncan's arch was a heavy and ponderous granite presence,

2 *Grand Army Plaza*

unrelieved by sculpture, and was unpopular. It also attempted to co-exist with the Victorian Gothic fountain. Critics bemoaned the infelicity of the juxtaposition of arch and fountain. Not only was Grand Army Plaza, as "the plaza" was now called, ugly, it was ugly in a lot of different ways. F. W. Darlington's Electric Fountain replaced the Gothic fountain in 1897. Charles Cyril Martin engineered the new, simpler fountain amid a new setting that the firm of Olmsted, Olmsted & Eliot designed. (This firm consisted of a doddering Frederick Law Olmsted, his stepson John, and Charles Eliot, son of the Harvard president.) The Bailey Fountain replaced the Electric Fountain in 1931.

The park entrance did not take its present form until George Brower hired McKim, Mead & White in 1889, four years before the Columbian Exposition in Chicago and four years before the competition for the design of the Brooklyn Museum. At Flatbush Avenue and at Prospect Park West had stood rustic shelters for those waiting for horsecars. Stanford White replaced these with the lovely, recently restored twelve-sided gazebos we see today. The gazebos have polished granite columns and tile roofs topped by pineapples, symbols of hospitality. Inside, the ceilings are of Guastavino tile. Stretching between the gazebos is a limestone fence with an open latticework design, with openings onto the pathways by which one enters the park toward either Meadowport Arch or Endale Arch. Atop the fence are marvelous bronze bowls with serpent handles. Four high columns, erected in 1892, with fasces at their bases and topped by bronze eagles, designed by MacMonnies and installed in 1901, range along the edge of the curving sidewalk in front of the fence. The eagles' wings point up and from a distance look like crab claws.

3 SOLDIERS' AND SAILORS' MONUMENT
1889–92, John H. Duncan
1894–1901, McKim, Mead & White

Grand Army Plaza did not begin to sing until Stanford White and Frederick MacMonnies came on the scene. Stanford White's brief was to bring the arch to life. To that end, he slightly remodeled the arch, creating "shelves" for statuary on the piers. Philip Martiny, who had worked with White on Madison Square Garden, carved the reliefs in the spandrels. Bronze relief panels were placed on each of the two inner walls of the abutments. One is an equestrian relief of Abraham Lincoln, the only known equestrian portrait of the sixteenth president. The other is an equestrian relief of Ulysses S. Grant (of whom there are many equestrian portraits, including the particularly fine one by William Ordway Partridge in Grant Square). These reliefs are attributed to two artists, William O'Donovan and Thomas Eakins. It is said that O'Donovan created the images of Lincoln and Grant, but that Eakins was brought in to sculpt the horses. Not everyone feels that these panels really belong where they are because their scale is incommensurate with other work on the arch and because they point in the opposite direction from the quadriga atop the arch. What makes the arch one of America's finest works of public art is the MacMonnies sculpture, the quadriga and the groups, *The Army* and *The Navy,* on the piers. The quadriga's official title is *The Triumphal Progress of Columbia.* The Army group's official name is *The Army: Genius of Patriotism Urging American Soldiers on to Victory.* The Navy group's official name is *The Navy: American Sailors Boarding a Vessel at Sea Urged on by the Genius of Patriotism.*

"The finest triumphal arch of modern times, second only to the Arc de Triomphe in Paris," wrote Henry Hope Reed. Grand Army Plaza, he said, is "about as good a collection of classical sculpture as you'll find anywhere in

3 *Soldiers' and Sailors' Monument, Grand Army Plaza*

America." In the bronze quadriga atop the arch is a stately woman—Columbia—standing in her chariot, the front of which is embossed with the Great Seal of the United States. She holds in her left hand a sword and in her right hand a wreathed flagstaff with billowing flag, and she wears a Phrygian cap. Four horses pull the chariot (hence "quadriga"). Compare these horses to the one nearby at the Slocum statue. In the latter, the horse is rendered with extreme realism. These, by the same sculptor, are simplified and idealized. Note that they are not actually hitched to the chariot, and that if they were, they would be attempting to pull it in several directions at once. There is nothing of realism to this work. It is, rather, an ideal classical composition. To either side of the horses is a winged and laurel-crowned female figure blowing a trumpet. The quadriga was installed in 1898 and is an unusual form in American civic art, perhaps the only other example in the United States being the one at Cass Gilbert's Minnesota State Capitol in St. Paul. On the west pedestal on the south side of the arch is *The Army,* installed in 1901. It is a tangled mess of humanity, a grisly scene of battle as realistic as anything in *Saving Private Ryan*—or in Stephen Crane's then recently published *The Red Badge of Courage* (1895), which Henry Hope Reed has suggested as an alternative title for MacMonnies's sculpture. Behind the compressed mass of standing and fallen figures—the fallen horse is a tour de force of equine sculpture—rises and trumpets the winged "Genius of Patriotism," or one presumes, given the title of the work, though she has the features of a Valkyrie. Etched against the granite background of the pier of the arch are numerous bayonets and other projecting elements, radiating from the central group like fireworks—MacMonnies said he wanted his sculpture to have the appearance of an explosion. He also cited Delacroix's *Liberty Guiding the People* as an inspiration. The central standing figure of the commander, a dashing figure, is very clearly a self-portrait of MacMonnies. We sense here not only a bit of Delacroix but also of François Rude and Auguste Rodin. In fact it is all quintessential MacMonnies, the sure and powerful blend of perfect naturalism with classical allegory and classical composition. On the east pedestal is *The Navy*. Not so complex as *The Army* (there is no fallen horse), nonetheless it, too, is filled with incident. Here the central standing figure of the commander, left arm pointing, is reminiscent of Saint-Gaudens's Admiral Farragut in Madison Square. Behind the group rises the helmeted, thick-bodied, trident-bearing female, Genius of Patriotism ("not one of MacMonnies' happiest choices of models," said M. M. Graff), beside whom is an outsized American eagle, wings far outspread. I must admit to being somewhat baffled by the title of this work. These sailors do not appear to me to be boarding a vessel. It is actually rather hard to figure out just what they're doing.

The arch, said Henry Hope Reed, is "one of the nation's great works of art."

FREDERICK WILLIAM MacMONNIES (1863–1937)

Frederick William MacMonnies was born September 20, 1863, at 111 Van Buren Street in Bedford-Stuyvesant. He was the son of a Scottish immigrant, a once wealthy grain merchant who had lost his fortune just before Frederick was born. At eighteen he got a job as an office boy and studio assistant for the sculptor Augustus Saint-Gaudens. MacMonnies attended evening classes at Cooper Union, the Art Students League, and the National Academy of Design until he was twenty, when he went to Paris to study at the École des Beaux-Arts. In this, Charles Follen McKim gave financial assistance to MacMonnies. There he studied under the sculptors Falguière and Mercié. In 1886, he won the Prix d'Atelier, the highest prize a foreigner was eligible to win. He then worked as an assistant to his teacher, Jean-Alexandre-Joseph Falguière (1831 1900). When MacMonnies returned to America, Saint-Gaudens said "the gentle, tender bird I had caressed out of its egg had turned into a proud eagle." Stanford White helped launch MacMonnies's career by hiring him in 1887 to create a set of kneeling angels for St. Paul's Roman Catholic Church on Columbus Avenue and 60th Street. White also secured commissions for MacMonnies for fountains in Seabright, New Jersey, and Stockbridge, Massachusetts. White, who had a history of collaboration with Saint-Gaudens, came to prefer working with MacMonnies. This may have had to do with the fact that MacMonnies, ten years White's junior, was clearly the subordinate partner in their collaborations, and also because he was as yet not so overworked as Saint-Gaudens and could meet deadlines. His *Diana* won an honorable mention at the Salon of 1889. Two years later he took second place at the Salon for two statues, one of Nathan Hale and the other of James S. T. Stranahan. The Nathan Hale statue, which the Sons of the American Revolution had commissioned, was erected in Manhattan's City Hall Park in 1893. Theodore Dreiser called it "one of the few notable public ornaments of New York." Henry Marquand, president of the Metropolitan Museum of Art, said it was "among the finest works we have ever produced in this country." Stanford White, who designed a very elegant base for the statue, said it was "a striking, lifelike and ideal representation of the man, and a work of art in every sense" and would "hold its own in fearlessness of conception and artistic character with any portrait-statue of modern times." Even with such encomia from Dreiser, Marquand and White, the art historian Matthew Baigell wrote, "Its lively texture, a feature of Falguière's neo-Rococo style, elicited disapproval from uninitiated New York critics." For his part, MacMonnies said, "I wanted to make something that would set the bootblacks and little clerks around there thinking, something that would make them want to be somebody and find life worth living." To our turn-of-the-millennium ears, that may sound slightly condescending. Nonetheless, his sentiments regarding the statue's role in the lives of little clerks were genuine and not ignoble. They expressed the view that statues, far from being the mere baubles of a prosperous civilization, had the power to make us better people Saint-Gaudens, for whom MacMonnies had worked, selected him to design one of the most important sculptures for the Columbian Exposition in Chicago in 1893, a group in the Court of Honor with twenty-seven figures.

MacMonnies's *Bacchante and Infant Faun* was shown at the Salon in 1893. The sculptor then gave the work to the architect Charles Follen McKim, who in 1896 installed it in the courtyard of his Boston Public Library. The nude woman dancing in drunken abandon elicited strong censure from certain staid Bostonians, led by Charles Eliot Norton and the Woman's Christian Temperance Union. The sculpture had to be removed and was placed in the Metropolitan Museum of Art. (A copy stood in Stanford White's studio in the tower of Madison Square Garden. Another copy is in the Brooklyn Museum.) It would not be the last time a public work by MacMonnies caused a sensation. In 1922, MacMonnies's *Civic Virtue* was installed in front of Manhattan's City Hall. This was an immense fountain, the centerpiece of which was a marble figure group the sculptor hoped would inspire New Yorkers with a vision of the probity and the rectitude that are—or should be—hallmarks of municipal government. The scene MacMonnies created, however, managed to convey a hundred different messages to people, none of them really having much to do with municipal government. In the center stood a muscular—and, truth to tell, slightly paunchy—lad of vaguely Roman mien. The *contrapposto* of this marble figure was highly refined—unsurprisingly, as MacMonnies was a master of modeling. That wasn't the problem. Rather, it was the scene depicted: the young fellow, with a stubby sword across his shoulder, represents, so the sculptor informed us, civic virtue. He is shown struggling with vice, symbolized by a pair of writhing, nubile female figures recumbent at the boy's feet. As he attempts to extricate himself from their grasp, he appears to trample one of their faces. For purposes of understanding the controversy caused by *Civic Virtue*, I think the description can end there. In 1922, one of the great waves of feminism was sweeping the land. The feminism of the 1920s, fresh from the victory for woman suffrage, was rhetorically strident. Feminists of the 1920s did not exactly cotton to the apparent symbolism of *Civic Virtue*. As every New Yorker knows, there is today no such sculpture in front of City Hall. *Civic Virtue*—the central, controversial figure group, at least—is with us still, however. In 1941, Parks Commissioner Robert Moses moved most of it (the fountain basins were destroyed) to an inconspicuous location near, though not right in front of or beside, the then new Queens Borough Hall on Queens Boulevard near Union Turnpike in Kew Gardens. Today *Civic Virtue* stands in a small plaza near the Queens Boulevard pedestrian bridge over the Interborough Parkway. The sculpture is at least so situated that it can easily be viewed in the round, though amid the roar of the expressway this is not a place to dawdle.

Between controversies, MacMonnies created some of the finest public sculpture in America, and much of it is right here around Prospect Park. Much of his work was executed in Giverny, France, where MacMonnies and his wife had chosen to settle. (He lived in that village at the same time as Claude Monet. According to the *Blue Guide,* "The village is also well-known for its *filet de boeuf en brioche.*") He created spandrel figures for White's Washington Memorial Arch, and pediment figures for White's Bowery Savings Bank. For Carrère & Hastings, MacMonnies created the fountains, *Truth* and *Beauty,* on either side of the main entrance to the New York Public Library. He did a Shakespeare for the Library of Congress, and the 130-foot-high *Battle of the Marne* in Meaux.

4 EQUESTRIAN STATUE OF HENRY WARNER SLOCUM
Grand Army Plaza, at northeast corner of intersection of
Flatbush Avenue, Eastern Parkway, and Plaza Street East
1905, Frederick W. MacMonnies

This marvelous equestrian statue was dedicated on May 30, 1905, at Eastern Parkway and Bedford Avenue. It was moved in 1924 to Prospect Park West and 15th Street, and moved again in 1928 to its present location. It was the second of Brooklyn's triumphant triumvirate of equestrian statues. The first was William Ordway Partridge's statue of Ulysses S. Grant at Grant Square. The third was Henry Merwin Shrady's statue of George Washington at

Williamsburg's Continental Army Plaza. This one brims with positivity in contrast to the world-weary quality of the others. If the Slocum lacks their psychological power, it is the better work as part of an urban ensemble. Like the
same sculptor's *Horse Tamers* at Park Circle, Slocum and his steed are viewed
against the sky. In outline it is a thrilling work, filled with spirit. The general so
beautifully commands his little hilltop along Plaza Street that it is hard to
believe the statue was originally in another location. Henry Warner Slocum
(1827–1894) was born in Onondaga County, New York, and was a graduate of
West Point. He resigned his commission in 1856, and worked as a lawyer in
Syracuse, New York, until called to return at the outbreak of the Civil War. He
commanded troops at Bull Run and Gettysburg and served in Sherman's
March to the Sea. After the war, he settled in Brooklyn, practicing law and
serving as a Democrat in the U.S. Congress from 1869 to 1873 and again from
1883 to 1885. He died in Brooklyn and is buried in Green-wood Cemetery.

Not everyone was pleased with the Slocum statue. Some who knew the
general said he was a retiring gentleman, not the show-offy type with raised
sword and open mouth that MacMonnies depicted. One commentator said of
Slocum, "He never played to the galleries . . . he never pointed his sword to
the skies." MacMonnies's depiction makes for a better, more exuberant work
when viewed from a distance, as indeed the statue usually is. Up close, the
open mouth leaves a little to be desired. The horse, however, is beautifully
modeled—in the opinion of some, it is MacMonnies's finest horse.

5 STATUE OF GOUVERNEUR KEMBLE WARREN
*Grand Army Plaza, northwest corner of Prospect Park West
    and Plaza Street West
1896, Henry Baerer*

The statue of General Warren was dedicated on July 4, 1896. Baerer's
Warren is stolidly Victorian in comparison with MacMonnies's exuberant
works. The general stands with left leg slightly bent, his field coat blowing in
the wind, right arm hanging at his side, while his cocked left arm holds binoculars. His gaze is set ahead, surveying the field of action. Warren commanded
troops at the fateful Battle of Little Round Top, the culmination, successful for
the Union, of the three-day Battle of Gettysburg. Warren was an engineer. His
sister was Emily Warren, who was married to an engineer, Washington
Roebling.

The right arm is an example of a peculiar problem in statuary, namely, what do you do with the figure's arms? The general's left arm is given the task of holding the binoculars. The right arm, though, seems a dangling, superfluous appendage. The object lesson in how to do it can be found across the plaza in MacMonnies's statue of Stranahan, where the arms, simply by being engaged in the mundane tasks of holding a hat and a walking stick, seem perfectly natural. Many sculptors get around the problem by having their figures hold something or gesture. John Quincy Adams Ward, in his Beecher statue in Cadman Plaza, basically conceals his figure's arms in the billowy sleeves of an Inverness cape, itself superbly rendered.

The sculptor Henry Baerer (1837–1908) came to America in 1854 and later returned to Munich where he created sculptures for the Royal Palace and for the Royal Opera. He worked in New York City from 1866. His works in the city include his busts of Beethoven in Central Park and Prospect Park.

6 MARY LOUISE BAILEY FOUNTAIN

Within the oval of Grand Army Plaza, behind (north of) the memorial arch, on the axis of Flatbush Avenue at the approximate line of Lincoln Place
1932, Eugene Savage, sculptor; Egerton Swartwout, architect

New York City, alas, is not a city notable for its fountains. This is among the most elaborate and enjoyable. Many people scoff at it, seeing it as an unintentionally comic *retardataire* of Rococo bombast. What these people don't realize is that it is quite *intentionally* comic. Why, indeed, should not the comic be a tool at the disposal of the public artist? The artists who created such works were not idiots, as many commentators seem to imply. Surely the artist intended this as a rollicking work. Surely he wishes us to laugh with surly Neptune. The fountain is set within a ring of London plane trees in the secluded oval north of the arch, contained within the elliptical berms that describe the inner arc of Plaza Street. It is a wonderful space, a public space, and rather a grand one at that, that comes as a complete surprise to the walker. Once this was the site of F. W. Darlington's electric fountain, which had seats all around it for Park Slopers and others who of a summer's evening would sit and relax and be entertained by the jets of color and water, in those palmy days when mindless entertainment at least reinforced the virtues of the public realm. The electric fountain was very simple. The Bailey Fountain is anything but—a riot of extravagant figuration and mythological and allegorical allusions. Seashell-blowing Tritons flank surly, potbellied Neptune, reclining with his trident. On the pedestal behind and above Neptune are standing nude figures of a man and a woman, back to back, symbolizing Felicity (female) and Wisdom (male). All the figures exhibit the exaggerated, even grotesque, musculature that was a hallmark of Eugene Savage's painting as well as his sculpture. Savage taught for many years at Yale and was extremely admired in the 1920s and 1930s, though recent auction records indicate that there is very little interest in his work today. The architect Swartwout—who had worked for McKim, Mead & White—and Savage were frequent collaborators, as at Chicago's Elks National Memorial and at New Haven's Yale Art Gallery.

To the north of the Bailey Fountain is a bronze bust of John F. Kennedy. Neil Estern designed the bust, dedicated in 1965 and, surprisingly, New York City's only official memorial to the thirty-fifth president. The bust is fine, but the setting is not. The bust sticks out from a marble stele by the architect Morris Ketchum, Jr. The head has a very unsupported, disembodied look to it—indeed, it looks kind of weird. Just to the north is another bronze bust, this one mounted masterfully. It is of Dr. Alexander J. C. Skene (1837–1900), a famous gynecologist who was the president of Long Island College Hospital in Cobble Hill. The memorial was dedicated in 1906. The work of the excellent sculptor J. Massey Rhind (1860-1936), the bust is set atop a pedestal in front of a stele and looks completely natural, not like a disembodied head hurtling through space.

Prospect Park

My preferred way of entering Prospect Park is from the entrance at Grand Army Plaza. One can take either of two paths leading to the Long Meadow, and either of these paths yields a thrilling experience. One can take the path to the east via Endale Arch, or the path to the west via Meadowport Arch. I slightly prefer the west path, because I prefer the design of **Meadowport Arch** (6a) to that of **Endale Arch** (6b).

Here's how to do it. Enter the park by the west path. For a while one's path is bordered by hillocks and berms and thick shrubs and canopied by trees. One feels closed in, sky is scarcely visible, the outside city disappears almost instantaneously when one enters the park. One can take this path a thousand times, as I have, and still each time feel just a tiny bit lost as one proceeds.

6A *Meadowport Arch*

When one enters the park, one is at the line of Park Slope's Union Street. One walks the exact equivalent of two blocks before reaching Meadowport Arch, which is on the line of Park Slope's Carroll Street. Along the way the path dips and curves, not a lot, but just enough to inspire that vague feeling of being a little lost. The way that, exactly one block in, at the line of Park Slope's President Street, the path forks in two around a hillock exacerbates this feeling. A thousand times one may have trod this path, yet each time that fork throws one for a little loop. The thing is, whichever way one goes, in a few moments one ends up at the same spot, on the south side of that hillock, with another block or so to go before Meadowport Arch. One first sees the structure of the arch on one's left before seeing through it to the other side. The arch has two openings onto the Long Meadow, and for maximum sensory impact I recommend bearing right. Meadowport Arch is a lovely structure of Ohio sandstone, with vaguely Oriental overtones, that Calvert Vaux designed and that was erected in 1868–70. So, one reaches the arch, enters the wood-lined tunnel, and bears right. The Long Meadow becomes visible through the frame of the arch, like a painting—a Barbizon painting, a Daubigny, a Théodore Rousseau, a Corot. Then: WHAM! One enters upon the Long Meadow. All that business of feeling slightly lost, closed in—then suddenly the light, the air, the vista, the openness. The effect is not so different from the way the Venetian *sottoportego* gives upon the *campo*. Though here, as nowhere else I've experienced, one has the feeling that one has stepped as if by magic right into that Corot canvas. It is the most intoxicating architectural experience in

New York City. Frederick Law Olmsted, Jr., the son of the codesigner of Prospect Park, described the approach to the Long Meadow as "a retired shady ante-chamber." M. M. Graff put it better, however, when she said it was "perhaps a subliminal image of a birth canal."

The Long Meadow of Prospect Park is a fantastic swath of green. At ninety acres and nearly a mile in length, it is the largest and longest meadow to be found in any New York City park. Central Park has nothing remotely approaching the Long Meadow. North Meadow was once Central Park's largest meadow at twenty-eight acres, but it is now covered with ballfields and seems un-meadow-like. The Great Lawn, which is not an original feature of Central Park, is fifteen acres. That leaves Sheep Meadow, at twelve acres, about the size of Prospect Park's Nethermead. Prospect Park can be viewed as divided in thirds. The westernmost third is meadow. The center third is mostly forest. The lake takes up most of the easternmost third. Meadow, forest, lake—these are the heart of Brooklyn. The park can also be viewed as divided into three ovals, of unequal size, formed by the circuitous paths of the eight park drives. So viewed, the Long Meadow occupies the western half of the westernmost and largest of these ovals. The forested areas of the Midwood, the Ravine, and Quaker Hill, as well as the watery areas of the Ravine, the Ambergill, and the Pools occupy the eastern half of this oval. The Pools connect via the Ambergill and the Ravine to the Lullwater, to the east of Center Drive and in the north-

6B *Endale Arch*

6C Pumas

ern part of the middle of the three ovals, thence to the Lake, which occupies most of the easternmost oval. The middle oval contains the aforementioned meadow called the Nethermead, as well as the forested Lookout Hill. The easternmost oval contains the lake and also the one formal area within the park, the Concert Grove, about which more anon.

To the east of East Drive, along a tangle of paths that lead to a point at which Flatbush Avenue's traffic is audible and intermittently visible, with the Brooklyn Botanic Garden right across the street, lies a hollow containing three formally designed lily pools, or would-be lily pools, for at this writing they are empty. Their setting is called the Rose Garden, which is an unfortunate name, for there appear to be no rosebushes, though I have it on good authority that there once were. The Rose Garden was placed here in 1896, and its designer is unknown. It was renovated in 1969 and according to the redoubtable M. M. Graff, the firm engaged to do the work created an unmanageable setting that shortly went to hell. For example, new fountains were installed in the Rose Garden in 1969. They were turned on only once, when Mayor John Lindsay appeared at the scene to extol his administration's record on park improvements. The fountains malfunctioned, flooding the garden, and have not been turned on since. This is an unusual and even slightly spooky little corner of the park, though fascinating. Further tangled paths lead west to the strangely named part of the park called the Vale of Cashmere. This is a deep and secluded hollow, a small glacial kettle with a free-form pool. The area is planted with azaleas and rhododendrons. It was originally the more rustic-looking Children's Playground, the water used for sailing toy boats. The space was made more formal when classical balustrades were added around the pool in 1896, at which time, to Olmsted's dismay, the area received its present name. A small fountain was also added. Frederick MacMonnies designed it, and some years later it was stolen. The balustrades, in need of repair, were instead removed. Surrounding elms died. The Vale of Cashmere became a neglected and seldom-visited part of the park. In recent years, however, the Friends of Prospect Park, under the leadership of M. M. Graff, has earmarked the Vale for community clean-up and restoration projects, and it is well worth the detour. As for that name, a *vale* is a valley, often with a stream running through it. "Cashmere" (or Kashmir) is a region in the Himalayas in northwest India. The name here is believed to have derived from a poem by Thomas Moore (1779–1852). Moore, born an Irish Catholic, was fashionable in Regency England, and his fame spread to America. He was a friend of Byron and an almost exact contemporary of Wordsworth, and the poem, *Lalla Rookh* (1817), from which "Vale of Cashmere" derives, was an Orientalist romance that enjoyed an enormous popular success on both sides of the Atlantic. Moore may be little read today, but his onetime stature is evident from the fact that there are busts of Moore in both Prospect Park (in the Concert Grove) and Central Park. The only other person so doubly honored was Beethoven. Anyway, in *Lalla Rookh,* travelers tell tales, one of which is set in Kashmir (which Moore calls Cashmere). This area in Prospect Park resembles a lake in Kashmir described in the poem.

To the south of the Vale of Cashmere, about midway across the Long Meadow at its eastern edge, begins the Ravine. Much of the forested region on either side of the Ravine is, at this writing and probably for about eight more years, closed off for desperately needed renovation. Decades of mismanagement by park tenders who were all too often patronage hacks with no real experience in the care of landscape caused severe erosion, the fixing of which under the auspices of the Prospect Park Alliance will require years during which no one is allowed to roam freely through the area. (The Prospect Park Alliance does offer excellent guided walking tours of the area, however.) For a scathing description of the mismanagement of this part of the park, the reader is directed to M. M. Graff's book *Central Park–Prospect Park: A New Perspective.* Another bit of mismanagement of an even more willful variety was the destruction, by Robert Moses in the 1930s, of Prospect Park's original plans. As a result, the restorers of the Ravine have proceeded with the aid of old photographs and a lot of educated guesswork. Anyway, the path east along the Quaker Hill, or south, side of the Ravine soon leads to one of the park's most impressive structures, the Nethermead Arches (three of them) that lead into the park's other meadow, the Nethermead. The arches carry the park's Center Drive. Designed by Vaux and built in 1868–70, the Ohio sandstone arches are of the segmental variety. The balustrades at the top running along Center Drive feature a Gothic trefoil motif, reminding us that Vaux was a major exponent of the Gothic Revival. The barrel-vaulted tunnels are faced in patterned brick, granite, and sandstone.

The Ravine feeds a body of water called the Lullwater, on the east bank of which is one of the park's most beguiling structures, the Boathouse.

THE BOATHOUSE

The Boathouse (6d) is an absolutely lovely structure designed by Brooklyn's great classicists Helmle & Huberty, who also designed the park's Tennis House and the addition to Litchfield Villa, as well as numerous structures throughout Brooklyn, including St. Gregory's Church in Crown Heights, St. Barbara's Church in Bushwick, and the Hotel Bossert in Brooklyn Heights. The Boathouse was a product of the turn-of-the-century classicizing of the park, when McKim, Mead & White (onetime employers of Helmle & Huberty's Frank Helmle) were hired to update the park's entrances along City Beautiful lines. Not only were the entrances classicized, but, under the later Parks Commissioner Michael J. Kennedy (appointed 1904), a few new classical structures, such as the Boathouse and Stanford White's Peristyle, were added to the interior of the park. Debate still rages over whether these additions, at least in the park interior, were appropriate. Certainly Olmsted and Vaux either would have hated them or, in the case of those in place before their deaths, did hate them. The definite outlines of this kind of architecture, as well as the gleaming City Beautiful whiteness, seem frankly unpastoral, thus flying in the face of everything Prospect Park was meant to stand for. Still, these structures are in themselves undeniably fine things. More than that, they are

6D *The Boathouse*

here; they are protected landmarks and aren't going anywhere soon; and for some of us, they have always been part of our experience and our idea of Prospect Park. Such structures as the Boathouse and the Peristyle, the architectural historian Leland M. Roth suggested, combined with the picturesque landscape to lend to the park "a rather pastoral Virgilian aspect." The architect Gregory F. Gilmartin suggested that these structures made the park "look more like the great English estates that had inspired Olmsted in the first place." However this may be, the Boathouse was erected in 1904 and is clad in a blindingly white glazed terra-cotta. Helmle & Huberty based the design of the first floor of the Boathouse on the first floor of Jacopo Sansovino's Library of St. Mark (1536–53) in Venice. The Doric arcade, the triglyphs and metopes of the entablature, and the style of the balustrade are similar to the Venetian prototype. Helmle & Huberty's building is less embellished, lacking, for example, the elaborate carvings of Sansovino's spandrels. The Boathouse has not fared well through much of its history. Misuse, disuse, general deterioration, and botched restorations have all taken their toll. In 1964, the Boathouse was very nearly pulled down, but was saved by local preservationists led by the poet Marianne Moore. The New York City Landmarks Preservation Commission then designated the Boathouse as a land-mark some years before the commission designated Prospect Park itself. The Boathouse closed in 1996, the result of water damage that was in turn the result of a botched 1971 restoration of the terra-cotta. (Interestingly, the St. Mark's Library on which the Boathouse design was partially based has a similarly checkered his-tory of constructional problems. Indeed, when part of it crumbled shortly after it was built, the architect Sansovino was sent to prison. I wonder when the last time was that an architect spent time in jail for one of his designs.) One is heartened, however, by the recent reports that the structure is to be renovated into a National Audubon Center. This joint undertaking of the National Audubon Society and the Prospect Park Alliance is scheduled to open on April 26, 2001, on the birthday shared by John James Audubon and Frederick Law Olmsted. The Audubon Society has declared Prospect Park an "Important Bird Area," and the center will be the society's first in an inner city. The park is a major stopover in spring and fall for migrating birds on the Great Atlantic Flyway. More than 240 species have been recorded in the park, including pied-billed grebes, great blue herons, great egrets, and kingfishers. This is not surprising given that the park contains by far the most bird-friendly conditions for miles around. As Prospect Park Administrator Tupper Thomas put it, "We're like Motel 8." The Audubon Center will offer birding tours and classes and will document sightings, which will be posted on the Internet. The center will also include exhibits and a gift shop.

Near the Boathouse is the park's most famous tree, the fabled **Camperdown elm** (6f, 6g). It is a freakish type of Scotch elm and this one at Prospect Park, a century and a half old, may be the direct scion of the original that appeared around 1850 on the grounds of the estate of the Earl of Camperdown in Dundee, Scotland. This variety lacks the gene for negative geotropism, which is to say that it has trouble standing up, and the understock of trees of this genus are typically grafted from normal Scotch elm. Here,

6E *Lullwater Bridge*

6F *Camperdown elm*

however, the tree appears about as trunkless as a tree can be and still be a tree. It is planted on a mound that allows the branches to spread. A. G. Burgess of East New York gave the Camperdown elm to Prospect Park, where the tree was planted in 1872. By then, it already had its fantastically gnarled appearance. In 1967, the architectural historian Clay Lancaster, who held the title of Curator of Prospect Park, discovered how decayed the Camperdown elm was. The City Parks Department seemed unwilling or unable to carry out the work needed to save the magnificent tree, so Lancaster and the Friends of Prospect Park raised the funds to study and repair it. The poet Marianne Moore of Cumberland Street in Fort Greene actively campaigned for the tree, writing in the *New York Times* of its plight and composing a poem, "The Camperdown Elm," in which she called it, as only a true poet could, "our crowning curio." M. M. Graff says that just as we should salute James Stranahan when we pass his statue upon entering the park from Grand Army Plaza, so should we salute Marianne Moore whenever we pass the Camperdown elm.

Just past the Camperdown elm is Calvert Vaux's beautiful Cleft Ridge Span, of molded concrete blocks, with the barrel-vaulted tunnel faced in red, yellow, and gray tiles. It was completed in 1872—the same year the Camperdown elm was planted in its present location. Through Cleft Ridge Span is the Oriental Pavilion. This part of the park, near its southeastern corner, used to be called the Concert Grove, and is now called the Flower Garden, probably because concerts are no longer held here. It is the one formal element that Vaux and Olmsted designed into the park. Its placement in Prospect Park

6G *Camperdown elm*

is very different from the placement of Central Park's formal element, the Mall
and Bethesda Terrace sequence. Where in Central Park, with its rectilinear
borders, the formal part is a kind of pivot around which the various, nonformal
features of the park are arrayed and by which they are accessed, here in
Prospect Park the formal bit serves no such function, being not in the center
of the park but at its periphery. Unfortunately, the insertion in 1961 of the
Wollman Memorial Rink, with its exposed refrigeration equipment, destroyed
the view from the Concert Grove toward the Lake. Calvert Vaux designed the
Oriental Pavilion, also known as the Concert Grove Pavilion, in 1874. It is, like
Thomas Moore's *Lalla Rookh*, an example of nineteenth-century Orientalist
romanticism. The broad, upswelling roof is actually somewhat reminiscent of

the gambrel roofs of old Dutch farmhouses that, in the 1870s, could be found in number very close to here. The eaves of the roof are carried on slender, ornately molded cast-iron columns of Hindu inspiration. The space within is open on all sides. The pavilion, which originally served as a café, has a grace and a picturesqueness befitting the pastoral landscape as envisioned by Vaux and Olmsted in a way that a structure such as Helmle & Huberty's Boathouse does not. The Oriental Pavilion stands at the north end of the Concert Grove, the formal, symmetrical, New Brunswick sandstone terraces of which slope down toward the Lake to the south.

SCULPTURE IN THE CONCERT GROVE

In the Concert Grove, as at the Mall and Bethesda Terrace in Central Park, Vaux and Olmsted felt sculpture appropriate. None of what is found here is a masterpiece, but there are some noteworthy specimens nonetheless. The most noteworthy is the statue of Abraham Lincoln facing south on axis with the Oriental Pavilion. The statue was dedicated on October 21, 1869 (a mere four years after Lincoln's death) but not here. It originally stood in Grand Army Plaza, as the physically rather inadequate centerpiece of that large space many years before John Duncan's massive granite arch was erected there. The Lincoln statue and the arch coexisted for a few years in awkward juxtaposition until 1895, when the statue was moved to its present location, where it seems it should have been all along. The sculptor, Henry Kirke Brown, was one of his generation's most significant in America. His undoubted masterpiece is the equestrian statue of George Washington in Manhattan's Union Square. Prospect Park's Lincoln is not nearly so exciting, though it is fine. The same can be said for Brown's *other* standing Lincoln, which is on the opposite end of Union Square from the equestrian Washington. The Union Square Lincoln was dedicated one year after the Brooklyn one. Though they are both bronze standing Lincolns done by the same sculptor at the same time, they are not from the same mold. In Union Square, Lincoln's right arm grasps his cloak and is pressed against his chest. His left arm dangles at his side. The Brooklyn Lincoln, on the other hand, appears to be delivering a speech, both his arms spread out in front of his body. Though the

6H *Oriental Pavilion*

figures are similarly attired, the Union Square Lincoln's marvelously rendered baggy trousers are not so baggy as the also marvelously rendered trousers of the Brooklyn figure.

A series of busts are arrayed semicircularly about the terrace between Lincoln and the Oriental Pavilion. Let us take them from west to east. First, there is Wolfgang Amadeus Mozart (1756-91). The bronze bust dates from 1897 and is the work of Augustus Mueller. Next is Ludwig van Beethoven (1770-1827) by Henry Baerer. We already met this sculptor, who produced the statue of Gouverneur Kemble Warren in Grand Army Plaza. Here, just as Henry Kirke Brown did standing Lincolns for both Manhattan and Brooklyn, so Henry Baerer produced bronze busts of Beethoven for each of the two independent cities. Baerer's Beethoven bust on the Mall in Central Park was dedicated in 1884. Brooklyn's Beethoven is from ten years later. Again, the works, though similar, are not from the same mold. Central Park's head is downcast, while Brooklyn's looks ahead, cocked slightly to the right, looking perhaps less dejected but no less dour than its Manhattan counterpart. Next east is a bust of Thomas Moore, the poet from whom derived the name of the Vale of Cashmere. Moore, as I said earlier, was once fantastically popular, though little read today. Here, too, the personage is similarly commemorated across the river in Central Park, though this time by a different sculptor. The Brooklyn bronze bust is from 1879, around the same time that the sculptor John G. Draddy (1833–1904) was contributing carvings to the new St. Patrick's Cathedral on Fifth Avenue. The Moore bust was dedicated in the year of the poet's centenary. That was also the occasion for Central Park's Moore bust by the sculptor D. B. Sheahan. Our theme in the Concert Grove, naturally, is musical, except of course for Lincoln, who is not original to the setting. (Moore was a poet, but equally as beloved as a writer of songs.) Next is a bronze bust of a thickly mustachioed Edvard Grieg (1843-1907), the nineteenth-century Norwegian composer of *Peer Gynt*. The Norwegian sculptor Sigvald Absjornsen created the bust, dedicated in 1914. By this time Brooklyn boasted New York City's largest Norwegian community. Finally, just to the south of Grieg is a bronze bust of the German composer Carl Maria von Weber (1786-1826). Chester Beach (1881–1956) created this bust, which was dedicated in 1909. Beach also created the bust of Brooklynite Walt Whitman that is part of the Hall of Fame Terrace at the old New York University campus in the Bronx. Once part of this grand sequence, though now cut off from the Concert Grove by the Wollman Rink's snack bar, is the elaborate World War I Memorial, erected in 1921 on the north bank of the Lake. Augustus Lukeman contributed the central bronze group, while Daniel Chester French did the flanking tablets. On the other side of East Lake Drive from the Concert Grove and near the Ocean Avenue edge of the park, is an 1871 bust of Washington Irving. James Wilson Alexander MacDonald, a commercially successful sculptor of household figurines in postbellum New York, created the bust; he was also the sculptor of the bronze seated figure of the poet Fitz-Greene Halleck on Central Park's Mall.

The Lake is a sixty-acre body of water at the southwestern end of the park along Parkside Avenue and Prospect Park Southwest. To the west of the Concert Grove is a peninsula, Breeze Hill, separating the Lullwater from the Lake. At the eastern end of Breeze Hill, spanning the narrow channel is Terrace Bridge. Completed in 1890, Terrace Bridge is an impressive structure with stately stone piers and a span of iron, carried on gracefully curving trusses, the spandrels on its sides bearing foliate designs in cast iron. This bridge was the last of Vaux's designs for the park and was done during the time of his partnership with George K. Radford. The bridge leads to Lookout Hill, where one will find the Maryland Society Battle Monument. Erected in 1895, this is the only known instance of Stanford White's work deep within the park. Indeed, this is a somewhat remote area and the monument, a polished granite Corinthian column surmounted by a marble globe, is typically overlooked in accounts of the park. The monument commemorates the Maryland volunteers who fought in the Battle of Long Island in August 1776. The most intense fighting in this battle raged in the wooded neck of parkland, known as Battle Pass, to the west of the Zoo.

On the east side of the park, near the intersection of Flatbush and Ocean Avenues, is the Willink Entrance, opposite the southern tip of the Botanic Garden. This recently restored entrance has none of the operatic intensity of Grand Army Plaza or Park Circle, but it is lovely nonetheless, with its granite pillars topped by bronze lanterns. It is actually the most heavily used of all the park's entrances, as it is closest to mass transportation. A number of interesting things can be viewed here within a short compass. Just inside the Willink Entrance is the carousel. Charles Carmel, a noted carver of horses, built the carousel in 1912 for Coney Island. It was moved to Prospect Park in 1952. In 1983, it stopped working and there were no funds for its repair. Four years later, the Prospect Park Alliance raised almost a million dollars to hire the noted carousel conservator Will Morton VIII to restore it, and it was reopened in and has been going strong since 1990. Prospect Park's is one of but twelve remaining Carmel carousels in the country. Nearby is the old Peter Lefferts farmhouse, or the

Lefferts Homestead as it is called. This lovely house was built in 1777–83 at the present site of Flatbush Avenue between Midwood and Maple Streets in the nearby neighborhood called Prospect–Lefferts Gardens, all of which was once part of the Lefferts family farm until it was subdivided in the late-nineteenth century. In the early-twentieth century, development in that northern neck of Flatbush was intensive, and to spare the historic house, it was relocated in 1918 to its present site within the park, just south of the zoo. The Lefferts house was built more than a hundred years after the Pieter Claesen Wyckoff house (part of which is the oldest surviving structure in New York State) at Clarendon Road and Ralph and Ditmas Avenues, yet the style of these "Dutch" farmhouses changed remarkably little. The dominant features are the same, with the gambrel roof sloping down to overhang a broad, welcoming porch screened by slender, widely spaced columns. Like the Wyckoff house, the Lefferts Homestead is a historic house museum. Operated by the Prospect Park Alliance, the Lefferts Homestead is oriented principally to children. Exhibits, workshops, and all kinds of family activities, including springtime sheep shearing, are part of the programs here. The Lefferts Homestead is open Friday, Saturday, and Sunday from April through November from 1:00 P.M. to 4:00 P.M. Call (718) 965-6505 for more details. North of the Lefferts Homestead is the Prospect Park Wildlife Center, like the Vale of Cashmere located within the hollow of a glacial kettle. Though the zoo is located within the park boundaries, the New York Zoological Society operates it, as they do its counterpart in Central Park. Also like the Central Park Zoo, Prospect Park's underwent a major renovation. Between 1989 and 1993, $36 million was spent to refurbish what had become a rundown mess of a zoo, insufficient in every way to house the large animals that lived there. Today, the Wildlife Center follows modern zoological practices and keeps only small animals in a highly educational setting. The shells of the original zoo buildings erected in 1935 by Aymar Embury II (Robert Moses's favorite architect and the designer of the Charles Neergaard house on Eighth Avenue and 3rd Street in Park Slope) remain, though their interiors have been thoroughly remodeled with all bars removed. These brick buildings arranged in a semicircle are adorned with bas-reliefs of scenes from Kipling's *Jungle Books* by such artists as the Brooklyn-based animalier Frederick George Richard Roth, whose numerous well-known works include the statue of Balto in Central Park. The charming *Lioness and Cubs* at the west entrance to the zoo dates from 1899 and was once misattributed to Frederick MacMonnies. It was in fact the work of August Peter, MacMonnies's pupil. MacMonnies purchased the work from Peter and made a gift of it to Prospect Park.

Over on the west side of the park one finds the Tennis House of Helmle & Huberty, completed in 1910. This is a meltingly beautiful brick-and-limestone structure in the Palladian style. The reader will remember that they also designed the Boathouse. The Tennis House, like Stanford White's Peristyle, is an open pavilion. Like the Peristyle, the ceiling is of Guastavino tile, here patterned as intricately and as beautifully as one will ever see. The Tennis House is home to an excellent organization called the Brooklyn Center for the Urban Environment (previously known as the Prospect Park Environmental Center). This group runs excellent walking tours, not only of the park but all over Brooklyn including its remotest reaches, and other educational programs under the leadership of John Muir. It is they who sponsor the cruises on the fetid yet at the same time mouth-watering Gowanus Canal. Walk all around the Tennis House, climb its porch and sit on its benches. The Tennis House is at the park's West Drive, on the line of Park Slope's 8th Street. To the north is another Palladian structure, the Picnic House, built in 1927. It lacks the pizzazz of the Helmle & Huberty structures, though it is handsome and, whether it truly belongs here or not, is used by many Park Slope organizations and schools for special programs including meetings, lectures, receptions, and fund-raising events. Its interesting architect, J. Sarsfield Kennedy, also designed the fine limestone Beaux-Arts town house at 631 - 1st Street in Park Slope (only a few blocks from here), built in 1909 and, in 1916–17, the unique, rocky and thatchy, Arts & Crafts–inspired Howard E. Jones house at 8220 Narrows Avenue (at 83rd Street) in Bay Ridge, a work that could not be more different either from the

Picnic House.

The part of the park to the west of West Drive, along Prospect Park West, Vaux called the "Very Expensive Lots." When Stranahan called upon Vaux to review Egbert Viele's plan for the park, just about the first thing Vaux recommended was that the City of Brooklyn purchase further land to the south and west so that the East Side Lands, divided from the rest by the pre-existing Flatbush Avenue, would not be needed for the park. To be precise, the original land purchased for the park was bounded on the north by Warren Street (now Prospect Place), on the east by Washington Avenue, on the south by 9th and 3rd Streets, and on the west by Vanderbilt, Ninth, and Tenth Avenues. Running smack through it all was Flatbush Avenue. Vaux proposed the present park boundaries, which included the purchase of a narrow strip of land along the west side of the park between Ninth and Tenth Avenues and 3rd and 15th Streets. These were the "Very Expensive Lots," accounting for $1.7 million of the total $4 million land-acquisition costs of the park. We're talking about what is perhaps 5 percent of the park's land accounting for more than 40 percent of the land acquisition costs—and it's the least inspiring part of the park! (By the way, Ninth Avenue is now Prospect Park West, and Tenth Avenue can be thought of as the park's West Drive.) Why was this land so expensive? A few years before planning for the park began, a very rich man named Edwin Clarke Litchfield built his country house on the plot bounded by 4th and 5th Streets and Ninth and Tenth Avenues. Oriented to the west to take in a vista of harbor, the Litchfield house, together with the new park planned for its backyard, placed huge upward pressure on the price of the building lots in this narrow strip of land, as people speculated that these would soon be some of the most desirable residential sites in Brooklyn. By the time Vaux convinced the City of Brooklyn that these lots were necessary for the park, their price had skyrocketed. Vaux felt them necessary—and he was, after all, right—chiefly for the effect on the visitor entering the park from the main, or Grand Army Plaza, entrance. That is, it wouldn't work to create that spectacular entry sequence described above if the whole west side of the park were truncated.

426

When we say that the Very Expensive Lots are a relatively unin-
spiring part of the park, we refer specifically to two misconceived
or at least misapplied uses to which much of this land has been
devoted. The first is a group of structures between the Tennis
House and the Picnic House. There we find the park-mainte-
nance buildings and garages. Necessary structures, it is true,
though their design and placement are such that they scar these
Very Expensive Lots in much the way that the Wollman Rink
scars the Concert Grove. We can say much the same of the Band
Shell between 10th and 11th Streets. The towering sound and
light stanchions are visually jarring. No one, though, would deny
the desirability of having some such facility there at park's edge.
Indeed, every summer the Celebrate Brooklyn! series brings to
Prospect Park a range of top-drawer performers, and the events
are not only well attended but make for a very pleasing scene of
neighborly urbanity, precisely of the sort that enlightened urban
planners work so hard to effect.

Across West Drive from the Picnic House is the stellar
attraction of the Very Expensive Lots: the house known as
Litchfield Villa.

LITCHFIELD VILLA

I've already mentioned Edwin Clarke Litchfield, the Very Rich
Man whose presence made these Very Expensive Lots. Litchfield
was a lawyer and a railroad financier who in mid-century must surely
have been one of the two or three wealthiest Brooklynites. In 1854,
he commissioned the architect Alexander Jackson Davis (1803–92),
arguably the most prestigious architect in the country at the time, to
design a country house, or "villa," on land that Litchfield owned
sloping down toward the harbor. The house was completed in 1857.
Litchfield's wife was named Grace Hill Hubbard, and "Grace Hill" is
what he called his property here. Davis pioneered the Italian Villa
style of country house in America, and here is one of the finest
examples. Houses such as this are a big tourist draw in the lower
Hudson River Valley. The style was one in the progression of romantic styles of the first half of the nineteenth century and followed the

Greek Revival and the Gothic Revival. Often the same architects, including Davis, worked in all three styles. The style was inspired by the vernacular farmhouse architecture of the Italian countryside, and like Gothic Revival revels in asymmetrical compositions of building parts. John Nash introduced the style into England at the beginning of the nineteenth century, and it made its way to this country thirty or so years later when the Philadelphia architect John Notman designed a house in the Italian Villa style for Bishop George Washington Doane in Burlington, New Jersey. The New York landscape gardener Andrew Jackson Downing, for whom the designer of Prospect Park, Calvert Vaux, worked, was a major proselytizer for the style. Davis, a close associate of Downing, became the most renowned designer of houses in the style. The Litchfield house, just inside the park and facing into Park Slope across Prospect Park West between 4th and 5th Streets, has a picturesque composition that makes it seem perfectly natural in its park setting. There are basically five distinct parts to its west-facing elevation. The most prominent is the second part from the right, a bold, projecting, octagonal pavilion, from the first floor of which projects a semicircular bay rising to a second-floor balustrade and balcony. A floor above is another balustraded balcony, this one straight across rather than curved, and, a floor above, a balustrade crowns the roof. Recessed to the left of this is a high square tower, in the base of which is the round-arched entrance. The tower rises a story above the octagonal pavilion and is crowned by a balustrade. To the left of the tower is a wing connecting to a lower, round corner tower set with narrow round-arched windows. To the right of the octagonal pavilion is a wing with a south-facing gable. At the base of this wing is a projecting porch with a fine colonnade featuring that quintessentially American feature, cornstalk capitals. The house is set upon a small hill with a generous garden separating it from Prospect Park West. Originally, Litchfield had an unobstructed view to the harbor to the west, including the Gowanus Canal, of which he was a major promoter and developer. Davis, in extolling the virtues of the Italian Villa style, said, "This style has the very great merit of allowing additions to be made in almost any direction, without injuring the effect of the original structure; indeed such is the variety of sizes and forms, which the different parts of the Italian villa may take, in perfect accordance with architectural propriety, that the original edifice frequently gains in beauty by additions of this description." This was borne out in 1911–13 when Helmle & Huberty designed the addition in the rear of the south side of the house. Litchfield continued to live in the house until his death in 1885, long after Prospect Park was completed. It was apparently part of the deal he struck with Stranahan and company when they acquired, at Vaux's suggestion, the Very Expensive Lots along the west side of the park. Nine years after Litchfield's death, under commissioner Frank Squier, the house became the headquarters of the Brooklyn Park Department. Four years after that, when Brooklyn became part of New York City, the house became the Brooklyn office of the New York City Parks Department, and it remains so to this day. The most unfortunate thing in the house's history occurred in the 1940s. Originally the house was coated in stucco, scored to imitate ashlar. The stucco had badly deteriorated by the 1940s, and when the city decided to restore it, they realized it had to be pulled off and replaced entirely. Half a century and more later, we are still waiting. Actually, when the idea was broached not long ago of finally replacing the stucco, some local architectural nabobs objected. Filled as they were with antiquated modernist notions of stucco sham, they insisted the house was finer for its naked brick, and effectively killed the possibility that A. J. Davis's vision will ever be restored.

Born in New York City, like James Renwick, Jr., and Stanford White, Alexander Jackson Davis had been drawing for most of his life when in 1823 at the age of twenty he began his formal training at the Antique School that the painter John Trumbull had established in New York. (It later became the National Academy of Design.) Trumbull persuaded Davis to pursue a career in architecture. In 1826, Davis went to work as a draftsman for the prominent New York City architect Josiah Brady, who had designed the second Trinity Church. Davis became, in 1829, a partner of Ithiel Town, one of the most important figures in the American Greek Revival. Town & Davis designed such buildings as the Indiana State Capitol (1831–35), the North Carolina State Capitol (1833–40), and, in New York City, the Custom House (later Federal Hall National Memorial, 1833–42) on

Wall Street. Davis began his own practice in 1835 and concentrated on the design of country houses. He and Andrew Jackson Downing became close, and Davis illustrated Downing's extremely influential books *Cottage Residences* (1842) and *The Architecture of Country Houses* (1850). Davis designed houses in the 1850s and 1860s for Llewellyn Park, the model suburb in West Orange, New Jersey, where he himself lived and where he died at the age of eighty-nine. It is rather startling to think that Davis lived until just one year before the Columbian Exposition. In Manhattan, Davis designed London Terrace on West 23rd Street in 1845. This elegant "colonnade row" of houses was replaced in the 1930s by the gigantic apartment complex of the same name. Indeed, Davis was a prolific designer of Manhattan row houses, mansions, and churches in the antebellum years, and were it not for his surviving country houses he might today be as little known as Josiah Brady and Calvin Pollard. Perhaps Davis's best-known work is the wonderful Gothic villa in Tarrytown, New York, called Lyndhurst. It was built in 1838 and Davis was retained twenty-seven years later to enlarge it. A seventy-five-year-old Davis participated, unsuccessfully, in the competition for the design of the Long Island Historical Society on Pierrepont Street.

A long detour now, to the south side of the park, facing into Flatbush.

7 THE HORSE TAMERS
1899, Frederick MacMonnies, bases by Stanford White
At Park Circle, intersection of Prospect Park Southwest,
Ocean Parkway, Coney Island Avenue, and Parkside Avenue

These are among the most thrilling works of public sculpture in New York City. This entrance at Park Circle is almost as fine as the one at Grand Army Plaza. *The Horse Tamers* comprises two sculptural groups flanking the roadway into the park. Each bronze group features a young man attempting to control two rearing horses. These are not wild horses, since their feet are shod, though they are nonetheless agitated. The original title was *The Triumph of Mind over Brute Force*, and we may presume that the young man symbolizes "mind." If it is not his intellect that at first strikes the viewer, I think it is because the notion of "mind" here symbolized is that of the intelligence that man employs, often in

7 *The Horse Tamers*

the service of physical exertion, in subduing "brute force." The sculptures are, at any rate, thrilling to behold and a tour de force such as one seldom sees in the modeling of equestrian forms. Be sure to savor the beautiful granite pedestals as well. Stanford White's elegant designs, at once so seemingly in contrast to the fury of the scene above and yet somehow so appropriate, are works of consummate elegance of the kind we expect from a designer whose fecundity extended to almost every conceivable type of object, such that his picture frames, or his sculpture pedestals, are in themselves exquisite works.

8 THE PERISTYLE
1904, McKim, Mead & White
> *Just inside the park opposite the Parade Ground, on Parkside Avenue*
> *just to the west of Parade Place, about midway between*
> *Coney Island Avenue and Ocean Avenue*

The Landmarks Preservation Commission insists on calling it the Croquet Shelter. The Friends of Prospect Park alternatively call it the Grecian

Shelter and the Peristyle. It was in fact originally a place for viewing the precision military drills that once took place on the Parade Ground across Parkside Avenue, when men would dress in historic military uniforms and perform intricately choreographed maneuvers, a form of entertainment that is not quite so popular today as it was at the turn of the twentieth century. The limestone structure itself is supremely beautiful, an essay in proportion. Open on all sides, it is surrounded by Corinthian columns, ten each on the north and south sides, four each on the east and west sides. The columns support an entablature with a beautiful foliated terra-cotta frieze, which is topped by a dentilated cornice, the whole surmounted by a fine balustrade. Inside, the roof is of Guastavino tile.

STANFORD WHITE (1853–1906)

Stanford White "was the greatest designer that this country has ever produced," wrote the lawyer and man of letters John Jay Chapman. White was born on November 9, 1853, at 110 East 10th Street in Manhattan. His father was Richard Grant White (1822–85), one of the most remarkable figures in New York's nineteenth-century literary culture. He was a drama and music critic and editor of an important twelve-volume edition of the works of Shakespeare. He wrote some seventy books. The Whites had been rich until Richard was twenty years old, and the family's fall from financial grace created a chip he was never quite able to get off his shoulder. Stanford's mother was Alexina Mease, who, though born in New York, was of proud Charleston, South Carolina, descent. She had been in line to inherit a plantation until the Civil War dashed all hopes of that. Richard and Alexina were married in 1850. The neighborhood in which Stanford was born had only recently been a fashionable area, but by 1853, it was part of "Kleindeutschland," a neighborhood filled with Germans who had been pouring into New York since the political upheavals of 1848. Perhaps because the recent German immigrants were a constant reminder to Richard Grant White of his own family's declining fortunes, he became vociferously anti-German in spite of his sensitive writings on Beethoven—he indeed wrote some of the first important essays in English on Beethoven's music. Richard was friends with many of New York's leading artists and intellectuals. When

young Stanford was thinking of becoming a painter, his father introduced him to his friend John LaFarge. LaFarge dissuaded young
Stanford from the uncertain life of a fine artist and advised him to
put his talent for drawing to use in an architect's office. Another
Richard Grant White friend, Frederick Law Olmsted (who was an
editor of the distinguished *Putnam's Monthly* at a time when
Richard was a contributor), suggested that Stanford seek employment with Henry Hobson Richardson. Stanford was sixteen when
he went to work in 1869 for Richardson at 6 Hanover Street in
Manhattan. The following year Stanford befriended a newcomer to
the office, fresh from the École des Beaux-Arts, Charles Follen
McKim. When Richardson moved his office to Boston in 1873,
White went with him and had a large role in the design of Trinity
Church (1872–77) at Copley Square. White left Richardson's office
to travel through Europe in 1878 and 1879, largely in the company
of the sculptor Augustus Saint-Gaudens. Also during this time,
White collaborated with Saint-Gaudens on the design of the
Admiral Farragut Monument for Madison Square, dedicated in
1881. The firm of McKim, Mead & White began in September
1879, just after White's return to the city from his European
sojourn. Though works were always credited to the firm as a whole,
typically either White or McKim was the principal designer.
White's credits include many of the greatest buildings of New York
City. He designed the following structures:

- the chancel renovation of Richard Upjohn's Church of the
  Ascension in 1885–88 at Fifth Avenue and 10th Street (with its
  spectacular mural by John LaFarge),
- the Goelet Building in 1886–87 on Broadway and 20th Street (a
  building much praised by Lewis Mumford, who felt White took
  a wrong turn after designing it),
- Madison Square Garden in 1887–91 at Madison Avenue and
  26th Street,
- the Judson Memorial Baptist Church in 1888–93 on
  Washington Square South,
- the Century Association clubhouse in 1889–91 on West 43rd
  Street,

- the Washington Arch (New York City's second greatest triumphal arch) in 1889–92,
- the Metropolitan Club in 1891–94 on Fifth Avenue and 60th Street,
- the Bowery Savings Bank in 1893–95 at the Bowery and Grand Street,
- the Gould Memorial Library (1896–1903) and the Hall of Fame for Great Americans (1900-01) at New York University's Bronx campus,
- the Joseph Pulitzer house in 1900–1903 on East 73rd Street,
- the portico of St. Bartholomew's Church in 1901–3 on Madison Avenue and 44th Street (later moved to Park Avenue and 50th Street),
- the Tiffany Building at Fifth Avenue and 37th Street (1903–6),
- the Gorham Building at Fifth Avenue and 36th Street (1903–6),
- the sadly demolished Madison Square Presbyterian Church at Madison Avenue and 24th Street (1903–6).

Much is made of White the playboy, the voluptuary, the philanderer, the corrupter of young girls. Much of this is probably exaggerated, or is at any rate conjectural and based on the testimony of those who stood to gain in some way from so painting White. What is indisputable was that he was shot and killed on June 25, 1906, in the roof garden of Madison Square Garden. The shooter was Harry Kendall Thaw, and the event has become a part of American folklore, inspiring the 1955 movie *The Girl in the Red Velvet Swing* (with Ray Milland as Stanford White, Farley Granger as Harry Thaw, and Joan Collins as Evelyn Nesbit) as well as a portion of E. L. Doctorow's 1975 novel *Ragtime*.

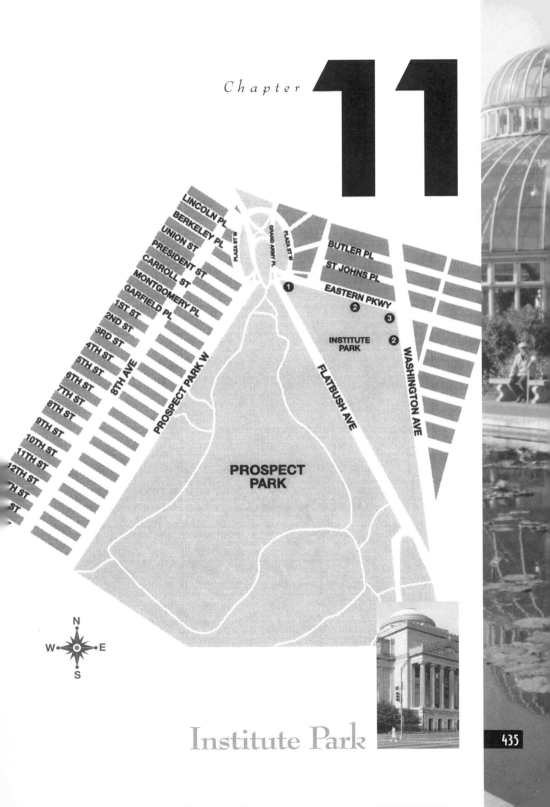

11

LINCOLN PL

BERKELEY PL

UNION ST

PRESIDENT ST

CARROLL ST

MONTGOMERY PL

GARFIELD PL

1ST ST

2ND ST

3RD ST

4TH ST

5TH ST

6TH ST

7TH ST

8TH ST

9TH ST

10TH ST

11TH ST

12TH ST

TH ST

ST

PLAZA ST W

GRAND ARMY PL

PLAZA ST E

BUTLER PL

ST JOHNS PL

EASTERN PKWY

① ② ③ ②

INSTITUTE
PARK

PROSPECT PARK W

8TH AVE

FLATBUSH AVE

WASHINGTON AVE

**PROSPECT
PARK**

N
W · E
S

Institute Park

1 Brooklyn Public
Library

Chapter **11**

Institute Park

1 BROOKLYN PUBLIC LIBRARY

Eastern Parkway, northeast corner of Flatbush Avenue
1937–41, Githens & Keally

Lewis Mumford said that as a work of architecture, the Brooklyn Public Library was superior to the New York Public Library and the Library of Congress. That overstated things a bit. While the Brooklyn Public Library may not be in the same league as those others, which are among the greatest buildings in America, nonetheless it is a very interesting building indeed, one that is increasingly admired by architects and architectural critics. The Brooklyn Public Library is a priceless municipal resource that has improved itself in recent years under its director Martín Gómez (since 1995). As a longtime resident of nearby Park Slope, I can say that my life would be seriously diminished without this library.

Brooklyn's public library system was founded in 1897, the year before Consolidation. There were forerunners, however. For example, the Apprentices' Library, founded in 1823 in a Fulton Street tavern, was a private subscription library intended to bring books into the lives of young workingmen. From a strictly genealogical standpoint, the Apprentices' Library was the progenitor of the Brooklyn Museum, not the Brooklyn Public Library. Still, throughout the nineteenth century, it was one of several efforts on the part of enlightened businessmen and philanthropists to create libraries to serve various segments of the public. Another such endeavor was the Mercantile Library, a private subscription library founded in 1857 and the first permanent home of which was a landmark building designed by Peter B. Wight and built in 1865–68 on Montague Street. In 1878, the name was changed to Brooklyn Library. Following the formation of the Brooklyn Public Library system, the Montague Street building became the system's first main branch, in 1903. When the Grand Army Plaza building was finally completed in 1941, the old Mercantile Library became the Brooklyn Heights Branch. (It was later demolished and replaced by the new Brooklyn Heights Branch and Business Library on Cadman Plaza West.) These forerunners were, as I said, private libraries that charged an annual fee for their use. Brooklyn's first completely free library, open to all Brooklyn residents over the age of fourteen, was the privately operated Free Library that opened in 1896 on Hall Street between DeKalb and Willoughby Avenues in Clinton Hill. Charles Pratt was the library's founder and benefactor, and it served its intended function until, again, the Grand Army Plaza building was finally completed, at which time use of Pratt's library was limited to students of Pratt Institute.

Note that I referred to when the Grand Army Plaza building was *finally* completed. For many, many years, the library's site at the foot of Mount Prospect was the most famous hole in the ground in New York City. In 1908, the library hired the gifted Brooklyn-born architect Raymond F. Almirall (1869–1939) to design the main branch. At that time, Almirall had already designed three of the Carnegie branch libraries for the system (the Pacific, Prospect, and Bushwick Branches) and would later design another (the Eastern Parkway Branch). These and all of Almirall's other works in Brooklyn and Manhattan were excellent. (Of particular note is his Emigrant Industrial Savings Bank on Chambers Street, one of New York's most beautiful skyscrapers.) Almirall, who attended Brooklyn Polytechnic Institute before spending four years (1892 to 1896) at the École des Beaux-Arts, returned to Paris in 1924 to assist William Welles Bosworth on the Rockefeller-funded restoration of Versailles, work that earned Almirall commendation as a Chevalier of the French Legion of Honor. At Grand Army Plaza, Almirall was thought to be just the man to design the building located between two of the city's most impressive classical monuments, the Soldiers' and Sailors' Memorial Arch and the Brooklyn Museum. A library in the Beaux-Arts classical style would make this one of the great City Beautiful sequences in America. Almirall designed his building and construction progressed until 1913, when funds ran out. By that time, the foundations had been dug and part of the west wall on Flatbush Avenue had risen. The hole in the ground and that one partial wall stood in their unfinished state for more than three decades, marking this as one of the great episodes in the history of municipal ineffectuality. Some have suggested another reason for foot-dragging on the Almirall building. Brooklyn's John Francis Hylan, a resident of Bushwick, was mayor of New York City from 1917 to 1924. A grand jury convened to investigate corruption charges against Hylan's administration. Raymond Almirall was the foreman of that grand jury and is said to have very aggressively sought to prove the claims against Hylan, who, some suggest, retaliated against Almirall by seeing to it that his building would never be completed. This is all speculation, of course, though we do know that Hylan and Almirall were none too fond of each other. In any event, Almirall's drawings, as well as photographs of the partially completed Flatbush Avenue wall, show that this would have been a magnificent building. The partial wall alone was replete with rusticated surfaces, monumental columns, pilasters, balustrades, pediments, and niches for statuary. Whatever the virtues of the present edifice, I think it a little sad that Almirall's building was never completed. What happened is that by 1937 when the city was prepared, at long last, to resume work on the building, no one was interested any longer in perpetuating the grand manner of Almirall's design. The period of streamlining had descended. This was the time when Raymond Loewy transformed the Twentieth-Century Limited, already the most famous train in America, into the sleek silver bullet that shot through the night. Art Deco, already using heavily stylized and streamlined forms, was made more spare under the increasing influence of European modernism, particularly the International Style that had been touted at the beginning of the decade by the Museum of Modern Art. In 1934–35, two years after MoMA's International Style exhibition, the Swiss modernist William Lescaze, an acolyte of his countryman Le Corbusier, mutilated—er, streamlined—the Brooklyn Museum. No, by 1937, the people in charge felt Almirall's design would no longer do, and in 1938, it was demolished.

New architects were called in—the firm of Alfred Morton Githens and Francis Keally. They scuttled Almirall's design, though they were required to make use of the foundations already dug as well as the framing that had already been erected. From that frame they stripped gorgeous marble ornament. Nonetheless, the original Almirall plan survives to the extent that it provided the basic dimensions, form, and orientation of the Githens & Keally building. The style of Githens & Keally's building is what has been termed "Modern Classical," the austere, stripped-down, sparsely ornamented classical design that we associate with the works of Paul Philippe Cret in Washington, D.C., and Philadelphia. The principal exterior material is beautiful Indiana lime-stone. One masterstroke on Githens & Keally's part was to make the library's entrance façade so sweepingly concave, something Almirall had not done. It makes sense facing the oval of Grand Army Plaza, and also echoes the concave form of the plaza entrance to Prospect Park, right across Flatbush Avenue. This concavity reappears inside in the inward-curving form of the monumen-tally scaled catalogue room. Here is a grandly proportioned space defined by massive three-story-high piers paneled in curving Appalachian white oak; a semi-elliptical second-floor balcony; and glass-block clerestory windows, adding up to what is probably the finest example of a monumental modernist interior space in New York City.

Back outside, the library's porch is a generous terraced space providing many shelves and ledges and steps for sitting. Many visitors are quite impressed by the exterior artwork. The streamlined form of the building has no use for projecting or modeled ornamentation, unlike Almirall's original, the monu-mental Beaux-Arts form of which was conceived in part as a carriage for sculp-ture that would stand against the sky. In Githens & Keally's building, the artwork is flat. The German-born Carl Paul Jennewein (1890–1978), who immigrated to America at the age of seventeen, designed the gilded, shallow reliefs on the giant curving piers on either side of the entrance—so shallow that if they weren't gilded they might not register to the eye. The reliefs' theme is the evolution of art and science. Jennewein was an important architectural artist. His productions throughout his long career were dauntingly varied both in style and in medium. In 1913, when he was but twenty-three years old, he painted the lunette murals—*Commerce* and *Labor*—in the lobby of the Woolworth Building. In 1933, Jennewein's glazed terra-cotta mythological fig-ures were installed in the pediment of the north "temple" of the Philadelphia Museum of Art. Jennewein also designed the bronze elevator doors inside that museum. Around the same time, he created the *Industries of the British Commonwealth* bronze figure screen over the entrance to the British Empire Building on Fifth Avenue at Rockefeller Center. That screen seems much like the bronze screen here, though that's *not* Jennewein's work, as we shall see. Perhaps my favorite work by Jennewein is his sculpture from the early 1920s for the ceiling of the magnificent Great Hall of the Cunard Line Building at 25 Broadway. The bronze screen at the library's entrance was the work of sculptor Thomas Hudson Jones, best known for his design of the *Tomb of the Unknown Soldier* in Arlington National Cemetery, Virginia. The screen comprises three columns of five figures each. The left column, from top to bottom, features Hester Prynne from Hawthorne's *The Scarlet Letter*, Babe the Blue Ox from the Paul Bunyan stories, Washington Irving's Rip Van Winkle Melville's Moby Dick, and Mark Twain's Tom Sawyer. The center column features, from top to bottom, the cockroaches archy and mehitabel from Don Marquis, Longfellow's Hiawatha, Brer Rabbit and the Tar Baby from the Uncle Remus stories of Joel Chandler Harris, Walt Whitman himself, and Eugene Field's Wynken, Blynken, and Nod. The right column features, from top to bottom, Louisa May Alcott's Meg from *Little Women,* Jack London's *White Fang,* James Fenimore Cooper's Natty Bumppo from *The Leatherstocking Tales,* Poe's *Raven,* and Charles Dana, author of the once immensely popular *Two Years Before the Mast.* It is fascinating to contemplate these figures that in the early 1940s were considered "canonical" enough to symbolize the library's mission. There is no question that the figures would be quite different today, with perhaps only Walt Whitman and Alcott's Meg making the cut. Note that no African American author is represented. Also interesting is that, excepting Whitman, none of these are "Brooklyn authors." (Irving, Melville, Cooper, Twain, Poe, and Marquis were in varying degrees "New York City authors," and Cooper did like to hang out at the Brooklyn Navy Yard.) I think that would be different today.

Just as in Manhattan where the New York Public Library stands where once the Croton Distributing Reservoir stood, so in Brooklyn the library was built on Mount Prospect, site of the onetime city reservoir. For many years, a high water-tower on the site was a landmark visible for miles around. The reservoir was replaced by Mount Prospect Park, which forms a kind of backyard for the library. The library is officially the Raymond V. Ingersoll Library, named for the Brooklyn borough president on whose watch it was built. It opened on February 1, 1941, and Mayor LaGuardia dedicated the building on March 29 of that year. For a number of years, only the first floor functioned. The second floor was not completed until 1955. The library was expanded in the rear in 1988, and in 1999–2000 the Children's Library to the east, with its own entrance next to Mount Prospect Park, was fully renovated. The gate leading to the children's entrance is adorned with gilded squirrels. All over the building are quotations inscribed into the stone. The principal quotations flanking the main entrance are from Roscoe C. E. Brown, president of the library's Board of Trustees at the time of construction. These quotations are quite prominent and so placed as to be easily read, unlike many such inscriptions on buildings. Indeed, they are of the correct size and placement to be read by the person ascending the steps of the building—a beautiful, unheralded bit of design. Countless library patrons over the years have, without trying to, have memorized these lines, and whenever one visits the library, one will always find somebody outside poring over them. I know of few other instances where text has been so ideally mated with architectural design. To the left of the entrance we read:

> *The Brooklyn Public Library through the joining of municipal enterprise and private generosity offers to all the people perpetual and free access to the knowledge and the thought of all the ages.*

On the right we read:

> *Here are enshrined the longing of great hearts and noble things that tower above the tide, the magic word that winged wonder starts, the garnered wisdom that never dies.*

By the way, the renowned Piccirilli brothers (of the Bronx!) produced the enormous, thirteen-foot-wide, cast-zinc eagle just inside the main entrance. It originally adorned the headquarters of the Brooklyn *Daily Eagle* at Washington and Johnson Streets.

2 BROOKLYN BOTANIC GARDEN
Main entrance at 1000 Washington Avenue

The Brooklyn Botanic Garden (not *Botanical Gardens* or *Botanical Garden* or *Botanic Gardens,* just to be clear) is one of the greatest treasures of New York City. It alone is reason for any visitor to New York City to take the subway to Brooklyn.

In 1910, the Parks Department set aside fifty acres, which it had been using as an ash dump, for the creation of a botanic garden. By this time, the Brooklyn Museum as we know it had only recently attained its form. The Botanic Garden was conceived from the first as symbiotic with the museum. Both the garden and the museum, indeed, were part of the same organization, the Brooklyn Institute of Arts and Sciences. The Parks Department may have donated the land, but private benefactors, beginning with the redoubtable

2B *Brooklyn Botanic Administration Building*

Alfred Tredway White, built up the collections, and today, while the land continues to be city property, about three quarters of the garden's operating budget comes from private sources. In addition to being a magnificent public garden, the Brooklyn Botanic Garden is a major research facility that operates three outreach stations, two in Westchester County and one in Nassau County. The Brooklyn Botanic Garden is the smallest in area of the nation's major botanical gardens. Nonetheless its reputation for the quality of its collections and the importance of its research and publications is worldwide. The visitor today can see thirteen thousand species of plants in thirteen specialized gardens. The Botanic Garden—small, manageable, and beautifully laid out—is the most accessible of all the world's great botanical gardens; the subway is right outside the garden's gates.

The official entrance to the Botanic Garden is on Washington Avenue, but I have always preferred—and many people prefer—to enter at the Eastern Parkway entrance, which is immediately west of the Brooklyn Museum. I have two reasons for preferring this entrance. First, since it is right next to the Brooklyn Museum, one experiences fully the architectural relationship of museum and garden, and so the careful interrelationship of all the parts of Institute Park. Second, I very much like the formal entrance provided by the Osborne Section of the Botanic Garden. So, we shall enter at Eastern Parkway.

The fanciful, Deco-ish iron gate was installed in 1946, the gift of Michael and Bessie Tuch, who lived directly across the street in Turner Towers, an enormous apartment building erected in 1928 at 135 Eastern Parkway. Originally called the Park Avenue Apartments, Turner Towers was simply the largest of a whole row of splendid, Park Avenue–style apartment houses to rise along Eastern Parkway in the 1920s. Many of these buildings have been renovated in recent years as nearby neighborhoods have prospered. Almost all of these buildings have stone bases with brick-faced upper floors and fine classically inspired decoration.

Straight ahead through the gate is the three-acre Osborne Section. On one's right, outside the boundaries of the garden, is Mount Prospect Park, the former site of the City of Brooklyn's water distributing reservoir. The park today separates the Botanic Garden from the Brooklyn Public Library. On one's left is the Brooklyn Museum, its stately forms flashing into view in a very pleasing manner. The Osborne Section is a formal, Italian Renaissance–style garden. It makes for a superb contrast with the very different, romantic landscape design of most of Prospect Park. Here, wisteria-covered pergolas edge both the west and the east sides of a large, 30,000-square-foot, oblong-shaped lawn. At the north end (nearer Eastern Parkway) is a semi-elliptical plaza with a water basin, sixteen feet in diameter, framed by curving stone benches and by 35-foot-high, freestanding classical columns. The column bases are carved with images of ginkgo leaves. At the south end is another semi-elliptical plaza with stone seats, this time with fourteen-foot-high columns. Here one finds another water basin, this one seventeen feet in diameter, with a fountain bowl carved from a single block of Indiana limestone. Spring brings daffodils and tulips to the Osborne Section, then crabapples and cherries followed by rhododendrons, azaleas, and wisterias. The Osborne Section is an excellent example of the work of Harold apRhys Caparn (1864–1945), who originally laid out the Botanic Garden with the firm of Olmsted Brothers. Caparn was born in England and trained in the classical tradition in the late nineteenth century at the École des Beaux-Arts in Paris. He came to America in 1900 and twelve years later began a long association with the Brooklyn Botanic Garden, serving as a consultant and designing the Osborne Section, which was completed to more or less its present form in the 1930s with the aid of Works Progress Administration labor. WPA workers completed the rock wall on the west side in 1934 just as other WPA workers were removing the front stairs of the Brooklyn Museum. (You win a few, you lose a few.) Caparn, by the way, was best known for his designs of formal grounds for mansions on Long

Island's North Shore. Though Caparn's Renaissance-inspired landscape designs could not have been more different from Olmsted and Vaux's romantic style, still Caparn, as a prominent member of the Municipal Art Society and other civic organizations, was a staunch defender of Central Park at times when it was threatened with inappropriate incursions. On the subject of ballfields there, for example, Caparn said that the park's true value to the community "is the most intangible and least understood by many self-styled practical men; that of the solace of beautiful scenery in the midst of the roar and bustle of the city." If ballfields were built, Caparn said, "there might appear . . . to be more going on because there would be more noise and more violent action. Two teams of boys playing baseball will create more bustle and excitement than 10,000 resting, strolling, or engaged in the milder forms of play. . . . This 'popularizing' would result in giving over the parks to one . . . class of the community—the boys of, say, eight to eighteen years of age. Not that the boys are at fault . . . it is merely that they are doing a perfectly proper thing in an improper place." (This is from a letter by Caparn to the *New York Times*, March 14, 1911, and is quoted in Gregory F. Gilmartin, *Shaping the City: New York and the Municipal Art Society*, 1995.) One wishes Caparn had been heeded by Robert Moses when he added ballfields in the southern part of the Long Meadow of Prospect Park!

Speaking of improper uses, the Brooklyn Botanic Garden posts a long list of rules that must be followed by visitors, and I, for one, am awfully glad they do. The rules enjoin the visitor to "Please remember that we are a living museum, not park or a playground. The flowers, shrubs, and trees are a beautiful, but fragile, 'living' collection." (I do not know why *living* is placed in quotations. It is literally true.) Among the rules are:

- No food or beverage can be brought into the Garden—except bottled water and baby bottles.
- Picnicking is not allowed anywhere in the Garden.
- Sit only on garden benches or the Cherry Esplanade lawn. Blankets and folding chairs are not permitted.
- Please do not pick flowers, walk on flower beds, or climb trees.
- Pets are not permitted in the Garden.
- Use radio, tape, and CD players with earphones only.
- Shirts and shoes are required.
- No ball playing, Frisbee tossing, biking, skating, rollerblading, jogging, or kite flying is allowed in the Garden.

It is rare and refreshing to find a list of rules like this, and it shows that the Botanic Garden is a very serious and dedicated institution that has drawn a line against modern, relaxed, and disrespectful ways of treating the public environment. While this makes me happy, it is only fair to point out that many others regard it as elitist and as disrespectful of the claims on public land of diversely acculturated peoples. Olmsted and Vaux believed strongly in enforcing rules of conduct in Central Park and Prospect Park. To the end of educating the public in the proper use of a park, Olmsted even helped to found the Park Rangers. The enforcement by the police of rules for the use of Prospect Park was satirized in 1908 by the Brooklyn *Daily Times:*

- Thou shalt not throw papers on the walks or lawns.
- Thou shalt not play with a ball.
- Thou shalt not walk on forbidden grass.
- Thou shalt not pick flowers nor shrubs nor break branches
   from the trees.
- Thou shalt not bring thy luncheon nor even bags of fruit.
- Thou shalt not loll about on the lawns or benches in
   unseemly attitudes.
- Thou shalt not be boisterous nor hilarious nor interfere with
   thy neighbor's peaceful enjoyment of the pleasures of the park.

Ellen M. Snyder-Grenier, in her excellent *Brooklyn: An Illustrated History* (from which the above commandments are quoted), says that most of the people arrested for breaking park rules were immigrants who could not read the signs. Snyder-Grenier refers to "the police's fear that the 'moral' tone of the park reserved for middle- and upper-middle-class users was being threatened. . . . the Lower East Side residents trying to escape the city heat wanted to use Prospect Park actively, for ball playing, walking on the cool grass, and if they were captured by the beauty of a flower on a branch, picking it to take home with them." In academia today, as attested to by books such as *Gotham* by Edwin G. Burrows and Mike Wallace, Olmsted and Vaux's creations had little or nothing to do with the real needs of the poor immigrant population of the city. The parks were elitist fantasies based on Olmsted's patronizing notion that a common laborer might wish to spend his scant free time sitting on a park bench, reading Emerson and listening to birdsong. This laborer, today's academics argue, wished rather to spend his scant free time drinking beer, shouting, and roughhousing. Today, the Central Park Conservancy comes under fire for closing off newly reseeded parts of Central Park so that grass can take hold without the soil being compacted by trampling feet. We have two extremely divergent opinions here about the proper use of our public spaces. For my part, I regard certain parks as works of art that exist in order to enrich the lives of all New Yorkers who are willing to make the minimal effort to educate themselves to the beauties that are theirs. If this is elitist, I'm not sure why. I, unlike most academics, do not presume that the common laborer is an aesthetic illiterate simply because he does not possess a Ph.D. Anyway, the Brooklyn Botanic Garden has taken sides.

Let us go back to the Osborne Section. At the south end, twenty-three granite steps lead down from the semi-elliptical plaza to the Louisa Clark Spencer Lilac Collection, which features twenty of the twenty-three known varieties of lilacs. From around here pathways lead to many different parts of the garden. To the right at the bottom of the steps is a fenced-off area known as the Local Flora Section. Begun in 1911, this section included only plants indigenous to within one hundred miles of the Botanic Garden. This section is an important resource in the Botanic Garden's pioneering efforts to catalogue the plant biodiversity of the New York metropolitan area. To the left once one descends the steps from the Osborne Section is the marvelous Cranford Rose Garden. Here five thousand rosebushes comprising 1,200 varieties bloom in early summer with tens of thousands of roses. To the east of the Cranford Rose Garden is the Cherry Esplanade, probably the most popular attraction in the Botanic Garden, at least from late March to mid-May. The collection of oriental flowering cherries at the Brooklyn Botanic Garden is believed to be the largest outside of Japan. At the Cherry Esplanade one finds the pink-petaled Kwanzan cherries, first planted here in 1941. Cherry trees were not introduced to the United States until the nineteenth century, though their Asian lineage is ancient. In Japan, the blossoming of the cherries is the occasion for ceremony, and the trees, with their intense, short-lived flowering, hold an honored place in the Buddhist scheme of things. On the north side of the Cherry Esplanade is an overlook with seating. The overlook leads down to the south to another of the garden's popular attractions, the Japanese Hill-and-Pond Garden.

THE JAPANESE HILL-AND-POND GARDEN

The **Japanese Garden** (2c) was constructed in 1914–15, the first Japanese garden created in an American public garden or park. Alfred Tredway White, the Brooklyn Heights philanthropist who built model workers' housing in Cobble Hill (the Tower and Home buildings and the Warren Place cottages) and Brooklyn Heights (the Riverside apartments), donated the funds for the Japanese Garden. Japanese landscape gardener Takeo Shiota (1881–1943) designed it. Shiota, born forty miles outside of Tokyo, came to America in 1907 at the age of twenty-six. He died in 1943 in an internment camp in South Carolina. According to the Brooklyn Botanic Garden, he was fired by an ambition to create, in his words, "a garden more beautiful than all others in the world." Whether or not he achieved his ambition in Brooklyn, there is no question that his garden here is exceptionally beautiful. It is said to be the finest Japanese garden outside Japan.

Within the space of a few city blocks, Brooklynites and visitors enjoy the rare opportunity to experience landscape designs of several traditions. In Prospect Park, Olmsted and Vaux created romantic landscapes heavily influenced by eighteenth- and nineteenth-century English practice. In the Brooklyn Botanic Garden, Harold Caparn created a formal, Italian Renaissance–style garden in the Osborne Section. Here, Shiota created a garden based on Japanese principles, very different from the European classical principles that inspired Caparn. Though traditional Japanese gardens such as this one are conceived as paeans to nature, it is well to note that their construction is often as artificial as any highly manicured Italian or French garden (or any Olmsted and Vaux garden, for that matter). Here, the hills, the waterfall, and the island, as well as the torii (the red gateway), the shrine to Inari (Shinto god of the harvest), the teahouse, the bridges, and the lanterns are all man-made. A common misconception is that the pond is also artificial, that it was formed to resemble the Chinese character for "heart." In fact, as M. M. Graff has pointed out, topographical maps from the nineteenth-century show this pond in its exact shape of today. It is actually a glacial kettle, like the Vale of Cashmere, the Lullwater, and

2C *Brooklyn Botanic Garden, Japanese Garden*

the hollow where the zoo is located in Prospect Park. If the pond is in the shape for "heart," Graff has written, it "is the only evidence that the Wisconsin ice sheet could write Chinese." The pond is lined with flowering oriental cherries, making this another must-stop in April and May, as well as with Japanese maples, white pines, and other trees. The Japanese Garden, which requires fanatical upkeep, was fully restored in 1999–2000 at a cost of $3.2 million. The pond contains about a hundred koi. The Hill-and-Pond Garden is an example of a "stroll garden," for perambulating, as contrasted with the other major type of Japanese garden, the "viewing garden," for contemplating. The stroll garden here is modeled on those of the Edo period, which extended from the seventeenth to the nineteenth century. (The great Edo-period artist Hiroshige, outstanding examples of whose woodblock prints are in the collection of the Brooklyn Museum next door, knew such stroll gardens.) Just outside the Japanese Garden is a seventeenth-century stone lantern, three tons in weight, a 1980 gift from the government of Japan to the people of Brooklyn. Not only is there much of Japanese influence in the Botanic Garden, but it is one of the major destinations of Japanese tourists in New York City, and I have been to the garden at times when Japanese visitors outnumber Americans.

To the south of the Japanese Garden is Celebrity Walk. Paved with stones commemorating famous Brooklynites, this path winds through Austrian pines, rhododendrons, and daffodils. Brooklyn is proud of its sons and daughters, though what sense does it make to have any context in which Walt Whitman and Dom DeLuise are honored together? Nonetheless, near here is **the fine memorial to the great Alfred Tredway White** (2a), featuring a circular stone bench and a stele bearing a Daniel Chester French bronze relief. French was in charge of the sculptural program on the exterior of the Brooklyn Museum. Continuing along the path to the east of the Japanese Garden, one arrives at the Botanic Garden's suite of buildings, whose backs face Washington Avenue. One first comes to the old Administration Building designed by McKim, Mead & White and built in 1918 when the firm was still quite active, though McKim and White had both been dead for several years. Better than the architecture of the Administration Building is the nearby garden work. Right in front of the Administration Building is Magnolia Plaza, a formal garden comprising sweet-smelling magnolias. When they blossom in March (white-flowered star magnolias), April (ivory, yellow, pink, and purple flowers of seventeen varieties of magnolias), and June (white-flowered sweetbay magnolias), they present a spectacle that competes with the cherries. Harold Caparn designed Magnolia Plaza which was first planted in 1932. A year later, the sculpture featuring the compass and armillary sphere was added, the design of Rhys Caparn, Harold Caparn's daughter. Just to the north of this formal garden is Daffodil Hill, where one finds thousands of trumpet daffodils that bloom yellow and gold in March. To the east of this and the north of the Administration Building are two specialty gardens of interest. The first is the Fragrance Garden, dedicated in 1955. Designed by Alice Ireys, this was the first garden in the country created specifically for the blind; the labels are in braille. The sighted and the sight-impaired can enjoy this garden equally. Next is the Shakespeare Garden. Brooklyn's original Shakespeare Garden was created in 1925 at the southern end of the Botanic Garden. Henry C. Folger, who established the Folger Shakespeare Library in Washington, D.C., donated the Shakespeare Garden to Brooklyn. Because of nearby growth that impinged on the garden, however, it was moved in 1979 to its present location. Designed in the style of an Elizabethan cottage garden, here are found eighty varieties of plants mentioned in the plays of Shakespeare. Labels provide quotations from the plays, placing the plants in their literary context. To the south of the Administration Building are the greenhouses designed by the prominent firm

2A *Brooklyn Botanic Gardens, Alfred Tredway White Memorial*

of modern architects Davis, Brody & Associates and opened in 1987. Some critics have suggested that these octagonal forms are a bit too aggressive for their garden context. The octagonal cupola atop the Administration Building suggested the form. Regardless of how these buildings appear on the outside, the exhibits within are very educational. The greenhouses have been described as "icebergs" because their exhibit gardens are sunken below grade. Plants re-create and educational text panels elucidate various ecosystems. There is the Desert Pavilion, the Robert W. Wilson Aquatic Pavilion, the Warm Temperate Pavilion, and the Tropical Pavilion (the largest of the pavilions, re-creating tropical rainforest conditions). Tying it all together is the Trail of Evolution, explaining four billion years of plant life. Located within the Steinhardt Conservatory is the Botanic Garden's famous C. V. Starr Bonsai Museum. Comprising 750 specimens, this is considered the largest and finest bonsai collection outside of Japan. Also within Steinhardt Conservatory is the Botanic Garden's superb, not-to-be-missed Garden Shop. In front of Steinhardt Conservatory is the **Lily Pool Terrace** (2d), which features water lilies, sacred lotuses, and other aquatic plants. The Lily Pool Terrace was built in 1919–21, following completion of the old conservatories. Directly west of the green-houses, on the west side of the Botanic Garden across Flatbush Avenue from Prospect Park's zoo, is the Rock Garden. Opened in 1917, this was the first

Japanese-style rock garden in an American public garden or park. Here one finds an excellent reproduction (erected in 1963) of the Ryoanji Temple, the original of which stands amid 500-year-old gardens in Kyoto. The Rock Garden is an example of a Japanese "viewing garden" for contemplation as opposed to a "stroll garden" for perambulation. The Hill-and-Pond Garden noted above is a stroll garden. The idea in a viewing garden is that there is a viewing platform. The designers of such a garden intend that it be viewed only from a specified fixed spot. Boulders are placed within a gravel "pond." In Japanese gardens, there is typically either water, as at the Hill-and-Pond Garden, or the *representation* of water, as here.

From the Rock Garden it is easy to exit the Botanic Garden at Flatbush Avenue and Empire Boulevard, where one will find the Prospect Park station of the D line subway.

The Brooklyn Botanic Garden is open from October through March on Tuesday through Friday from 8:00 A.M. to 4:30 P.M. and on Saturday, Sunday, and holidays from 10:00 A.M. to 4:30 P.M.; and from April through September on Tuesday through Friday from 8:00 A.M. to 6:00 P.M. and on Saturday, Sunday, and holidays from 10:00 A.M. to 6:00 P.M. Park guides offer free walking tours on Saturday and Sunday (except on major holiday weekends) at 1:00 P.M., leaving from the Administration Building.

2D *Brooklyn Botanic Garden, Lily Pool Terrace*

3 BROOKLYN MUSEUM

200 Eastern Parkway, southwest corner of Washington Avenue
1893–1915, McKim, Mead & White
Front stairs removed 1934–35

McKim, Mead & White won the Brooklyn Museum competition in May 1893. Their design was for a building that would be simply enormous, but designed in such a way that it could easily be built in stages and not appear to be unfinished. Construction began on the northwest wing in 1895; when this wing was finished two years later, the museum formally opened. The center pavilion of this front, with its Guastavino dome, and the hall behind it were built in 1900–05. The east half of the front was built in 1904–06. The grand staircase came in 1906, and further additions were made in 1913–15, by which time McKim had been dead for a few years.

Besides McKim, Mead & White, the Brooklyn Museum competition entrants included the Parfitt Brothers, Josiah Cleveland Cady, Carrère & Hastings, Boring & Tilton, and Brockway & Cromwell. The judges included A. D. F. Hamlin, Franklin W. Hooper, Robert W. Peabody (of the Boston architectural firm of Peabody & Stearns), and George L. Morse.

In McKim's original plan, the north and south entrances would define the main axis of the building, which was to be 560 feet per side. In the center

3 *Brooklyn Museum*

would be a rotunda eighty feet in diameter and 180 feet high. There would have been low saucer domes over each of the four quadrants (such as the one dome now present), and, in the center, an enormous, high dome would be set upon a colonnaded drum. In the museum's collections can be found a marvelous watercolor and pen-and-ink rendering of McKim's proposed design by Francis Hoppin, the gifted draftsman who worked for McKim, Mead & White at the time and who went on to form his own firm of Hoppin & Koen, designing Manhattan's magnificent Police Headquarters on Centre Street as well as Edith Wharton's house, the Mount, in Lenox, Massachusetts.

Though only one of the four quadrants was built, it was the principal quadrant in the sense that it was the one to face Eastern Parkway and to contain the museum's main entrance, including, originally, its monumental stairway. The stairway, completed in 1906 and leading to the museum's third floor, was removed in 1934–35 as part of a WPA project under the direction of the Swiss-born modernist architect William Lescaze. The idea allegedly was to make the museum seem less forbidding to the ordinary Brooklynite, though there is a strong suspicion it was all just something someone thought up to give otherwise unemployed construction workers something to do. In any event, it was a major act of architectural vandalism.

The museum was conceived in 1888, a full decade before Consolidation, as an encyclopedic museum to rival New York City's Metropolitan. McKim's grand scheme of 1893 was appealing to the civic pride of Brooklyn leaders. Construction, however, was slowed at first by the onset of the depression of 1893.

It has often been noted that McKim's design was similar to his Agriculture Building at the World's Columbian Exposition, opened just as the competition drawings for Brooklyn were being done. There are indeed many similarities between the two works, but just as many differences. It is important to note that the Brooklyn Museum was not in any way a knockoff of the Chicago design. One building that is never mentioned in conjunction with the Brooklyn Museum and that perhaps ought to be is Brooklyn City Hall. I have never come across anything that would indicate that McKim was influenced at all by the City Hall, but it has two very important features in common with the much grander Brooklyn Museum. First, both buildings have Ionic hexastyle porticoes reached by grand stairways and topped by broad triangular pediments. The Chicago building, on the other hand, had a main entrance portico that was Corinthian and tetrastyle, and the stair was relatively low. Second, the similarity between the Brooklyn City Hall and the Brooklyn Museum in the manner in which their façades are molded is very important and quite different from the Chicago building. In the Chicago building, the main façade, facing the lagoon, featured eighteen high, arched windows in six bays of three windows each. There is nothing at all like this at the Brooklyn Museum. In Brooklyn City Hall, however, Doric pilasters ring the building and lend an enlivening plasticity to the façades. Just so, the Brooklyn Museum similarly uses pilasters extensively to enliven the façades, though here they are employed in the Beaux-Arts manner to support visually the plinths of the numerous statues that ring the building at attic level. That manner of using statues is more like the Agriculture Building in Chicago than it is like Brooklyn City Hall, as is the general manner of embellishment such as the sculptural pediment over the entrance portico. We know from his expansion of Isaiah Rogers' Merchants' Exchange on Wall Street, some years after the Brooklyn Museum, that McKim had an obvious sympathy for the the early-nineteenth-century Greek Revival of which Brooklyn City Hall is a superb example, and I cannot help thinking that thoughts of City Hall affected to some slight degree McKim's design of the museum. So too might the Brooklyn Museum's earlier home have suggested a thing or two to McKim. The building housing what was at the time called the Brooklyn Institute stood at Washington and Concord Streets in downtown Brooklyn and was roughly contemporary with City Hall. The simple design featured four prominent Ionic three-quarter columns rising from an astylar base.

The Brooklyn Museum had its origin in the Apprentices' Library, founded in 1823 in a tavern on Fulton Street. In addition to being a library, it would offer courses and "lectures upon Mechanics and Sciences," and would be a museum for the exhibition of scientific and mechanical apparatus, "with specimens of the arts and natural productions." The Apprentices' Library was founded mainly by relatively recently arrived Brooklyn businessmen, among them the potash merchant Robert Snow, newspaper publisher (*Long Island Star*) Alden Spooner, rope tycoon Joshua Sands, and distiller and paint manufacturer Augustus Graham. Their idea for the Apprentices' Library was to promote the professional advancement and the moral edification of young apprentices. In the early-nineteenth-century, in a fast-industrializing society, the traditional, highly paternalistic system of apprenticeship in trades was breaking down amid the increasingly fluid labor markets created by the factory system. While young workingmen were no longer bound to masters and enjoyed more freedom, at the same time many of the elements of young work-ingmen's lives that had been well provided by the apprenticeship system—including training, general education, moral uplift and religious involvement, developing social bonds, and so on—were falling by the wayside. The Apprentices' Library was an attempt to establish an institution that would pro-vide young workingmen with some of the things once provided in the tradi-tional master-apprentice relationship. It is interesting to see that the Brooklyn Museum had its origin in an attempt at the systematic edification of the young. The library's founders said the purpose was "to cultivate a taste for reading and the acquisition of knowledge, and generally to promote those studies which would tend to enlarge their minds, improve their morals and make them emi-nent in their several stations and professions."

Inspiration for the Apprentices' Library came from across the river, where two institutions, still going strong, had already been founded: the General Society of Mechanics and Tradesmen, and the Mercantile Library. The Apprentices' Library's first permanent building was erected on the corner of Henry and Cranberry Streets in 1825. The cornerstone was laid on July 4 of that year, and the Marquis de Lafayette, in the midst of his famous return visit to America, attended the ceremony. Also present was a six-year-old neighbor-hood boy named Walt Whitman, who later recalled being lifted up by Lafayette in order to get a better view. Once the building was up, it became the epicen-ter of official village life, housing government offices, a post office, a court-room, and even a savings bank. The only problem was that few apprentices were interested in the library's offerings. In 1836, the building was sold to the newly formed City of Brooklyn.

In 1843, the Apprentices' Library changed its name to the Brooklyn Institute. In 1848, the Institute purchased the building erected at Washington and Concord Streets by another institution, the Brooklyn Lyceum, which had been founded in 1833. The Apprentices' Library had moved into the Lyceum building in 1841, and established a general evening school of what we would call "continuing education." The Brooklyn Institute appears to have been a very enterprising operation. Women were admitted to its courses. The range and quality of lecturers was impressive. Horace Greeley, Louis Agassiz, Richard Salter Storrs, Ralph Waldo Emerson, and Henry Ward Beecher all lectured there. It remained at Washington and Concord Streets (an intersection demapped in the 1950s for the creation of Cadman Plaza) until 1890.

At that time, the Institute's new director, Franklin W. Hooper, a zoologist who had been a student of Louis Agassiz at Harvard, led the aging and somewhat tired organization on a new path. He merged it with other educational organizations to form the Brooklyn Institute of Arts and Sciences. It was at first housed in the building at Washington and Concord Streets, but that building burned down in September 1890. When they sold the site of the burned-down building a year later, they decided to rebuild, though not in the downtown area. When the Institute was first formed, downtown was the only conceivable location. But by the 1890s, Brooklyn was growing in all directions. The neighborhoods bordering Prospect Park were becoming the most desirable residential neighborhoods in the city. Hooper and the trustees of the Brooklyn Institute decided on a tract of land on Eastern Parkway, a twelve-acre parcel that was part of the "East Side Lands," separated from Prospect Park proper by Flatbush Avenue, that Olmsted and Vaux had set aside for just such an eventuality as the construction of a museum. (Their concern was not to make the same mistake they had made in designing Central Park, in which the Metropolitan Museum of Art was actually within, rather than just outside, the park.) Hooper organized the competition that selected Charles Follen McKim as the museum's architect.

The museum was to be encyclopedic—not an encyclopedic museum of art, but of all realms of knowledge. Painting, architecture, photography (many years before the Museum of Modern Art made a splash by including it among its departments), architecture, yes, but also departments we are not accustomed to seeing in museums, such as literature and music, and beyond that the sciences and natural history, with separate departments of electricity, chemistry, and engineering. The museum would also house schools of painting, sculpture, architecture, and photography. Had it been completed according to plan, it would have been the largest museum in the world and would have covered a broader spectrum of human endeavor than any other museum. Ultimately, approximately one-sixth of the museum as envisioned was built. Even at one-sixth its intended size, it ranks as one of the largest art museums in the world.

Once it was apparent that, as far as consolidated Greater New York was concerned, the Brooklyn Museum was always going to be regarded as second banana to the Metropolitan Museum of Art, Brooklyn got down to building its unique collections and refining its strengths. Central to the process of creating an identity for the museum was a remarkable curator named Stewart Culin, an ethnologist whose travels brought back to Brooklyn countless artworks and artifacts of North American, Far Eastern, African, and Oceanic peoples. The museum's renowned period rooms were collected and installed between 1917 and 1929. In the 1930s, the scientific and natural history collections were dispersed, as the museum chose to concentrate on art. Some of the old collections were shifted to the Brooklyn Children's Museum, another branch of the Brooklyn Institute of Arts and Sciences and the premier institution of its kind in the country. In 1931, the museum was given an endowment for building up and maintaining its now world-renowned Egyptological collections.

CHARLES FOLLEN McKIM (1847–1909)

Charles Follen McKim, the architect of the Brooklyn Museum, was born August 27, 1847, in Chester County, Pennsylvania. His father, Miller McKim, a Pennsylvanian of Scottish descent, became an abolitionist after reading William Lloyd Garrison. Miller married Sarah Speakman, a Chester County Quaker, abolitionist, and close friend of Lucretia Mott. Charles was named after Karl Follen, a Harvard professor who lost his job because of his outspoken antislavery views. When Miller became involved in relief work for freed slaves and had to work in Manhattan, the McKims moved in 1866 to Llewellyn Park, New Jersey, America's first landscaped suburb, founded in 1853 by an admirer of Andrew Jackson Downing and Calvert Vaux and based on Downing's ideas. It was in what is now West Orange. Alexander Jackson Davis, architect of Litchfield Villa in Park Slope, lived in Llewellyn Park and designed most of its houses, including the McKims', built 1858–59. Several leading abolitionists and Fourierists settled in Llewellyn Park. Miller put up a quarter of the money to found the *Nation*. William Lloyd Garrison, Unitarian minister William Henry Furness (father of the Philadelphia architect), Henry Villard (Garrison's son-in-law), and other well-known people were regular visitors to the McKim home. Charles's sister married William Lloyd Garrison's son. Another friend of Miller's and visitor to the house was Russell Sturgis, art critic for the *Nation*.

Charles was soft-spoken in a way said to be learned from his mother. He entered Harvard's Lawrence Scientific School in the fall of 1866, planning to become an engineer. He soon changed his sights to architecture because of his love of drawing. In 1867, Charles went to work in the New York office of Russell Sturgis prior to setting off in the fall of that year for the École des Beaux-Arts in Paris. One of his close friends at the École was Robert Swain Peabody, who would later be a partner in the Boston architectural firm of Peabody & Stearns. In 1893, Peabody would also be one of the judges of the competition for the design of the Brooklyn Museum. Charles learned from reading Ruskin that the architect should be trained not with the engineer but with the sculptor. He remained at the École from 1867 to 1870, in the atelier of Pierre-Gérôme-Honoré Daumet (1826–1911). Charles was there just after the time when a geometrically pure Roman classicism had yielded to a much broader, richer historical allusionism. Great emphasis was placed on logical planning of interior space as well as on a logical, historically based program of symbolic expression. The two went hand in hand, and both are clearly apparent in the Brooklyn Museum. After returning to New York in 1870, Charles went to work for Henry Hobson Richardson, the architect who would have such a profound impact on Brooklyn architecture. In 1872, Charles struck out on his own. Five years later the firm of McKim, Bigelow & Mead formed. William Bigelow was McKim's brother-in-law. When McKim and his wife divorced, Bigelow left the firm and, in 1879, Stanford White, another Richardson protégé, joined to form McKim, Mead & White.

Among the works that McKim designed for the firm, we may cite the Boston Public Library (1887–95), the Agriculture Building and the New York State Pavilion at the Columbian Exposition of 1893, the Harvard Club (1893–94) on West 44th Street, the master plan of Columbia University including Low Memorial Library (1894–97, named by Columbia's president, Brooklyn's Seth Low, for his father, Abiel Abbot Low), the University Club (1896–1900) on Fifth Avenue and 54th Street, the restoration of and additions to the White House (1902–3, for Theodore Roosevelt), the Pierpont Morgan Library (1902–7), the remodeling of the Merchants' Exchange (1904–10) on Wall Street, and Pennsylvania Station (1902–11).

The exterior of McKim's building is a showcase of sculpture outstanding enough that if it were all the museum possessed this would still be one of Brooklyn's major artistic destinations. The thirty figures ranged along the attic make the Brooklyn Museum the peer of that handful of New York buildings where we see the full realization of the Beaux-Arts ideal of the integration of the arts. Other such buildings include Cass Gilbert's U.S. Custom House, James Brown Lord's Appellate Division Courthouse at Madison Square, and Carrère & Hastings's New York Public Library. At the Brooklyn Museum, five figures are ranged along the attic on the east side of the building. They are, from south to north:

- *Zoroaster* (symbolizing Persian philosophy) by Edmond T. Quinn. A statue of Zoroaster (aka Zarathustra) can also be seen atop the Appellate Division Courthouse at Madison Square. Who would ever guess that New York City boasts not one but two statues of Zoroaster?
- *Sankara* (Indian philosophy) by Edward Clark Potter (sculptor of the lions in front of the New York Public Library).
- *Kalidasa* (Indian literature) by Attilio Piccirilli. Piccirilli was the sculptor of the Maine Monument in Columbus Circle, among much else.
- *Manu* (Indian law) by Piccirilli. Manu also appears on the Appellate Division Courthouse.
- *Buddha* (Indian religion) by Potter.

On the north side, to the east of the pediment, from east to west, we have:

- Confucius (Chinese philosophy) by Karl Bitter. Confucius also appears on the Appellate Division Courthouse. Karl Bitter did the façade sculptures of Manhattan's Metropolitan Museum of Art.
- Lao-Tse (Chinese religion) by Bitter.
- Chinese art by Bitter.
- Chinese law by Bitter.
- Japanese art by Janet Scudder.
- Moses (Hebrew law) by Augustus Lukeman. Moses also appears on the Appellate Division Courthouse. Lukeman was

the sculptor of the World War I Memorial by the Lake in Prospect Park.

- *David* (Hebrew psalmist) by Lukeman.
- *Isaiah* (Hebrew prophet) by Lukeman.
- *Saint Paul* (Hebrew apostle) by Lukeman.
- Mohammed by Charles Keck. A statue of Mohammed once appeared on the Appellate Division Courthouse, but Moslem nations asked the State of New York to remove it, citing the fact that Islam is an iconoclastic religion. The statue was duly removed. Yet Brooklyn's remains! Many years later, Keck was the sculptor of the figures of the War Memorial in Cadman Plaza.

On the north side, to the west of the pediment, from east to west, we have:

- Homer (Greek epic) by Daniel Chester French.
- Pindar (Greek lyric poetry) by French.
- Aeschylus (Greek drama) by George T. Brewster.
- Pericles (Greek statecraft) by Brewster.
- Archimedes (Greek science) by Kenyon Cox. Known primarily as a mural painter, Cox was the author of *The Classic Point of View,* one of the best primers on the art of painting.
- Athena (Greek religion) by French.
- Plato (Greek philosophy) by Herbert Adams.
- Phidias (Greek architecture) by Adams.
- Praxiteles (Greek sculpture) by Adams.
- Demosthenes (Greek letters) by Adams.

On the west side, from north to south, we have:

- Justinian (Roman law) by Johannes Gelert. Justinian also appears on the Appellate Division Courthouse.
- Julius Caesar (Roman statecraft) by Gelert.
- Augustus Caesar (Roman emperor) by Gelert.
- Cicero (Roman oratory) by Gelert.
- Virgil (Roman epic poetry) by Carl Heber.

461

Daniel Chester French and his assistant, Adolph Alexander Weinman, sculpted the central triangular pediment. The figures on the right (west) symbolize Painting, Sculpture, and Architecture. The figures on the left (east) symbolize Geology, Astronomy, and Biology. We see from these figures that the scope of the Brooklyn Museum was once much broader than today. At the extreme left is a sphinx, symbolizing Knowledge. At the right, a peacock symbolizes Art. The pediment was complete in 1914. Charles Follen McKim chose French not only to sculpt the pediment, but also to hire the other sculptors, establish the subject matter, and supervise the work. He also created the two large allegorical sculptures flanking the main entrance. These granite groups, however, were not executed for the museum, but were placed in 1916 at the Brooklyn entrance to the Manhattan Bridge. When the approach roadways to the bridge were widened, the sculptures were removed in 1963 to their present location in front of the museum. On the left is an allegorical seated female figure of Manhattan. On the right is Brooklyn. On Manhattan's lap is a winged globe, a symbol of dominion. To her left is a peacock, symbol of pride. Her right foot rests on a treasure chest. Brooklyn is quite different. She wears a laurel crown, and her left hand holds a book. At her feet to the left is a nude child reading a book. Behind her on the right is a model of a church. The figures are, in the manner characteristic of French, beautifully modeled. We see a gifted artist's vision of the differences between Manhattan and Brooklyn in the early years after Consolidation. Manhattan is all about worldliness and progress. Brooklyn is about domesticity, piety, and culture.

The Brooklyn Museum's collections are of course among the greatest treasures of Brooklyn. A proper guide to the museum's outstanding collections would double or treble the length of the present volume. Therefore, I shall give the lay of the land and highlight a few of those things that I, personally, enjoy showing to visitors. In the old days when the front stair was in place, one entered the museum onto its third floor, where there is a wonderful skylit court under the saucer dome. Today we enter at the ground floor into the Grand Lobby, as it is called, which is not McKim, Mead & White but rather William Lescaze, the Swiss modernist engaged in the 1930s to renovate the building. He oversaw the stair removal and also designed the Wilbour Library of Egyptology on the third floor. The Grand Lobby is an austere space with the sort of cool contours that make it easy to think it was designed by the co-architect of the Philadelphia Saving Fund Society skyscraper of only a couple of years earlier in Philadelphia. The first floor contains art of the Americas, of

Africa, and of the Pacific Islands—a lot of the Stewart Culin stuff. One also finds on the first floor the renowned museum shop, selling all manner of books, scarves, jewelry, posters, reproduction pieces, and so on. The second floor contains Chinese, Korean, Japanese, Indian, Southeast Asian, and Islamic art. This is also the floor for the museum's excellent Art Reference Library and Archives, a resource available to the public by appointment. The third floor is for many the museum's pièce de résistance. Here are found the Egyptian, Classical, and ancient Middle Eastern galleries, containing collections generally reckoned among the best of their kind in the world. Three other things, all of architectural note, can be found on this floor. First, to the far east, is the aforementioned Wilbour Library. In 1916, the heirs of the pioneering American Egyptologist Charles Edwin Wilbour donated to the museum his collection of Egyptian art as well as his library. The Egyptian collections were further augmented when the museum purchased the holdings in that area belonging to the New-York Historical Society. (How and why the New-York Historical Society had an Egyptian collection is a long and interesting story, but best left for another time.) In the 1930s, Lescaze, an acolyte of his countryman Le Corbusier, designed the present rooms of the Wilbour Library. Also on this floor is that central court, mentioned earlier, by McKim, Mead & White; recently restored, its skylight, elegant arcades, stately Corinthian columns, bronze chandelier, and bronze lanterns look better than they have in a very long time. To the south of the court is the Iris and B. Gerald Cantor Auditorium, opened in April 1991 as the first part of a new master plan by the famous Japanese architect Arata Isozaki to be constructed. For the architectural buff, the fourth floor is a treat. Here are the decorative arts, including the museum's outstanding collection of "period rooms," an indispensable resource for anyone studying the history of American architecture. The rooms include ones from the seventeenth-century Jan Martense Schenck house (which stood at Avenue U and 63rd in Flatlands); fine eighteenth-century specimens from the South and New England; the exotic smoking-room that Arabella Worsham installed in her 1860s town house, later the home of John D. Rockefeller, at 4 West 54th Street in Manhattan; and the stylish Art Deco study from the Worgelt apartment of the late 1920s in Manhattan. Space constraints preclude the more expansive treatment that these rooms demand. Of special interest in the decorative arts collections is the Century Vase that Karl Müller designed for Thomas C. Smith's Union Porcelain Works of Greenpoint in 1876. Union Porcelain exhibited this vase in their booth at the Centennial Exposition in

Philadelphia. The vase celebrates America, with bison-head handles, painted scenes of American life, a fabulous golden eagle set within a pattern of zig-zagging rays, and, in bisque relief, a profile portrait of George Washington and further scenes of American life. The exceptional quality of this showpiece was indicative of the excellence of this firm's work when Brooklyn was one of the ceramics capitals of America.

For me, the museum's pièce de résistance is its fifth floor. Here are the galleries of European and of American paintings. Among the best-known of the European paintings are *A Shepherd Tending His Flock,* from the 1860s by Jean-François Millet (1814–75), and *Mademoiselle Fiocre in the Ballet "La Source,"* also from the 1860s, by Edgar Degas (1834–1917). What most excites me on this floor are the American painting and sculpture galleries, which are reason enough to visit Brooklyn.

THE AMERICAN LANDSCAPE

Perhaps the museum's most celebrated paintings are its American landscapes. A good place to start is *Winter Scene in Brooklyn,* by Francis Guy (ca. 1760–1820), from sometime around 1817 to 1820. Here we see the fledgling waterfront town. In the foreground are figures—men standing and talking, a horse-drawn cart, frolicking dogs, a man feeding chickens, another man sawing wood, another shoveling coal, and so on—on snow-covered streets. A series of handsome clapboard houses, some of them quite substantial, recedes into the background, smoke rising from the many chimneys. Though the feeling of the scene is that of small-town America, still there is something, perhaps in the piling up of houses, perhaps in all the conversations that seem to be going on, that portends growth. Guy was born in the Lake District of England and came to America in 1795, settling in Brooklyn. He worked as a silk-dyer and tried his hand at dentistry (!) in addition to being a painter. He lived in Baltimore from 1798 to 1817, when he returned to Brooklyn. It was sometime between his return to Brooklyn and his death three years later that he painted *Winter Scene in Brooklyn.*

Here is *The Pic-Nic,* 1846, by Thomas Cole (1801–48), who

is considered the father of the Hudson River School. Like Francis Guy, Cole was born in England. He came to America at the age of seventeen. After studying painting at the Pennsylvania Academy of the Fine Arts, he moved to New York City. He made his first sketching trip up the Hudson River in 1825, and eleven years later settled in the town of Catskill, New York. Cole's works of the 1820s tended toward topographical views, and were not so different from the works of a painter such as Francis Guy. In the 1830s, his style matured in such works as his epic five-panel *Course of Empire* series at the New-York Historical Society. *The Pic-Nic*, which Cole painted only two years before his death, is an outstanding example of his mature style. Also here is another work by Cole from around the same time, a study for his epic cycle *The Cross and the World*.

Other painters considered part of the Hudson River School are represented here, including Frederic Edwin Church (1826–1900) and John Frederick Kensett (1816–72). Church was a pupil of Cole from 1844 to 1846, the year of *The Pic-Nic*. Church, born in Hartford, Connecticut, did not go abroad until he was twenty-seven, and then he went not to Europe but to South America, which would form the subject matter of many of his most renowned works. John Ruskin was among the many admirers of Church's landscapes. In the 1870s, Church collaborated with Calvert Vaux, the planner of Prospect Park, on the design of Olana, Church's house in Hudson, New York. The Brooklyn Museum is home to Church's *Tropical Scenery*, 1873, painted when he was at the height of his fame and influence.

A favorite among visitors to the museum is *A Storm in the Rocky Mountains, Mount Rosalie*, 1866, by Albert Bierstadt (1830–1902), more the Byronic evocation of nature's majestic authority than is Cole's more Wordsworthian, pastoral idyll of lakeside picnickers. Bierstadt was born in Germany and came to America when he was two years old, settling with his family in New Bedford, Massachusetts. He went to Germany in 1853 to study painting in Düsseldorf, then one of the major centers for the training of young artists. He returned to America in 1857 and the following year made his first trip to the West. He became famous as a painter of western landscapes, the northern counterparts to Frederic Edwin Church's South American views. Generally, Bierstadt's work was excellent in line and form, reflecting his meticulous Düsseldorf training. Color, however, was not his forte. Many consider his painting in the Brooklyn Museum his greatest accomplishment, in which his characteristic dryness was ameliorated by the influence of J. M. W. Turner. The painting dropped from public view when a private collector purchased it in 1867, and it was not publicly exhibited again until 1974. Bierstadt was extremely popular at the time of this painting, though in the next decade his popularity waned as the public came to prefer smaller, more intimate, Barbizon-influenced landscapes; by the time of his death he was totally forgotten. The rediscovery of the painting now hanging in the Brooklyn Museum led to a resurgence of interest in Bierstadt's art.

Portraiture receives its due in a couple of outstanding pieces. Thomas Eakins (1844–1916) painted Letitia Wilson Jordan in 1888, and John Singer Sargent (1856–1925) gave us *Paul Helleu Sketching with His Wife* in 1889. The French painter Paul Helleu, a friend of Sargent, designed the Sky Ceiling of Grand Central Terminal and is said to have been an inspiration for his friend Proust's character of Elstir in *A la recherches du temps perdu.* As for Eakins, the portrait of Letitia Wilson Jordan together with his *William Rush Carving His Allegorical Figure of the Schuylkill River* make the Brooklyn Museum a must for lovers of the great painter from Philadelphia. (Eakins studied at the École des Beaux-Arts in Paris from 1866 to 1869, at the same time as Charles Follen McKim.) In 1895, while commuting from Philadelphia to teach at New York's Cooper Union, and well after he had created his most famous paintings, Eakins provided relief sculptures for the inner walls of the abutments of the Soldiers' and Sailors' Memorial Arch in Grand Army Plaza, a couple of blocks away from the Brooklyn Museum. This is the only known instance of a direct association between Eakins and Brooklyn. The equestrian reliefs are of Lincoln and of Grant. Apparently, William O'Donovan executed the human figures, while Eakins, renowned for his understanding of animal anatomy, was called in to work on the horses.

Among the American sculpture, note the two bronze busts by Olin Levi Warner (1844-96), both from 1880. One is of his friend, the painter J. Alden

Weir. The other is of Maud Morgan. The gifted Warner, who died so young, created the portrait heads on the exterior of the Long Island Historical Society on Pierrepont Street. (See chapter 3 for a brief biography of Warner.)

It is hard to do even minimal justice to the collections exhibited on the fifth floor. There are excellent works by Eastman Johnson, George Inness, Daniel Huntington (including a marvelous portrait of William Cullen Bryant), Childe Hassam, Winslow Homer, Thomas Wilmer Dewing, William Glackens, Randolph Rogers, Frederick MacMonnies, Augustus Saint-Gaudens, Hiram Powers, Frank Duveneck, Louis Comfort Tiffany, and many others. A sampling of post–World War II abstract art by Mark Rothko, Hans Hofmann, Ad Reinhardt, David Smith, Willem de Kooning, Richard Diebenkorn, and others rounds out the fifth-floor galleries.

The fifth-floor elevator vestibule contains one of my favorite things in the museum: *Religion Enthroned* (1910), a magnificent stained-glass window by the remarkable Frederick Stymetz Lamb (1863–1928). Executed in the opalescent technique that John LaFarge taught to his friend Lamb, this is as rich, as luminous, and as vibrantly colored an example of its genre as one is ever likely to encounter. Lamb's work can be seen elsewhere in Brooklyn, too. He did eighteen windows for Plymouth Church on Orange Street in Brooklyn Heights. Irving Bush, developer of Bush Terminal, donated *Religion Enthroned* to the Brooklyn Museum.

14B *Sanctuary, Christ Church*

Index

Note: This index contains all names of persons that appear in the text. Names of buildings, sites, etc., refer only to their appearance as main entries.